The Tourism Education Futures Initiative

As the world faces many serious challenges informed, courageous and mindful leadership is needed for a better future. The Tourism Education Futures Initiative (TEFI) is the collective effort of a group of innovative, thoughtful and committed scholars and industry leaders seeking to provide vision, knowledge, and a framework for tourism education programs that promote global citizenship and optimism for a better world. This book consolidates some of TEFI's work as it seeks to be the leading, forward-looking network that inspires, informs and supports tourism educators and students to passionately and courageously transform the world for the better. It makes the case for why change is needed, and how tourism educators can respond to that change with strategies and values-based tools. The book contains papers published in special TEFI issues of the *Journal of Teaching in Travel & Tourism* (*JTTT*), which question and explore some of the most important theoretical, conceptual and practical issues facing tourism education now and into the future. The book concludes by integrating the special issues' key contributions with a brief conceptualisation of education futures before it outlines TEFI's framework for action over the coming years. Tourism educators worldwide will find that this volume serves two important purposes. On the one hand, it challenges educators to think both critically and proactively about tourism education, while on the other sharing examples of teaching and learning tools that seek to prepare our students for the future and to be global citizens that live lives of consequence.

This book is a collection of articles from the *Journal of Teaching in Travel and Tourism*.

Darko Prebežac is a Professor of Tourism Marketing Management and Transportation Management at the University of Zagreb, Faculty of Economics & Business (Croatia). His research interests include marketing management (services, tourism, air transportation, airline companies and airports), transport and tourism and airline industry trends (globalization, consolidation, alliances, strategies and business models).

Christian Schott is TEFI Vice Chair (since April 2013) and a Senior Lecturer in the Victoria Business School at Victoria University of Wellington (NZ). His current research interests span: youth travel and self-development, sustainable tourism with a particular focus on climate change, and teaching and learning.

Pauline J. Sheldon is a co-founder of TEFI and is Emeritus Professor of Tourism at the School of Travel Industry Management at the University of Hawaii, USA. Her areas

The Tourism Education Futures Initiative

Activating Change in Tourism Education

Edited by
Darko Prebežac, Christian Schott and
Pauline J. Sheldon

Routledge
Taylor & Francis Group

LONDON AND NEW YORK

First published 2014
by Routledge
2 Park Square, Milton Park, Abingdon, Oxon OX14 4RN

Simultaneously published in the USA and Canada
by Routledge
711 Third Avenue, New York, NY10017

Routledge is an imprint of the Taylor & Francis Group, an informa business

First issued in paperback 2014

© 2014 Taylor & Francis

British Library Cataloguing in Publication Data
A catalogue record for this book is available from the British Library

ISBN 13: 978-0-415-84416-1 (hbk)
ISBN 13: 978-0-415-72196-7 (pbk)

Typeset in Garamond
by Taylor & Francis Books

Publisher's Note
The publisher accepts responsibility for any inconsistencies that may have arisen during the conversion of this book from journal articles to book chapters, namely the possible inclusion of journal terminology.

Disclaimer
Every effort has been made to contact copyright holders for their permission to reprint material in this book. The publishers would be grateful to hear from any copyright holder who is not here acknowledged and will undertake to rectify any errors or omissions in future editions of this book.

Contents

Part III: TEFI Papers – Case Studies

CONTENTS

Citation Information

The following chapters were originally published in various issues of the *Journal of Teaching in Travel and Tourism*. When citing this material, please use the original page numbering for each article, as follows:

Chapter 2
Tourism Education Futures, 2010–2030: Building the Capacity to Lead
Pauline Sheldon, Dan Fesenmaier, Karl Woeber, Chris Cooper, and Magda Antonioli
Journal of Teaching in Travel and Tourism, volume 7, issue 3 (2007) pp. 61–68

Chapter 3
The Tourism Education Futures Initiative (TEFI): Activating Change in Tourism Education
Pauline J. Sheldon, Daniel R. Fesenmaier and John Tribe
Journal of Teaching in Travel and Tourism, volume 11, issue 1 (2011) pp. 2–23

Chapter 4
Academic Agency and Leadership in Tourism Higher Education
Dianne Dredge and Christian Schott
Journal of Teaching in Travel and Tourism, volume 13, issue 2 (2013) pp. 105–129

Chapter 5
A Learning Theory Framework for Sustainability Education in Tourism
Bonnie Farber Canziani, Sevil Sönmez, Yuchin (Jerrie) Hsieh, and Erick T. Byrd
Journal of Teaching in Travel and Tourism, volume 12, issue 1 (2012) pp. 3–20

Chapter 6
Toward Values Education in Tourism: The Challenge of Measuring the Values
Gianna Moscardo and Laurie Murphy
Journal of Teaching in Travel and Tourism, volume 11, issue 1 (2011) pp. 76–93

Chapter 20

Reforming Higher Education: The Case of Jordan's Hospitality and Tourism Sector
Donald E. Hawkins, Joseph Ruddy and Amin Ardah
Journal of Teaching in Travel and Tourism, volume 12, issue 1 (2012)
pp. 105–117

Please direct any queries you may have about the citations to
clsuk.permissions@cengage.com

Notes on Contributors

Magda Antonioli Corigliano is a Professor of Tourism Policy, Director of the Master in Tourism and Economics at Bocconi University, Milan, and Senior Professor at the Bocconi Business School. She serves as a special adviser for the EU Commissioner for Tourism and her current research includes tourism, industrial and environmental policy.

Amin Ardah is an Industry Training Specialist with the USAID/Jordan Tourism Development Project. He has coordinated industry based training activities and the development of standards for personnel in the hospitality and tourism sector. He also serves as liaison with the Higher Education Accreditation Commission in Jordan.

Elizabeth H. Barber is the Associate Dean of Temple University's School of Tourism and Hospitality Management. She is a Certified Hospitality Educator (CHE). Her areas of research have included values education, curriculum development, instructional adequacy, teaching and learning styles, and customer and personnel satisfaction within an organization.

Pierre Benckendorff is Senior Lecturer and social scientist in the School of Tourism, The University of Queensland, Australia. His research interests include consumer behavior in tourism and leisure, the impact of new technologies on tourism, tourism education and tourism scholarship and epistemology.

Gillian Bowser is a Research Scientist at Colorado State University in the Natural Resource Ecological Laboratory where her research is focused on biodiversity, sustainability and women scholarship. She is the lead investigator on four National Science Foundation grants related to sustainability and undergraduate education.

Zélia Breda is Invited Assistant Professor at the Department of Economics, Management and Industrial Engineering and a member of the Research Unit 'Governance, Competitiveness and Public Policies' of the University of Aveiro (Portugal). Her research interests include governance, networks, gender, tourism in China and Goa, and internationalization.

Erick T. Byrd is an Associate Professor in the Department of Marketing, Entrepreneurship, Hospitality and Tourism in the Bryan School of Business and Economics at the University of North Carolina Greensboro. His current research interests focus on community participation in sustainable tourism development, tourism marketing and destination planning.

Sandra Caçador is Research Assistant at the Department of Economics, Management and Industrial Engineering of the University of Aveiro (Portugal). She holds a Master in Management and a BSc in Mathematics from the University of Aveiro. Her current research interests include organization theory, corporate finance and quantitative methodologies.

Bonnie Farber Canziani is an Associate Professor in the Bryan School of Business and Economics at the University of North Carolina Greensboro. Her current research foci include: services management and marketing in the hospitality and wine industries, cultural sustainability, and hospitality entrepreneurship. She also has a background in academic assessment and program evaluation.

Inês Carvalho is a Ph.D. candidate in Tourism studies at the University of Aveiro (Portugal) and visiting Ph.D. student at the Unit of Gender Studies at Linköping University (Sweden). Her current research interests include gender and tourism organizations, as well as literary tourism.

Inger-Marie F. Christensen is an E-learning Consultant at the University of Southern Denmark. She holds a Master's degree in ICT and learning. Her field of interest is teacher training and educational design of blended learning and distance learning with a particular focus on collaborative learning processes and feedback.

Chris Cooper is a Professor and the co-editor of Current Issues in Tourism, the co-series editor of Channelview's influential book series 'Aspects of Tourism' and series editor of Goodfellow Publisher's Contemporary Tourism Reviews. He was awarded the UN Ulysses Medal for contributions to tourism education and policy in 2009.

Carlos Costa is a Professor (Professor Catedrático) based at the University of Aveiro (Portugal). He is leader of the PhD Programme and of the Tourism Research Unit. He is also Editor of the Portuguese Tourism & Development Journal.

Rui Costa is a member of the Research Unit 'Governance, Competitiveness and Public Policies' at the University of Aveiro (Portugal), Department of Economics, Management and Industrial Engineering. His research interests include small and micro enterprises, networks, strategic planning and development, and evaluation of tourism public policies.

Dianne Dredge is Adjunct Professor, Urban Research Program, Griffith University, Australia. She was project leader on an Australia-wide project examining the balance between liberal and vocational education in tourism and hospitality curriculum. She was First Vice Chair of CAUTHE and is Chair of TEFI since April 2013.

Daniel R. Fesenmaier is a Professor in the School of Tourism and Hospitality Management and Director of the National Laboratory for Tourism & eCommerce, Temple University. His research focuses on tourism marketing, advertising evaluation and the use of information technology by travelers and the travel industry. He is co-founder of TEFI.

Linda Joyce Forristal is an Assistant Professor in the Department of Hospitality Management, Culinary Arts and Food Science at Drexel University. She teaches undergraduate and graduate courses in tourism, including Introduction to Tourism, Cultural Heritage Tourism, The Global Tourism System, Literary Tourism, and Tourism Geography. She also guides graduate hospitality research.

Ulrike Gretzel is an Associate Professor at the University of Wollongong. She received her PhD in Communications from the University of Illinois at Urbana Champaign and holds a Masters degree in International Business from the Vienna University of Economics and Business. Her research focuses on the design and implementation of intelligent systems in tourism.

Donald E. Hawkins is the Eisenhower Professor of Tourism Policy at the George Washington University School of Business. In 2003, he received the first United Nations World Tourism Organization Ulysses Prize and serves as the Special Advisor to the UNWTO Secretary General for the Knowledge Network.

Tania von der Heidt is a Senior Lecturer in Marketing at Southern Cross University. Her research interests include innovating the marketing curriculum by embedding creative problem solving and education for sustainability. Tania has led a number of research projects and has published over 35 refereed journal articles and conference papers.

Anne-Mette Hjalager is a Professor and Head of Center at the Danish Center for Rural Research, University of Southern Denmark. Her areas of interest are local development, innovation and labor market issues in tourism. She is involved in transnational research in rural wellbeing, ecosystems services and innovation issues in tourism.

Yuchin "Jerrie" Hsieh is an Associate Professor in the Bryan School of Business and Economics at UNC Greensboro. Prior to her return to academia, Dr. Hsieh held managerial positions in the lodging industry. Her research interests include hotel employees' occupational health, hospitality sustainability and education.

Annica Isacsson is a Principal Lecturer at HAAGA-HELIA University of Applied Sciences, Finland. Annica has managed her own tourism company, designed and implemented a tourism bachelor level degree curriculum, managed a number of tourism related projects and programs and actively integrated research and development projects into tourism implementations and teaching.

Montserrat Iglesias Xamaní is a Senior Lecturer of English as a Foreign Language at the School of Hospitality and Tourism Management CETT-UB (University of Barcelona, Spain) and the Head of Studies at CETT Language School. Her research focuses on Oral Communicative Competence in English and on Language Tourism.

Janne J. Liburd is Director of the Centre for Tourism, Innovation and Culture at the University of Southern Denmark. She is a cultural anthropologist and her research interests are in the fields of higher education and sustainable tourism development.

Rico Maggi is the Dean of the Faculty of Economics at University of Lugano. He teaches microeconomics, international economics and tourism economics and oversees research in transportation and mobility, urban development and tourism. He is the President of the Swiss Science Transport Association.

David Matarrita-Cascante is an Assistant Professor in the Department of Recreation, Park, and Tourism Sciences at Texas A&M University, USA. His interest in tourism lies at the intersection of community development, rural sustainable natural tourism, and development of study abroad opportunities for students interested in sustainability, tourism, and rural development.

Gianna Moscardo is a Professor in the School of Business at James Cook University. Prior to joining JCU Gianna was the Tourism Research project leader for the CRC Reef Research for eight years. Her research interests include understanding tourist behaviour and experiences and evaluating tourism as a sustainable development strategy.

Edna Mrnjavac is a Professor at the University of Rijeka, Croatia, Faculty of Tourism and Hospitality Management, specializing in the field of transport and logistics in tourism. She wrote the university books *Maritime System*, *Traffic in Tourism*, and *Logistics Management in Tourism* and is a member of the Croatian Academy of Technical Sciences.

Laurie Murphy is an Associate Professor in the School of Business at James Cook University. Her research interests focus on improving tourism's contribution to regional communities with an emphasis on tourism marketing, including the backpacker market, destination image, choice and branding, tourist shopping villages and community well-being.

Loredana Padurean is Professor of Management at Lasell College in Newton, MA, USA, focusing on the area of operations and entrepreneurship in services. She is actively teaching and consulting internationally in USA, Switzerland, Italy and India.

Nadia Pavia is a Professor at the University of Rijeka, Croatia, Faculty of Management in Tourism and Hospitality, specialising in the field of organization and management in hotel industry. She is the author of the university books *Organization and Categorization of Hospitality Facilities* and *Management of Processing Functions in the Hotel Industry*.

David Peguero Manzanares graduated from Ecole Hoteliere de Lausanne and IESE (University of Navarra, Spain). He is the Director of CETT Consultancy Division and has 20 years' experience in Tourism Consultancy and Hospitality Management, as well as broad experience in Education Management and in the business development of educational programs.

Darko Prebežac, is a Professor of Tourism Marketing Management and Transportation Management at the University of Zagreb, Faculty of Economics & Business (Croatia). His research interests include marketing management (services, tourism, air transportation, airline companies and airports), transport and tourism and airline industry trends (globalization, consolidation, alliances, strategies and business models).

Nicholas 'Joseph' Ruddy is a development specialist in tourism education, training and development with experience in Europe, Asia and Africa. He holds a Ph.D, MA, BSc and is currently serving as Component Leader for USAID Jordan Tourism Development. He has 25 years' experience in management at technical and university levels.

Gloria Sanmartín Antolín is a Senior Lecturer of Hospitality Management at the School of Hospitality and Tourism Management CETT-UB (University of Barcelona, Spain) and a Senior Consultant of CETT Consultancy Division. Her areas of expertise include all aspects of Hospitality Management, especially Operations Management, Revenue Management and Quality Systems.

Christian Schott is a Senior Lecturer in Victoria Business School at Victoria University of Wellington (NZ). His current research interests span: youth travel and self development, sustainable tourism with a particular focus on climate change, and teaching and learning. He is Vice Chair of TEFI since April 2013.

Pauline J. Sheldon is a co-founder of TEFI and Emeritus Professor of tourism at the School of Travel Industry Management, at the University of Hawaii, USA. Her areas of research are sustainable tourism, corporate social responsibility in tourism, wellness tourism, and knowledge management in tourism.

Sevil Sönmez is Professor in the Bryan School of Business and Economics at UNC Greensboro. Her research focuses on the preventive medicine role of travel and occupational health of tourism and hospitality sector workers. She examines health risks and benefits of tourism and impacts on destination sustainability.

John Tribe is Professor and Head of Tourism at the University of Surrey, UK. His research concentrates on sustainability, epistemology and education. He is editor of *Annals of Tourism Research* and the *Journal of Hospitality, Leisure Sport and Tourism Education (JOHLSTE)*.

Vidoje Vujić is a Professor at the Faculty of Tourism and Hospitality Management, Opatija, Croatia. In his field of research (entrepreneurship, management of human capital and business culture) he has written several university books: *Management of Human Capital, Entrepreneurship and Management in Service Industries, Change Management* and *Business Ethics and Multiculture*.

Elina Wainio, M.Sc. (Economics), born 1968 in Finland, has worked as a Senior Lecturer of business and tourism since 1999. Prior to her academic career, she worked within sales and marketing in tourism business for a decade. The mother of two sons enjoys broadening her perspectives by reading and traveling.

Erica Wilson is Senior Lecturer and Deputy Head of School in the School of Tourism and Hospitality Management at Southern Cross University. She has published over 40 refereed or edited outputs. Her scholarly interests include sustainable tourism, gender and tourism, food studies, and the use of critical/qualitative approaches in tourism.

Karl Wober is Full Professor and Founding President of MODUL University Vienna. Since 2012 he is the chairman of the Austrian Private University Conference. His research on decision support systems for tourism marketing and planning led to the development of the leading tourism marketing information system in Europe (www.tourmis.info).

Preface

Today's radical global changes are a catalyst for the dramatic changes in tourism around the world. Not only is it imperative that tourism education adapts to match these external shifts in order for graduates to succeed as leaders and stewards of the future industry, but it is also important to give space and time to imagine, discuss and create the future we want for tourism education.

In 2007, a small group of international tourism educators joined forces to respond to this challenge over time inviting others to join the initiative. Out of this meeting (which took place at Modul University, Vienna, Austria) the Tourism Education Futures Initiative (TEFI) was born. TEFI seeks to be the leading, forward-looking network that inspires, informs, supports and gives voice to tourism educators and students to passionately and courageously transform the world for the better.

Since that initial meeting TEFI has held annual conferences all over the world: in 2008 (Hawaii, USA), 2009 (Lugano, Switzerland), 2010 (San Sebastian, Spain), 2011 (Philadelphia, USA), 2012 (Milan, Italy) and 2013 (Oxford, England). Although each conference has had a different theme, the glue that binds them together is a commitment and passion for the future of tourism education.

This book represents some of the thinking of the educators who have been involved with TEFI in re-designing tourism education with a future focus and a focus on values. It represents content from the annual conferences that were subsequently published in three special issues of *Journal of Teaching in Travel and Tourism* (JTTT), and also contains a few papers published in earlier issues.

The book's structure has a logical order and gradually introduces the reader to the challenges of tourism education. The Introduction explains the role of TEFI in future tourism education and its influence in building the capacity needed to lead the necessary changes. Parts I to III contain inspiring work from TEFI conference research sessions, which are a thought-provoking demonstration of the high quality theoretical and conceptual papers, education-relevant applications and interdisciplinary case studies throughout the world. In the Epilogue the authors synthesise the collective TEFI learnings as well as the dilemmas facing tourism education. This aims to develop strategies for creating a sustainable approach to tourism education and the world at large.

It is anticipated that the provision of this book will enable the wider academic and student community to access the TEFI-relevant special issue scholarship in one location. The book aims to inspire tourism educators and industry alike, as they seek to engage their students or employees with the values and knowledge necessary in preparing them to be destination stewards.

We would like to thank Dr. Daniel Fesenmaier for his inspiration and leadership since the very beginning of TEFI, and Dr. Dianne Dredge for her recent contributions and her efforts in defining the future of TEFI. Thanks also goes to each contributor of this book, for sharing their ideas and creativity to improve tourism education. Special thanks go to Dr. Cathy Hsu, editor of JTTT, who saw the value of our work and each year assigned a special issue of her journal to publish papers from our conferences.

Numerous universities have sponsored the TEFI conferences over the last seven years and we would like to thank them also (in alphabetical order): Bocconi University (Milan, Italy), Hong Kong Polytechnic University (Hong Kong, China), Modul University (Vienna, Austria), Oxford Brookes University (Oxford, England), Southern Cross University (Gold Coast, Australia), Temple University (Philadelphia, USA), University of Deusto, (San Sebastian, Spain), University of Lugano (Lugano, Switzerland), University of Hawai'i (Honolulu USA), University of Queensland (Brisbane, Australia), Virginia Tech University (Blacksburg, USA).

Finally, thanks to the Publisher for giving us a chance to provide another forum with which to communicate our vision and the challenges we face in shaping tourism education for the future.

Darko Prebežac
Christian Schott
Pauline J. Sheldon

The Tourism Education Futures Initiative: An Introduction

PAULINE J. SHELDON

School of Travel Industry Management, University of Hawaii, Honolulu, HI, USA

DARKO PREBEŽAC

Faculty of Economics & Business, Department for Tourism, University of Zagreb, Zagreb, Croatia

DANIEL R. FESENMAIER

School of Hotel and Tourism Management, Temple University, Philadelphia, PA, USA

The impetus for this book is the need to transform tourism educational programs so as both to prepare students for a different world and to help them contribute to and create this world. Students entering the uncertain world of the future and in particular, the vulnerable tourism sector, need different skills, aptitudes and knowledge to succeed. Educational systems in general need radical change to meet the challenge of the next few decades (Wallis and Steptoe, 2006). Skills and knowledge sets must be redefined, structures and assumptions need to be questioned, and old ways of doing things must be transcended. Tourism employment in the coming decades must have a very different profile than it does today. In 2030 students will be applying for jobs that do not even exist today, and much of what we teach our students is obsolete by the time they graduate. These pressures and the increasing need for responsible stewardship of tourism destinations call out for a new paradigm of values-based tourism education. We believe that university level tourism programs must build the capacity in our graduates to lead in a new and different way.

In an attempt to address these issues, the Tourism Education Futures Initiative (TEFI) was born in 2007 by a few concerned tourism educators (Sheldon et al, 2008). This book provides a consolidation of TEFI's work, and a framework for the future development of tourism education. Its content is based on the writings of about fifty experienced educators who have attended TEFI conferences over the last six years.

They inquire into the need for change and recommend diverse approaches that constitute a framework for a new tourism curriculum. Therefore, the vision of TEFI is to not only work to reshape tourism education worldwide, but to help the leaders of the tourism industry follow practices that are rooted in basic values. For an introduction to TEFI, please see our website: www.tourismeducationfutures.org

Perspectives of different stakeholder groups have been important to TEFI discussions. Industry members, graduate students, central university administrators and community representatives have participated in our conferences, albeit in the minority. Their presentations and opinions have informed the outcomes. The value shift that TEFI advocates must happen, and is happening, in these stakeholder groups making it easier for students upon graduation to find positions that support their education experience. For many graduates, this may not be the case and they must be the changemakers in their future work environments.

The first TEFI meeting was in 2007 at Modul University, Vienna, Austria, to discuss the status of tourism education and to assess whether there was consensus on the need to develop alternative models for tourism education. During this meeting, a process emerged that is both proactive and action oriented to create a fundamental change in tourism education. The TEFI process includes two important action settings: first, an annual conference, which brings together innovators and keynote speakers from around the world to consider issues related to the future of tourism education. Second, we have working groups, which throughout the year develop tools that can be used to affect tourism education.

The Annual Conference is generally comprised of 40 – 50 leading scholars and industry professionals and includes keynote presentations and breakout groups. Each conference has a specific theme relating to the future of tourism education. The keynote presentations stimulate thinking and challenge the status quo related to that theme. While the lectures provide the starting point of discussion, the main work of the TEFI annual conference is in the breakout groups that provide the setting for ideation, creativity, dialogue and problem resolution. The results of these breakout groups are presented to the entire TEFI body for clarification, refinement and concensus.

The Working Groups move the TEFI agenda forward between conferences by providing essential energy and direction resulting in concrete action-oriented tools that can be used by tourism educators. For example, one Working Group conducted a pre-meeting survey of participants regarding key knowledge and skill sets needed for the tourism graduate of the future. Another group developed a 'values inventory' which may be used as part of program assessment.

The first TEFI Conference at Modul University, Vienna explored various futuristic scenarios of society to which tourism education programs would need to adapt. Modifying tourism education programs to fit a multitude of possible world scenarios, or even a single preferred scenario was found to be a task fraught with too much specificity and uncertainty. Instead, TEFI participants concluded that whatever world scenario emerges in the future, certain values would provide the students with the foundation to meet the multitude of uncertainties presented by that the future. Given this consensus, the work of TEFI moved to define these value sets.

At the second TEFI Conference at the University of Hawai'i, USA, five values-based principles were identified to be embodied in tourism education programs ensuring students became responsible leaders and stewards for destinations in Figure 1 (see below)

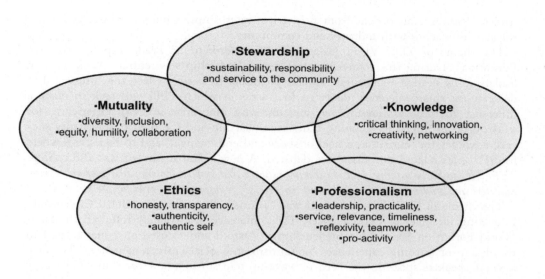

Figure 1 TEFI Values

Specifically the five values are: 1. Ethics, 2. Stewardship, 3. Knowledge, 4. Professionalism and 5. Mutuality. They are conceptually portrayed as interlocking value principles demonstrating their interconnectedness and permeability. TEFI members envisioned that educators can use subsets of the five value principles to integrate into their courses as appropriate.

During the third TEFI Conference at the University of Lugano, Switzerland, delegates considered each value in more detail and designed learning objectives and knowledge content that could be used to teach these values in a tourism context. The outcome of their work resulted in detailed descriptions of specific learning experiences and learning objectives for each value-based principle. These can be found on our website in the White Paper. We are grateful to the delegates of TEFI II and III for their contributions during the conference and after the conference ended. Another focus of TEFI III was the consideration of Outcome-Based teaching, and whether this would provide a useful resource for furthering the TEFI agenda. The group decided not to accept this approach, as the rigidity of the outcomes-based approach was too restrictive to the creative development that was required to transform tourism education.

The Theme of TEFI IV at University of Deusto in San Sebastian, Spain was "Tools for Change and New Challenges". The delegates at this conference heard from keynote speakers about new challenges that tourism education will face in the years ahead. The working groups focused on designing new tools that could be shared with other educators wishing to provide a future oriented values-based education for their students. It was at this conference that the concept of the global online courses was developed.

The theme of TEFI V in Philadelphia was "Activating Change in Tourism Education" with the goal of implementing the changes discussed so far, and bringing them to action. In line with this thinking, TEFI V was the first meeting where delegates presented their research and initiatives. Presentations addressed how we should engage industry, communities and students in learning experiences. Complementing the presentations and discussions, very enlightening field trips forced us to imagine how student learning can benefit from field trips, internships, service learning, and other ways of interfacing with industry and community.

The theme of TEFI VI in Milan was "Transformational Leadership for Tourism Education". During this conference the issue of leadership was central. What type of leadership is needed to change tourism programs to better reflect the future? The delegates at this conference identified four areas in which TEFI will seek to make a difference in the years ahead; they are: fostering innovative learning experiences for students at all levels, re-visioning tourism scholarship and the metrics for faculty success, advocacy for tourism as a field of study and employment, and to be a place where futures issues related to tourism are debated. A new vision statement was also crafted: *TEFI seeks to be the leading, forward-looking network that inspires, informs and supports tourism educators and students to passionately and courageously transform the world for the better.*

The theme of TEFI VII in Oxford was "Tourism Education for Global Citizenship: Educating for Lives of Consequence". The conference immediately followed the Skoll World Forum on Social Entrepreneurship in Oxford and focused on issues related to the design of learning experiences for tourism and social entrepreneurship. The three keynote speakers spoke to the need to wake-up tourism to a new paradigm and recognize the significant policy shifts that are occurring at the international level. Delegates were also challenged to re-examine their understanding of global citizenship and discover ways to include new dimensions in the classroom. The proposal for a TEFI Change Conference that embodied faculty learning about social entrepreneurship in a tourism setting while walking in Nepal was proposed and eagerly received. Many new initiatives were born at this exciting meeting.

The key articles from these seven conferences have been captured in special issues of the *Journal of Teaching in Travel & Tourism (JTTT)*, which are reprinted here in this book. Editor-in-Chief Cathy Hsu designated three thematic issues of JTTT to TEFI's work, and the interest in this topic has been strong. An article introducing TEFI's work published less than a year after the first TEFI Conference is still the most cited and downloaded article of the Journal indicating strong interest and concern for tourism education's future (Sheldon, Fesenmaier, Woeber, Cooper, & Antonioli, 2008).

This book is divided into three sections and represents the work of innovative, thoughtful, and committed scholars and industry leaders, who have contributed to TEFI. The book is structured such that it first introduces the reader to TEFI and then systematically discusses the challenges facing tourism education at the university level. The focus of the book is both conceptual and pragmatic in nature, and covers a wide range of issues facing tourism education not only in the future, but also at present.

Part I entitled "TEFI PAPERS – Theoretical and Conceptual" consists of four high quality and inspiring works seeking to provide vision, knowledge and frameworks for tourism education programs that promote global citizenship and examine critically the context of the neo-liberal university. The papers also report on different initiatives examining the future of tourism education into the years 2010 -2030, explore the leadership in tourism higher education and provide a conceptual framework for sustainable education that moves beyond current models in tourism education.

Part II entitled "TEFI PAPERS – Applications" presents eight education-relevant applications of TEFI philosophy. The authors deal with the conceptual framework of tourism values, the creation of a TEFI values inventory, examine barriers to transformational changes of the tourism curriculum, implementation of new technology and new pedagogies, environmental attitudes, gender perspectives and the communication of role models to tourism students.

Part III entitled "TEFI PAPERS – Case Studies" provides seven interdisciplinary case studies dealing with the implementation of core values into the undergraduate curriculum, value-based teaching in the context of sustainable tourism, inter-disciplinarity and reform policies and practices in higher tourism education, students' integration in innovative research and development projects, educational leadership, and career development of tourism graduates. The case studies illustrate important tourism education issues in a variety of English and non-English speaking countries in different parts of the world, including USA, Scandinavia, Southern Europe, the Caribbean and the Middle East.

In the last chapter "The Way Forward" the authors synthesise the collective TEFI learnings over the past seven years in an effort to address some important shifts needed to provide an education of quality and relevance to tomorrow's tourism industry.

It is our hope that this book will encourage the reader to reflect on the many socio-economic, political, cultural, environmental and industry issues affecting tourism education. It is also our hope that readers will be stimulated by the book to create their own solutions to the challenge of creating real leaders and stewards for the tourism industry of the future.

REFERENCES

Sheldon, P., Fesenmaier, D., Woeber, K., Cooper, C., & Antonioli, M. (2008). Tourism Education Futures – 2010–2030: Building the Capacity to Lead. *Journal of Teaching in Travel & Tourism*, 7(3), 61–68.

Wallis, C., and Steptoe, S. (2006). How to bring our Schools out of the 20th Century. Time, Sunday, 10th December.

Tourism Education Futures, 2010–2030: Building the Capacity to Lead

Pauline Sheldon
Dan Fesenmaier
Karl Woeber
Chris Cooper
Magda Antonioli

ABSTRACT. This paper reports on an initiative to examine the future of tourism education into the years 2010–2030. A group of 45 senior tourism educators and industry experts came together for a summit at Modul University, Vienna, Austria to discuss how tourism education needs to adapt to significant societal and industry changes. The theme of the summit was how to build the capacity for tourism students to lead the industry into the future as it faces increasing pressures for responsibility and stewardship. This paper discusses the pre-summit and summit processes and their outcomes, and explains future plans for this Tourism Education Futures Initiative (TEFI). Among other outcomes was a listing of values that could create the foundation for future tourism education programs, and also five categories of skills that participants felt would be important for students of the future to master. These are destination stewardship skills, political skills, ethical skills, enhanced human resource skills, and dynamic business skills.

... for business leaders to succeed in the global economy will require new kinds of management processes and analytical frameworks. Their decision rules will need to be more rigorous and open to a wider set of measures and realities than in the past. The old decision rules and assumptions won't do. In fact a new definition of rigor is needed. (Samuelson, 2006, p. 356)

Logical and precise, left-brain thinking gave us the Information-Age. Now comes the Conceptual-Age—ruled by artistry, empathy, and emotion. (Pink, 2005, p. 70)

INTRODUCTION

The world is experiencing seismic changes. We know what they are, and we know they are happening with increasing frequency. Society and tourism are being shaken by these external shocks and need to adjust to the impacts and prepare to act, think, and plan differently. Students who enter this uncertain world and, in particular, the fragile and vulnerable tourism sector, need different skills, aptitudes, and knowledge, implying that educational systems need to change radically to meet this need (Wallis & Steptoe, 2006). Tourism educational programs need to fundamentally retool and redesign—not incrementally by adding new courses or simply by putting courses on-line—but by changing the nature of what is taught and how it is taught. Skills and knowledge sets must be redefined, structures and assumptions need to be questioned, and old ways of doing things must be transcended. Tourism employment in the coming decades will have a very different profile than it does today. For example, the key jobs in 2015 may not even exist today, and much of what we teach our students may be obsolete by the time they graduate. These pressures and the increasing need for responsible stewardship of tourism call out for a new paradigm for values-based tourism education.

TOURISM EDUCATION FUTURES SUMMIT

In an attempt to address these issues, five sponsoring universities (Temple University and University of Hawaii, USA; The University of Queensland, Australia; Bocconi University, Italy; and Modul University, Austria) invited experienced educators and industry members to meet to discuss recommendations for a framework for a new tourism curriculum for 2010–2030. Specifically they came together with the following intention:

> To understand the changing environment that future students of tourism and hospitality will enter upon graduation. To identify the values, knowledge, and capabilities that graduates will need to lead positively, responsibly and effectively. Time frame for discussions: 2010–2030.

This initiative began with a summit in April 2007 at Modul University in Vienna, Austria, which was attended by 48 academics and industry members from 13 countries. Many of those in attendance were at the top of their careers and brought a wealth of experience and forethought to the discussions. Prior to the meeting, participants were sent readings to inform and focus their thinking process. These readings (Coles, Hall, & Duval, 2006; Pink, 2005; Samuelson, 2006; Wallis & Steptoe, 2006 listed in the references) were mostly chosen in the general field of education rather than in tourism. About two months prior to the summit, the participants were also surveyed regarding their perceptions of skills and knowledge sets that graduates of the future would need. The topics posed to them were:

- Please identify and explain the *four key issues* that you feel will most dramatically change the world of tourism in the period 2010–2030.
- Please identify and explain the *four key capabilities and knowledge areas* that graduates (undergraduate and master's students) entering the world of the future will need to acquire in their education.
- Please identify and explain the *four key capabilities and knowledge areas* that graduates entering the world of the future will need but do not currently acquire in their education.

The summit meeting began with a presentation by a futurist (Jim Dator) who laid the foundation for futures studies; he stressed the importance of considering different futures and creating the most preferable one. He identified the main threats or tsunamis that we need to be aware of as we project ourselves into 2030. They are demographic, environmental, techno-logical, economic, cultural, and governmental in nature. His detailed talk on each of these megatrends can be played on http://www.tourismeducation summit.com. This was followed by a tourism-specific presentation on "Implications of Global Megatrends for Tourism" by the Sustainable Tourism Cooperative Research Centre (ST CRC) in Australia (presented by Chris Cooper) (Dwyer et al., 2007). Many of the identified trends reflected those addressed by Dator. The main ones were social (e.g., age complexity, urbanization, feminization of workforce), political (e.g., safety and security, immigration issues), environmental and resources (e.g., climate change, land use changes), and technical (e.g., increasing impor-tance of knowledge, continued fast pace of technological development).

The next presentation by Gerry Fernandez highlighted the expected increases in social diversity in the future. The demographic shifts occurring in ethnicity, age, family status, religion, gender, sexual orientation, etc. will change the nature of the work force and the traveler by 2030. He explained how knowledge on diversity will become a competitive advantage and how leadership in the future will need to be more culturally competent.

Scott Meis developed the work force trends further and gave a human resource view of tourism considering education, labor, and jobs in tour-ism. He shared many results of statistical analysis and forecasting of the tourism labor market in Canada. The slide presentations of all the present-ers are available on http://www.tourismeducationsummit.com.

To start the hard work of the summit and to break the participants' comfort zones, Jim Dator presented five different geopolitical, social, and environmental scenarios for the delegates' consideration as they envisioned tourism in 2030. Part of the first day was spent in small groups working with these five possible futures and their impact on tourism.

The second day began by focusing on creating a set of values upon which future tourism education systems should be based. The values that emerged from participants' discussions are as follows:

- Managing/celebrating cultural diversity
- Pluralism
- Ethics
- Experiential learning
- Valuing people
- People's multifaceted capabilities
- Creativity, innovation, and ideas
- Emotional intelligence
- Self-actualization
- Inclusion
- Respect for education
- Value critical thinking
- Value knowledge and complexity
- Value of arts, sciences, and fundamental disciplines
- Openness
- Optimism
- Gender equity
- Educational diversity
- Instrumental education
- Good citizenship

The final step of the summit considered how program structures, curriculum design, and interactions between faculty, students, and industry should shift based on the previous sessions that had envisioned the future. This last step did not progress as far or as smoothly as the organizers had hoped. It was clear that more time was needed and more work needed to be put in.

Despite this sense of incompleteness, the summit ended with a sense that progress had been made and that futures thinking had begun. Many participants stated that they would take the findings of the summit home to their institutions and implement futures studies in their tourism programs (see the Website for these comments). The intended, and rather optimistic, goal of drafting a White Paper to provide a framework for the future of tourism education was not achieved. The summit therefore, rather than being a stand-alone event with an outcome, became an initial step in what is now realized needs to be a necessarily longer process taking two to three years to complete.

SURVEY RESULTS

One of the richest outcomes of the summit was the participants' responses to the pre-summit survey. The full responses are on the Website; however a consolidation of the comments is worth reporting here to guide future activities. It is hoped that it will be useful to tourism educators in general as they think through their own curricula. The responses of 16 participants were summarized and the following four categories emerged:

Destination Stewardship Skills

- Management of real and virtual networks
- Knowledge sharing skills
- Ability to respect and work with all stakeholders
- Managing complex adaptive systems
- Environmental management skills

Political and Ethical Skills

- Ethical behavior: demonstration and motivation
- Integration of basic human values into the workplace
- Lobbying and the ability to influence the political process

Enhanced Human Resource Skills

- Team building
- Effective listening and negotiation
- Motivation and leadership
- Working with distributed, virtual project teams
- Emotional intelligence

Dynamic Business Skills

- Flexibility
- Multitasking
- Critical thinking
- Optimal use of common sense
- Innovation/entrepreneurship

- Communication skills using new multimedia technologies
- Cross-cultural competencies
- Risk identification, estimation, and control
- Avoiding problems rather than solving them

SUMMARY AND NEXT STEPS

All the activities of the summit (including keynote speeches, scenarios, pre-summit survey responses, readings, etc.) can be found on the Website http://www.tourismeducationsummit.com. The sponsoring universities of the summit consider it vitally important to continue this initiative and the work that began in Vienna. To do this, it was felt that the initiative needed both a name and an organizational home. The initiative will now be called the Tourism Education Futures Initiative (TEFI) and is now incorporated into the BEST Education Network whose mission fits with the intent of the initiative:

> The BEST Education Network (BEST EN) is an international consortium of educators committed to furthering the development and dissemination of knowledge in the field of sustainable tourism (http://www.besteducationnetwork.org).

The goal of TEFI remains to create a framework for a values-based tourism curriculum that will be relevant and effective in creating responsible leaders for tourism in the coming decades. At the BESTEN Think Tank in Flagstaff, Arizona, June 2007, various members of the summit met to determine future steps in the initiative. Others who could not be present were also asked for their opinions on next steps. The next steps are well under way and are as follows:

- A small task force consisting of Dan Fesenmaier, Pauline Sheldon, Chris Cooper, Leo Jago, Sue Beeton, Janne Liburd, and John Tribe has been formed to guide the progress of the initiative.
- This report summarizing the progress to date will be circulated to all summit participants to inform them of the next steps.
- Two team members will research in depth the latest thinking, concepts, and ideas from the field of education regarding futures.
- One team member will research in depth the futures literature to ensure that all possible future trends and impacts are included in the initiative.
- The core task force met in October 2007 to discuss the findings and the next steps.

- One university has offered to be a pilot for the recommendations that emerge.
- BEST EN will give an award for Innovative Tourism Education Programs.
- Input from an Austrian graduate student's thesis will inform the process.
- A second summit is planned at the University of Hawaii, School of Travel Industry Management, April 11–14th, 2008 with the participants of the first summit. This summit will be entitled "Towards a Values-Based Tourism Education Program."
- A final summit in 2009 will complete the work, and the White Paper on a Future Curriculum for Tourism Education will be released by the end of 2009. The location of this summit is not yet determined.

REFERENCES

Coles, T., Hall, M. C., & Duval, D. T. (2006). Tourism and post-disciplinary enquiry. *Current Issues in Tourism, 9*(4/5), 293--319. Retrieved April 3, 2007, from the Future of Tourism Education Summit 2007 Web site: http://www.tourism.wu-wien.ac.at/Summit/Material/Tourism_and_Education.pdf.

Dwyer, L., Edwards, D., Mistilis, N., Scott, N., Cooper, C., & Roman, C. (2007). Trends Underpinning Tourism until 2020: An analysis for key drivers for change. Queensland, Australia: Sustainable Tourism CRC. Retrieved April 3, 2007, from the Future of Tourism Education Summit 2007 Web site: http://www.tourism.wu-wien.ac.at/Summit/Material/Tourism_Megatrends_2007.pdf.

Pink, D. H. (2005). Revenge of the right brain. *Wired, 2*, 70--72. Retrieved April 3, 2007, from the Future of Tourism Education Summit 2007 Web site: http://www.tourism.wu-wien.ac.at/Summit/Material/Revenge_of_the_Right_Brain.pdf.

Samuelson, J. (2006). The new rigor: Beyond the right answer. *Academy of Management, Learning, and Education, 5*(3), 356--365. Retrieved April 3, 2007, from the Future of Tourism Education Summit 2007 Web site: http://www.tourism.wu-wien.ac.at/Summit/Material/The_new_Rigor.pdf.

Wallis, C., & Steptoe, S. (2006, December 10). How to bring our schools out of the 20th century. *Time*. Retrieved April 3, 2007, from the Future of Tourism Education Summit 2007 Web site: http://www.tourism.wu-wien.ac.at/Summit/Material/How_to_bring_our_schools_out_of_the_20th_Century.pdf.

The Tourism Education Futures Initiative (TEFI): Activating Change in Tourism Education

PAULINE J. SHELDON
University of Hawaii, Honolulu, Hawaii, USA

DANIEL R. FESENMAIER
Temple University, Philadelphia, Pennsylvania, USA

JOHN TRIBE
University of Surrey, Surrey, UK

The Tourism Education Futures Initiative (TEFI) seeks to provide vision, knowledge, and a framework for tourism education programs that promote global citizenship and optimism for a better world. This article provides background on TEFI, its inception, its development and its future. The article argues that a fundamental shift in tourism education is necessary to respond to global challenges impacting tourism at a fundamental level. These shifts demand higher levels of responsibility and stewardship by graduates and industry leaders. TEFI attempts to address the complexity and diversity of the shifts required by educational institutions and industry. TEFI's work began by defining a set of foundational values for tourism education programs worldwide (stewardship, ethics, knowledge, mutuality, professionalism). TEFI is now addressing other important shifts needed to provide an education of quality and relevance to tomorrow's tourism industry.

INTRODUCTION

Tourism is a hallmark activity of the postmodern world. As such, it is a significant factor in world-making and people-making. The same can be said for universities—they are major enterprises and, historically, have been important sources of innovative thinking and change. The intersection of tourism and universities is, therefore, a powerful nexus of potential influence. From an industry perspective, tourism employment in the coming decades must have a very different profile than it does today. In 2020, students will be applying for jobs that do not even exist today, and much of what we teach our students is obsolete by the time they graduate. Students entering the uncertain world of the future and, in particular, the vulnerable tourism sector need different skills, aptitudes, and knowledge to succeed. To meet the challenges of the next few decades, tourism educational systems, however, are in need of radical change. Indeed, Wallis and Steptoe (2006) and many others argued that a fundamental re-tool and re-design is necessary; not incremental change, but change in the nature of what is taught and how it is taught. Further, skills and knowledge sets must be redefined, structures and assumptions need to be questioned; thus, the "old ways of doing things" must be transcended.

The challenges facing the tourism industry and tourism educators call out for a new paradigm of tourism education. In an attempt to address these challenges, the Tourism Education Futures Initiative (TEFI) was born by a few concerned tourism educators (Sheldon et al., 2008). The purpose of this article is to outline a framework developed by TEFI for the future development of tourism education. Its content is based on the input of about 80 experienced educators and industry leaders who met four times between 2007 an 2010 to discuss and debate the need for change and to provide recommendations for a framework for a new tourism curriculum for 2015–2030. Specifically TEFI has the following mission: "TEFI seeks to provide vision, knowledge and a framework for tourism education programs to promote global citizenship and optimism for a better world." The vision of TEFI is to not only work to reshape tourism education worldwide, but to help the leaders of the tourism industry follow practices that are rooted in basic values.

The TEFI was born in 2007 when a few tourism educators and industry met in Vienna, Austria to discuss the status of tourism education. During this meeting, a process emerged that provides a framework for the development of TEFI. Subsequent meetings in Hawaii, USA, Lugano, Switzerland, and San Sebastian, Spain built on the work in Vienna. TEFI is organized around a process that is both proactive and action oriented, focusing on translating the core values articulated by the participants into implementation to bring about fundamental change in tourism education.

An important initial outcome of the TEFI process is a set of five values-based principles that tourism students should embody upon graduation to become responsible leaders and stewards for the destinations (including hospitality and other tourism-related businesses and organizations) where they work or live. The five value sets are ethics, stewardship, knowledge, professionalism, and mutuality and are discussed in more detail later in this article. They are portrayed as interlocking values because of their interconnectedness and their permeability. This article provides more detail on these value sets, how they can be incorporated into the learning experience for tourism students, and examples of courses incorporating these values.

Another dimension of the TEFI process is the Working Groups that develop a range of tools for educating tourism students. These Working Groups are now involved in a number of activities including a faculty and student code of ethics; an outreach pilot program to universities worldwide; and a values inventory to be used as part of program assessment. Working Groups are currently finalizing their tools and outcomes. The next TEFI meeting will be the *TEFI World Congress: Activating Change in Tourism Education* at Temple University Philadelphia, Pennsylvania on May 18–21, 2011. Educators and industry leaders from around the world are invited to attend.

BACKGROUND AND RATIONALE

The intersection of the tourism industry and universities is a powerful nexus for tourism education in that both universities and tourism are products of the world—hence, a paradox exists in that they are both shaped by the world and have the potential to shape it. This paradox presents a challenge for tourism educators. Being part of the world, and not distant or removed from it, is of course important so that academics do not retreat to ineffectual ivory towers. That is to say, they should offer participation as well as critique and therefore universities should not just become places of critique. They should contribute to a productive world by developing a highly skilled workforce. But being shaped by the world also means that tourism education faces a number of challenges.

The first of these challenges is avoidance of unthinking reproduction (Apple, 1990). Here, the existing world model and machine, buttressed with solid structures and deeply impregnated by ideology (Althusser, 1984) has an innate tendency to reproduce itself in its current form. If caught in this simple, yet possibly blind cycle of reproduction, students learn to fit in passively to the world that exists (Minogue, 1973) rather than to create challenging vistas.

Related to this is a second tendency to concentrate on means rather than ends. That is to say, our present configuration of the tourism world tends to create a number of immediate problems that need solving (e.g., in marketing, operations, service quality, and logistics). Universities are called upon to produce human resources that can solve these problems. The urgency of the day-to-day inevitably competes for space with the equally urgent, but never quite so pressing issues of the future. Here, we can allow the vocational to supplant the philosophical (Tribe, 2002b), giving insufficient attention to questions of desirable ends and the kind of tourism world we wish to create.

The late 1980s saw the crisis of communism marked by the symbolic fall of the Berlin Wall. The year 2008 saw the crystallization of a third significant challenge: the crisis of capitalism marked by the symbolic fall of major banks including Lehman Brothers. This has surfaced the challenge of appropriate corporate and broader societal values. Here, university business schools have been fiercely criticized for a failure to give adequate attention or leadership to this part of the curriculum for future business leaders.

The fourth challenge relates to sustainability and is neatly captured by Giddens' Paradox (Giddens, 2009). This is the paradox of climate change where Giddens noted that because we are not currently unduly affected by the outcomes of climate change we fail to act. But when we are finally pressed into action by its consequences it will be too late to do anything about them.

The fifth challenge is that tourism might be read as another product of some form of Washington Consensus (Williamson, 1997). For example, its terms of trade (between supplier and consumer), its rules of engagement, its allowed and disallowed moves, its tolerance of inequality, indeed its general configuration performs to generate a predictable structure of winners and losers legitimized by a script of neoliberalist values.

A sixth and final challenge is that of extent and pace of change. Patterns of consumption, technological change, and supply innovation in tourism as elsewhere are in a constant state of transformation. This mean that graduates may find that their degrees only offer a few years of currency rather than a lifetime of expertise (Cooper, Hofheinz, & Purdy, 2007). This clearly stresses the need to understand and promote lifelong learning to underpin professional expertise.

These challenges set the context for TEFI. A central task is to educate tourism graduates (e.g., undergraduate and graduate students) to satisfy the demands of the market place as productive employees for a fast-changing world. The tourism industry expects its workforce to be well trained, and society might expect a contribution from universities in terms of enhanced economic performance. But any deep consideration of the term society generates other inescapable questions about what kind of tourism is to be developed. Here, it is argued that we need to re-think and re-engineer our tourism courses and our students' experiences. Further, it is argued that we need ourselves and our graduates to lead the debate about a set of values that should govern the development of the tourism world. If we achieve this, we would be at the forefront of people-making and world-making through tourism.

THE TEFI PROCESS

As highlighted previously, the seeds of TEFI are based upon the general recognition that higher education and more particularly, tourism education, must change in order to meet the challenges that face tourism and society. Additionally, it was recognized that many people (e.g., academicians, teachers, industry professionals, and government leaders) throughout the world have expressed their concerns regarding the future. Led by these voices, a number of innovators concerned about the future of tourism education met in Vienna, Austria to discuss the status of tourism education and to assess the degree to which there was an agreement concerning the need to develop alternative models for tourism education. During this meeting, a process emerged that provides a framework for the growth and development of TEFI. That is, TEFI is largely organized around a process which is both proactive and action oriented, focusing on translating the core values it has articulated into action and implementation to create a fundamental change in tourism education. The TEFI process includes two important action settings: (a) an Annual Summit, which brings together innovators from around the world to consider issues related to tourism education; and (b) Working Groups, which throughout the year seek to develop tools that can be used to affect tourism education.

The Annual Summit has been comprised of 30–40 leading scholars and industry professionals and has included a series of lectures and breakout discussion groups. The lectures are conducted to stimulate thinking and to challenge the status quo. For example, in the first Summit, Dr. Jim Dator (a leading futurist from the University of Hawaii) challenged the TEFI members to develop scenarios of future worlds and then to propose possible solutions/responses to these scenarios. In the second Summit, Dr. John Tribe (University of Surrey) articulated a vision of hope for the future of society and tourism education, in particular. But he also challenged the group to take personal responsibility in shaping this future world. Dr. Gianna Moscardo (James Cook University) focused on the learning styles of the next generation, arguing that how we teach is just as important as what we teach. And, Scott Meis (former director of research for the Tourism Industry Association of Canada) demonstrated quite conclusively that the industry need for qualified employees will become even more critical over the next decade. The third Summit focused on barriers to change within the university (as discussed by Dr. Thomas Bieger of the University of St. Gallen) and strategies for programmatic change (as exemplified in lectures by Drs. Irena Ateljevic, Simon Wong, Loredana Padurean, and Betsy Barber). These presentations clearly demonstrated barriers and potential strategies for changing educational processes within the university; they also highlighted a number of conflicts within higher education in realizing the changes. The fourth Summit in San Sebastian, Spain focused on the status of the Working Groups and the various tasks they have considered over the year, and on preparation for the TEFI World Congress to be held at Temple University, Philadelphia, Pennsylvania on May 18–21, 2011.

While the lectures provide the starting point of discussion, the main work of TEFI is in the breakout groups that provide the setting for ideation, creativity, dialog, and problem resolution. Throughout the TEFI Summits, the group members are tasked to develop position statements regarding the various issues related to the theme of the annual meeting. Then, the results of these efforts were presented to the entire TEFI body for clarification and ultimate approval.

The second pillar of the TEFI process is the Working Group. These Groups are tasked to move the TEFI agenda forward between Summits by providing essential energy and direction resulting in concrete action-oriented tools that can be used by TEFI. For example, prior to the first TEFI Summit, a Working Group identified a core set of readings that established a foundation—a common language and set of ideas and ideals—for discussion. In addition, the Working Group conducted a pre-meeting survey of participants regarding key knowledge and skill sets needed for the tourism graduate of the future. Three different Working Groups emerged from the first Summit, focusing on defining a set of values to drive the TEFI agenda forward, identifying case studies in values-based education, and evaluating outcome-based education as a tool to assess programmatic changes. Each of the Working Groups developed working papers and presentations that are then presented and discussed at the next TEFI Summit.

And finally, as the result of the Third Summit, a series of Working Groups were identified to create concrete "tools" for supporting TEFI-based initiatives. These Working Groups included proposing a Faculty Code of Ethics, developing an outreach pilot program to universities worldwide, and developing a values inventory, which may be used as part of program assessment.

TEFI VALUES

The first TEFI Summit explored various futuristic scenarios of society that tourism education programs would need to adapt to. It was decided that attempting to modify tourism education programs to fit a multitude of possible world scenarios, or even a single preferred scenario was a task fraught

FIGURE 1 The TEFI values of tourism education.

with too much specificity and too much uncertainty. Instead, a consensus among TEFI participants concluded that whatever the world scenario in the future, certain values would provide the students with the foundation to meet the multitude of uncertainties of the future. Given this consensus, the work of TEFI moved to define these value sets.

The five values-based principles that TEFI identified to be embodied in tourism education programs so that students become responsible leaders and stewards for the destinations where they work or live are shown in Figure 1. Specifically the five values are ethics, stewardship, knowledge, professionalism, and mutuality. They are conceptually portrayed as interlocking Value Principles demonstrating their interconnectedness and permeability. It is envisioned by TEFI members that educators can use subsets of the five value principles to integrate into their courses as appropriate. Each values-based principle is discussed below with an emphasis on how that concept can be incorporated into the tourism student learning process. For each principle we describe its definition, the content that should be included in the learning experience, and specific learning objectives.

Ethics

DEFINITION

Ethics is concerned with distinguishing between behavior that is right and behavior that is wrong. It is the basis for good action and provides a framework for judging actions that are questionable. *Ethical behavior* means striving for actions that are deemed "good" based on principles and values (Jamal & Menzel, 2008). It also involves making such principles and values explicit and rendering the processes that leads to decisions transparent (Fennell, 2000; Hudson & Miller, 2005). Recognizing that good actions do not occur in a vacuum but are derived from specific value systems further requires understanding and respect for actions based on different systems.

CONTENT

Teaching ethics involves the following:

1. Introducing students to Ethics as a field of study with practical importance by
    a. defining Ethics;
    b. encouraging reflexivity and decolonization of the self;
    c. recognizing diversity;
    d. outlining the practical importance of ethical behavior;
    e. discussing the specific issues and challenges in the context of tourism;
    f. exemplifying the implications of unethical behavior; and
    g. identifying the stakeholders in certain ethical dilemmas.
2. Exposing students to different ethical traditions and principles by
    a. helping students understand what traditions and principles exist (e.g., Utilitarianism, Kantian ethic of respect for others, Aristotelian virtue ethics, religion, principles of benevolence, honesty, autonomy, justice, etc.);
    b. explaining the evolution of these traditions;
    c. illustrating how these traditions and principles influence actions; and
    d. highlighting differences and potential areas of conflict.
3. Equipping students with the means to achieve reconciliation by
    a. explaining how Ethics informs judgment;
    b. engaging students in principles of negotiation; and
    c. illustrating ways in which conflicts can be resolved and compromises reached.
4. Drawing connections to issues of power and politics by
    a. identifying sources of power;
    b. discussing the importance and principles of the legitimization of power; and
    c. emphasizing the role of existing power structures in determining ethical outcomes.
5. Evoking actions by
    a. exposing students to sources which can guide their actions;
    b. encouraging students to develop their own Codes of Conduct; and
    c. having students identify and implement good actions.

Students who study Ethics in the tourism context should be able to:

- recognize its importance in general and specifically for tourism,
- judge their own and others' actions,
- value transparency,
- respect different ethical traditions/approaches,
- identify potential and actual conflicts and set actions in place to mitigate them,
- know which resources are available when dealing with ethical concerns, and
- provide ethical leadership and initiate changes for the better.

Knowledge

DEFINITION

Knowledge can be described as (a) expertise and skills acquired by a person through experience or education; (b) the theoretical or practical understanding of a subject; (c) facts and information about a field; or (d) awareness or familiarity gained by experience of a fact or situation. This implies that knowledge is more than data (summary descriptions of parts of the world around us) and more than information (data put into a context). Knowledge comes in both explicit and tacit formats. In most instances, it is not possible to have an exhaustive understanding of an information domain so knowledge is ceaselessly incomplete. Knowledge is created through processes of selecting, connecting, and reflecting. Knowledge is always already predicated by existing knowledge, which means that knowledge involves interpretation and contextualization and existing knowledge should be challenged.

CONTENT

The knowledge creation process should address *creativity*, *critical thinking*, and *networking* for change and innovation through complex cognitive processes of perception, reasoning, learning, communication, association, and application.

CREATIVITY

Creativity has been identified as a key factor to adequately address the seismic changes facing contemporary society and as a driving force toward knowledge creation and socio-economic advancements (European

University Association, 2007). It is often useful to explicitly distinguish between creativity and innovation. Creativity is typically used to refer to the act of producing new ideas, approaches, or actions that are appropriate to the problem at hand, while innovation often begins with creative ideas and involves a process of both generating and applying such creative ideas in a specific context for a human, cultural, or economic purposes. The ethical dimension of creativity and creative knowledge should be addressed. Dealing with future insecurity and uncertainty requires "thinking outside the box", looking at existing domains and problems from a new angle. Promoting such a culture of creativity that acknowledges and seeks to learn from failure encourages students to move from hypothesis and conventional knowledge toward possibilities and originality. Creativity and knowledge formation takes place in an organizational set-up, for example but not exclusively, in the format of educational institutions or business organizations. It is essential to envisage outcomes consisting of both factual and procedural knowledge, and that finding a balance between the two are essential for the comprehension and application of knowledge.

CRITICAL THINKING

Critical thinking calls for an unrelenting examination of any form of knowledge and the knowledge creation process to recognize the existence (or non-existence) of the use and power that supports it and the further conclusions to which it tends. It is important that knowledge is contextualized in order to recognize unstated assumptions and values. Critical thinking is not only about criticizing but being critical of the constitution of knowledge and underlying dogmas. Students should therefore be encouraged to make the implicit explicit and identify ethnocentric bias and prejudice whenever deciding upon or solving a problem. Embodying an ethical dimension in mainstream disciplines in social sciences can enrich the thinking and add relevant dimensions of critical thinking, not only for the critique as an academic exercise, but critique as part of a constructive pursuit. Responsible citizenship evolves through knowledge-enhancing critical thinking.

NETWORKING

The dissemination and development of knowledge take place in social environments. Social networks can create or assist in refining the use of knowledge. Bridging social networks can link different repositories of knowledge with the potential innovation effects. Networks and knowledge repositories become more open as a consequence of the development of technical and institutional remedies connected to the social media. Hereby, problem solving and identification increasingly take place through sharing and cooperation in open knowledge systems, where providers and users of knowledge meet and exchange information. Students and higher institutions of education must understand and address the issues of open knowledge sources and open innovation, which are in contrast to issues of knowledge hoarding, protection and monopolizing in closed learning environments. New ways of thinking about the professions are essential. Higher educational institutions must prepare students to become practitioners, researchers, philosophical scholars, and knowledge brokers throughout their studies and in their subsequent careers.

SPECIFIC STUDENT LEARNING OBJECTIVES IN THE TOURISM CONTEXT

As a phenomenon, industry, career, and lifestyle tourism constitutes exceptional learning opportunities. The specific student learning objectives in the tourism context are

- understanding the value and power of knowledge rather than data or information;
- the art and skill of sharing knowledge, including new codes of conduct;
- harvesting from new knowledge intermediaries;
- developing equitable ways of communication with industry and community—across national borders and disciplines;
- humility and courage in the fields of data creation and management, information management and knowledge creation and management;
- the art of questioning the answer - challenge what is taken for granted;
- letting go—risking the adventure of creative journeys, using creativity tools and new ways of collaboration;
- strengthening students' critical thinking skills through interactive teaching processes; and
- shifting from solely valuing and rewarding individual achievement toward collective action, participation and contribution.

Stewardship

DEFINITION

Stewardship implies the responsibility to care for something, or someone, and the accountability to exercise responsibility. The value of stewardship is deeply reflected in sustainable development (Liburd, 2010). It implies that the earth is a divine gift, which we are permitted to use and take care of for the benefit of future generations. This definition also suggests that tourism faculty and students should learn to take leadership in three distinct aspects of stewardship:

- sustainability,
- responsibility, and
- service to the community

All stakeholders have responsibility for the environment and the society and power and/or influence are necessary to exercise responsibility. Responsibility also implies the existence of rights. If all stakeholders are to take responsibility for the future of the planet in tourism, empowerment of those who are currently in a position of powerlessness is called for, just as the restraint of power of others may be necessary. Whereas local communities may help facilitate liaison building based on a shared sense of contextual responsibility, it is important to recognize that communities are not homogenous units that easily reach consensus. Service to the community is one way that stakeholders can demonstrate their commitment to taking responsibility.

CONTENT

A frequent claim made in the literature is that sustainable tourism development can be achieved. Arguing that sustainability is achievable over a period of time fails to understand that change and ever-evolving processes are the norm rather than the exception. Choice in life style, cultural preferences, and patterns of consumption and communication are not the same between generations and these are rather unpredictable. Similarly, it is not feasible to assume that tourism that stays the same "will go on forever" (C. M. Hall & Butler, 1995, p. 102). These arguments indicate that the very idea of striking a balance in which the environment, economy, and social and cultural elements are in equilibrium can be seen as an oxymoron. Appreciating the complexities of socio-cultural values, quality of life aspirations, and the bio-physical and economic systems in which tourism takes place over time, an integrated approach to stewardship is of importance. Consequently also discarding the notion of sustainable development as a goal that can be achieved is called for.

Stewardship implies that individuals and organizations acknowledge their responsibilities and act accordingly. All stakeholders have responsibility for the environment and the society, requiring the use of influence or power. Responsibility and stewardship also imply the existence of rights. If all stakeholders take responsibility for the future of the planet in tourism, empowerment of those who are currently powerless is necessary, as is the restraint of power of other groups. The stakeholders with responsibilities include destination governments, generating country governments, tourism industry firms and organizations, employees, tourists, host communities, media, and investors.

Finally, stewardship includes service to the destination community, allowing stakeholders to take responsibility. In the context of tourism education, in addition to the destination host community other communities worthy of consideration are students, graduates, and the global tourism academic community. Volunteer-tourism is an example of implementing service to the destination community.

In order to implement knowledge of stewardship in the tourism curriculum we propose that students are exposed to debates, which will challenge conventional ideas and taken-for-granted discourses. Educators must also consider whether they have the right or the responsibility to inculcate particular values in students. Including stewardship in the tourism curriculum will require this self-reflection by the educators.

The specific learning objectives are:

1. understand social and ecological systems;
2. be able to explain environmental governance and policies;
3. be able to apply adaptive management and adaptive co-management concepts;
4. understand tourists' ecological footprint;
5. understand the precautionary principle;
6. know environmental management systems;
7. understand the relationship between climate change and tourism;
8. understand different kinds of sustainable business practices and operations;
9. know how destinations can be managed to become more sustainable;
10. critically evaluate the impact of their own vacations;
11. undertake tourism-related projects that serve a community; and
12. understand the various motivators of stakeholders in the tourism system, and the various power structures between these stakeholders.

Professionalism

DEFINITION

Professionalism is a rather nebulous term as it implies not only a profession and the skills, competencies, or standards associated with it, but also an attitude and behavior that reflect these. It has also been defined as the ability to align personal and organizational conduct with ethical and professional standards that include a responsibility to the customer or guest and community, a service orientation, and a commitment to lifelong learning and improvement (Haga, 1976).

Professionalism is defined as incorporating leadership, a practical approach (practicality), attention to services, concern for the relevance and timeliness of evidence, reflexivity, teamwork and partnership building skills, and pro-activity. Pro-activity involves taking the initiative to address problems in one's service domain and a commitment to excellence in one's domain of expertise. According to Bateman and Crant (1993), "[p]roactive people scan for opportunities, show initiative, take action, and persevere until they reach closure by bringing about change. They are pathfinders (Levitt, 1988) who change their organization's mission or find and solve problems" (p. 105). This is in keeping with leadership, which is the ability to inspire individual and organizational excellence, to create and attain a shared vision, and to successfully manage change to attain the organization's strategic ends and successful performance.

CONTENT

The core values of professionalism are a requirement for all tourism and hospitality academic programs. It is educators' responsibility to expose students to high quality and appropriate professionalism. The term *new professionalism* is used by Sachs (2003) to distinguish between old forms of professionalism, which debate characteristics of professions and the extent to which occupational groups might be acknowledged as professions, and new forms, which, claimed Sachs, assume a "changed analytical perspective" and are seen to be more "positive, principled and postmodern" (p. 182). The distinction between old and new forms of professionalism is useful, although the notion that new forms of professionalism are necessarily positive and principled should be considered with caution, as there is also evidence of a less principled discourse in action.

While there is no overall agreement as to what constitutes a profession, certain key aspects are commonly cited that seek claim to professional status. These generally include reference to specialist knowledge, autonomy, and responsibility (Hoyle & John, 1995). Professionalism, therefore, implies that such characteristics are evident in an individual's work. It is also linked to ethics or ethical behavior. Some refer to it as an emotion, or a feeling of being professional. TEFI appears to include some of both, where professionalism is a series of behaviors and beliefs. To achieve success in the behavior of professionalism requires an attitude (ethical belief) of what makes a true professional. It also seems that leadership is key; because the professional that exhibits the most positive leadership often displays the other components in a positive manner as well.

SPECIFIC STUDENT LEARNING OBJECTIVES IN THE TOURISM CONTEXT

The desired learning outcome can be synthesized as having students aspire to the highest levels of professionalism and committed to continuous improvement of that professionalism. The two sections below identify the content to be transferred in the learning process. The way in which this can be done is discussed in general at the end of the two sections.

Relevance, timeliness, reflexivity. The rapid evolution of the demand and supply characteristics in the tourism industry require the professional to constantly think in terms of innovation and improvement to their own professionalism and also to the product, the processes and the services delivered. The learning environment must encourage students to understand the importance of timeliness in a variety of professional situations. It must also ensure that students understand that their work must be relevant to the ever-changing environments in the travel industry. It must also introduce the students to the importance of reflecting on their work and contributions.

The learning process must help students understand which information is relevant to address the issue at hand, the importance of timeliness in the decision-making process, and the need to reflect on the outcome once decisions have been made. It is critical that students understand the options available and can assess the appropriateness of each of the areas that might require attention and/or investment in the quest for professionalism. These three qualities of relevance, timeliness, and reflexivity are important in their contribution to tourism product, process, and service innovation and improvement. Innovation is often high risk, and involves substantial investment in people, time, and money. All dimensions of professionalism can be introduced in a sector by adopting accreditation and certification schemes.

Practicality, partnership, leadership. Tourism is an inherently conservative industry; slowly reacting to market trends and demands rather than predicting and preparing for them. Within reason and practicality, the ability of operators to discard their risk aversion is one of the first steps to take in becoming more innovative and, ultimately, more successful. Professionalism is critical when we look at the roles played inside the organization at all levels. It is the tertiary sector where the organizational competencies such as leadership, practicality, relevance, timeliness, reflexivity, teamwork, and partnership are critical needs.

Innovation pivots on intrinsically motivated individuals, within a supportive culture, informed by a broad sense of the future. Intrinsic innovation in the workplace evolves from an environment in which new ideas and creative thinking are genuinely encouraged. It requires an environment and leadership that allows ideas to be aired, tested, and allowed to flourish. Students must gain a full appreciation of the types of innovation that exist, the costs and benefits associated with each, the partnerships or team approaches required to bring them to fruition, and the leadership role that, in time, they will be called upon to exhibit within their organization. Various types of innovation are business model innovation, marketing innovation, supply chain innovation, and organizational innovation that involves the creation or alteration of business structures, practices, and models.

Learning objectives for the professionalism value would be knowledge and comprehension of the concepts underpinning professionalism (students should be able to list, define, describe, identify, show, label, collect, examine, summarize, describe, interpret, contrast, differentiate, and discuss). Then the skills involving application and analysis must be introduced (apply, demonstrate, calculate, illustrate, show, solve, examine, classify, experiment, discover, analyze, separate, order, explain, connect, compare, and select). Finally synthesis and evaluation must be introduced (combine, integrate, modify, plan, create, design, invent, compose, prepare, generalize, rewrite, assess, decide, grade, test, measure, recommend, convince, judge, explain, discriminate, support, conclude, and, summarize; Bloom, 1956). Students could either be exposed to a case study or an actual experiential learning environment (e.g., internship) where the assessment criteria would be incorporated into the learning objectives and the assignments given.

Mutual Respect

DEFINITION

Within the TEFI framework, *mutual respect* has been initially defined as diversity, inclusion, equity, humility, and collaboration. However, during the TEFI III Summit the meaning of this value was refined and extended by the participants: Mutual respect is seen as a value grounded in human relationships that requires attitudinal developments that are evolving, dynamic and involve acceptance, self-awareness of structural inequalities, open-mindedness, empowerment, and ability to revisit one' cultural understanding of the world.

CONTENT

Several important elements of the mutuality value are highlighted:

1. Mutuality is a process that is evolving and dynamic, emphasizing that achieving mutual respect is a long-term and even life-long learning process that can be developed at different levels, starting from the individual to the society and global levels. It also can apply to human–animal relationships particularly in the context of how animals are used in tourism. This development from survival values of one's own isolated existence to relational/global consciousness of mutuality has been researched for the last 25 years by eminent sociologist Ronald Inglehart (1990, 1997). In his longitudinal World Values Survey covering two-thirds of world population, he has been capturing global evolution of the personal, social, public, and cultural values, which he conceptualized under a theory of a "Spiral of Values" (see also Webster, 2001).

2. Mutuality starts with self-awareness and understanding of own identity, values, cultural drivers and behavioural patterns. Understanding self-identity is a prerequisite to understanding values and believes of other people, and developing positive attitudes to diverse identities. It is important to recognize that structural inequalities exist, including race, sex, gender, religion etc, and acknowledge these inequalities to eliminate the bias. Self-awareness also helps to question "I versus Them" attitude and move from comparing and contrasting to accepting and sharing. Self-awareness also helps to perceive self as a positive change agent.

3. Mutual respect is about behaviors and attitudes. Respect of self and others is an attitude that involves recognition and acknowledgement of other people's views. It goes beyond formal structures and legal frameworks for social inclusion and diversity, and it is grounded into early age education.

4. Mutuality is grounded in human relationships. Respect of self and others is developed through open interactions, through constructive communication and discussions, conflict avoidance and management, empathy and acceptance. Mutuality is about developing respectful relationships between self and people through sharing and understanding values and attitudes. Mutuality starts with changing our own mindset and the way of constructing and perceiving reality. It involves open discussions and appreciation of diverse opinions.

Tourism education is a medium through which mutual respect can be promoted. However, we believe that mutuality is a process that starts from self and therefore cannot be taught directly as a subject but rather facilitated through the whole variety of general self-awareness and conflict resolution courses which would need to be compulsory part of the whole tourism program (undergraduate and postgraduate). Another way of incorporating mutual respect into the tourism curricula is to ensure that students are exposed to diverse social and cultural values and behaviors, and to encourage positive attitude towards diversity.

SPECIFIC LEARNING OBJECTIVES

- The promotion of respect and the feeling of recognition.
- Innovative thinking and learning methods.
- Closer cooperation with "real life" through joint development projects with the industry.
- Students as active participants and decision makers, creating an atmosphere of mutual respect and support.
- The role of teachers should change from "fact tellers" to facilitators of a student's own development.

- A learning environment that is inclusive, safe, and dynamic, where students are not afraid to take the initiative should be created.
- Self-awareness as a prerequisite to mutual respect should involve faculty, because teachers should understand their role as a positive change agents to promote mutuality.
- Continuous training is needed for all staff members to build an understanding of diverse cultural backgrounds and value systems.
- Teachers should be able to recognize their own values and be open to question and revisit these values.
- Mutual respect should be promoted between staff members as well as between teachers and students.

Mutual respect is a process of self-development and thus is unique for every individual. Therefore, mutuality cannot be measured and assessed as a learning outcome in the curriculum. However, it is vital to incorporate mutuality elements and principles into study modules. Tourism curricula should be based on a variety of approaches, experiences, and knowledge. It should incorporate courses related to professional and personal development, sociology, theology, and cultural studies to facilitate students' understanding of drivers for change. Critical thinking skills should be emphasized in the curricula, and student's ability to initiate open dialog, manage conflicts, and reach mutually beneficial agreements should be rewarded. Programs promoting cooperation, inclusion, and diversity should be included into tourism studies.

Summary of Value-Based Principles

The ideas presented above are meant to be used creatively by educators in their course materials. The specifics of how to incorporate them are left to the educator. Ways in which the TEFI values can be incorporated into student learning and industry operations are discussed below.

THE WAY FORWARD

With the goal to fundamentally transform tourism education, TEFI is poised to progress in a number of ways. First, as we move forward it is critical that we engage all stakeholders. In particular, TEFI will work with leading university educators and industry professionals to define a new model of education for the tourism industry. In addition, we will invite students into the process to add their understanding to the redesign of education. Finally, we will also invite those in the upper levels of administration of university programs including deans, rectors, chancellors, provosts, etc., to gain their unique perspective and implementation possibilities.

TEFI fellows are already creating linkages with other organizations with similar visions, distributing a White Paper broadly to educators, industry, students, and associations of educators worldwide. TEFI fellows are beginning to develop pilot programs in the university context to test the values framework and are planning two future TEFI Summits to bring their initiatives to its fruition. Each of these initiatives is discussed below.

1. Networking with other organizations:
   - To influence accreditation and certification agencies such as United Nations World Tourism Organization (UNWTO) through the TedQual certification, Accreditation Commission for Programs in Hospitality Administration (ACPHA) and others.
   - To share outcomes with other agencies/groups working to change education such as Principles for Responsible Management Education (www.unprme.org), Academy of Hope.
   - To present the TEFI Guidelines at international, national and regional conferences such as International Society of Travel and Tourism Educators (ISTTE), Business Enterprises for Sustainable Tourism Education Network (BESTEN), Council of Australian Universities in Tourism and Hospitality Education (CAUTHE)—particularly those focusing on education and future leadership of the industry.
   - To partner with industry associations such as World Travel and Tourism Council (WTTC).
   - To partner with the International Academy for the Study of Tourism.
   - The creation of online TEFI courses where faculty and students at multiple campuses engage in professional course delivery and assignments based on the TEFI values.
2. Grants: Numerous funding agencies have been identified for possible funding of the TEFI initiative. In particular, proposals will be written to obtain funds to support the development and evaluation of alternative educational strategies/programs/methods for integrating TEFI values into tourism curricula.
3. Future TEFI Summits: TEFI will hold a World Congress open to all tourism educators and industry leaders. It will be titled "TEFI World Congress: Activating Change in Tourism Education" and will be held at Temple University, Philadelphia, Pennsylvania on May 18–21, 2011. This World Congress will be an opportunity for all involved in the tourism education process from around the world (educators, administrators at all levels, industry, students, and governments) to come together to learn about the initiative, to design strategy for its implementation on a global scale, and

to identify new challenges and opportunities that tourism education is likely to face between now and 2030.

4. Pilot projects: A few universities are beginning to structurally infuse their programs with TEFI values. For example, Modul University Vienna is using the values to create an oath that all students agree to upon graduation. Temple University is already using the values-based framework in its course design ensuring that each value set and its sub-values get coverage. James Cook University in Australia and University of Hawaii are both in the initial stages of implementing the values-based framework. Many individual members of TEFI are changing their individual courses to reflect the TEFI initiative. Additionally, a TEFI Scholarship of Hope has been created at Modul University Vienna to encourage excellent students to continue their tourism studies. This scholarship is given to the winner of an essay competition in which the students must show how the values relate to stewardship and leadership in their lives.

5. TEFI Faculty Code of Ethics/Conduct and Student Oath: The need for faculty to "walk the talk" in addition to "talking the talk" has been discussed numerous times at the various TEFI Summits. The role of faculty as mentors, role models and a source inspiration and knowledge for students is paramount in this initiative. The creation of a Code of Ethics will be developed to help guide faculty in playing this larger role in students' lives. In line with this code, examples of student codes that imbibe the TEFI values will be created.

6. TEFI Values Assessment Inventory: Tools to assess how students' values are being advanced within the TEFI framework are being developed and will be an important guideline to measure the success of the program. A TEFI Values Assessment Inventory currently under development will measure the values of students prior to being exposed to TEFI courses and also upon completion of the courses.

In summary, the TEFI initiative is dynamic with many institutions and players involved. It is our hope that this collaborative effort succeed in shifting the focus of tourism education worldwide to provide more responsible graduates and better stewardship for destinations and their environmental and socio-cultural resources. We invite as many people as possible to walk this path with us and help to redefine tourism education and provide leadership for this vital field into the future.

TEFI has benefitted from the incredible participation of educators and industry members from around the world. This article reflects their insight, creativity, and concern for the future of tourism education. Working Groups have been led by various individuals who have played a key role in bringing the initiative to this point. Four meetings have been held to date that have been financially sponsored by universities from around the world with strong tourism programs: Temple University, University of Hawaii, and Virginia Polytechnic Institute and State University, in the United States; University of Queensland, La Trobe University, and University of Victoria, in Australia; Bocconi University, in Italy; Modul University Vienna, in Austria; University of Lugano, in Switzerland; and CICtourGUNE, University of Duesto, in San Sebastian, Spain. They have also been sponsored by the *International Academy for the Study of Tourism,* and the *BEST Education Network*. The Steering Committee that has guided TEFI includes Drs. Leo Jago, Janne Liburd, John Tribe, Karl Wöber, Pauline Sheldon, and Daniel Fesenmaier. We would also like to thank numerous TEFI participants who have contributed significantly to this article: They include but are not limited to Drs. Marion Joppe, Irena Ateljevic, Betsy Barber, John Swarbrooke, Ulli Gretzel, Darko Prebezac, Julia Nevemrzhitskaya, Rico Maggi, Gianna Moscardo, Anne-Mette Hjalager, Christina Mottirini, Loredana Padurean, and Tiger Wu. We also owe a special thank you to David Fennell for his thoughtful review of this article and the suggestions he made.

REFERENCES

Althusser, L. (1984). *Essays on ideology*. London, UK: Verso.

Apple, M. (1990). *Ideology and the curriculum*. London, UK: Routledge and Kegan Paul.

Bloom, B. S. (Ed.). (1956). *Taxonomy of educational objectives: The classification of educational goals*. New York, NY: D. McKay.

Cooper, T., Hofheinz, P., & Purdy, M. (2007). *Skills for the future*. London, UK: Accenture.

Fennell, D. A. (2000). Tourism and applied ethics. *Tourism Recreation Research, 25*(1), 59–69.

Giddens, A. (2009). *The politics of climate change*. London, UK: Polity Press.

Haga, W. J. (1976). Managerial professionalism and the use of organization resources. *American Journal of Economics and Sociology, 35*, 337–347.

Hall, C. M., & Butler, R. W. (1995). In search of common ground: Reflections on sustainability, complexity and process in the tourism system—a discussion between C. Michael Hall and Richard W. Butler. *Journal of Sustainable Tourism, 3*(2), 99–105.

Hoyle, E., & John, P. D. (1995). *Professional knowledge and professional practice*. London, UK: Cassell.

Hudson, S., & Miller, G. (2005). Ethical orientation and awareness of tourism students. *Journal of Business Ethics, 62*, 383–396.

Inglehart, R. (1990). *Culture shift in advanced industrial society*. Princeton, NJ: Princeton University Press.

Inglehart, R. (1997). *Modernisation and postmodernisation*. Princeton, NJ: Princeton University Press.

Jamal, T., & Menzel, C. (2008). Good actions in tourism. In J. Tribe (Ed.), *Philosophical issues in tourism* (pp. 227–243). Bristol, UK: Channel View Publications.

Liburd, J. J. (2010). Introduction to sustainable tourism development. In J. J. Liburd & D. Edwards (Eds.), *Understanding the sustainable development of tourism* (pp. 1–18). Oxford, UK: Goodfellow.

Sachs, J. (2003). Teacher professional standards: Controlling or developing teaching. *Teachers and Teaching: Theory and Practice, 9*(2), 175–186.

Sheldon, P., Fesenmaier, D., Wöeber, K., Cooper, C., & Antonioli, M. (2008). Tourism education futures, 2010–2030: Building the capacity to lead. *Journal of Teaching in Tourism and Travel, 7*(3), 61–68.

Tribe, J. (2002a). Education for ethical tourism action. *Journal of Sustainable Tourism, 10*(4), 309–324.

Tribe, J. (2002b). The philosophic practitioner. *Annals of Tourism Research, 29,* 338–357.

Wallis, C., & Steptoe, S. (2006, December 10). How to bring our schools out of the 20th century. *New York Times,* pp. 21–22.

Webster, A. (2001). *Spiral of values: The flow from survival values to global consciousness in New Zealand.* Hawera, New Zealand: Alpha.

Williamson, J. (1997). The Washington consensus revisited. In L. Emmerij (Ed.), *Economic and social development into the XXI century* (pp. 48–61). Washington, DC: Inter-American Development Bank.

Academic Agency and Leadership in Tourism Higher Education

DIANNE DREDGE

Southern Cross University, Gold Coast, Australia

CHRISTIAN SCHOTT

Victoria University of Wellington, Wellington, New Zealand

This article explores the leadership agency of tourism faculty in higher education and recommends actions to enhance leadership for social change. Based on a review of literature grounded within an agency perspective, a conceptual framework is presented that identifies systemic and individual influences on leadership. Three types of freedom for faculty to engage in leadership behaviors arise: (1) the capacity of the individual to lead; (2) the freedom afforded by the organizational context to lead in accordance with one's capacity to lead; and (3) the social freedom to lead derived from each faculty member's disciplinary and departmental norms and structures.

INTRODUCTION

Leadership in higher education has received increasing attention at both the theoretical and practical levels during the last 20 years (Kezar, Carducci, & Contreras-McGavin, 2006; Marshall, Orrell, Cameron, Bosanquet, & Thomas, 2011; Ramsden, 2003). This interest is driven in part by the push for higher education institutions in both developed and emerging economies to adopt

---

We wish to thank Dr. Paul McDonald and Dr. Sarah Proctor-Thompson of the Victoria Business School for their valuable comments on previous versions of this article.

business management and corporate governance practices, as well as by increasing pressure to improve transparency and accountability in meeting a broad range of teaching, learning, research, and engagement objectives (Marginson & Considine, 2000). For example, higher education institutions in developed economies are expected to deliver on a range of national economic objectives to help fill employment gaps, promote innovation, and improve competitiveness (Pusser, Kempner, Marginson, & Ordorika, 2012). In emerging economies, improved access to and participation in higher education is seen as a key to improving living standards through increased employment and higher incomes. Despite these diverse expectations placed on universities in both developed and emerging economies, the wide adoption of new public management practices has generally resulted in a flattening of organizational structures, larger faculties, and fewer hierarchical leadership roles (e.g., heads of school, deans, etc.). Instead, leadership roles have been distributed in a proliferation of nonhierarchical leadership positions including, for example, program directors, 1st-year advisors, directors of teaching and learning, directors of research, and so on. As a result, it has become increasingly apparent that universities across the world have dispersed leadership beyond the traditional hierarchical management structures (Acker, 2012; Drew, 2010; Inman, 2011; Seeber, 2011). This situation creates leadership opportunities for a broad range of academics at all levels in the academic hierarchy, but because such positions often lack formal recognition and power, academics in these roles need to be aware of where their agency lies.

The aim of this article is to explore the leadership agency of academic faculty in tourism higher education and to recommend actions that enhance leadership for social change. The concept of agency—or the effective capacity of an individual faculty member to make choices about when, where, why, and how to lead—is key to understanding leadership. The article seeks to explicitly build awareness of the leadership agency of tourism academics in their teaching, research, and service roles through a synthesis of the literature and subsequent development of a conceptual framework. To date, there has been very little attention to the potential leadership roles that tourism academics can play in the rapidly changing context of higher education (Pearce, 2005b). There are, however, related discussions about hopeful tourism and several reflexive accounts of tourism academics' career development that contour around the edges of leadership (e.g., Ateljevic, Pritchard, & Morgan, 2007; Gill, 2012; Nash, 2007). We choose to focus less on these personal characteristics, traits, and behaviors of tourism academics who lead (e.g., see Nash [2007] in the anthropology of tourism, Smith [2010] in tourism geography, and Pearce [2011] in tourism psychology), and instead, we focus more on how human agency is socially constructed within the higher education environment. We argue that these reflexive personal explanations of career development provide little theoretical understanding about how cultural, social, and institutional systems in higher education shape leadership. As an alternative, we ground our work within an agency perspective and argue that the calculative action of tourism (and indeed all) academic faculty to lead is socially constructed through the interplay of the personal values, behaviors, and qualities of individuals, and the range of social, organizational, political, economic, and other factors. We argue that understanding the leadership agency of tourism academic faculty in their teaching, research, and service activities is an important first step in pursuing social change through tourism.

In addressing this aim, this article will first explore the key concepts of leadership and academic agency. Following this, a range of systemic influences, which operate at multiple scales to influence the freedom of faculty to lead, will then be discussed. The article will then engage with the values and aspirations of the tourism academy with respect to worldmaking, a discourse that is shaping the way leadership is socially constructed and collectively framed. Finally, we undertake a discussion of academic freedom to better understand the influences upon individuals, academic collectives, and higher education institutions in terms of how leadership is enhanced and constrained. Drawing from these threads, a conceptual framework is presented that outlines the influences on leadership.

LEADERSHIP AND ACADEMIC AGENCY

Leadership

While definitions of leadership abound (e.g., see Jackson & Parry, 2008; Northouse, 2009), for the purposes of this article, leadership is broadly conceptualized as the mobilizing of human, intellectual, and social capital and resources to achieve some desired future state. Three dimensions are inherent in this conceptualization of leadership: (1) The exercise of leadership requires both *leaders and followers*; (2) the capacity to mobilize requires *communication and interpersonal skills*; and (3) to lead requires *actions toward goals* (Jackson & Parry, 2008). Jackson and Parry (2008) argue that simple transactions, such as undertaking tasks to fulfill a contract or obligation, are a form of management or "transactional leadership" (see Bass, 2008). Transactional leadership is distinguished from transformational leadership because the latter involves multiple decisions and tradeoffs between alternative consequences where there is usually no clear solution or path to follow. The leader needs to influence and inspire those around her/him (i.e., followers) into individual and collective action, the sum of which is more than if individuals acted alone. This notion of transformational leadership has been described as a form of leadership that inspires action, ignites passion in followers, and leads to transformation (Bass, 2008).

In the business studies literature, where leadership has been a theme of research for some decades, a highly developed body of theory has evolved that predominantly focuses on the behaviors of individual leaders (Bass, 2008). In this literature, leadership is synonymous with improved profitability, competitiveness, market position, brand awareness, and other such goals. In organizational psychology, there is also a rich body of research that interrogates the personal characteristics and humanistic qualities of leaders (Haslam, Reicher, & Platow, 2011; Maslow, 1987; Messick & Kramer, 2005). Leadership has also been widely examined within sociology, politics, public policy, and organizational studies, with theoretical developments grouped into four main perspectives reflecting how leadership has historically been explained:

- Trait theories argue that leadership is derived from the personality traits and characteristics of leaders and generally hold that leaders are charismatic, born that way, and cannot be trained.
- Behavioral theories hold that leadership is exercised through patterns of behavior that can be learned (i.e., leaders are not just born that way).
- Contingency theories argue that effective leadership depends upon context and, thus, is distinguished from trait and behavioral theories that focus on the individual. Contingency theories focus on understanding specific situations and the influence of exogenous and endogenous influences.
- Integrative theories combine the first three theories, but also attempt to acknowledge relationships between leaders and followers, with transformational and distributive leadership theories being the most well-known of this group (see Bass & Riggio, 2005; Rafferty & Griffith, 2004). An integrative theory that has recently gained considerable momentum in the management literature is authentic leadership, which places a strong focus on awareness of the self, others, and contexts (see Avolio & Gardner, 2005; Walumbwa, Avolio, Gardner, Wernsing, & Peterson, 2008).

Although much discussed in the broader higher education context (e.g., see Inman, 2011; Jones, Applebee, Harvey, & Lefoe, 2010; Kezar et al., 2006; Richards, 2012), understandings of leadership have generally focused on formally designated roles such as heads of schools, deans, research chairs, and other senior managers (Kezar, 2000; Macfarlane, 2011). Leadership, however, has not been directly discussed in relation to tourism, let alone tourism education. Despite this gap, there is a growing discourse around the need to frame tourism education in terms of producing graduates who are mindful of tourism's impacts and can manage tourism to improve the human condition (Hollinshead, 2009; Morgan, 2012; Pritchard, Morgan, & Ateljevic, 2011). Contemplating how to achieve social change through tourism, and who drives this, suggests that a discussion about leadership is overdue. Here, the agency of academic faculty becomes relevant and a number of questions emerge, such as: How can individual academics lead and drive social change? What are the opportunities for collectives of tourism academics to demonstrate leadership? What are the impediments to exercising leadership?

Agency and Action

Theories of action have historically been discussed in philosophy in terms of the purpose, reasons, and motivations for individual action, but they made little impact in the social sciences until the 1970s and 1980s. This is because these discussions focused on the individual realm and did not pay much attention to the influence of broader sociocultural and institutional conditions that influence social change (Giddens, 1979). By the 1980s, agency theory, which explores the freedom and capacity of agents to act within the social context, began to receive increasing attention. In sociology, for example, Giddens (1984) proposed a structure–agency theory wherein agency and structure were theorized in a dialectical relationship. Agency was defined not as the sum of discrete acts, but as the flow of conduct. The capacity of individuals to independently develop this flow of conduct was shaped by structures (i.e., rules, routines, and other patterned arrangements) that shape the choices available to them to act. Further, agency resides not only in individuals, but also in institutions and things. Sen (1985, 1999) outlined a theory of capability development, which explored how different dimensions of freedom shape human capability; and in psychology, there are theories of control, self-regulation, and self-efficacy (e.g., Crockett, 2002). Further, in business and economics, the principal–agent approach has explored the nature of the transactional relationship between principals (who delegate work) and agents (who perform the work on the principal's behalf). This transactional relationship is metaphorically known as a contract (Eisenhardt, 1989), and how a contract is enacted is influenced by a range of factors including alignment of goals, obligation, reciprocity, risk, and self-interest between principal and agent (Jensen & Meckling, 1976; Ross, 1973).

These streams of research have delivered understandings about how individual and collective perceptions of the capacity to act are shaped by an interlocking network of social, cultural, economic, and political forces. However, application of this agency perspective in higher education has received limited attention and is made more difficult because principal and agency roles are unclear (Marginson, 2008). For example, governments (principals) require universities (agents) to deliver on national education policy objectives. At the same time, universities (principals) require individual academic staff (agents) to deliver on a range of teaching and research objectives. Further, fee-paying students (principals) expect their teachers (agents) to meet high-quality teaching standards and deliver course objectives. All have agency, make choices, and undertake purposive action based on (1) perceptions of their own resources, levels of control, and capacity to act or lead; and (2) evaluations of the benefits and consequences of alternative actions. Despite these difficulties in conceptualizing agency, it is useful in considering leadership in higher education because it reminds us that leadership exists in a variety of relationships and in multiple actors and does not exist outside the social context. That is, agency (in our case, the capacity to lead) does not just reside in those formally appointed to leadership roles but can be distributed in individuals, universities, government, and in the marketplace.

However, conceptualizing leadership and understanding the agency of academics, either as individuals or as a collective, are two very different things. Leadership can be a person, a result, a position, or a process, which makes it difficult to identify, explain, and understand leadership in action (Jackson & Parry, 2008). Grint (2005) argues that we have become far too focused on leaders and their individual qualities and that focusing on leadership in a more holistic sense, which takes into account social, cultural, and institutional influences, is also needed. Grint argues that the social construction of the context (e.g., in many developed economies, higher education is characterized as a regulated neoliberal market-driven system) legitimates particular types of actions and constitutes the world and the leadership challenge in the process. For example, the neoliberal agenda dictates an emphasis on competition, cost-effectiveness, and mass-market efficiencies, so leadership that delivers on this agenda will be deemed "good leadership." However, different renderings of the context (e.g., an emphasis on effective learning, access to socioeconomically disadvantaged groups, or employability) will produce different leadership orientations and opportunities for academic agency.

For Jackson and Parry (2008), constructing the leadership context is complex; there are multiple competing agendas, problems, and solutions. The challenge of leadership is to appreciate the complexity of the problem space and to take action, sometimes without a clear understanding of where such actions will lead. The rapidly globalizing higher education sector discussed in the next section, with its attendant pressures on teaching, research, and service, exemplifies the complex system of social forces at play.

SYSTEMIC INFLUENCES ON HIGHER EDUCATION

Across the world, higher education has been in a constant state of reform for five decades (Van Der Wende, 2007). After World War II, many developing countries began to actively restructure their economies to position themselves in a rapidly globalizing and increasingly mobile world (Gamage & Mininberg, 2003; Teichler, 2003; Tynan & Mark, 2009). By the 1970s, many of these countries started to deindustrialize and shift their economic emphasis from manufacturing to the tertiary sectors. Higher education policy became increasingly tied to national economic objectives such as developing the knowledge economy, meeting new labor force needs, and promoting innovation and economic diversity. Pressures including globalization, increased competition, shifting student markets and consumer trends, the increasing imperative of sustainability, changing work patterns, and characteristics of work and innovations in the information and communications technology arena have resulted in transcendental change in higher education (Marginson, 1999; Marginson & Considine, 2000; Marginson & Sawir, 2005). Further, new public management has contributed to a decrease in public funding in most higher education systems relative to private revenue streams; there is upward pressure on student fees to cover ballooning costs, and new public management practices have been adopted that focus predominantly on performance, productivity, and profitability (Van Der Wende, 2007).

Although this article focuses on developed countries, since 2000, the role of higher education in improving living standards and progressing economic development, competitiveness, and globalization objectives in emerging economies has been increasingly emphasized (Van Der Wende, 2007). As a result, parallels can be drawn between the evolution of higher education systems in developed countries and the present paths of developing countries, which are predicted to follow similar trajectories (Marginson & Rhoades, 2002).

Implications for Organizations

In many universities in developed economies, the result of all these intersecting pressures has been the decline in Socratic and craft-based teaching practices; the industrialization of teaching processes, practices, and materials; and the development of highly diversified mass student markets (Marginson & Considine, 2000; Trowler, 2010). Larger numbers of students can attend universities in different study modes (i.e., internal, external, and offshore). Academic educators are under increasing pressure to deliver on a range of performance measures including teaching evaluations, research outputs, significance, and measures of esteem (Phillips, 2005). Consistent with new public management approaches that seek to facilitate and enable the achievement of goals through partnerships and shared responsibility, university managers have become responsible for steering their institutions toward measurable outcomes (Coaldrake & Stedman, 1999; Tynan & Mark, 2009). One important consequence has been that leadership within many higher education institutions has become overly focused on "command and control" systems geared toward achieving corporate and commercial objectives (Sharrock, 2012). Less attention has been placed on the agency of academic faculty to lead in their teaching, research, and service activities (Jones et al., 2010).

Tourism programs find themselves in a vexed situation under these conditions. Tourism programs largely emerged out of a need to produce graduates to fill growing industry demands during the 1980s and 1990s (Pearce, 2005a). Located predominantly within business studies focusing on management with a social sciences flavor (Dredge et al., 2012; Tribe, 2002), and quite often heavily vocational in their curriculum orientation, tourism programs have struggled to gain academic credibility and contribute to measures of university reputation (i.e., rankings, significance) or to attract substantial external funding and sponsorship (Pearce, 2005b; Tribe, 1997). As a result, tourism has received little profile in many universities, with managers responding by increasing support for publication outputs and the writing of grant applications to maximize their tourism faculty's contribution to corporate and commercial objectives, or by merging tourism into larger faculties so they strengthen outcomes in other fields such as business. This emphasis on corporate objectives has anecdotally drawn academic faculty attention away from engagement with industry and community stakeholders, diverted efforts away from engagement with external communities toward "ivory tower" pursuits in some cases, and inhibited interest in formal leadership positions (e.g., head of school positions)

Given the extent and depth of these reform processes and the different stages through which developed and emerging economies are passing, it is important that universities not only deal effectively with the current pressures, but that they also position themselves as leaders into the future, anticipating and strategically positioning themselves to confront the challenges ahead (World Development Bank, 1999). Yet, it is also true that universities have been around for hundreds of years, and although the modern university is quite different at both operational and structural levels, universities for the most part remain organized into disciplines with established cultures and academic practices (Tynan & Mark, 2009, pp. 98–99). These disciplinary structures promote a certain level of stability within universities (Becher & Trowler, 2001; Latour, 1987), thus opening up opportunities for academic collectives to provide leadership on important societal issues that transcend short-term political cycles associated with government elections.

Implications for the Academy

PROFESSIONAL IDENTITY

There has been substantial discussion about the origins and development of tourism as a field of study (e.g., see Coles, Hall, & Duval, 2006; Holden, 2005; Jafari, 1991, 2001, 2003; Tribe, 1997, 2006), with agreement that there are two broad but interrelated camps within tourism higher education research and teaching: The first is devoted to framing tourism as a business activity and teaching, where research and engagement activities are hinged on improving productivity, competitiveness, and innovation; the second is characterized by a social science focus where teaching, research, and engagement activities focus on the transformative qualities and effects of tourism on society (Tribe, 1997). Studies into academic identity and disciplinary location reveal that the level of socialization within "disciplinary tribes" is significant in shaping how individual academics see and engage in the world (Becher & Trowler, 2001). In Tribe's analysis of tourism, he found that the field was characterized by a divergent community wherein a diversity of approaches is tolerated; however, universities and departmentalism often force convergence and "tribal allegiances" to certain forms of knowledge and practice (Tribe, 2010). His findings also reiterated observations in the broader literature that suggest an academic faculty member's agency (i.e., their capacity to lead in this case) is inextricably tied to the effective agency that exists in the system in which they work (Calvert, Lewis, & Spindler, 2011; Henkel, 2000, 2005; Whitchurch, 2012).

Academic identity in tourism centers on a unique shared sense of purpose, practices, and knowledge. The capacity of tourism to contribute to social change is increasingly acknowledged as a central interest with researchers arguing that academics need to embrace research and teaching practices that make a difference to societal issues and to produce graduates that can create a better world (Hollinshead, 2009; Hollinshead, Ateljevic, & Ali, 2009; Pritchard et al., 2011; Ren, Pritchard, & Morgan, 2010). In this vein, the Hopeful Tourism Academy is an alternative to the neoliberal, business-orientated hegemony of tourism studies. The Hopeful Tourism Academy is based on practices of "cooperation, reciprocity, interdependence, activism and support" and seeks to emphasize responsibilities to each other and to global sustainability (Pritchard et al., 2011, p. 945). Tourism education, and by corollary, its institutions, academics, and students, are placed squarely at the center of this challenge by virtue of the contribution higher education makes to the tourism industry's "talent pool."

Yet there is a gap between what should be (i.e., social change) and how to get there (i.e., leadership by whom and how). Pritchard et al. (2011, p. 945) and Sheldon, Fesenmaier, and Tribe (2011) argue that to make a difference, academic faculty can pursue hopeful tourism by engaging in real problems, with real people, and can make a positive difference by addressing issues such as oppression, displacement, marginalization, and social injustice. According to Higgins-Desbiolles and Whyte (2013), however, "people can hope for a world with greater justice while simultaneously failing to understand the need to confront the role their own privileges can play in reproducing injustice" (p. 428). Hopefulness, they rightfully argue, "can be rife with insensitivity, ignorance and serious deficits in moral imagination" (p. 428). Mindful attention and reflexive engagement are needed in what hopefulness is, and how it can be given meaning through teaching, research, and community engagement practices.

TABLE 1 TEFI Values

Value	Explanation
Ethics	Involves striving for actions that are deemed "good" based on principles and values of honesty
Stewardship	Involves the pursuit of sustainability, responsibility, and service to the community
Knowledge	Includes the expertise and skills acquired by education and experience, and what is known in a particular field, including facts, information, theories, and models
Professionalism	Refers to conduct that is aligned with ethical and professional behavior and incorporates principles such as leadership, practicality, concern for relevance, and timeliness
Mutuality	Incorporates respect for diversity, inclusion, equity, humility, and collaboration, wherein the long-term benefits are respect, self-awareness, and appreciation of diverse opinions, cultures, and practices

Sources. Barber, 2011; Sheldon et al., 2011.

VALUES

Building on a long history of interest in values-based education (Harland & Pickering, 2011), the Tourism Education Futures Initiative (TEFI) has turned its attention to the importance of values in unlocking leadership in tourism higher education (see Table 1; Sheldon et al., 2011). Values are abstract ideals, positive or negative, that shape both individual and collective beliefs and attitudes about what is important (Sheldon et al., 2011). Ultimately, values guide leadership although they often remain implicit and their effects are overlooked in the daily business of teaching, research, and community service (Moscardo & Murphy, 2011). TEFI has argued that a focus on values-based education provides an important foundation for tourism programs so that graduates develop the knowledge, skills, and capacity to lead. It is also a collective response from educators to ensure that higher education meets its responsibilities to society, now and in the future.

A number of educators have taken a leadership role, integrating these TEFI values within their teaching and incorporating them within program planning and curriculum design (e.g., Gretzel, Isacsson, Matarrita, & Wainio, 2011; Liburd, 2012). Moscardo and Murphy (2011) have focused on developing a tool to measure values by embarking on the development of a TEFI Values Inventory. Although this work is still in its early stages, it has nevertheless become clear that a great deal more work is required in interpreting and giving meaning to these values within the curriculum space, within students' learning experiences and environments, and in how to measure these values in ways that are respectful to different cultural contexts and learning opportunities available to students. Accordingly, there is a need to better understand these values and to better link them to a more cohesive and philosophical approach to leadership in tourism education.

The agency of academic faculty to lead in all facets of their academic work and the development of graduates with the skills and capacity to lead are closely aligned. Higgins-Desbiolles (2010), Dredge and Hales (2012), and Lew (2007) argue for an engaged academic activist role in tourism research and service, a role that is deliberatively formed and mindful of the values embedded in research approaches, styles, and tools of community engagement. Such academic activism provides important opportunities to link teaching and research and to demonstrate leadership. However, beyond this, "there is silence on the question of exactly how the academic's role in academia and research itself can serve as tools for communities to change their own conditions on their own terms" (Higgins-Desbiolles & Whyte, 2013, p. 430). Addressing this question is even more difficult because of the rapid and sustained change in the higher education system and the way in which these changes shape academic work.

Implications for Individual Faculty Members

ACADEMIC WORK PROFILES

The changing nature of academic work has influenced the agency of academics in the following ways: First, the adoption of market models of higher education provision and performance-based measures in many countries have emphasized metrics, such as student satisfaction and graduate outcomes, which are increasingly used to classify universities for the purposes of funding and market comparison (Buchen, 2005). As a result, consumers now wield more weight in terms of what programs are offered and how they are delivered. The impact on academic work has been both positive and negative: On one hand, there is increasing pressure on academics to teach better and more creatively and to engage their students; on the other hand, rising student numbers and staff–student ratios have increased workload pressures (Davis, 2005; Trowler, 2010).

Second, performance measures have become inputs for university marketing and branding. So important have these performance measures become that academic staff appraisals and professional development plans are increasingly shaped by these metrics (Bexley, James, & Arkoudis, 2011). The impact on academic work has been increased time spent on collecting, documenting, and analyzing metrics. However, on a positive note, academics' self-reflexive processes along with institutional support can often result in improved performance and emergent forms of leadership as academics discover their strengths.

Third, and related to the previous two points, increased internationalization, liberalization, harmonization, and competition have increased awareness of higher educational products and services (Coaldrake & Stedman, 1999). Not only is there increased competition among institutions for enrollments, but the sector is characterized by increasing mobility of the academic workforce, of academic institutions (onshore and offshore student cohorts, overseas campuses, partner institutions) and of students (Bok, 2003). The impact on academic work can be viewed both positively and negatively: Personal and professional growth, and potentially global leadership, can result from increased mobility; however, travel and developing cross-cultural work practices can be time-consuming and can detract from efforts to develop international leadership opportunities.

Fourth, an emphasis on the consumer, increased mobility of the student market, and diversity in student markets has simulated demand for more customized and personalized learning services and environments (Atkins, 2005; Hazelkorn, 2011). Larger classes and higher student–staff ratios have dictated the need for greater flexibility and creativity in the use of mobile technologies and byte-sized learning packages with which students can engage during their own time. In many institutions, responses have been to replace the traditional lecture format with more interactive and personalized learning activities. The implications for academic work include a need for staff to up-skill in mobile technologies, changes to the way they prepare and implement lesson plans, and the development and maintenance of online learning materials (Kogan & Teichler, 2007).

Fifth, these changes have also led to increased openness and collaboration both for students in their learning and for academic staff in their research, with potential for collectives of academics to lead. Important trends shaping the way learning takes place include the democratization of learning opportunities (e.g., University of the People, http://www.uopeople.org); the global delivery of massive open online courses (e.g., Coursera, http://www.coursera.org; Udacity, http://www.udacity.com); and community-driven collaborative learning (e.g., unclasses). Although the effects of these innovations on academic work and leadership are not yet clear, the longer-term implications of these offerings are expected to bring positive and negative transformation to higher education.

Sixth, the pressure for academics to produce high-quality research with demonstrated significance and impact is significant (Atkins, 2005; Dale, 2000). Research excellence frameworks in many countries have placed considerable pressure on academics to become more effective and efficient in the way they produce research and to gather evidence of their esteem (e.g., leadership; Smith, Ward, & House, 2011). The impact on academic work has been in the transformation of research practices, particularly in the social sciences, from individualist craft-based approaches to more industrialized team-based approaches that require leaders. The impact of these changes can also be viewed in both positive and negative terms. For example, these shifts have resulted in many academics becoming more active and productive in their research endeavors by virtue of their engagement in larger teams of researchers where specialist skills can be pooled and greater learning opportunities can be leveraged. On the negative side, where academics have not been able to navigate this new playing field, the impact on some academics has been marginalization and reallocation of their research workload component to other researchers (Coles, 2009). Anecdotal evidence suggests that there are cases of academics who are deemed research-"inactive" and are receiving very strong encouragement to leave the institution. By virtue of these pressures, academic leaders have emerged across the higher education sector in teaching, research, and service activities.

These pressures on academic work, generated by a range of external and institutional conditions, have implications for the individual agency of academic faculty members to exercise leadership in their teaching, research, and service commitments. In an attempt to make sense of academic work, and to better identify where leadership agency exists and has the potential to develop, it is useful to consider Boyer's four dimensions of academic scholarship. Boyer (1990) called for a repositioning of academic work to pursue four key dimensions of scholarship:

- the scholarship of discovery, traditional research that builds new knowledge;
- the scholarship of integration, which interprets and gives meaning to knowledge making connections across disciplines;
- the scholarship of application, which is application of knowledge to help solve societal problems; and
- the scholarship of teaching, intellectual engagement in the practice of teaching to educate and entice future scholars.

Following Nussbaum's (1997, 2010) arguments for the humanities and social sciences to address pressing social, civic, economic, and moral problems, Boyer's (1990) dimensions of scholarship have been widely endorsed because they refocus academic work on society's "big questions," such as how tourism can contribute to poverty alleviation and improve equity, tolerance, self-determination, and quality of life. Very real questions have been raised with respect to the agency of academic faculty members in addressing these "big questions" given the neoliberal values embedded in university vision statements, values, and management plans (Pritchard et al., 2011; Pusser et al., 2012).

ACADEMIC FREEDOM, INDIVIDUAL AGENCY, AND WORK PROFILE

The principle of academic freedom, originally articulated by W. von Humboldt in the establishment of the Berlin University in 1809, remains a fundamental plank of the modern university and is intimately tied to the modern concept of academic agency. The original ideal of academic free-dom envisioned freedom of research and teaching, integrated in such a way that students build an intellectual life—the highest form of moral life—and a commitment to humanity (McCarty, 2011). In the modern university, McInnis (2000) found that academics are highly socialized into their professional roles through their disciplinary experience and location, but they also tend to exercise a high degree of self-direction in terms of their teaching approaches and research activities (see also Adams, 1998; Calvert et al., 2011; Henkel, 2005). However, this academic freedom has resulted in a range of issues for university managers, including, for example, difficulty in managing the academic workforce, a lack of quality control, and large variations in degree standards. Neoliberal management practices introduced during the last 10 years have sought to address these issues, and in the process, they have limited some academic freedoms previously enjoyed.

In this neoliberal university, academic freedom is now tempered by the pressures of "deliverables," employment contracts, union agreements, modern work practices, students' expectations for professional degrees, and work readiness, all of which distract from the moral ideal of education for humanity. To illustrate, an interesting insight into the neoliberal reforms on New Zealand universities, which are declared as both "critic and conscience of society" by the *Education Act* (New Zealand Government, 1989), is offered by Harland, Tidswell, Everett, Hale, and Pickering (2010). These authors conclude that the reforms "leave academics with less freedom to act as critic and conscience and may finally threaten the democratic role the university plays in society" (p. 95).

As a result, earlier conceptions of academic freedom described above have been revisited by those interested in how the freedom to act is shaped by: (1) the capacity of the individual to act (agency freedom) and (2) the freedom afforded by the organizational context or setting (effective freedom) to act in accordance with one's own beliefs (Marginson & Rhoades, 2002). To this, we also add (3) the notion of a social freedom derived from the disciplinary norms and structures within which an academic operates. With respect to agency freedom, leadership theories can highlight the behavioral characteristics, traits, and the relationships between leaders and followers that are necessary for an individual to exercise leadership. However, individual agency to lead is deeply entwined with social (e.g., academic tribes, departmentalism, etc.) and organizational (e.g., university) environments, and the latitude that these arrangements afford individual faculty members to take action.

For example, studies of the academic workforce are replete with observations about the way new public management practices, neoliberalism, and globalization have depleted the agency of academics. Studies of the academic workforce reveal an aging workforce across many developed countries (Ackers & Gill, 2005; Hugo & Morriss, 2010; Koopman-Boyden

& Macdonald, 2003; Magner, 1999) and a desire by completed Ph.D.s and early career academics to leave the academy (Ackers & Gill, 2005; Bexley, Arkoudis, & James, 2013; Huisman, Weert, & Bartelse, 2002). There is also a casualization of the workforce occurring (Coates, Dobson, Goedegebuure, & Meek, 2010; McInnis, 2000). A large study of the U.S. higher education system, for example, revealed that 60% of today's 1,138,734 faculty members are in full- and part-time appointments outside the tenure system, while in 1975, this proportion was 42% (Gappa, Austin, & Trice, 2007; Schuster & Finkelstein, 2006). In many other countries, academics are poorly paid and many need to hold down more than one job, or permanent posts are not available and academics need what are called "portfolio careers" (Bexley et al., 2011; Coaldrake & Stedman, 1999). These portfolio careers require an individual to develop portfolios of expertise directed at different opportunities inside and outside the university (e.g., academics might act as consultants in addition to their academic duties or they might contribute to a family business; Anderson, Johnson, & Saha, 2002; Kogan & Teichler, 2007; Lyons, 2010). These conditions both constrain and provide opportunities for academics to embrace leadership inside and outside the university.

DISCUSSION

The aim of this article was to explore the factors that affect the leadership agency of tourism faculty and to recommend actions to promote leadership. The article was premised on the idea that academic agency, which is shaped by organizational, social, and individual factors, is key to better understanding how leadership opportunities emerge. From this review, a conceptual framework has been developed (see Figure 1).

In the introduction to this article, we noted that individual traits and behaviors, identity, and personal circumstances are important in shaping the agency of academic faculty (see Bass, 2008; Jackson & Parry, 2008). These are noted in the top right of Figure 1. However, given the attention already devoted to these factors in the leadership literature and in the reflexive accounts of tourism academics (e.g., see Nash, 2007; Pearce, 2011; Smith, 2010), we chose not to explore these aspects but instead to focus on the systemic influences that we argue have not yet been sufficiently explored in the literature (indicated in the top left of Figure 1).

Figure 1 conceptualizes leadership as being filtered through layers of interdependent factors starting with these systemic and individual influences. The factors influence (1) the organizational setting, (2) the disciplinary/departmental setting (i.e., the academy), and (3) the individual faculty member's goals, values, and identity. Leadership agency is produced through a process of mindful and reflexive engagement with these three contexts to identify what leadership opportunities and impediments are at play.

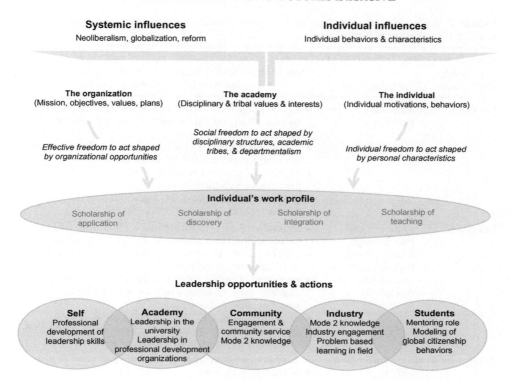

FIGURE 1 Factors contributing to tourism faculty leadership opportunities.

These insights are then translated into the individual's work profile. This work profile includes a range of activities that can be broadly categorized into the four dimensions of leadership, as proposed by Boyer (1990) and the Carnegie Foundation: scholarship of discovery, scholarship of integration, scholarship of application, and scholarship of teaching.

In Figure 1, we have sketched out a framework that reflects these insights drawn from literature, but the question remains, "How can tourism faculty lead positive social change?" To seed dialogue on this important question, we propose an exploratory list of actions that illustrate opportunities and strategies for leadership in tourism. To align this basic catalogue of actions with the conceptual framework, we revisit Boyer's (1990) four dimensions of scholarship to position each action in a meaningful context. However, as clearly evident in Table 2, the placement of actions necessitates numerous instances of overlap across dimensions. On one hand, this is a reminder of the multitude of functions, both realized and potential, that academic roles perform. At the same time, it is in keeping with the concept of scholarship, which for most academics is an overarching approach that finds application in all domains of academic life, including, but importantly not limited to, "research."

TABLE 2 Boyer's (1990) Scholarship Dimensions and Opportunities and Strategies for Academic Leadership in Tourism

Boyer Scholarship Dimensions	Explanation	Opportunities and Strategies for Academic Leadership in Tourism (an Exploratory List)
Discovery	Advancing knowledge	• Challenging what "types of knowledge" are deemed worthy of advancing by institutions and funding bodies; • furthering insightful new approaches to knowledge generation and analysis of information; • coproducing new knowledge using "Mode 2" knowledge production; and • publishing in peer-reviewed academic forums, industry journals, and other media
Integration	Positioning and interpreting knowledge in broader contexts and across disciplines	• Multidisciplinary/transdisciplinary literature reviews, research books, or textbooks for a broad audience; • collaboration outside the discipline/field of study in a multidisciplinary project; • engaging in public intellectualism by positioning and making sense of knowledge for the benefit of a nonspecialist audience; and • communicating and disseminating knowledge in places and spaces where it can assist in understanding or solving complex real-world problems
Application	Aiding society, industry, professions, and government in addressing problems	• Industry or government consultancies; • academic activism; • leadership roles in professional organizations; • mentoring students' professional growth; • incorporating research/problem-based learning scenarios that require learners to apply theory, confront complexities, and collaborate with external stakeholders; • media engagement and contribution to political discourses about an issue; and • actively supporting the creation of meaningful volunteering opportunities for learners to aid society by applying and enhancing their knowledge and skills
Teaching	Designing, evaluating, and reflexively engaging in teaching curriculum and practices	• Engaging in critical, reflexive teaching practice; • developing and testing teaching materials; • stimulating active learning and fostering critical and creative thinking in learners; • informing teaching through (multidisciplinary and/or transdisciplinary) research; • engaging in research on effective teaching and learning; • mentoring graduate students in their teaching activities; • designing staged assessment for a program; • performing service/instructional teaching in the profession; and • engaging and learning from stakeholders, including students, in curriculum and assessment design

As highlighted earlier, by devising this exploratory list, we seek to stimulate dialogue about leadership in tourism higher education rather than suggest it be an authoritative or exhaustive list. Further, although we are not explicit about this in the table, it is inherent to all actions that opportunities for both individual and collective leadership exist, with the synchronization of several academics' agency to achieve collective leadership presenting particular challenges but offering powerful outcomes.

Although it is not possible to expand on each of the suggested actions due to space constraints, we wish to briefly synthesize key themes in Table 2. In the context of discovery, challenging the common parameters of what neoliberal universities deem appropriate or discussing valuable topics and techniques of inquiry present opportunities for academic leadership. Equally, leadership and academic agency are called on to catalyze the transition of tourism-related knowledge generation from Mode 1, characterized by the hegemony of experimental science, by an internally driven taxonomy of disciplines, and by the autonomy of scientists and their universities to Mode 2 knowledge production, which is socially distributed, application-oriented, transdisciplinary, and subject to multiple accountabilities (Gibbons et al., 1994). Opportunities that we envisage in the domain of the scholarship of integration include the translation, integration, and dissemination of tourism-related knowledge in the contexts and forums in which it has relevance and meaning. This undoubtedly includes transmitting knowledge to our tourism students and disseminating it in academic publications that fall under the tourism theme. However, the relevance and meaning of tourism-related knowledge branches far beyond these spheres by crossing disciplinary, geographical, and cultural boundaries, and reaches a heterogeneous cohort of individuals who are nonspecialists of tourism knowledge but who are important stakeholders in the generation and use of such knowledge.

The application domain provides a large platform for academics to apply their knowledge and skills to support positive social change. Academics can lead social change by critically commenting and contributing to government policy and practice and industry projects and needs, by advising nongovernmental organizations, and by actively supporting their work for social change and a better world. They can also lead social change crucially through their roles as teachers, mentors, and role models to undergraduate and postgraduate students. The ability of academics to act as powerful facilitators of meaningful and deep learning is also of great significance here, as is academic activism and the role of an agent of institutionally focused change. Naturally, some of these opportunities and strategies are also highly relevant to our learners and other stakeholders in tourism education, as well as to the domain of the scholarship of teaching, which is characterized by critical (self) reflection, active engagement with the generation of knowledge, and continual learning about the field. The opportunities for leadership arise out of these facets of the scholarship of teaching.

CONCLUSION

In tourism, there is increasing discussion about the "worldmaking" role of tourism, within which academic faculty have an important role and a responsibility to students, the global community, and industry to unlock the potential of tourism to improve the human condition. The leadership of academic faculty in pursuing social change is constituted through their interactions with students at both the undergraduate and postgraduate levels, with their disciplinary communities and external communities, and within the reflexive and mindful engagement in their own institutional contexts. Accordingly, we argue that leadership in tourism higher education is distributed across the different roles that academics undertake within their work and in different members of staff depending upon their institutional responsibilities and personal characteristics.

This article has sought to review and synthesize the literature and in the process has opened up several opportunities for further research and empirical study. In particular, we have drawn inspiration and broad license from theories of agency and leadership, which provide stimulus for future research. Additionally, this review and synthesis has provided a starting point for dialogue about strategies and opportunities to catalyze, and hopefully lead, transformation of tourism higher education using the power of collective action. Additionally, we sought to develop a foundation for more robust theoretical and empirical study of leadership in tourism, which is needed if we are to address the challenges outlined by advocates of hopeful tourism.

Finally, in terms of implications for management, it is important to understand how tourism academics produce different renderings of the higher education environment that open up perceptions of their own agency and the type of leadership actions opened or closed off by their rendering. We need to better understand how to enhance and facilitate the agency of individual academics to progress their role in social change in the reflexive and sensitive manner called for by Higgins-Desbiolles and Whyte (2013). This may require an active reconstruction of the current polemic in higher education that seeks to reproduce ideas about the ascendancy of neoliberal public management and the attendant loss of academic faculty power and authority. Instead, we need a more textured, fine-grained, and situated understanding of agency within different higher education contexts.

REFERENCES

Acker, S. (2012). Chairing and caring: Gendered dimensions of leadership in academe. *Gender and Education, 24*(4), 411–428.

Ackers, L., & Gill, B. (2005). Attracting and retaining 'early career' researchers in English higher education institutions. *Innovation, 18*(3), 277–299.

Adams, D. (1998). Examining the fabric of academic life: An analysis of three decades of research on the perceptions of Australian academics about their roles. *Higher Education, 36*(4), 421–435.

Anderson, D., Johnson, R., & Saha, L. (2002). *Changes in academic work: Implications for universities of the changing age distribution and work roles of academic staff*. Canberra, Australia: Commonwealth of Australia.

Ateljevic, I., Pritchard, A., & Morgan, N. (Eds.). (2007). *The critical turn in tourism studies: Innovative research methodologies*. Oxford, UK: Elsevier.

Atkins, D. (2005). *University futures and new technologies: Possibilities and issues*. Paris, France: Organization for Economic Co-operation and Development/ Centre for Education Research and Innovation. Retrieved from http://www. oecd.org/education/highereducationandadultlearning/36758866.pdf

Avolio, B. J., & Gardner, W. L. (2005). Authentic leadership development: Getting to the root of positive forms of leadership. *The Leadership Quarterly, 16*(3), 315–338.

Barber, E. (2011). Case study: Integrating TEFI (Tourism Education Futures Initiative) core values into the undergraduate curriculum. *Journal of Teaching in Travel & Tourism, 11*, 38–75.

Bass, B. (2008). *The Bass handbook of leadership: Theory, research and managerial applications*. New York, NY: Free Press.

Bass, B., & Riggio, R. (2005). *Transformational leadership* (2nd ed.). Mahwah, NJ: Lawrence Erlbaum.

Becher, T., & Trowler, P. R. (2001). *Academic tribes and territories: Intellectual enquiry and the culture of disciplines*. Buckingham, UK: The Society for Research Into Higher Education and Open University Press.

Bexley, E., Arkoudis, S., & James, R. (2013). The motivations, values and future plans of Australian academics. *Higher Education, 65*(3), 385–400.

Bexley, E., James, R., & Arkoudis, S. (2011). *The Australian academic profession in transition*. Melbourne, Australia: Centre for the Study of Higher Education, University of Melbourne.

Bok, D. (2003). *Universities in the marketplace: The commercialization of higher education*. Princeton, NJ: Princeton University Press.

Boyer, E. L. (1990). *Scholarship reconsidered: Priorities of the professoriate*. San Francisco, CA: Jossey-Bass.

Buchen, I. H. (2005). Finding time for the future and overcoming future avoidance. *Foresight, 7*(6), 3–7.

Calvert, M., Lewis, T., & Spindler, J. (2011). Negotiating professional identities in higher education: Dilemmas and priorities of academic staff. *Research in Education, 86*, 25–38.

Coaldrake, P., & Stedman, L. (1999). *Academic work in the twenty-first century: Changing roles and policies*. Canberra, Australia: Department of Education, Training, and Youth Affairs, Higher Education Division.

Coates, H., Dobson, I. R., Goedegebuure, L., & Meek, L. (2010). Across the great divide: What do Australian academics think of university leadership? Advice from the CAP survey. *Journal of Higher Education Policy & Management, 32*(4), 379–387.

Coles, T. (2009). Tourism studies and the governance of higher education in the United Kingdom. *Tourism Geographies, 11*(1), 23–42.

Coles, T., Hall, C. M., & Duval, D. T. (2006). Tourism and post-disciplinary enquiry. *Current Issues in Tourism*, *9*(4/5), 293–319.

Crockett, L. (2002). Agency in the life course: Concepts and processes. In R. Dienstbier & L. Crockett (Eds.), *Nebraska Symposium on Motivation: Vol. 48. Agency, motivation, and the life course* (pp. 1–31). Lincoln, NE: University of Nebraska Press.

Dale, R. (2000). Globalization and education: Demonstrating a common world educational culture or locating a globally structured educational agenda? *Educational Theory*, *50*(4), 427–448.

Davis, G. (2005, April). *Regulating universities: An assumption and three propositions*. Paper presented at Sustaining Prosperity, Melbourne, Australia.

Dredge, D., Benckendorff, P., Day, M., Gross, M. J., Walo, M., Weeks, P., & Whitelaw, P. (2012). The philosophic practitioner and the curriculum space. *Annals of Tourism Research*, *39*(4), 2154–2176.

Dredge, D., & Hales, R. (2012). Embedded community case study. In L. Dwyer, A. Gill, & N. Seetaram (Eds.), *Handbook of research methods in tourism: Quantitative and qualitative approaches* (pp. 417–433). Northampton, MA: Edward Elgar.

Drew, G. (2010). Issues and challenges in higher education leadership: Engaging for change. *Australian Educational Researcher*, *37*(3), 57–76.

Eisenhardt, K. (1989). Agency theory: An assessment and review. *The Academy of Management Review*, *14*(1), 57–74.

Gamage, D. T., & Mininberg, E. (2003). The Australian and American higher education: Key issues of the first decade of the 21st century. *Higher Education*, *45*(2), 183–202.

Gappa, J. M., Austin, A. E., & Trice, A. G. (2007). *Rethinking faculty work: Higher education's strategic imperative*. San Francisco, CA: John Wiley and Sons.

Gibbons, M., Limoges, C., Nowotny, H., Schwartzman, S., Scott, P., & Trow, M. (1994). *The new production of knowledge: The dynamics of science and research in contemporary societies*. London, UK: Sage.

Giddens, A. (1979). *Central problems in social theory: Action, structure and contradiction in social analysis*. Berkeley, CA: University of California Press.

Giddens, A. (1984). *The constitution of society: Outline of the theory of structuration*. Cambridge, UK: Polity Press.

Gill, A. (2012). Travelling down the road to postdisciplinarity? Reflections of a tourism geographer. *Canadian Geographer*, *56*(1), 3–17.

Gretzel, U., Isacsson, A., Matarrita, D., & Wainio, E. (2011). Teaching based on TEFI values: A case study. *Journal of Teaching in Travel & Tourism*, *11*, 94–106.

Grint, K. (2005). Problems, problems, problems: The social construction of leadership. *Human Relations*, *58*(11), 1467–1494.

Harland, T., & Pickering, N. (2011). *Values in higher education teaching*. Abingdon, UK: Routledge.

Harland, T., Tidswell, T., Everett, D., Hale, L., & Pickering, N. (2010). Neoliberalism and the academic as critic and conscience of society. *Teaching in Higher Education*, *15*(1), 85–96.

Haslam, S. A., Reicher, S., & Platow, M. (2011). *The new psychology of leadership: Identity, influence and power*. New York, NY: Psychology Press.

Hazelkorn, E. (2011). *Rankings and the reshaping of higher education: The battle for world-class excellence*. Basingstoke, UK: Palgrave Macmillan.

Henkel, M. (2000). *Academic identities and policy change in higher education*. London, UK: Jessica Kingsley.

Henkel, M. (2005). Academic identity and autonomy in a changing policy environment. *Higher Education, 49*(1/2), 155–176.

Higgins-Desbiolles, F. (2010). In the eye of the beholder? Tourism and the activist academic. In P. M. Burns, C. A. Palmer, & J. M. Lester (Eds.), *Tourism and visual culture: Vol. 1. Theories and concepts* (pp. 98–106). Wallingford, UK: CABI.

Higgins-Desbiolles, F., & Whyte, K. P. (2013). No high hopes for hopeful tourism: A critical comment. *Annals of Tourism Research, 40*, 428–433.

Holden, A. (2005). *Tourism studies and the social sciences*. Abingdon, UK: Routledge.

Hollinshead, K. (2009). The 'worldmaking' prodigy of tourism: The reach and power of tourism in the dynamics of change and transformation. *Tourism Analysis, 14*(1), 139–152.

Hollinshead, K., Ateljevic, I., & Ali, N. (2009). Worldmaking agency-worldmaking authority: The sovereign constitutive role of tourism. *Tourism Geographies, 11*(4), 427–443.

Hugo, G., & Morriss, A. (2010). *Investigating the ageing academic workforce: Stocktake*. Adelaide, Australia: The National Centre for Social Applications of Geographic Information Systems, The University of Adelaide, and Anama Morriss Consulting & Associates. Retrieved from http://www.professions.com.au/Files/Academic_Workforce_Study.pdf

Huisman, J., Weert, E. D., & Bartelse, J. (2002). Academic careers from a European perspective: The declining desirability of the faculty position. *The Journal of Higher Education, 73*(1), 141–160.

Inman, M. (2011). The journey to leadership for academics in higher education. *Educational Management Administration & Leadership, 39*(2), 228–241.

Jackson, B., & Parry, K. (2008). *A very short, interesting and reasonably cheap book about leadership*. London, UK: Sage.

Jafari, J. (1991). Tourism social science. *Annals of Tourism Research, 8*(1), 13–33.

Jafari, J. (2001). The scientification of tourism. In V. Smith & M. Brent (Eds.), *Hosts and guests revisited: Tourism issues of the 21st century* (pp. 28–41). Elmsford, NY: Cognizant Communications.

Jafari, J. (2003). Research and scholarship. *The Journal of Tourism Studies, 14*(1), 6–16.

Jensen, M., & Meckling, W. (1976). Theory of the firm: Managerial behavior, agency costs and ownership structure. *Journal of Financial Economics, 3*(4), 305–360.

Jones, S., Applebee, A., Harvey, M., & Lefoe, G. (2010, July). *Scoping a distributed leadership matrix for higher education*. Paper presented at the 33rd Higher Education Research and Development Society of Australasia, Melbourne, Australia.

Kezar, A. (2000). Pluralistic leadership: Incorporating diverse voices. *The Journal of Higher Education, 71*(6), 722–743.

Kezar, A., Carducci, M., & Contreras-McGavin, M. (2006). *Rethinking the 'L' word in higher education: The revolution of research in leadership* (ASHE Higher Education Report). San Fransisco, CA: Jossey-Bass.

Kogan, M., & Teichler, U. (2007). *Key challenges to the academic profession*. Paris, France: UN Educational, Scientific and Cultural Organization Forum on High Education Research and Knowledge.

Koopman-Boyden, P. G., & Macdonald, L. (2003). Ageing, work performance and managing ageing academics. *Journal of Higher Education Policy and Management, 25*(1), 29–40.

Latour, B. (1987). *Science in action: How to follow scientists and engineers through society*. Milton Keynes, UK: Open University Press.

Lew, A. (2007). Invited commentary: Tourism planning and traditional urban planning theory: Planners as agents of social change. *Leisure/Loisir: Journal of the Canadian Association of Leisure Studies in Higher Education, 31*(2), 383–392.

Liburd, J. (2012). Tourism research 2.0. *Annals of Tourism Research, 39*(2), 883–907.

Lyons, K. (2010). Room to move? The challenges of career mobility for tourism education. *Journal of Hospitality & Tourism Education, 22*(2), 51–55.

Macfarlane, B. (2011). Professors as intellectual leaders: Formation, identity and role. *Studies in Higher Education, 36*(1), 57–73.

Magner, D. (1999, September). The graying professoriate. *The Chronicle of Higher Education, 3*, A18–A21.

Marginson, S. (1999, November). *The enterprise university comes to Australia*. Paper presented at the Australian Association for Research in Education, Melbourne, Australia.

Marginson, S. (2008). Academic creativity under new public management foundations for an investigation. *Educational Theory, 58*(3), 269–286.

Marginson, S., & Considine, M. (2000). *The enterprise university: Power governance and reinvention in Australia*. Cambridge, UK: Cambridge University Press.

Marginson, S., & Rhoades, G. (2002). Beyond national states, markets, and systems of higher education: A glonacal agency heuristic. *Higher Education, 43*, 281–309.

Marginson, S., & Sawir, E. (2005). Interrogating global flows in higher education. *Globalisation, Societies and Education, 3*(3), 281–309.

Marshall, S. J., Orrell, J., Cameron, A., Bosanquet, A., & Thomas, S. (2011). Leading and managing learning and teaching in higher education. *Higher Education Research & Development, 30*(2), 87–103.

Maslow, A. (1987). *Motivation and personality* (3rd ed.). New York, NY: Harper & Row.

McCarty, L. P. (2011). Cosmopolitan education. *Colleagues, 6*(1), article 5. Retrieved from http://scholarworks.gvsu.edu/colleagues/vol6/iss1/5

McInnis, C. (2000). Changing academic work roles: The everyday realities challenging quality in teaching. *Quality in Higher Education, 6*(2), 143–152.

Messick, D., & Kramer, R. (2005). *The psychology of leadership: New perspectives and research*. Mahwah, NJ: Lawrence Erlbaum.

Morgan, N. (2012). Time for 'mindful' destination management and marketing. *Journal of Destination Marketing & Management, 1*, 8–9.

Moscardo, G., & Murphy, L. (2011). Toward values education in tourism: The challenge of measuring the values. *Journal of Teaching in Travel & Tourism, 11*(1), 76–93.

Nash, D. (2007). *The study of tourism: Anthropological and sociological beginnings*. Oxford, UK: Elsevier.

New Zealand Government. (1989). *Education Act*. Wellington, New Zealand: Author.

Northouse, P. G. (2009). *Leadership: Theory and practice*. London, UK: Sage.

Nussbaum, M. (1997). *Cultivating humanity: A classical defense of reform in liberal education*. Cambridge, MA: Harvard University Press.

Nussbaum, M. (2010). *Not for profit: Why democracy needs the humanities*. Princeton, NJ: Princeton University Press.

Pearce, P. (2005a). Australian tourism education: The quest for status. In C. H. Hsu (Ed.), *Global tourism higher education: Past, present, and future* (pp. 251–267). Binghamton, NY: Haworth Information Press.

Pearce, P. (2005b). Professing tourism: Tourism academics as educators, researchers and change leaders. *Journal of Tourism Studies, 16*(2), 21–33.

Pearce, P. (2011). *The study of tourism: Foundations from psychology*. Oxford, UK: Emerald.

Phillips, R. (2005). Challenging the primacy of lectures: The dissonance between theory and practice in university lecturing. *Journal of University Teaching and Learning Practice, 2*(1). Retrieved from http://jutlp.uow.edu.au/2005_v02_i01/pdf/phillips_003.pdf

Pritchard, A., Morgan, N., & Ateljevic, I. (2011). Hopeful tourism: A new transformative perspective. *Annals of Tourism Research, 38*(3), 941–963.

Pusser, B., Kempner, K., Marginson, S., & Ordorika, I. (2012). *Universities and the public sphere: Knowledge creation and state building in an era of globalization*. London, UK: Routledge.

Rafferty, A., & Griffith, M. (2004). Dimensions of transformational leadership: Conceptual and empirical extensions. *The Leadership Quarterly, 15*, 329–354.

Ramsden, P. (2003). *Learning to teach in higher education* (2nd ed.). Abingdon, UK: Routledge Falmer.

Ren, C., Pritchard, A., & Morgan, N. (2010). Constructing tourism research: A critical inquiry. *Annals of Tourism Research, 37*(4), 885–904.

Richards, D. (2012). Leadership for learning in higher education: The student perspective. *Educational Management Administration & Leadership, 40*(1), 84–108.

Ross, S. (1973). The economic theory of agency: The principal's problem. *American Economic Review, 63*(1), 7–63.

Schuster, J. H., & Finkelstein, M. J. (2006). *The American faculty: The restructuring of academic work and careers*. Baltimore, MD: Johns Hopkins University Press.

Seeber, M. (2011). Efficacy and limitations of research steering in different disciplines. *Studies in Higher Education, 38*(1), 20–38.

Sen, A. (1985). Well-being, agency and freedom: The Dewey Lectures 1984. *The Journal of Philosophy, 82*(4), 169–221.

Sen, A. (1999). *Development as freedom*. Oxford, UK: Oxford University Press.

Sharrock, G. (2012). Four management agendas for Australian universities. *Journal of Higher Education Policy and Management, 34*(3), 323–337.

Sheldon, P. J., Fesenmaier, D. R., & Tribe, J. (2011). The Tourism Education Futures Initiative (TEFI): Activating change in tourism education. *Journal of Teaching in Travel & Tourism, 11*, 2–23.

Smith, S. L. J. (2010). *The discovery of tourism*. Oxford, UK: Emerald.

Smith, S., Ward, V., & House, A. (2011). 'Impact' in the proposals for the UK's research excellence framework: Shifting the boundaries of academic autonomy. *Research Policy, 40*(10), 1369–1379.

Teichler, U. (2003). The future of higher education and the future of higher education research. *Tertiary Education and Management, 9*(3), 171–185.

Tribe, J. (1997). The indiscipline of tourism. *Annals of Tourism Reserach, 24*(3), 638–657.

Tribe, J. (2002). The philosophic practitioner. *Annals of Tourism Research, 29*(2), 228–257.

Tribe, J. (2006). The truth about tourism. *Annals of Tourism Research, 33*(2), 360–381.

Tribe, J. (2010). Tribes, territories and networks in the tourism academy. *Annals of Tourism Research, 37*(1), 7–33.

Trowler, P. (2010). UK higher education: Captured by new managerialist ideology? In V. L. Meek, L. Goedegebuure, R. Santiago, & T. Carvalho (Eds.), *The changing dynamics of higher education middle management* (Vol. 33, pp. 197–211). Dordrecht, the Netherlands: Springer Netherlands.

Tynan, B., & Mark, J. W. L. (2009). Tales of adventure and change: Academic staff members' future visions of higher education and their professional development needs. *On the Horizon, 17*(2), 98–108.

Van Der Wende, M. (2007). Internationalization of higher education in the OECD countries: Challenges and opportunities for the coming decade. *Journal of Studies in International Education, 11*(3/4), 274–289.

Walumbwa, F. O., Avolio, B. J., Gardner, W. L., Wernsing, T. S., & Peterson, S. J. (2008). Authentic leadership: Development and validation of a theory-based measure. *Journal of Management, 34*, 89–126.

Whitchurch, C. (2012). Expanding the parameters of academia. *Higher Education, 64*(1), 99–117.

World Development Bank. (1999). *World Development Bank: Knowledge for development*. Washington, DC: World Development Bank.

A Learning Theory Framework for Sustainability Education in Tourism

BONNIE FARBER CANZIANI, SEVIL SÖNMEZ,
YUCHIN (JERRIE) HSIEH, and ERICK T. BYRD
*University of North Carolina Greensboro, Greensboro,
North Carolina, USA*

*As efforts abound across tourism educator networks to craft plans
for guiding educational responses to the threats of tourism to people and the planet, it is worth exploring areas in which such labors
might be made more efficient, and thus more timely and productive. In this article, we examine how the concept of learning systems
can serve as a useful tool for identifying opportunities to improve
sustainability education planning in tourism. We provide a conceptual framework for sustainability education that moves beyond
current models by incorporating additional concepts from learning
theory and from a 2-year curricular revision process.*

INTRODUCTION

The sustainability movement exhibits the inductive nature of a learning
system, given that concerned individuals are joining together in attempts to
collect and systematize knowledge and guide action to protect people and
the planet. Learning systems are composed of inputs in the forms of *learners* and the influences of *communities of practice*; similarly, learning systems
deploy processes in the form of *cognition* (of learning content, including
awareness of context and impacts) and *action* (implying implementation

methods and measurement; Hall & Paradice, 2005). Networks of tourism educators such as the Building Excellence in Sustainable Tourism (BEST) Education Network (EN) and Tourism Education Futures Initiative (TEFI) can be viewed as part of the emerging and complex sustainability learning system. Educators in TEFI have strongly supported the insertion of sustainability concepts and values into tourism education (Sheldon, Fesenmaier, & Tribe, 2009); TEFI and BEST EN demonstrate the type of global and collective leadership that is required to formulate sustainability-focused educational strategies that assist tourism educators at the local levels in preparing students to manage with an eye to achieving a sustainable future and a profitable present.

Specific guiding value sets have been identified within the TEFI framework: ethics, knowledge, professionalism, mutuality, and stewardship (Liburd & Edwards, 2010). Clearly, there has been momentum among BEST EN and TEFI researchers toward the goal of embedding sustainability principles into what tourism students are learning (BEST EN, n.d.). Nonetheless, there are still questions remaining about how best to transform existing hospitality and tourism education so it meets the challenges and promises of sustainability.

For the purpose of this article, two primary issues for planning sustainability education in tourism are discussed. First, employing the perspectives of the literature on learning systems and communities of practice, the authors draw attention to sources of inefficiency that have influenced their own 2-year curricular revision process at the authors' university. Secondly, the need for additional reflection on specific learning theories (i.e., Bloom's revised taxonomy in Krathwohl, 2002; Kirkpatrick & Kirkpatrick, 2005) is addressed to help educators define the learning goals for sustainability education in the tourism field (Espinoza & Porter, 2011). *Sustainability education in tourism* is broadly defined herein and encompasses any level of education or training related to environmental, social-cultural, and economic issues in the conduct of tourism enterprise and tourism development.

In this article, the authors examine how the concept of learning systems can serve as a useful tool for identifying opportunities to improve sustainability education planning in tourism. A conceptual framework for sustainability education is provided that moves beyond current models by incorporating additional concepts from learning theory. The presented framework aligns a variety of content foci of sustainability education that have appeared within the tourism literature (ranging from teaching philosophy/values to operational management skill training to leadership development) with Bloom's taxonomic ladders of knowledge and cognitive processes (Krathwohl, 2002). Furthermore, the framework incorporates Kirkpatrick and Kirkpatrick's (2005) model of evaluation to suggest appropriate evaluation criteria for each of three learning goals for sustainability education that are presented in this article. The authors' current work in revising a university-level hospitality and tourism program to deliver comprehensive sustainability education will exemplify significant uses and issues related to these learning theories and systems concepts.

SUSTAINABILITY EDUCATION AS A LEARNING SYSTEM

Through the continuous endeavors of educational leaders and researchers in a variety of fields (i.e., Lewis, 2005; Tribe, 2002), sustainability education, both within and beyond the field of tourism, has advanced steadily as a complexity of overlapping learning initiatives. Nkhata and Breen (2010) stated that "understanding of an integrated learning system is essential if we are to successfully promote learning across multiple scales as a fundamental component of adaptability in the governance and management of protected areas" (p. 403). This statement is equally applicable in the context of tourism. However, Henry (2009) finds no systematic treatments of learning for sustainability in the literature and concludes that "the development of strategies to promote learning for sustainability remains an elusive goal" (p. 131).

As efforts abound across tourism educator networks to craft plans for guiding educational responses to the threats of tourism to people and the planet, it is worth exploring areas in which such labors might be made more efficient and thus more timely and productive. To examine inefficiencies, the authors have conceptualized sustainability education as a learning system with various components. Figure 1 presents the authors' view of

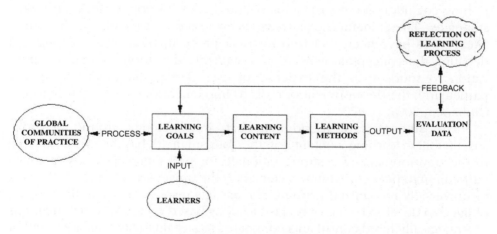

FIGURE 1 Learning system with feedback loop.

a holistic learning system and incorporates global communities of practice (of educators, practitioners, and agencies), inputs from learners, goals, implementation, evaluation of the learning, and a feedback loop.

The system concept generally employs a feedback loop to permit both cognitive reflection and measurement data to feed back to the learning process in terms of changes in learning goals, content, or instructional methods. Learning systems can be examined as a local phenomenon or can be conceived of as the more abstract global learning system for a field or discipline. More importantly, learning systems are construed as existing by thoughtful design, rather than due to random manifestations of goals, content, or activities.

In the context of the authors' curricular revision work, the natural first step for understanding sustainability education in tourism as a learning system involved a comprehensive examination of existing learning content and learning goal statements. The authors anticipated finding a coherent learning process for sustainability education already applied to tourism due to the numerous publications, course syllabi, and conference materials readily available through Internet and physical searches. A sizable effort was made to access materials globally, through means of a review of leading sustainability organizations, best-practice tourism and hospitality academic programs and professional associations, and organizational development efforts of tourism and hospitality agencies and businesses.

The basic premise of a cohesive learning system guiding sustainability education foundered upon review of the materials accessed. Faculty appraisal of existing sustainability learning content and learning goals for tourism and hospitality uncovered two principal sources of system inefficiency: (a) lack of consensus around (or unnecessary revision of) core learning content, and (b) lack of good fit between global resources supporting cognition about sustainability and the local priorities for educational strategies. These inefficiencies have been noted in the tourism literature. "Academics have been criticized for their preoccupation with defining and debating the conceptual aspects of sustainable development and its application to tourism, at the expense of considering the practical aspects, particularly, the development of tools to implement the concept in practice" (Ruhanen, 2008, p. 429).

The authors have found that such inconsistency around desirable sustainability learning content for the tourism field has been detrimental to the development of a strong rationale for presenting new sustainability curriculum to peer curriculum reviewers at the university. Ultimately, the lack of universally recognized learning content has resulted in the authors being obliged to develop background justifications based on the recommendations of strategically hired consultants committed to sustainability education, rather than being able to point to a systematic and cogent argument supported by the industry or the tourism and hospitality academic community as a whole.

Based on the authors' experience, it is particularly important to address inefficiencies in three areas: the development of core learning constructs, learning-goal prioritization, and content classification systems.

MAKING SENSE OF SUSTAINABILITY EDUCATION LEARNING CONTENT

The development of core learning constructs is the first area of concern that significantly impacts a faculty's ability to define learning goals for a sustainability education program in tourism and hospitality. Construct utility is a vital consideration for instructional development as well as for research modeling. Without careful attention to the creation of discrete and meaningful core concepts, educators cannot hope to move learners from initial cognition phases forward to action phases and on to cognitive reflection. Furthermore, useful learning goals for formal sustainability education initiatives cannot be developed when the core concepts in a field are weakly constructed. Because of the importance of good construct development, much of the academic community's effort has historically been spent on attempting to refine theoretical definitions and scientific principles that will be used to design instructional lessons and research studies (i.e., Jaccard & Jacoby, 2009; Smith & Hitt, 2005; Styhre, 2003).

In this vein, the authors note that tourism leaders and educators have devoted significant effort to defining the core sustainability principles that leaders believe ought to guide actions in the tourism field. As noted in the introduction, the TEFI has taken a step forward in crafting an array of five value sets (ethics, knowledge, professionalism, mutuality, and stewardship) that are positioned broadly as principles, which can be converted into relevant learning goals for the education of both tourism publics and tourism professionals around the globe. It became apparent, however, as the authors attempted to incorporate these value sets into the design of learning goals for their program, that the constructs underlying the five value sets were not sufficiently discrete, and thus, it became difficult in practical terms to use these value sets to underpin the new curriculum.

Definitional issues can be seen in terms of construct overlap across the TEFI value sets. For example, social equity is addressed in the discussion of the *ethics* value set (Liburd & Edwards, 2010, p. 9) in the context of making good versus bad choices; similar arguments for impartiality and equality are found again in the presentation of the *mutual respect* (*mutuality*) value set (Liburd & Edwards, p. 11). What the reader takes away is that in the world of tourism education, one of the classical ethical reasoning theories (*justice* or *fairness*) is to be reintroduced as the separate value construct of *mutuality*. Repositioning *justice/fairness* theory in this manner could be construed as an impediment for actually teaching ethical decision making to tourism students, particularly those students who might also take a classical ethics course as part of their academic programs. The utility of the *mutuality* construct as a primary sustainability value would be diminished due to its lack of uniqueness as a construct. Having redundant treatments of justice/fairness in this array of sustainability values might add to confusion on the part of the student, if not the educator attempting to develop a lesson plan.

Continuing the examination of the value sets described by Liburd and Edwards (2010), one sees that the value set associated with *knowledge* (p. 10) overlaps with the value set of *professionalism* (p. 10), in that both focus on the use of evidence, reflective activity, and collective responses, with perhaps the former being more macro-oriented in the form of networks and the latter being more micro-oriented in that it concerns team member performance. Although the examples of conceptual overlap in this article are isolated ones, the underlying concern the authors had in the curricular development process is that core content should be founded on conceptually discrete constructs, each of which add separate utility to critical thinking and decision processes in the development of students.

With this in mind, another source of inefficiency with respect to the development of core content is the assumption that completely new models for teaching and learning sustainability curriculum must be developed for tourism. At the minimum, educators will need to use care in making decisions about how to adapt previously codified systems of learning and practice to the goals of sustainability education in tourism. Returning to the *professionalism* value set in Liburd and Edwards (2010), we see that a model based on the philosophy of continuous improvement is partially adapted rather than fully integrated into the plan for sustainability education. Concepts such as attention to the customer and services and timeliness of evidence might best be laid at the door of already well-known quality control mechanisms. The need to identify appropriate learning content for sustainability education in tourism is real, but there is an equally valid need to recognize and adopt existing decision tools (i.e., ethical and quality improvement decision tools) in their entirety rather than absorbing bits and pieces into newly constructed sustainable tourism models. By retaining the whole of previously codified systems of learning and practice, tourism educators will be able to focus energy on applying such tools to tourism sustainability contexts, rather than linger unnecessarily in a stage of continuous tweaking of core content.

A second concern that emerged during the development of primary learning goals for the program was that of a lack of clear prioritization of learning goals in sustainability education for the tourism field. What has been absent from the literature on sustainability education in tourism seems to be the negotiation of critical core sustainability learning goals for the tourism higher education community that are durable and universal. Sustainability education priorities can be influenced by individual and organizational agendas as well as by broader sea changes in the concerns of a society—this is unavoidable. Wright's (2007) comment that in the general higher education sector there is a "lack of cohesion amongst researchers due to the interdisciplinary nature of the emerging [sustainability] field and few opportunities for international intellectual exchange (p. 35)" applies to the tourism sector as well. Educators from varying disciplinary backgrounds studying tourism are likely overwhelmed by the numerous disparate and possible sustainability foci and may be unnerved by differing senses of urgency among academic, practitioner, and public bodies.

Even when the sense of urgency to take specific actions about sustainability has been high and ongoing, say for recycling education or water conservation in a community, Bramwell and Lane (2008) concede that sustainability priorities in society will inevitably evolve and point to shifts from environmental sustainability to "just sustainability" (*just* in the sense of fairness; Agyeman & Evans, 2004, p.157). They also point to Beck's (1992) belief that some countries have moved from social equity issues to focus on issues primarily associated with the notion of risk management.

Thus, either real or perceived shifts in priorities can cause individual tourism educators to avoid sinking personal investments of time and resources into curricular priorities perceived as transitory, particularly if these sustainability programs appear to lack adequate support from governments, businesses, or citizens. The lack of universal or durable core concepts and terminology has been particularly troublesome to the authors' efforts in devising core curriculum in sustainable tourism and hospitality at the university. The tendency of benchmarked existing tourism programs to specialize in certain aspects of sustainability—for example, the sciences of green tourism or the issues of destination development and stakeholder concerns—is very evident across tourism curricula reviewed in the present curricular revision process. Added to this is the very real resource constraint of current faculty skill bases and personal motivations in the area of sustainability, as well as general obligations to seek grants and endowments that tend to be largely narrow in focus and intent and driven by donor interests.

Additional forces such as being within a school of business and having natural existing partnerships with programs such as entrepreneurship are also impact factors when exploring priorities for learning goal and course development at the university. Lastly, the competition for terminology (i.e., responsible tourism, sustainable tourism, eco-tourism, ethical tourism) haunts faculty efforts in not only assigning titles to prospective courses, but in deciding on a suitable new academic program name that will go beyond trendiness.

A third source of inefficiency in compiling and organizing core content in a learning system is found when competing classification systems exist for filing and accessing learning content in sustainability. Generally, academic disciplines attempt to guide learners toward core disciplinary content by using distinct categorization labels that demonstrate easily comprehended hierarchical or typological logic (e.g., genre, historical, or geographical classifications of written literature). In the case of sustainability education in tourism, guiding frameworks in the form of compendia of practices in education and training for sustainable development have been compiled by leading organizations such as the United Nations Educational, Scientific, and Cultural Organization's International Center for Technical and Vocational Education and Training (UNESCO-UNEVOC) and the BEST EN.

These compendia organize the vast issues surfacing in discussions of sustainability education into digestible chunks of information. BEST-EN's Think Tanks have been organized by topics ranging across *sector interests* such as transportation, events, and marketing; *skills* such as strategic management and networking; *issues* such as risk, values, and corporate social responsibility; and *result areas* such as quality of life. UNESCO-UNEVOC's annotated bibliography positions practices under categories such as *education and training, employment, sustainable livelihoods, stewardship,* and *the triple bottom line* (UNESCO, 2004). Neither of these two major repositories' classification schemes have a clear classification logic, nor do they attempt to integrate learning theories into their categorization of the materials or suggestions for sustainability education. It was the authors' exposure to this vast "bits and pieces" disorganization of learning content and materials that prompted faculty interest in exploring how more specific learning theories (i.e., Bloom, 1956; Kirkpatrick & Kirkpatrick, 2005) might be applied in organizing learning goals and content for sustainability education in tourism and hospitality. The ensuing discussion may be construed as aligning the *what* of learning goals and content with the *who* and *when* of learning in sustainability education.

LEARNING THEORY AND DESIGN OF SUSTAINABILITY EDUCATION

Having experienced considerable difficulties in deciding what core learning goals and learning content ought to be for the curricular initiatives at the university due to content-related inefficiencies in the field, the authors wish now to explain how specific learning theories helped the faculty determine their primary learning goals for the revised program. This section of the article will introduce a learning theory perspective into the design of sustainability education initiatives by focusing on three interdependent learning goals drafted by the authors; these learning goals directly correspond with Bloom's (1956) hierarchical classification of knowledge levels, under which sustainability content from the tourism literature (e.g., Liburd & Edwards, 2010) may be organized.

The classic (1956) text edited by Benjamin Bloom (commonly referred to as "Bloom's Taxonomy") was introduced to teachers as a device for the classification of educational objectives. Bloom expressed the clear desire to support teachers' conversations around the concepts of curricular design and instructional innovation. It is the idea that the taxonomy can help guide the conversation about learners and content in the sustainability field that makes Bloom's work so appealing, given the aforementioned deficiencies in the way the tourism community has organized sustainability content and concepts to date. Bloom's model is useful primarily because it offers a way to arrange learning content across a continuum of learner development within a field of study. The authors of the current article offer this device principally as an organizing tool and a conversation starter rather than meaning to debate the validity of the taxonomy or to urge strict adherence to its component parts.

The 2001 revised Bloom's taxonomy has been selected for the purpose of this article to take advantage of research-based enhancements in its design (Krathwohl, 2002); the revised taxonomy differentiates between: (a) levels of knowledge in a field and (b) levels of cognitive processing exhibited by a learner. A major portion of the original taxonomy has been incorporated into a "cognitive process dimension" that specifies six subdimensions in order of learners' progressive cognitive processing of a knowledge domain. *Remembering* is described as the lowest stage of cognitive processing, and *creating* is deemed the highest stage. Table 1 shows the four levels of the theorized knowledge dimension, and Table 2 displays the six levels of the cognitive process dimension of the revised Bloom's taxonomy.

The knowledge dimension of the revised Bloom's taxonomy, presented in Krathwohl (2002), has been particularly valuable for the authors' curriculum development task. Knowledge levels are seen to run from more basic factual knowledge to the highest level of metacognitive knowledge. It is in contemplation of the knowledge dimension in the revised taxonomy that the authors were able to see more clearly how to organize a curriculum in

TABLE 1 Levels of the Knowledge Dimension of the Revised Bloom's Taxonomy[a]

Factual Knowledge	Conceptual Knowledge	Procedural Knowledge	Metacognitive Knowledge
"The basic elements students must know to be acquainted with a discipline or solve problems in it."	"The interrelationships among the basic elements within a larger structure that enable them to function together."	"How to do something, methods of inquiry, and criteria for using skills, algorithms, techniques, and methods."	"Knowledge of cognition in general as well as awareness and knowledge of one's own cognition."

[a]Krathwohl (2002, p. 214).

TABLE 2 Components of the Cognitive Process Dimension of the Revised Bloom's Taxonomy[a]

Cognitive Process	Learner Action
Remember	Retrieve relevant knowledge from long-term memory.
Understand	Construct meaning from instructional messages, including oral, written, and graphic communication.
Apply	Carry out or use a procedure in a given situation.
Analyze	Break material into its constituent parts and determine how the parts relate to one another and to an overall structure or purpose.
Evaluate	Make judgments based on criteria and standards.
Create	Put elements together to form a coherent or functional whole; reorganize elements into a new pattern or structure.

[a]Krathwohl (2002, p. 215).

sustainable tourism and hospitality. Using Bloom's terminology, an initial priority is to have students conceptualize what sustainability is about and what the (competing) guiding frameworks are in terms of ethics and values in the industry and among educators and advocates. From a practical standpoint, students are also expected to do something in terms of actively practicing what they learn—through class activities, internships, and eventually job placement. And lastly, students are expected to critically self-reflect on what sustainability means to them personally and how they might champion and lead others to pursue sustainable actions. This led to three critical overarching learning goals; these learning goals are closely aligned with Bloom, as depicted in Table 3.

Learning Goal 1 is centered on philosophical debates and socially constructed regulatory systems in the tourism field. It is evident that sustainability knowledge is built upon a foundation of political activity. Through lobbying and grassroots activism, stakeholders in the tourism industry, and

TABLE 3 Levels of Sustainability Knowledge for the Revised Academic Program Aligned with Bloom's Knowledge Dimension[a]

Factual Knowledge	Conceptual Knowledge	Procedural Knowledge	Metacognitive Knowledge
"The basic elements students must know to be acquainted with a discipline or solve problems in it."	"The interrelationships among the basic elements within a larger structure that enable them to function together."	"How to do something, methods of inquiry, and criteria for using skills, algorithms, techniques, and methods."	"Knowledge of cognition in general as well as awareness and knowledge of one's own cognition."
The Philosophical Debates and Socially Constructed Regulatory Systems		The Tourism and Hospitality Supply Chain	Producing the Advocates, the Leaders, the Champions

[a]Krathwohl (2002, p. 214).

in the social environment that surrounds it, argue their cases before the world (MacLellan, 1997). Communities face off against developers, the public reacts against tourists, operators react against regulators, and the scientific community studies it all. As a primary learning goal for college students, and perhaps the greater public at large, the tourism field must design an education strategy to prepare stakeholders from all possible sectors to recognize and anticipate the agendas and rhetoric of all interested persons (Mckenzie-Mohr, 2000; Sheldon et al., 2009). Such learning will require constant reinforcement of theories of ethical reasoning, ecological systems, responsible development, and interdependence. Learners additionally must recognize the intents and sources of regulatory systems and comprehend these as social constructions that are enacted when organizations and individuals prompted by sustainability principles successfully influence societies and their industries.

Overall, the field of tourism education has benefitted by the preponderance of expertise focused on devising philosophical statements and guidelines for sustainable practice. Sustainability education efforts, however, must eventually teach human agents to recognize opportunities in the supply chain system for transforming inputs, outputs, and processes in ways that support sustainability goals (Seuring & Müller, 2008). Learning Goal 2 concentrates on the doing aspect of sustainability in tourism and hospitality by vigorously dissecting the tourism and hospitality supply chain and its inputs, outputs, and processes. In the curricular revision at the authors' university, it was critical to identify the various actors in the supply chain in both tourism and hospitality enterprises and to determine which of these actors to target for educational interventions (Jithendran & Baum, 2000). It can be predicted that educators reduce inefficiencies in the learning system when they collaborate closely with practitioner and community education partners to deliver sustainability education to the right person at the right time, thereby avoiding lack of good fit between learning content and application setting. Internal actors typically include employees, guests, suppliers, and the greater public (Perron, Côté, & Duffy, 2006). It is obvious that all of these actors in the sustainability learning system potentially may have contact with sustainability curriculum through studies at the campus or the university's community outreach efforts.

Sustainability education requires a multidisciplinary approach that spans the core skill sets of any individual set of actors, to expose the whole of the supply chain system to analysis to find operational improvements that yield sustainability results. External agents impact the tourism field as well; such agents include sustainability specialists or contractors from other sectors who need to be familiarized with the industry's supply chain. Educators must leverage partnerships with these external actors to encourage (or adopt) best practices in other relevant fields. In the limited context of the present curricular revision, the faculty are planning for such strategic networking and bridging with external fields by broadening the scope of the program advisory board members and by reviewing what students will take from related disciplines through strategic minors, related area electives, and internships.

Learning Goal 3 focuses on producing the sustainability advocates, the leaders, and the champions for the tourism and hospitality field. The development of advocacy for sustainability is an attitudinal development goal, complemented by skill development in communication and negotiation, whereby leaders exhibit not merely core knowledge and skills, but also metacognition of how personal values impact willingness to learn and act. Furthermore, this third learning goal invites personal transformation and the development of sustainability education leadership for the future of the tourism industry.

ENHANCING THE MODEL OF SUSTAINABILITY EDUCATION

Beyond setting the overarching learning goals for curricular revision, the authors also looked to learning theory to guide the faculty in determining other critical features of the curriculum. Table 4 displays the faculty's current thinking on how additional components of the curricular design are organized under the three primary learning goals. Examples are provided as follows with temporary course titles as fillers for the purpose of the

TABLE 4 A Systems Perspective on Learning Goals in Sustainability Education

Design Elements	Learning Goal 1: Philosophy	Learning Goal 2: Transformation	Learning Goal 3: Stewardship
Targeted learner	Stakeholders	Systems Actors	Champions
Content focus	Ecological systems	Supply chains and processes	Industry environments
Scope of education	Broad and continuous	Narrow and finite	Narrow and periodic
Critical Discourses	Ethical reasoning Interdependence	Operations management Entrepreneurship	Communication Leadership
Bloom's Cognitive Levels[a]	Remembering Understanding	Applying Analyzing	Evaluating Creating
Kirkpatrick's Evaluation Levels[b]	Learner recall Learner reaction Triple Bottom Line criteria	Scientific indices Product/Project impacts Tactical investments	Strengthened networks Enhanced missions Holistic enterprises
Example of Planned Course (Draft Title)	Principles of Sustainable Development	Sustainable Lodging Management	Corporate Social Responsibility

[a]Krathwohl (2002).

[b]Kirkpatrick & Kirkpatrick (2005).

article. The full curriculum is not yet finalized, and therefore, the discussion will draw upon subset examples only. In terms of critical discourses that will be used to attain the desired learning goals, the authors anticipate that within courses that introduce the philosophical knowledge base underpinning sustainability (e.g., Principles of Sustainable Development), the discourses used will be heavy on ethical reasoning and interdependence of ecological entities.

Courses such as Sustainable Lodging or Sustainable Food and Beverage are meant to inspire students to question the current supply chain activity of tourism enterprises. Such curricula will require learners to focus on operational analysis of inputs, outputs, and processes and to search for entrepreneurial funding for innovative practices that are sustainable. Lastly, a course such as Corporate Social Responsibility will expand students' use of communication and leadership strategies to foster within themselves a metacognitive phase of personal development moving them potentially into roles of sustainability advocacy.

Although the revised Bloom's taxonomy (Krathwohl, 2002) does not exclusively pair specific cognitive processes with specific knowledge levels, the authors have done so only as a way of expressing that, for the most part, they expect courses in the revised curriculum to advance students across the various levels of cognitive processing in a thoughtful way. In courses that introduce the philosophical knowledge base, a majority of course activities will be geared toward students remembering and understanding the different frameworks and arguments about sustainability that have surfaced across the globe. In like manner, in courses that focus on transformative reengineering of the supply chain, students will apply and analyze operations using a variety of scientific and operational techniques to foster continuous achievement of sustainability goals at the enterprise level. Lastly, in courses that focus on developing students as the new wave of leadership in sustainability, considerable attention will be paid to activities that ask students to evaluate existing live operations and/or to create new examples of sustainable enterprises using holistic thinking and long-term horizons.

An additional source from the learning theory literature is Kirkpatrick and Kirkpatrick's (2005) updated seminal model of evaluating training. Their work offers useful insights in terms of the most appropriate ways to measure the impact of sustainability education. Four levels of evaluation are described: measures that address learner reaction to or liking of the learning experience, measures of competency improvement taken within or right after the educational intervention, measures of transference of learning to relevant settings and situations (i.e., the workplace), and longer-horizon organizational or ecological results that may be attributed to the educational intervention.

In Table 4, the authors have suggested that the most relevant measures for courses that focus on the philosophy of sustainability are those measures that focus on reactions of learners to sustainability as a mission as well as their degree of acceptance of balanced criteria for measuring business performance. Moving on to the goal of transformations along the supply chain, the authors posit that relevant evaluation criteria in this context include learning transfer, behavioral change, and ideally results evidenced by environmental indices and measures (Štreimikienė, Girdzijauskas, & Stoškus, 2009), such as air quality, reduced cradle-to-grave impact of products, and reduced project impacts on regions. Finally, in terms of measuring curricular impact on the development of leadership and champions for sustainability in the tourism and hospitality field, it is presumed that relevant measures of learning in this context include program graduates' abilities to craft sustainability-oriented mission statements and demonstrate increased investments in training, innovation, and entrepreneurship supporting sustainability in their future tourism businesses and providing leadership to social networks sponsoring sustainability initiatives.

CONCLUSION

It was noted at the outset of this article that communities of practice in tourism education are compiling resources and encouraging learners to embrace sustainability values and to implement sustainable procedures in the tourism supply chain. As agents within a learning system, educators have come together to broadcast critical sustainability value concepts and unify the educational community in identifying and prioritizing high-utility sustainability education strategies. Like every system, sustainability education in tourism possesses the potential for inefficiencies. Ambiguities in the definition of core learning constructs, for example, can make curricular and instructional design decisions more difficult. Competing or shifting priorities in the establishment of learning goals for sustainability education in tourism are another source of inefficiency in the learning system. Finally, the efficiency of searches for learning content that is being made available across the globe is hindered due to weakly constructed classification schemes.

This article has tried to advance the theory underlying sustainability education by specifying a systems approach to learning design. The article also calls for learning goals to be aligned with relevant learning theory, such as Bloom's taxonomy, and with learning evaluation criteria, such as Kirkpatrick and Kirkpatrick's (2005) model of evaluation, to build a holistic model of sustainability education for the future. The authors provide concrete examples of learning system inefficiencies encountered while engaging in a 2-year process of curricular revision that moved a hospitality and tourism program toward a strengthened position in sustainability education. While the primary goal of the article has been to share the learning system framework that was devised during the curricular revision, a few additional remarks are in order. These remarks follow on the heels of the authors' continued inability to find reasonably organized learning content in the area of sustainability in tourism and hospitality.

The first remark is targeted to readers who find themselves engaged in activities meant to coordinate the vast collections of learning content in the area of sustainability in tourism and hospitality. There is a notion separate from that of *communities of practice* that is called *shared epistemic agency*; the latter "emphasizes the capacity that enables people to be more than mere knowledge 'carriers' . . . to be productive participants in these knowledge-laden, object-driven collaborative activities and to be in charge of their own [and the system's] knowledge advancement" (Damşa, Kirschner, Andriessen, Erkens, & Sins, 2010, p. 146). The difference between generic communities of practice and shared epistemic agency (i.e., Glasser, 2010; Hildreth, Kimble, & Wright, 2000; Wenger, McDermott, & Snyder, 2002) is that the latter is intentional in its striving to be more than the sum of collective parts. Shared epistemic agents are expected to join together to create new and robust knowledge objects, rather than merely amass individual knowledge into a central location. Educators in the tourism field may strive to move what they are currently doing in amassing information on the Web and in published works from merely centralizing its location to a more cautious and inspired conceptualization of its alignment with the various learning theories discussed in this article.

A second remark expands on the finding that it is nigh to impossible to develop curriculum in the absence of agendas and prioritizations. In cases where time to deliver curriculum is limited and educators must limit learning content in courses, the authors remind the reader that access to the whole range of learning can still be facilitated through centralized data collection and curricular development efforts of large-scale international groups such as BEST EN and TEFI. Following the thought process of Liburd and Hjalager (2010), it may be that educator networks have the potential to combat the instability and inconsistency of sustainability education learning priorities by establishing open-source depositories of learning content. With these collective actions, educators at the micro-level would be able to view the learning system as able to expand exponentially (e.g., though the low-cost use of technology storage space), rather than be obligated to view learning content development as a zero-sum game limited by number of weeks in a semester or the local priorities of the institution. When learning content is made continually available through cloud computing, educators can choose or not choose to employ specific content as their programs require and, more importantly, can refer learners to other relevant content that was not specifically covered in the lesson plan.

The authors want to underscore the importance of aligning instructional activities with learning goals; more research is needed on this topic. Wright (2007) found that among 35 international higher education sustainability (HES) experts gathered in Halifax, Canada in October 2005, out of 19 possible research agenda items, respondents ranked studying teaching and learning methods in the sustainability education context as the top research agenda item for the higher education sector to be able to move the cause of sustainability forward. Wright also noted that "an investigation of what epistemologies and research methodologies are best suited for HES was considered of utmost importance to the group" (p. 40).

Equally necessary is the expansion of formal assessment devices to track sustainability learning impacts over time (e.g., Wallis, Kelly, & Graymore, 2010) to foster in educators and institutions a longer-term commitment to any particular sustainability education strategy they may choose to implement. Assessment, like low-cost cloud computing, has a beneficial dampening effect on the tendency to update unnecessarily one's syllabus or instructional plan in ways that toss out critical and still applicable core constructs solely because they were first conceived of years earlier. According to Wallis et al., activities related to devising assessment procedures and reviewing outcomes are vital to construct robustness as well.

In summation, the authors have shown that sustainability education progresses both at the local development and the system development levels, and they have sought to facilitate educational planning activity by specifying learning goals and their relevant elements. While the first two learning goals presented in our model are tightly coupled to existing and emerging practices in the field, the authors additionally believe that the development of champions must be a learning goal for sustainability education to make even sustainability education sustainable.

REFERENCES

Agyeman, J., & Evans, B. (2004). Just sustainability: The emerging discourse of environmental justice in Britain? *The Geographical Journal*, *170*(2), 155–164.

Beck, U. (1992). *The Risk Society: Towards a new modernity*. London, UK: Sage.

Bloom, B. (1956). *Taxonomy of educational objectives. Book 1: Cognitive domain*. White Plains, NY: Longman.

Bramwell, B., & Lane, B. (2008). Priorities in sustainable tourism research. *Journal of Sustainable Tourism*, *16*(1), 1–4.

Building Excellence in Sustainable Tourism Education Network. (n.d.). *Past Think Tanks*. Retrieved from http://www.besteducationnetwork.org/past_tt.php

Damşa, C. I., Kirschner, P. A., Andriessen, J. E. B., Erkens, G., & Sins, P. H. M. (2010). Shared epistemic agency: An empirical study of an emergent construct. *Journal of the Learning Sciences*, *19*(2), 143–186.

Espinoza, A., & Porter, T. (2011). Sustainability, complexity, and learning insights from complex systems approaches. *The Learning Organization*, *18*(1), 54–72.

Glasser, H. (2010). An early look at building a social learning for sustainability community of practice: RCE Grand Rapids' Flagship Project. *Journal of Education for Sustainable Development*, 4(1), 61–72.

Hall, D. J., & Paradice, D. (2005). Philosophical foundations for a learning-oriented knowledge management system for decision support. *Decision Support Systems*, 39(3), 445–461.

Henry, A. D. (2009). The challenge of learning for sustainability: A prolegomenon to theory. *Human Ecology Review*, 16(2), 131–140.

Hildreth, P., Kimble, C., & Wright, P. (2000). Communities of practice in the distributed international environment. *Journal of Knowledge Management*, 4(1), 27–38.

Jaccard, J., & Jacoby, J. (2009). *Theory construction and model-building skills (methodology in the social sciences)*. London, UK: Guilford Press.

Jithendran, K. J., & Baum, T. (2000). Human resources development and sustainability: The case of Indian tourism. *International Journal of Tourism Research*, 2(6), 403–421.

Kirkpatrick, D. L., & Kirkpatrick, J. D. (2005). *Evaluating training programs: The four levels* (3rd ed.). San Francisco, CA: Berrett-Koehler.

Krathwohl, D. R. (2002). A revision of Bloom's taxonomy: An overview. *Theory into Practice*, 41(4), 212–218.

Lewis, A. (2005). Rationalizing a tourism curriculum for sustainable tourism development in small island states: A stakeholder perspective. *Journal of Hospitality, Leisure, Sport, & Tourism Education*, 4(2), 4–15.

Liburd, J. J., & Edwards, D. (Eds.). (2010). *Understanding the sustainable development of tourism*. Oxford, UK: Goodfellow Publishers Limited.

Liburd, J. J., & Hjalager, A. M. (2010). Changing approaches towards open education, innovation, and research in tourism. *Journal of Hospitality and Tourism Management*, 17(1), 12–20.

MacLellan, L. R. (1997). The tourism and the environment debate, from idealism to cynicism. In M. Foley, J. Lennon, & G. Maxwell (Eds.), *Hospitality, tourism, and leisure management* (pp. 177–194). London, UK: Cassell.

Mckenzie-Mohr, D. (2000). Fostering sustainable behavior through community-based social marketing. *American Psychologist*, 55(5), 531–537.

Nkhata, B. M., & Breen, C. (2010). A framework for exploring integrated learning systems for the governance and management of public protected areas. *Environmental Management*, 45(2), 403–413.

Perron, G., Côté, R. P., & Duffy, J. F. (2006). Improving environmental awareness training in business. *Journal of Cleaner Production*, 14(6/7), 551–562.

Ruhanen, L. (2008). Progressing the sustainability debate: A knowledge management approach to sustainable tourism planning. *Current Issues in Tourism*, 11(5), 429–455.

Seuring, S., & Müller, M. (2008). From a literature review to a conceptual framework for sustainable supply chain management. *Journal of Cleaner Production*, 16(15), 1699–1710.

Sheldon, P., Fesenmaier, D., & Tribe, J. (2009). The Tourism Education Futures Initiative. *E-Review of Tourism Research*, 7(3), 39–44.

Smith, K. G., & Hitt, M. A. (Eds.). (2005). *Great minds in management: The process of theory development*. Oxford, UK: Oxford University Press.

Štreimikienė, D., Girdzijauskas, S., & Stoškus, L. (2009). Sustainability assessment methods and their application to harmonization of policies and sustainability monitoring. *Environmental Research, Engineering, and Management*, *48*(2), 51–62.

Styhre, A. (2003). *Understanding knowledge management: Critical and postmodern perspectives*. Copenhagen, Denmark: Copenhagen Business School Press.

Tribe, J. (2002). The philosophic practitioner. *Annals of Tourism Research*, *29*(2), 338–357.

United Nations Educational, Scientific, and Cultural Organization. (2004). *Technical and vocational education and training for sustainable development: An annotated bibliography of research and related literature (1998–2004)*. Retrieved from http://www.unevoc.unesco.org/fileadmin/user_upload/pubs/AB1_TVETforSD.pdf

Wallis, A. M., Kelly, A. R., & Graymore, M. L. M. (2010). Assessing sustainability: A technical fix or a means of social learning? *International Journal of Sustainable Development & World Ecology*, *17*(1), 67–75.

Wenger, E., McDermott, R., & Snyder, W. M. (2002). *Cultivating communities of practice*. Boston, MA: Harvard Business School Press.

Wright, T. S. A. (2007). Developing research priorities with a cohort of higher education for sustainability experts. *International Journal of Sustainability in Higher Education*, *8*(1), 34–43.

Toward Values Education in Tourism: The Challenge of Measuring the Values

GIANNA MOSCARDO and LAURIE MURPHY

James Cook University, Townsville, Queensland, Australia

Values are implicit in our education systems and practices—they are reflected in the choices that we make about what to teach, how to teach, and who to teach it to. Values education is about making values explicit and about focusing education on a particular set of values. This article reports on part of such an initiative within tourism education in universities and colleges, the Tourism Education Futures Initiative (TEFI), the development of tools to measure values. In particular it reports on an exercise conducted with university students to develop a pool of items for the development of a TEFI Values Inventory.

INTRODUCTION

"Values are the glue that holds societies together" (Coyne & Coyne, 2001, p. 58) and there is a long history of discussions about the importance of values in education (Halstead & Taylor, 2000). But in this history, the prominence of values in educational practice has changed on a regular basis going through cycles of popularity and neglect (Howard, Berkowitz, & Schaeffer, 2004). In the last 10 to 15 years the inclusion of values in educational practice has made something of a comeback in all levels of education (T. M. Jones, 2009; Ladwig, 2010), but especially in university education (Grundstein-Amado, 1995). Arguably this resurgence reflects growing community concerns about the actions of business and government leaders (Meier, 2003). A number of recent corporate failures including those associated with the global financial crisis and environmental disasters have highlighted this issue for many in tertiary education (Sharrock, 2010).

The Tourism Education Futures Initiative (TEFI) reflects these forces and seeks to provide a framework that promotes the introduction of values into the tourism curriculum at the university level (Sheldon, Fesenmaier, Woeber, Cooper, & Antonioli, 2008). This article reports on one element of this initiative, the development of a Values Inventory as part of a larger program to support the adoption of a values education approach in tourism education in colleges and universities. In particular, the article explores the roles and importance of a values scale or inventory in the development and evaluation of these efforts and reports on some of the challenges of operationalizing value concepts.

APPROACHES TO VALUE EDUCATION

Values have been formally defined in the social sciences as "abstract ideals, positive or negative, not tied to any specific object or situation, representing a person's beliefs about modes of conduct and ideal terminal modes" (Rokeach, 1968, p. 124). Values are broad and abstract ideas about desirable global end states and the means of achieving these end states (Becker & Connor, 1983). They are fundamental to the way individuals view their world and they guide attitudes toward more specific topics and objects and, through attitudes, direct behavior (Becker & Connor, 1983). Figure 1

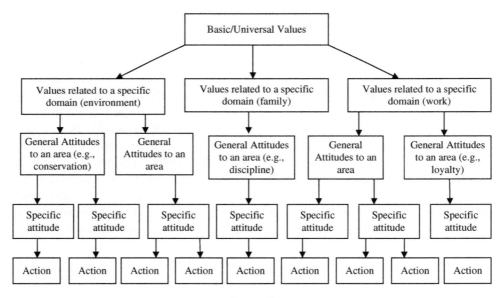

FIGURE 1 Linking values to actions.

provides an overview of the links between values, attitudes, and actions. Essentially there is an increasing level of specificity as you move down the ladder from values to actions and a greater influence from personal experience and context. Thus the most universal or basic values are at the top of the ladder and these are stable and important. There is debate amongst social scientists about where the label values is most suitably applied in such a ladder with some preferring to reserve it only for the highest levels (Rokeach, 1968) and others prepared to accept values in more specific domains (see Dunlap & van Liere, 2008, for values related to the environment). There is also some debate over the values that should be in the highest level with different systems proposed by Rokeach (1968) and Schwartz (Lindeman & Verkasalo, 2005).

Values education describes the explicit consideration of values and their transmission in educational organizations. Values education is an umbrella term that incorporates a number of general education movements, such as civics and citizenship education, character education, moral education, and environmental education (Halstead & Taylor, 2000; Howard et al., 2004; Veugelers, 2000) and specific programs such as "community of caring" (S. C. Jones & Stoodley, 1999).

T. M. Jones (2009) identified 16 distinctive approaches to values education that could be organized into four categories. The first category are conservative approaches that focus on the direct transmission of values from teacher to student and these include religious instruction, values inculcation, character education, and citizenship and civic education (T. M. Jones, 2009). In these approaches, especially character education and values inculcation, the desired values are presented in specific teaching activities and programs and then reinforced through the actions of both the teacher and the student (Howard et al., 2004; T. M. Jones, 2009).

T. M. Jones (2009) labeled the second category as liberal/development approaches and included four approaches: confluent education, laissez faire, moral development, and values clarification. The moral development approach was advocated by, and based on the psychological research of, Kohlberg and was especially concerned with the presentation of moral dilemmas to students (Kohlberg & Higgins, 1987). The argument was that discussion of these dilemmas encouraged students to think more deeply about decisions and their own moral development (Halstead & Taylor, 2000). This is similar to the values clarification approach of Kirschenbaum (1976). In values clarification a number of different techniques are used to encourage students to think about and identify their own values and to assess how their values are connected with their decision making (Halstead & Taylor, 2000). These techniques can include the use of a values journal (Grundstein-Amado, 1995), the development of personal value narratives (Eriksen, 2009) and the combination of these techniques with the completion of value scales (Payne & Pettingill, 1987). Both cases advocate a Socratic approach to education (Howard et al., 2004). The third category is critical approaches and includes caring community, cultural heritage programs, peace education, and social action learning (T. M. Jones, 2009). These approaches focus on relationships and the welfare of others (Howard et al., 2004). Finally there are post-modern approaches that include ethical inquiry, the discursive school, values analysis, and values stimulation (T. M. Jones, 2009).

Howard et al. (2004) provided a history of the development of these various approaches to values education and describes an ongoing tension in this history between those who advocate the transmission of prescriptive values (such as in values inculcation and character education approaches) and those who support participation processes that encourage the development of capacity to identify and think about values (such as found in the moral development and values clarification approaches). Howard et al. (2004) described this as a tension between action and habit and knowing and doing. This tension contributes to a situation where the proponents of the different approaches tend not to communicate with each other and for educators this creates a situation where they are faced with a plethora of different programs (Veugelers, 2000). This results in confusion and encourages education institutions to see values education programs as stand-alone units that are additional to, rather than part of, the main curriculum (Veugelers, 2000).

Adding values education as a separate unit is problematic as the available evidence suggests that a core element in the success of values education is that values are embedded in the entire educational system (Halstead & Taylor, 2000). Halstead and Taylor (2000) argued that values need to be embedded in the entire life of the organisation—in specific values programs, integrated into other content, in the social interactions of people, in the way conflicts are resolved, in the organization's aims, mission, and policies and in the expectations of and from staff. Brandes and Stuber (2004) described an example of such an approach taken with a U.S. college. This program involved the development of a set of values after extensive consultation with key stakeholders. These values were then integrated throughout the institution with:

- A branding strategy in which a logo depicting the values were created and used on all correspondence and stationary and in posters and banners;
- The inclusion of values into the mission and vision of the institution and all other planning and strategy documents;
- The development of a set of principles for staff supported by a recognition program and the use of the values in faculty recruitment;
- The integration of the values into the curriculum and teaching practice of each academic unit; and
- The development of partnerships to proactively pursue the values beyond the college (Brandes & Stuber, 2004).

Brandes and Stuber (2004) went on to describe both the factors that contribute to the success of the program and the challenges. The success factors included support from senior leaders and management, extensive consultation, clear strategies for change, and support for the change process. The two main challenges identified were finding time in tight work schedules to implement the change and getting the support of some academics who see themselves as individuals rather than part of a collective or community (Brandes & Stuber, 2004). Coyne and Coyne (2001) noted these issues in their analysis of the barriers to adopting character education. They also added some other challenges including concerns about deciding upon whose values or a common set of values to adopt and beliefs by educators that time spent on values education can detract from other learning. In this latter case they argued that the available evidence suggests that values education can enhance student learning across a range of areas, a conclusion supported by Eriksen (2009) in his evaluation of a values based activity conducted with MBA students.

THE ROLE OF VALUES MEASUREMENT

While there exists a number of papers reporting on specific values education initiatives undertaken by teachers in various institutions, a continuing issue for values education is the lack of research both into the values themselves and that systematically evaluates the outcomes of these different programs (Ladwig, 2010). One key area required for the advancement of values education is the development of tools to measure values. Such tools have two important roles. Firstly, they allow for the assessment and investigation of the existing values of all involved in education including students, teachers, managers/administrators, families, employers, and other community members. Bulach (2002) argued that we need to know the values already held to be able to guide the development of new curricula and other activities. Secondly, tools to measure values are important to evaluate the effectiveness of actions taken to implement values education programs. Such evaluations could be conducted with all the participants in a values education program including teachers and administrators as well as students. They could also be used to evaluate whole programs or parts of the programs beyond the classroom, as well as specific teaching activities.

It is important here to distinguish between evaluation and assessment. One important element of integrating values into a curriculum is the development of appropriate assessment. Indeed such assessments can be tools for value education in that they may require students to demonstrate their understanding and use of values in different ways (cf. Eriksen, 2009; Grundstein-Amado, 1995; Payne & Pettingill, 1987). But it is possible that students may do well in such assessments without changing their own values by temporarily adopting the stance they perceive is necessary for the assessment. Howard et al. (2004) reported that this possibility is one of the criticisms of the transmission and inculcation approaches to values education—it may be able to force students to adopt a particular value temporarily but have little impact on their long-term views. It is also possible that the reverse is true that students may have changed their values but for various other reasons may not do well on the assessments. Further, if the assessment is itself part of the educational process then to demonstrate its effectiveness it is important to have an independent means of evaluating changes in values. In short, assessment is a critical element of values education but is separate from evaluation.

THE PROCESS OF DEVELOPING A VALUES INVENTORY OR SCALE

Scales or inventories are very commonly used in social science research and there is consensus about how they should be developed (de Vaus, 1990; Kerlinger, 1973; Oppenheim, 1992). There are five main steps in the development process:

1. Create a set of questions or an item pool that reflect an orientation to the topic of interest (de Vaus, 1990; Kerlinger, 1973; Oppenheim, 1992). Rowan and Wulff (2007) noted that the generation of items for a scale is often given little attention in the textbooks, but there are a number of options. Some researchers generate the items themselves by writing statements about different aspects of the topic. Others seek statements from experts in the area or from the literature describing the topic. Rowan and Wulff described the use of different qualitative techniques in which members of the population of interest provide insights into the topic that allow for statements to be generated. Regardless of the technique used, the key is to ensure that the sufficient statements are generated to cover all the aspects or dimensions of the topic (Oppenheim, 1992).
2. Get it completed by an appropriate sample (de Vaus, 1990; Kerlinger, 1973; Oppenheim, 1992).
3. Test the scale for various aspects of reliability. (de Vaus, 1990; Kerlinger, 1973; Oppenheim, 1992). Reliability testing typically involves the use of Cronbach's alpha coefficient to assess the internal consistency of scales (de Vaus, 1990; Oppenheim, 1992). But reliability can also be analyzed by calculating the consistency of responses for a test-retest situation where the sample is asked to complete the test at least twice in a limited time span (Oppenheim, 1992), and split-tests or parallel forms testing where

the responses to two sets of questions designed to measure the same things are administered and then responses compared.

4. Examine the dimensionality of the scale items using principal components factor analysis (de Vaus, 1990; Kerlinger, 1973; Oppenheim, 1992).

5. Confirm the validity of the scale or inventory (Oppenheim, 1992). There are four types of validity that can be explored. The first is *content validity*, which refers to the extent to which the test items cover the relevant aspects of the topic. The second is *predictive validity* or the ability of scores on the scale to be used to predict relevant behaviours. The third is *concurrent validity,* which is the extent to which scores on the scale are correlated with other external measures of the topic. Finally there is *construct validity* in which scores on the scale are compared to measures of related concepts (Oppenheim, 1992).

TEFI AND ITS VALUES

The aim of this article is to report on the development of a values scale or inventory to use to investigate, support and evaluate the implementation of the values identified as part of the TEFI. The TEFI mission is "to provide vision, knowledge and a framework for tourism education programs to promote global citizenship and optimism for a better world" (TEFI, n.d.). The initiative has developed over four years, starting in 2007, and is driven by a concern about the quality of tourism education and its ability to prepare graduates for the future of tourism (Sheldon et al., 2008). In discussing issues around tourism, the initiative identified the need to focus on vales education and through a series of workshops, with a group of educators and some industry representatives, developed a set of six values (see Figure 1 in the lead article of this issue).

These six values are described in more detail in a White Paper (TEFI, 2009). Table 1 provides a comparison of the TEFI values to the universal values of Rokeach (1968) and Schwartz (Lindeman & Verkasalo, 2005). In this table comparable values are italicized. The table shows that the TEFI values are a mixture of some universal or broad values and then more domain specific values or attitudes. There are also some very specific attitudes, particularly within the professional grouping where relevance, timeliness, and service are listed. This places the TEFI values as mostly within the first two levels of the ladder in Figure 1. It could also be argued that some of the TEFI elements are skills, for example, critical thinking and networking, and it is not clear whether it is the skill itself that is important or the attitudes toward the importance of the skill. There is still potential to further develop and clarify some of these TEFI groupings and elements.

TABLE 1 Comparison of the TEFI Values to Rokeach's and Schwartz's Universal Values

TEFI values	Rokeach values	Schwartz values

Stewardship
• Sustainability
 	
• Responsibility
• Service to the community
 	
Knowledge
• Critical thinking
• Innovation
• Creativity
• Networking
Professionalism
• Leadership
• Practicality
• Service
• Relevance
 	
• Timeliness
• Reflexivity
• Team work
• Proactive
Ethics
• Honesty
• Transparency
• Authenticity
• Authentic self
Mutuality
• Diversity
• Inclusion
• Equity
• Humility
• Collaboration
	Terminal values (end states)
	• A comfortable life
	
	• Equality
	• An exciting life
	
	• Family security
	• Freedom
	• Health
	• Inner harmony
	• Mature love
	• National security
	• Pleasure
	• Salvation
	• Self-respect
	• A sense of
	  accomplishment
	• Social recognition
	• True friendship
	• Wisdom
	• A world at peace
	• A world of beauty
	Instrumental values
	(means)
	• Ambitious
	• Broad-minded
	• Capable
	• Clean
	• Courageous
	• Forgiving
	• Helpful
	• Honest
	• Imaginative
	• Independent
	• Intellectual
	• Logical
	• Loving
	• Loyal
	• Obedient
	• Polite
	• Responsible
	• Self-controlled
		Power
		• Authority over
		  others
		• Recognition
		• Positive public
		  image
		Achievement
		• Success
		• Ambition
		• Self-respect
		Hedonism
		• Pleasure
		• Enjoyment
		Stimulation
		• Excitement
		• Challenge
		
		Self-direction
		• Creativity
		• Curiosity
		• Freedom
		Universalism
		• Protecting the
		  environment
		• World of beauty
		• Social justice
		• Equality
		• Inner harmony
		• Wisdom
		Benevolence
		• Helpful
		• Honest
		• Responsible
		• Mature love
		• True friendship
		Tradition
		• Respect for tradition
		• Humility
		• Being devout
		Conformity
		• Politeness
		• Obedience
		• Self-discipline
		Security
		• Social order
		• Family security
		• Sense of belonging
		• Good health
		• Reciprocation of
		  favours

MEASURING THE TEFI VALUES

The development of the TEFI Values Inventory is part of a larger program of activities including a faculty code of ethics and examples or case studies of the implementation of the values into curricula (TEFI, 2009). The primary aim of the TEFI Values Inventory is as an evaluation tool to determine the effectiveness of implementation programs and activities. But it can also be used to assess the importance of the values to different stakeholders and so it can contribute to the clarification and extension of the values themselves and in turn widen the debate and discussion of the values of the tourism phenomena. Table 2 provides a summary of the steps to be taken in the development of the TEFI Values Inventory. The rest of this section reports on the first step of this process.

Review of Existing Scales

After examining the more detailed descriptions of the TEFI values provided in the White Paper, a list of the values and their components and possible

TABLE 2 Summary of the Development of the TEFI Values Inventory

Step in inventory development	Process for the TEFI Values Inventory
Create an item pool	Understand what the TEFI values are from the workshops
	Review existing scales in related areas to both generate items but also to determine possible items for testing construct and concurrent validity
	Generate items from interviews with a sample from a relevant population
Get the inventory completed	Conduct studies with samples from relevant populations focusing on students. But if possible conduct studies with educators and other stakeholders such as tourism industry managers and leaders.
Test the scale of various aspects of reliability	Conduct a series of analyses on the data from samples completing the inventory. In order to conduct a full range of reliability tests it would be useful to generate two versions of each of the measures.
Examine the dimensionality of the scale	Conduct factor analysis on the data from samples completing the inventory focusing on the extent to which the items contribute to factors that are consistent with the six TEFI value groupings.
Confirm the validity of the inventory	Conduct a series of studies where samples from the relevant populations complete the inventory and also provide information on external criteria including completion of existing scales for similar and relevant concepts and reporting on relevant actions.

related concepts was generated and used in a search of the academic literature to identify existing scales or inventories. This exercise had two aims: to generate potential inventory items and also to identify scales that could be used to evaluate both concurrent and construct validity of the TEFI Values Inventory. This review focused on identifying scales that had been tested and widely used and which were publicly available.

In the first value grouping of stewardship three existing scales were identified: the New Environmental Paradigm (NEP) scale of Dunlap and van Liere (2008), the Environmental Attitudes Inventory (EAI) of Milfont and Duckitt (2010), in its long, short and brief versions, and Shafer, Fukukawa, and Lee's (2007) Perceived Importance of Ethics and Social Responsibility (PRESOR) scale. All three have been tested and used extensively. The first two concentrate on the environmental dimensions of sustainability, while the third looks at social responsibility and service to the community.

In the second value grouping of ethics one widely used and well-developed test is the Ethical Positions Questionnaire developed by Forsyth (1980), which covers all of the elements of this grouping except for authenticity/authentic self options. Further investigation of the descriptions of these items suggests that the concepts being described here are similar to what has been called *existential authenticity* (Steiner & Reisinger, 2006) and *dispositional authenticity* (Kernis & Goldman, 2006). A scale by Kernis and Goldman, the Authenticity Inventory, seems to cover this component. The third values grouping of mutuality, which includes the components of diversity, inclusion, and equity, seemed to be most closely connected to the concepts measured in the well-established and commonly used Miville-Guzman Universality-Diversity Scales (M-GUDS-S; Fuertes, Miville, Mohr, Sedlacek, & Gretchen, 2000).

The final two values groupings, professionalism and knowledge, were more difficult. In the case of professionalism there exists a generic scale, Halls Professionalism Inventory (Snizek, 1972), that is meant to be adapted to specific types of profession (see Shafer, Park, & Liao, 2002, for an example of the inventory adapted for accountants). But this scale does not include any items related to leadership which is listed as a main element in the Professionalism value for TEFI. There exist a large number of published leadership scales but they are focused on the type and style of leadership rather than the value of leadership qualities. In the case of knowledge the review of existing scales was not fruitful. There are tests of creativity and methods for testing actual cognitive skills and abilities, but as with leadership there do not appear to be scales measuring how much people value creativity and critical thinking. In the case of innovation the focus of existing scales is on adoption and response to innovation in the ICT area, rather than attitudes toward innovation in general.

Student Perspectives

The second step in the generation of item pool for the TEFI Values Inventory was conducted in a second-year business research methods class in a regional Australian university. This class is a core element of the business program at this institution and is taken by students from a range of diverse majors including tourism, hospitality, and sports and events management. The students in this class can be seen as representative of some of the target populations for the TEFI initiatives. The Values Inventory development activity was conducted as a practical exercise aimed at helping students learn and practice skills in survey questionnaire design and scale development. For several years the authors have been involved in teaching this class and offering students the opportunity to learn through participation in real research activities focused on areas of interest or personal relevance to them.

The activity consisted of two steps. Firstly, the students were given a background to the TEFI initiative and access to the TEFI White Paper (TEFI, 2009) and the review of existing scales. After the teaching staff presented these documents and described the process of questionnaire and scale development, the students were asked to think about one of the TEFI values sub-elements and to write the features they thought someone would have to be considered as a person that valued the sub-element. That is, what would a person who demonstrated leadership have to be and do? Or how would we know that a person valued networking? Once they had completed a list of these features for the sub-element, the list was passed to another student who read it, ticked those they agreed with, and then added more to the list. Once this was completed the student then went to the next sub-element on their list and started this process again. Each student started at a different sub-element and so all were covered. The aim of swapping the responses was to provide prompts to generate as wide a range of responses as possible. The resulting lists were summarized and the summary provided to the class.

Table 3 contains a summary of the first stage of the exercise, which involved listing the features the students associated with each of the values and their sub-elements. Several features of these lists are noteworthy. Firstly, the number of items generated for each sub-element varied with students able to generate more features for elements such as leadership and sustainability than for equity, creative, and reflexive. Two factors could be involved here in that a short listing could indicate that there is clarity and consensus about what the element means or it could reflect difficulties in understanding the element. Secondly, the lists are a mixture of personal characteristics, skills, behaviors, and value or attitude orientations. This is not surprising because the elements themselves are a mixture. Nor is it necessarily a problem in that the lists of features could be used both for developing scale items

TABLE 3 Summary of Features Students Associate with the TEFI Values

TEFI value	Sub-elements		
Professionalism	Leadership	Partnership building	Service oriented
	• Not abusing power	• Works on building relationships	• Professional customer service
	• Driven	• Networks	• Thoughtful
	• Helpful	• Builds relationships	• Ability to think in a variety of positions
	• Good at delegating	• Bonding	• Values service
	• Available	• Understanding each other/people	• Focused on company performance
	• Ethical	• Mutual respect	• Ability to communicate with diverse people
	• Unbiased	• Forming trust	• Actively provides service
	• Understanding	• Supportive	• Focused on customer satisfaction
	• Overcoming conflict	• Effective communication	• Task performance
	• Influence and inspires others	• Tolerance	• Customer is always right
	• Charismatic	• Honesty	• Aware of how actions affect customer experience
	• Respectful	Practical & responsive	• Good customer service
	• Confident	• Think on feet	Reflexive
	• Shows initiative	• Forward thinker	• Reflects on work
	• Takes control	• Thinks of most effective strategy/solution	• Desire to improve
	• Mentor	• Decisive	• Being flexible in actions
	• Manage people	• Attentive	• Goal driven
	• Approachable	• Awareness of variety of methods	• Monitors performance
	• Value equality	• Effective use of resources	• Asks for feedback
	• Motivate others	• Flexible	• Critical of ones self
	Teamwork	• Provides feedback	• Look for continuous ways of improvement
	• Being focused on the task at hand	• Enthusiastic	
	• Encouraging	Proactive	

(Continued)

TABLE 3 (Continued)

TEFI value	Sub-elements		
	• Good communication	• Self-motivated	
	• Inclusive and tolerant of diversity	• Keen to get things done	
	• Understanding others	• Thinks and plans ahead	
	• Common purpose/goal	• Visualises problems and reacts positively	
	• Cooperative	• Taking the initiative	
	• Active involvement in the team	• Enthusiastic	
	• Collaboration	• Innovative	
	• Working together	• Time management	
	• Active listener		
	• Divide jobs among team members		
	• Open-minded		
Ethics	Honesty	Awareness of self	Transparency
	• Truthful/trust worthy	• Self-identity	• Clear and precise
	• Body language	• High self-esteem	• Confident in decisions
	• Integrity	• Self-respect	• Research to support what is said
	• Loyal	• Pride in work	• Communicating effectively (verbally and non-verbally)
	• Respect for others	• Understanding own values and views	• Open
	• Tactful	• Reflective	• Accountable
	• Transparency	• Open to feedback	• Willing to discuss various topics
	• Open for discussion	• Accept criticism	• No hidden agendas
	• Admits when wrong		• Honest
	• Provides feedback		
	Authenticity of interactions		
	• Communication		
	• Strong sense of purpose		
	• Straightforward		
	• Genuine		
	• Open and honest		

(Continued)

TABLE 3 (Continued)

TEFI value	Sub-elements		
	• Good listener • Enthusiastic		
Stewardship	Sustainability • Environmentally friendly and aware	Community service • Desire to help others	Responsibility • Accountable
	• Looking toward the future	• Concerned about well-being of community	• Takes action when necessary
	• Caring for the future	• Look at bigger picture	• Shows initiative
	• Continual improvement	• Considering others	• Completing tasks on time
	• Knowledge of important issues	• Selfless	• Organized
	• Aware of organizational impacts on environment	• Friendly	• Ethical
	• Involved in projects that protect the environment	• Value the community	• Honest
	• Long-term view	• Aware of community's affect on organization	• Confident
	• Future consequences for environment	• Volunteer	• Take control of situation
	• Leadership • Innovative • Improving current strategies for the future	• Help out when needed	• Assertive
Mutuality	Tolerant of diversity • Accepting of others	Equity • Pleases others	Humility • Kind
	• Willingness to work with diverse people	• Ensures decisions are utilitarian	• Respectful
	• Equality	• Includes and listens to everyone	• Humble
	• Geocentric	• Fair	• Including others
	• Aware of differences	• Treats everyone equally	• Listener
	• Aware of international affairs	Collaboration	• Admits when wrong
	• Open to new ways of learning	• Working with others to obtain maximum results	• Easy to interact with

(*Continued*)

TABLE 3 (Continued)

TEFI value	Sub-elements		
	Supportive of inclusiveness	• Good information with results	• Modest
	• Including others in activities	• Allows everyone to have an input	• Make fun/joke about one's self
	• Being supportive	• Gathering all ideas together	
	• Values all opinions	• Discussion	
	• Accept other cultures and work with them	• Analyse situation	
	• Encourages others	• Supportive	
	• Teamwork focused	• Group work	
	• Motivates others		
Knowledge	Critical thinker	Innovative	Networking
	• Intelligent	• Improvements	• Good communication skills
	• Problem solver	• Consumers needs high priority	• Likeable personality
	• Good analyser	• Use new knowledge to improve current situation	• Ability to communicate knowledge
	• Ability to process knowledge	• Creative	• Building and sustaining relationships
	• Observes and evaluates	• Resourceful	• Connect with others from different backgrounds
	• Brainstorms	• Enthusiastic	• Connecting ideas
	• Strategist	• Realistic	• Social
	• Self-aware	• Recognizes unmet needs	• People person
	• Evaluative	• Approaches problems from multiple views	• Friendly
	• Adaptive		• Outgoing
	• Values feedback		• Ability to use technology Approachable
	• Values challenges		• Good interpersonal skills
	Creative		
	• Work with a team		
	• Think outside the box		
	• Make knowledge useful		

(Continued)

TABLE 3 (Continued)

TEFI value	Sub-elements
<ul><li>Artistic</li><li>Numerous ideas</li><li>Enthusiastic</li><li>Problem solver</li><li>Open-minded</li><li>Unique ideas</li><li>Trying new designs</li></ul>	

but also for creating potential questions for testing the validity of the scale. The final feature of note is that there is some overlap between the items. There are two types of overlap that are evident: overlap of actual values, which have been highlighted in the table in bold, and overlap of features across different values and their sub-elements. In the first case, being ethical and tolerant of diversity are examples where values are seen as connected to each other. In the second case, good communication and confidence are features listed several times across different areas. Similarly, ethics and tolerance of diversity are values that are listed under other values. While this is consistent with the presentation of the values as interconnected and overlapping (TEFI, 2009), it could be problematic in the development of inventory in terms of developing scales that have the appropriate psychometric properties.

In the second stage the teachers went through the summary list with the students and then the students were required to use these statements as a resource to generate a survey questionnaire that would measure one of the five TEFI value groupings. Students were free to pick whichever one of the TEFI values they were most interested in. Overall this step of the exercise generated a substantial pool of more than 500 statements from over 90 students. Unfortunately the distribution of these items across the values was very uneven with half of the items generated for stewardship (51%), a further 20% for professionalism, 18% for ethics, 6% for knowledge, and 5% for mutuality. This uneven distribution could reflect either different levels of student interest in the values or different levels of difficulty in constructing items in the different areas or some combination of both this factors. This is an issue that needs further exploration.

SUMMARY AND IMPLICATIONS FOR THE TEFI VALUES

This student exercise generated a large item pool to assist in the development of the TEFI Values Inventory. While more work needs to be done on this item pool, it is likely that a draft instrument will be ready for testing in the near future. But the exercise generated more than simply an item pool for the inventory—it also provided some insights into the nature of the TEFI values. Two implications can be described from these insights. Firstly, there was variation between the values in terms of the number of features and items that students generated. This suggests that there are some issues with understanding some of the values and this is an area that needs further attention. Secondly, there was overlap in both the features and items generated to measure the different values and there was a clear perception that some values are dependent upon the others. For example to be a professional one has to be ethical and authentic. This means that the values need to be considered a whole and integrated as a whole into educational practice.

REFERENCES

Becker, B. W., & Connor, P. E. (1983). A course on human values for the management curriculum. *Journal of Management Education, 8*(1), 10–16.

Brandes, P. J., & Stuber, L. (2004). Towards becoming a values-based organization. *College Quarterly, 7*(2). Retrieved from http://www.senecac.on.ca/quarterly/2004-vol07-num02-spring/brandes_stuber.html

Bulach, C. R. (2002). Implementing a character education curriculum and assessing its impact on student behaviour. *The Clearinghouse, 76*(2), 79–83.

Coyne, K., & Coyne, R. (2001). Dispelling the myths of character education. *Principal Leadership, 2*(3), 58–61.

de Vaus, D. A. (1990). *Surveys in social research* (2nd ed.). Sydney, Australia: Allen & Unwin.

Dunlap, R. E., & van Liere, K. D. (2008). The "New Environmental Paradigm." *Journal of Environmental Education, 40*(1), 19–28.

Eriksen, M. (2009). Authentic leadership: Practical reflexivity, self-awareness, and self-authorship. *Journal of Management Education, 33*(6), 747–771.

Forsyth, D. R. (1980). A taxonomy of ethical ideologies. *Journal of Personality & Social Psychology, 39*, 175–184.

Fuertes, J. N., Miville, M. L., Moher, J. J., Sedlacek, W. E., & Gretchen, D. (2000). Factor structure and short form of the Miville-Guzman Universality-Diversity Scale. *Measurement & Evaluation in Counseling & Development, 33*, 157–169.

Grundstein-Amado, R. (1995). Values education: A new direction for medical education. *Journal of Medical Ethics, 21*, 174–178.

Halstead, J. M., & Taylor, M. J. (2000). Learning and teaching about values: A review of recent research. *Cambridge Journal of Education, 30*(2), 169–202.

Howard, R. W., Berkowitz, M. W., & Schaeffer, E. F. (2004). Politics of character education. *Educational Policy, 18*(1), 188–215.

Jones, S. C., & Stoodley, J. (1999). Community of caring: A character education program designed to integrate values into a school community. *National Association of Secondary School Principals Bulletin, 83*, 46–51.

Jones, T. M. (2009). Framing the framework: Discourse in Australia's national values education policy. *Educational Research for Policy & Practice, 8*, 35–57.

Kerlinger, F. N. (1973). *Foundations of behavioural research* (2nd ed.). New York, NY: Holt, Rinehart & Winston.

Kernis, M. H., & Goldman, B. M. (2006). A multi-component conceptualization of authenticity: Theory and research. *Advances in Experimental Social Psychology, 38*, 283–357.

Kirschenbaum, H. (1976). Clarifying values clarification: Some theoretical issues and a review of research. *Group & Organization Studies, 1*(1), 99–116.

Kohlberg, L., & Higgins, A. (1987). School democracy and social interaction. In W. M. Kurtines & J. L. Gewirtz (Eds.), *Moral development through social interaction* (pp. 102–128). New York, NY: Wiley.

Ladwig, J. G. (2010). Beyond academic outcomes. *Review of Research in Education, 34*, 113–141.

Lindeman, M., & Verkasalo, M. (2005). Measuring values with the short Schwartz's value survey. *Journal of Personality Assessment, 85*(2), 170–178.

Meier, D. W. (2003). Becoming educated: The power of ideas. *Principal Leadership, 3*(7), 16–19.

Milfont, T. L., & Duckitt, J. (2010). The environmental attitudes inventory: A valid and reliable measure to assess the structure of environmental attitudes. *Journal of Environmental Psychology, 30*(1), 80–94.

Oppenheim, A. N. (1992). *Questionnaire design, interviewing and attitude measurement* (2nd ed.). London, UK: Pinter.

Payne, S. L., & Pettingill, B. F. (1987). Management and values/ethics education. *Journal of Management Education, 11*, 18–27.

Rokeach, M. (1968). *Belief, attitudes and values*. San Francisco, CA: Jossey-Bass.

Rowan, N., & Wulff, D. (2007). Using qualitative methods to inform scale development. *The Qualitative Report, 12*(3), 450–466.

Shafer, W. E., Fukukawa, K., & Lee, G. M. (2007). Values and perceived importance of ethics and social responsibility: The US versus China. *Journal of Business Ethics, 70*, 265–284.

Shafer, W. E., Park, L. J., & Liao, W. M. (2002). Professionalism, organizational-professional conflict and work outcomes. *Accounting, Auditing & Accountability Journal, 15*(1), 46–68.

Sharrock, G. (2010). Two Hippocratic oaths for higher education. *Journal of Higher Education Policy and Management, 32*(4), 365–377.

Sheldon, P., Fesenmaier, D., Woeber, K., Cooper, C., & Antonioli, A. (2008). Tourism education futures, 2010–2030: Building the capacity to lead. *Journal of Teaching in Travel and Tourism, 7*(3), 61–68.

Snizek, W. E. (1972). Hall's professionalism scale: An empirical assessment. *American Sociological Review, 37*(1), 109–114.

Steiner, C. J., & Reisinger, Y. (2006). Understanding existential authenticity. *Annals of Tourism Research, 33*(2), 299–318.

TEFI. (n.d.). *Tourism Education Futures Initiative*. Retrieved from http://quovadis. wu-wien.ac.at/drupal/index.php?q=node/8

TEFI. (2009). *A values-based framework for tourism education: Building the capacity to lead*. Retrieved from http://quovadis.wu-wien.ac.at/drupal/ files/White%20Paper%20May22_0.pdf

Veugelers, W. (2000). Different ways of teaching values. *Educational Review, 52*(1), 37–47.

Business as Usual? Barriers to Education for Sustainability in the Tourism Curriculum

ERICA WILSON and TANIA VON DER HEIDT

Southern Cross University, Lismore, Australia

There is little research on how "sustainability" is embedded within tourism programs. This article draws on findings from a study of education for sustainability within the 1st-year business/tourism curriculum at an Australian regional university. Using an interpretive methodology, interviews took place with 16 academics regarding the barriers in trying to incorporate sustainability. Three key themes were revealed: (1) a crowded curriculum; (2) staff and student resistance to sustainability; and (3) the realities of a complex, multicampus institution. These impediments will be important to consider if we want to engender a more transformational approach to sustainability leadership in tourism education.

INTRODUCTION

It has been argued that integrating sustainability education in the curriculum better prepares students to face the significant environmental and societal challenges we now face (Albinsson, Perera, & Sautter, 2011; Hasan, 1993; Munilla, Bleicken, & Miles, 1998). Yet the concept of "sustainable development" offers a tremendous challenge for the higher education curriculum.

The authors would like to acknowledge that the study on which this article is based was funded through a Southern Cross University Vice Chancellor's Small Grant Award for Teaching and Learning, 2011. They would also like to thank the two anonymous reviewers for their helpful and constructive feedback.

Working from a critical, values-based pedagogy, "sustainability" in education may mean a radical rethink of how institutions operate, how teachers teach, and how learners learn (Brookfield & Holst, 2010). Here, we define sustainable development (or, more broadly, sustainability) in the sense of the "Brundtland" report—that is, "development" that does not impact upon the needs of future generations and that is based on a firm cautionary awareness of the social, cultural, and ecological crises and complexities that the planet currently faces in a resource-scarce environment (World Commission on Environment and Development, 1987).

The integration of sustainable development principles in higher education also presents a number of interesting opportunities. A move toward "sustainability" can prepare students, teachers, and the whole campus community to be more creative and innovative leaders in the face of complex social and biological problems, including climate change (Galea, 2007; Glasser, Calder, & Fadeeva, 2005; Kearins & Springett, 2003). As the organizational and educational research demonstrates, "transformational leadership" relies upon individuals who are passionate, energized, and charismatic in inspiring others to think differently and critically about global issues and problems (Bass & Riggio, 2006; Leithwood & Jantzi, 2005). In teaching sustainability, which is premised on action and change in the educational context, "instructional" or "transactional" leadership styles may no longer work. The transformational educator in sustainability must lead that action and be actively reflexive and clear in the ways in which their values and worldviews influence their pedagogical approach. However, the ability to embrace transformational leadership in teaching tourism (or sustainable tourism) at the higher education level is always mediated by external factors such as institutional support and culture, educational market factors, and political imperatives (Hallinger, 2003; Leithwood & Jantzi, 2005).

Education for sustainable development (ESD) is a holistic concept that draws together the tenets of sustainable development and education, and it has been most widely promulgated via the UN Decade of Education for Sustainable Development (UNDESD) 2005–2014 campaign. The UNDESD "seeks to mobilize the educational resources of the world to help create a more sustainable future" (UN Education, Scientific and Cultural Organization, 2012). ESD attempts to transgress education merely *about* the environment and sustainable development, although this is still important. ESD strives for a more environmentally sustainable world through encouraging individuals and social groups to take action and make behavioral changes in their everyday lives (Fien & Tilbury, 1996; Tilbury, Crawley, & Berry, 2004).

As the UNDESD draws to a close, it is pertinent to reflect upon the extent to which education for sustainability (EfS) and sustainable development principles are now "embedded" within higher education pedagogy and curricula. This applies equally to the university tourism studies context. "Sustainable tourism" has indeed been a prominent feature on the tourism research agenda during the last four decades (Bramwell & Lane, 2008), as the cautionary and postcautionary platforms have prevailed (Jafari, 2003) and scholars have become increasingly concerned about tourism's impacts on society, culture, and the environment (Busby, 2003; Weaver, 2006). That said, little research has explored how sustainable development principles have been embedded within the tourism curricula, embraced by students, and taught in the "classroom" (some exceptions include Benckendorff, Moscardo, & Murphy, 2012; Canziani, Sonmez, Hsieh, & Byrd, 2012; Jamal, 2004; Wilson, 2010).

In the context of tourism education and this Tourism Education Futures Initiative (TEFI) special issue, there is a need to explore how tourism curricula might be rethought, reshaped, and refigured to help teach our students (who are our future transformational tourism leaders) to act in sustainable, ethical, and environmentally responsible ways. TEFI values like stewardship, ethics, and mutuality (Sheldon, Fesenmaier, & Tribe, 2009) are also integral to a sustainable pedagogy and are attributes that many of us hope our tourism graduates attain. But how do we *teach* sustainable development in the context of a values-based tourism education? What does *sustainability* look like in a tourism curriculum, particularly one that is situated within a business faculty? And at what level or point in a course/degree do we introduce concepts like sustainability? Although sustainability is generally viewed as a "higher-order" concept (Canziani et al., 2012), some argue that as a concept, it is better placed in the later years of a degree, or even at the graduate level, when students will assumedly be more receptive (Greenspoon, 2008); others suggest that sustainability must be incorporated from the very start, in the 1st-year curriculum (Springett, 2005). In this way, the 1st-year experience becomes an exceptionally important foundation point in student learning (Pitkethly & Prosser, 2001), where students may be gradually exposed to higher-order learning and concepts like sustainability.

Yet these are not curricular or chronological issues alone. The role of the academic teacher as a transformational agent and leader is particularly important in thinking about EDS, as he or she brings with them their own personal and political values, beliefs, and worldviews (Brookfield, 2005). As stated by Stergiou, Airey, and Riley (2008), "the teacher has special responsibilities in relation to subject-knowledge . . . This responsibility places special demands not only on the depth, but also on the understanding of how it should be ordered in ways that will be clear and accessible" (p. 635).

Stemming from these issues and debates, this article draws on selected findings from an empirical analysis of how sustainability is embedded within the 1st-year business (including tourism) curriculum at a regional, multicampus university in Australia (see von der Heidt, Lamberton, Wilson, & Morrison, 2012). The focus here is on insights gained from a set of qualitative interviews with individual academics, who teach 1st-year subjects.

Of particular interest are their experiences of teaching or embedding sustainability in a business/tourism program and the barriers and challenges inherent in doing so.

EDUCATION FOR SUSTAINABILITY IN BUSINESS AND TOURISM HIGHER EDUCATION

As indicated in the introduction, a number of terms abound in the literature on sustainability as it relates to education. These include ESD, ecologically sustainable development (another ESD acronym, which emerged from the Rio Earth Summit and the ensuing Agenda 21), EfS, education about sustainability (EaS), and education for and about sustainability. For the purposes of this article, we use the term education for sustainability. EfS is a term originating in Britain and is now used widely in Australian policy and educational contexts (Leihy & Salazar, 2011).

It is important to distinguish briefly between EaS and EfS. This is not merely a matter of wording, but a significant difference in pedagogical approach. EaS focuses on teaching students about the *content matter* of sustainable development, such as overconsumption, climate change, and biodiversity loss (Tilbury et al., 2004). While these content issues are indeed important, EfS is a holistic, pedagogical concept that motivates and equips individuals in making reflective, informed decisions to work toward a more sustainable world (Tilbury et al., 2004). Underpinned by the principles of critical theory and critical-thinking skills, EfS seeks to engage and empower people to implement systemic change and action. In this way, both student and teacher can become transformational agents of change in their own lives and in the world around them.

Although certainly a paradigm shift has been noted in the education sector, EfS is not taken up widely in universities. More than a decade ago, Filho (2000) identified a number of factors that might explain why sustainability is not being integrated. First, sustainability is not a subject *per se* because it is viewed as too abstract, too theoretical, and too broad. Second, there is a lack of resources and qualified staff to teach it; and third, "sustainability" is perceived as a mere fashion of fad. Further, there are often other political and institutional reasons why teachers may find it difficult to "embed" sustainability principles into their curricula (Leihy & Salazar, 2011). These constraints and barriers need exploration if EfS is desired.

According to some (Barlett, 2008; Bates, Silverblatt, & Kleban, 2009; Springett, 2005), business schools in particular are lagging behind other disciplines in "going green." In previous research, von der Heidt and Lamberton (2011) discussed the sustainability imperative and the role of business in the transition to sustainability. Although "business" is commonly cited as the culprit of unsustainable consumption, adoption of sustainable business practices can provide solutions to many of these problems (Ferraro & Sands, 2009; Nidumolu, Prahalad, & Rangaswami, 2009), particularly when managers have the requisite education and motivation to implement such practices (Bridges & Wilhelm, 2008).

In many universities, tourism schools are located in business or management departments and faculties (Dredge et al., 2010; Wilson, Harris, & Small, 2008). As such, tourism students are predominantly business/management students, graduating with business/management degrees. This is no doubt a product of the history and development of tourism in higher education during the last three decades. While some tourism programs emerged from the anthropological, geographical, or sociological disciplines, many were tied to the hotel school model popular in Europe and the United States (Inui, Wheeler, & Lankford, 2006) or from the polytechnic system prominent in the United Kingdom and Australia (McKercher, 2002). Striving to be taken seriously as a subject of university study, tourism scholars and curriculum developers have turned to theoretical frameworks offered in the fields of business, management, and economics for guidance (Fidgeon, 2010; Jafari, 2003).

As a result, vocational and professional skills were seen as paramount to receiving a "good" tourism (business/management) education (Airey & Johnson, 1999; Busby, 2001; Inui et al., 2006). Indeed, a content analysis of tourism course prospectuses in the United Kingdom in the early 2000s revealed a predominantly vocational focus, with no words, phrases, or subjects related to sustainability, the environment, or tourism impacts (Busby & Fiedel, 2001). More recent studies show that the vocational model still reigns in tourism programs in Australia (Dredge et al., 2010). Vigorous debate has ensued around the idea of whether tourism education should follow a vocational or philosophical path (Ayikoru, Tribe, & Airey, 2009; Dredge et al., 2012; Stergiou et al., 2008; Tribe, 2002). Studies have also revealed that students themselves predominantly desire a tourism degree in the vocational mould (Busby, 2001), leaving scholars to argue over whether today's students are being adequately exposed to reflective, critical, and philosophical perspectives (Jamal, 2004; Tribe, 2002).

EfS would usually align more closely with a liberal, philosophical ontological view toward teaching and curriculum, which exposes students to the complex, multidisciplinary nature of tourism (Ayikoru et al., 2009; Tribe, 2002) and its associated social, cultural, and environmental impacts (Belhassen & Caton, 2011; Canziani et al., 2012). Uncovering and unmasking these complexities is the goal of the critical tourism scholar and educator (Fallon, 2006; Fullagar & Wilson, 2012); thus, many teaching in sustainability would be overtly critical and, ultimately, transformative in their approach to teaching and learning. The critical educator's view contrasts sharply with that of the university as a neoliberal, market-driven institution that is highly conservative and managerial in nature (James, 2002). This instrumentalist view of education works to sustain and reinforce the dominant capitalist paradigm through seeing education as a product that can be bought by the consumer (the "student"; Ayikoru et al., 2009; Biggs, 2002).

An Audit of Sustainability in the 1st-Year Business/Tourism Curriculum: The Case of Southern Cross University

Southern Cross University (SCU) is a midsized regional university with the main campus located in Lismore, in the far Northeastern corner of the state of New South Wales. It also has campuses in Coffs Harbour and Sydney, as well as a newer campus at the Southern end of the Gold Coast (Queensland), and a number of educational articulations with other domestic and international institutions. Like many universities in Australia, SCU is a signatory to the Talloires Declaration and has a stated strategic commitment to sustainability and the "triple bottom line." Of the four recently articulated goals in the SCU Strategic Plan 2010–2015 (SCU, 2011, p. 10), Goal 4 states: "We will enhance our performance in a sustainable and responsible manner" with the corresponding strategy to "embed a commitment to the triple-bottom line to enhance the economic, social and environmental sustainability of the University."

This article presents selected aspects of an empirical study of this commitment. In 2011, an audit and evaluation was undertaken into how "sustainability" was embedded into the curriculum and assessment of the 1st-year Bachelor of Business (BBus) program courses held in the Southern Cross Business School and the Bachelor of Business in Tourism Management (BBusTM) program courses held in the School of Tourism and Hospitality Management (STHM; von der Heidt et al., 2012). Although these two courses are housed in different schools, they share some elements of the core 1st year. Further, several of STHM's degrees are grounded in the business/management paradigm, and carry the "BBus" preface; thus, an analysis across both schools was logical.

METHODOLOGY

For the overall study, a mixed-methods approach was used to enable a full audit of the 1st-year BBus and BBusTM courses. This involved a content analysis of the fourteen 1st-year unit statements and learning materials as to the presence of key sustainability concepts, as well as semistructured interviews with 16 academics involved in teaching the 1st-year curriculum (14 unit assessors [UA] or "subject lecturers," and 2 course/degree coordinators [CC]). As outlined earlier, this article focuses solely on the interview data and on one research question, which pertained to the barriers and challenges that academics faced in incorporating sustainability in their teaching practices and curricula. Thus, it should be noted that the findings of the content analysis are not presented here, but they can be found in the full report (von der Heidt et al., 2012). The 1st-year business and tourism course curriculum at SCU is shown in Table 1.

The focus in the interviews was on exploring the academics' attitudes toward and experiences of EfS in their units. As experts on their curriculum design and delivery, the UAs/CCs were knowledgeable key informants who were best able to provide insights (Miller, Cardinal, & Glick, 1997; Seidler, 1974). Approval to undertake the interview study was obtained from the university's human research ethics committee. All 1st-year UAs and CCs were included in the sample to obtain a representative view of the 1st year. Semistructured interviews allowed the researchers to find out what academics were thinking, feeling, and "doing" regarding EfS to allow for a richer understanding of their experiences of sustainability (Kvale & Brinkmann, 2009). In particular, the in-depth interview guide asked participants to reflect on how they conceptualized "sustainability," their knowledge of EfS and sustainable development, how they incorporated sustainability principles into their units and curriculum, and any barriers or challenges they faced in trying to incorporate sustainability (or EfS) into the business/tourism curriculum, or into their own practices as a teacher. It is this latter question that forms the focus of the current analysis.

It should be noted that academics perceived and taught sustainability in a variety of ways; the researchers did not want to "structure" participants' views or definitions of sustainability. However, our wider study

TABLE 1 The 1st-Year Curriculum (BBus and BBusTM, Southern Cross University)

Unit Name	School	Course (Degree)
Financial Information for Decision-Making	SCBS	Both
Communication in Organizations	STHM	Both
Economic Analysis for Tourism and Hospitality	STHM	BBusTM
Economics	SCBS	BBus
Introduction to Business Law	SLJ	BBus
Quantitative Analysis	SCBS	BBus
Marketing Principles	SCBS	BBus
Tourism and Hospitality Marketing	STHM	BBusTM
Introduction to Tourism and Hospitality Management	STHM	BBusTM
Managing Organizations in a Global Context	SCBS	BBus
Human Resource and Workplace Management	STHM	BBusTM
Hospitality Services Management	STHM	BBusTM
Tourism Theories and Practices	STHM	BBusTM
Ethics and Sustainability	SCBS	BBus

SCBS = Southern Cross Business School; STHM = School of Tourism and Hospitality Management; SLJ = School of Law and Justice; BBus = Bachelor of Business; BBusTM = Bachelor of Business in Tourism Management.

results reveal that most academics (10 out of 14) viewed sustainability as a holistic concept incorporating social, cultural, ethical, and/or environmental dimensions, and many identified it as aligning with "triple bottom line" thinking. Furthermore, 4 academics clearly resonated with a "strong" sustainability focus on ecological/environmental awareness, and a challenge to the dominant economic model of consumptive business and tourism practices (von der Heidt et al., 2012).

The interviews were conducted by an experienced interviewer who was knowledgeable about the interview topic and also a teacher of sustainable business ethics herself. The interviewer controlled the course of the semistructured interview, was sensitive to the nuances in meaning, and sought to have these clarified where possible. Each recorded interview was transcribed by an experienced transcriber from oral speech to written text (the transcript) to prepare the interview material for analysis. All interview transcripts were checked by interviewees, thereby providing additional support for the validity of their words and experiences. Drawing on Braun and Clarke (2006) and Attride-Stirling (2001), the researchers then identified, analyzed, and reported patterns and themes within the data. To do this, the researchers first fully familiarized themselves with the transcribed data. The material was then coded manually on the basis of the research questions; individual transcripts were dissected and reorganized in terms of the codes. Codes were analyzed, discussed, refined, and then combined to form a core group of broader themes; in this case, three overarching themes were elicited that best reflected the experiences and perspectives of academics in trying to teach sustainability in tourism.

FINDINGS: BARRIERS AND CHALLENGES IN TEACHING SUSTAINABILITY

Based on a thematic analysis of interviews, it was evident that key challenges emerged in terms of academics trying to embrace and embed sustainability, environmental awareness, and/or the principles of EfS. These were: (a) *a crowded curriculum*, (b) *staff and student resistance* to the concepts of sustainability, and (c) the realities of learning in a *complex, multicampus institution*. These will now be discussed in turn.

A Crowded Curriculum

When asked about barriers and challenges, a common theme discussed by participants (11 out of 16) related to a lack of time or a lack of space in the curriculum, or what we have termed here the "crowded curriculum" dilemma. That is, academics may have had the interest or motivation to incorporate sustainability into their unit/course, but it was deemed that there was not sufficient time or space within what was already seen as a very tight 1st-year business/tourism syllabus.

Several participants felt that it was outside the scope of their unit syllabus or semester timeframe to "fit" sustainability within it. This applied particularly to those units that promoted a practical orientation, such as economics, marketing, finance and accounting, and business law, where certain core skills and graduate attributes needed to be covered. As participants who taught in these "practical" areas noted: "I'd dearly love to, but I think it's the time, space factor. We have to cover all the different aspects . . . Consequently we only scratch the surface" (Participant 14). "[It's a] 1st-year unit; hard to incorporate [sustainability] when laying down foundations, directions" (Participant 8). "I could do more on sustainability, but this is a class that is very practical" (Participant 1).

Professional qualifications and accreditation were also part of this. "The content is dictated by the needs of the school, and the degree needs to meet certain professional qualifications, such as accounting . . . but in the unit I teach, there's no room for any of that" (Participant 5). Another tourism academic also noted difficulties with fitting everything in to a new "shortened" semester model introduced recently by the university: "We have such a short teaching term that we have to be careful that we don't make our syllabuses too crowded for our students" (Participant 12). Other participants shared similar frustrations: "The most obvious barrier is the amount of weeks in the semester. Sustainability is still at that level where if you have to prioritize, it's one of the things that might get cut" (Participant 3). "We've got a very condensed course, and very condensed time" (Participant 15).

Some teachers thought that sustainability was better placed in later years of the degree progression. Students were not seen as "mature" enough to engage with the philosophical and critical issues that sustainability posed: "It's a 1st-year, first-semester unit and a lot of them are quite young and their heads are not yet in that space. I'd like to do more of that but I think maybe they need to walk before they can run" (Participant 6).

Time was not only an issue related to shortened semesters or a tight curriculum. Several academics talked in general about their lack of time in a workload that has many competing priorities (e.g., research, community engagement, academic governance). As such, sustainability was seen as something that might have been desired, but like many things, it was a matter of time and space for reflection. "It's time for lecturers to do things differently than what they've done before" (Participant 15). "You just don't have enough time . . . And it's all assessment-driven . . . we're so used to doing [it] that way" (Participant 6).

And although university employment was still considered the "promised land" by Participant 5, he acknowledged that "there is so much pressure on us to just keep our heads above water, particularly the teaching." As one CC noted, the industry-ready graduates that business and tourism schools now foster did not leave much time for "higher-order" concepts like sustainability: "We are working within industries that are used to having people that can come in and do things straight away, whereas we're trying to produce graduates that have these higher-order skills" (Participant 16).

Another participant felt that more time was needed for his own professional development and thinking regarding sustainability: "[It's] my own lack of understanding. I think that will develop as long as there's an opportunity for staff or colleagues to get together and talk about these issues" (Participant 3).

Staff and Student Resistance

Another key theme that emerged was a perceived resistance by other departmental staff and students to the incorporation of sustainability in the business/tourism curriculum. Eight of the 16 participants talked about a sense of resistance, often expressed in terms of a lack of support and interest from colleagues and/or students regarding the incorporation of sustainability principles into the 1st-year curriculum.

According to some academics, it was a matter of challenging the status quo, or a traditional business-focused teaching paradigm. "The barriers I suppose are the traditional lecturers that are set in their ways and some who don't get it" (Participant 2). Another participant perceived that sustainability was overtly marginalized:

> Some of our colleagues would not know how to embed sustainability and there's probably a general culture of people [who] work on their own and we don't have a lot of cross-disciplinary dialogue . . . I think they (lecturers) should recognize that sustainability is not a fad but it's an important part. But I just don't think that they're there yet. (Participant 10)

It was also felt that sustainability had to be championed by individual teaching staff, rather than having broad organizational or departmental support. "If I'd kept quiet in the last two years . . . those units would have been eliminated in the last review" (Participant 10). "There's a bit of 'well, we have a sustainability subject that's in there so why are we worrying about putting it into all of our other subjects?'" (Participant 11). Another academic also mentioned a need to look outside of the "silo": "We tend to be a bit silo-ish. We do our units in isolation . . . Is sustainability something we want to teach across all of our units, or just something a particular subject will take carriage of?" (Participant 13).

In addition to staff or collegial resistance, a number of participants also spoke of student resistance to the incorporation or embeddedness of sustainability. "[Students] see it as an isolated thing. It's a bit 'out there,'

I'm afraid . . . . I think maybe the history of the word 'sustainable' equaling something to do with, you know, greenies running up trees" (Participant 13). "To be honest I don't think enough people know what sustainability is. If you threw that at them, it would freak the hell out of a lot of people!" (Participant 3). Others thought that business students generally tended to avoid a curriculum that was too "different" or "innovative." "They (business students) don't like anything different . . . They want all the answers, they don't want to have to think, they don't like doing reflection . . . Any sort of critical thinking, reflection" (Participant 4). "Also, a lot of students really resist new 'innovative' approaches, assessment" (Participant 15).

Complex, Multicampus Institution

SCU has a high intake of distance (or external) education students. In the business and tourism schools in particular, academic staff teach across a number of campuses and deal with a range of domestic and international partners. This was noted by some interviewees: "We're across five campuses and the lead time to prepare [is long] . . . We have to moderate each others' work" (Participant 7). A high level of familiarity with converged/distance learning practices and online technology was required. For one teacher, good online technology was an opportunity for innovation in sustainability teaching: "[We need] better support for those types of technologies. In terms of sustainability, there would be real opportunities to do really clever stuff using online resources" (Participant 2). Some considered interactive, face-to-face involvement with their students to be germane to developing an appreciation of sustainability and lamented the limited time available to communicate with students directly: "I don't have enough time with them . . . . When it comes to actually think[ing] about the complexities of sustainability in a holistic sense, it kind of helps to be in the same room with them for a while" (Participant 6).

DISCUSSION

A number of barriers and challenges were evident in the academics' desire and ability to embed sustainability within the BBus and BBusTM programs. These constraints related to perceived curriculum crowding, the realities of working across complex programs and multiple campuses, as well as a feeling of staff and student resistance to the ideas of sustainability in the business program.

There is some broad support for these findings in the wider literature and policy on sustainable business/tourism education. Concerns about the "crowded curriculum" have been noted in many disciplines, including in tourism studies (Ayikoru et al., 2009; Biggs, 2002). Pressures from institutional or other political forces (e.g., accreditation) can mean that the space for thorough planning, innovation, and teacher-led curriculum can become squeezed. In many tourism schools housed within business departments or faculties, there is also the desire for students to be "work-ready," via industry placements and internships (Canziani et al., 2012). In Australia, federal university funding is now tied to performance criteria that include "graduate employability" and placement in full-time work (Department of Education, Employment, and Workplace Relations, 2012).

As could be seen in the interviews with academics, "sustainability" was construed as something separate from the rest of the business degree, where individual teachers were left to incorporate sustainable development and EfS principles according to their own interests. This led to teachers feeling that they were only able to "scratch the surface" with sustainability (as one interviewee put it). As noted by Benckendorff et al. (2012, pp. 64–65) in their study of tourism undergraduates' environmental attitudes, sustainability should be "integrated throughout a curriculum, as having [it] as a separate component is unlikely to encourage changes in attitudes." Clear strategies that support staff and curriculum visioning and strategic planning are required, with commitment from the top down.

Several academics also described resistance from staff and students toward the concept of sustainability in the business/tourism curriculum. This could be partly explained by wider assertions that business and business/tourism students are career-focused and tend to prefer a results-oriented teaching style to a discursive, philosophical mode of inquiry (Busby, 2001; Macquarie University, 2009). Some studies have countered this view and have revealed that business/tourism undergraduate students had strong environmental awareness and were receptive to issues of sustainability within the curriculum (Benckendorff et al., 2012; Busby, 2003). The present study did not collect data on the student experience, but lecturers did note a lack of student engagement with the philosophical and critical thinking required for EfS.

An additional finding of interest to this theme was the perception that other staff (or the respective school) did not prioritize sustainability at the course or curriculum levels. Perceived reasons for this included a lack of knowledge or interest in sustainability on the part of business colleagues, a lack of a sustainability-related value system, and the ever-present lack of time. Similar concerns have been raised in other tourism research. For example, Canziani et al. (2012, p. 9) noted that tourism academics may be "overwhelmed" and "unnerved" by the urgency and complexity that sustainability teaching brings with it. They also add to this "the very real resource constraints of current faculty skills bases and personal motivations in the area of sustainability" (p. 9).

The constraints of working across multiple campuses and with a variety of cohorts (internal/external; international/domestic) may be endemic to the SCU case. However, other universities in Australia and around the world may share these realities, and the impacts would extend beyond incorporating EfS. The neoliberal higher education landscape is, naturally, focused on cost and scale efficiencies in offering its business and tourism programs (Ayikoru et al., 2009); the teaching and learning vernacular has followed suit with concepts like "converged delivery," "distance learning," and "internationalization." Although these have been important in globalizing and democratizing higher education, they have also led to an increasingly complex and fractured teaching environment (Biggs, 2002).

As in the world of organizational behavior, transformational leadership in education is evident through academic "leaders" (lecturers, senior management, unit and curriculum developers) being passionate, charismatic in their approach to teaching, learning, and governance, and concerned with intellectually motivating students and staff to embrace new ways of thinking (Bass & Riggio, 2006; Leithwood & Jantzi, 2005). Critical thinking, EfS, and other values-based teaching approaches rely upon transformational leaders and educators to inspire the future of tourism education. As the findings of our study suggest, however, transformational leadership and education may be hampered by a number of external factors, including political, institutional, and curricular constraints.

If transformational change is desired in tourism and business higher education, and we want to train our students as future transformational leaders, a radical rethink of how we "do" sustainability is called for. The starting point is for a tourism school/department to commit to EfS, and this must be evident in its values and mission statement to provide the basis for shared understanding and action from all stakeholders involved (e.g., all academic and professional staff, students, etc.). The biggest challenge, of course, is operationalizing this commitment.

Benn and Bubna-Litic (2004) outlined two main ways to embed EfS in a curriculum, and these provide a useful framework here: (1) The *incremental* (or first-generation) approach involves integrating EfS in existing units and/or degrees. Teaching and learning techniques fostering active engagement germane to higher-order learning are emphasized. (2) The *radical* (second-generation) approach is to create revolutionary new units or degrees designed to break out of the "technocratic" mindset and to move toward a more "ecocentric" ideology (Beder, 1996; Harding, 1998). The aim is to "develop graduates able to span both worlds and who have the ability to think critically and act creatively and reflectively to transform current business practices" (Benn & Bubna-Litic, 2004, p. 90). The challenge for the first-generation approach is overcoming the dominant worldview of exploitation of nature in existing curricula. Further, unless the sustainability content and examples are salient to the core curriculum, they will add to curriculum crowding. As with any radical (vs. incremental) change or creation, achieving the second-generation approach to EfS seems even more daunting. Benn and Bubna-Litic argue that either approach can be used to take students "beyond reflex" action to an active reflection about the purpose of business, hence achieving a core objective of EfS.

CONCLUSION

The findings from this review of the 1st-year SCU business/tourism curriculum reveal that, despite the articulated institutional commitment to sustainability, neither the first- nor second-generation approach to EfS has been fully considered (Benn & Bubna-Litic, 2004). Rather, it appears that sustainability is undertaken in an ad-hoc way, often dependant on the interest, passions, and personal values of the individual teacher.

Certainly, there is potential for "radical" new units and even degrees, but these initiatives may be constrained by the complexities of individual departments and schools and the bureaucratic processes that any curriculum changes must address. Further, in the neoliberal university business school, these complexities and constraints can work to limit transformational change and leadership efforts, reproducing socially and ecologically unsustainable values (Ayikoru et al., 2009; Biggs, 2002).

Critical and transformational approaches are needed for EfS to occur within the business and tourism curriculum. To fully embrace the tenets of "strong" sustainability in the 1st year and throughout the entire academic program, teachers and curriculum developers need to embody the values of sustainability and "practice what they teach" (Wilson, 2010). They will need to have room to make some challenging changes to the curriculum, which makes students think and can encourage them to question, change, or take action in their lives to work toward a more environmentally and socially just world. For this, students will need the support of their teachers and other academic leaders. Teachers will also need the support of sustainability experts to capacity-build on sustainability concepts and their "fit" within disciplines. Without these purposeful actions, tourism curricula may continue to be just "business as usual."

REFERENCES

Airey, D., & Johnson, S. (1999). The content of tourism degree courses in the UK. *Tourism Management*, *20*, 229–235.

Albinsson, P., Perera, B., & Sautter, P. (2011). Integrating sustainability into the business curriculum through e-learning. *Journal of Online Learning and Teaching*, *7*(1), 117–127.

Attride-Stirling, J. (2001). Thematic networks: An analytic tool for qualitative research. *Qualitative Research*, *1*(3), 385–405.

Ayikoru, M., Tribe, J., & Airey, D. (2009). Reading tourism education: Neoliberalism unveiled. *Annals of Tourism Research, 36*(2), 191–221.

Barlett, P. F. (2008). Reason and reenchantment. *Current Anthropology, 49*(6), 1077–1098.

Bass, B. M., & Riggio, R. E. (2006). *Transformational leadership.* Mahwah, NJ: Lawrence Erlbaum.

Bates, C., Silverblatt, R., & Kleban, J. (2009). Creating a new green management course. *The Business Review, Cambridge, 12*(1), 60–66.

Beder, S. (1996). *The nature of sustainable development.* Newham, Australia: Scribe Publications.

Belhassen, Y., & Caton, K. (2011). On the need for critical pedagogy in tourism education. *Tourism Management, 32,* 1389–1396.

Benckendorff, P., Moscardo, G., & Murphy, L. (2012). Environmental attitudes of Generation Y students: Foundations for sustainability education in tourism. *Journal of Teaching in Travel & Tourism, 12,* 44–69.

Benn, S., & Bubna-Litic, D. (2004). Is the MBA sustainable? Degrees of change. In C. Galea (Ed.), *Teaching business sustainability: Vol. 1. From theory to practice* (pp. 82–94). Sheffield, UK: Greenleaf.

Biggs, J. (2002). Corporatised universities: An educational and cultural disaster. In J. Biggs & R. Davis (Eds.), *The subversion of Australian universities* (pp. 184–222). Wollongong, Australia: Fund for Educational Dissent, University of Wollongong.

Bramwell, B., & Lane, B. (2008). Priorities in sustainable tourism research. *Journal of Sustainable Tourism, 16*(1), 1–4.

Braun, V., & Clarke, V. (2006). Using thematic analysis in psychology. *Qualitative Research in Psychology, 3,* 77–101.

Bridges, C. M., & Wilhelm, W. B. (2008). Going beyond green: The 'why and how' of integrating sustainability into the marketing curriculum. *Journal of Marketing Education, 30*(1), 33–46.

Brookfield, S. D. (2005). *The power of critical theory: Liberating adult learning and teaching.* San Francisco, CA: Jossey-Bass.

Brookfield, S. D., & Holst, J. D. (2010). *Radicalizing learning: Adult education for a just world.* San Francisco, CA: Jossey-Bass.

Busby, G. (2001). Vocationalism in higher level tourism courses: The British perspective. *Journal of Further and Higher Education, 25*(1), 29–43.

Busby, G. (2003). The concept of sustainable tourism within the higher education curriculum: A British case study. *Journal of Hospitality, Leisure, Sport and Tourism Education, 2*(2), 48–58.

Busby, G., & Fiedel, J. (2001). A contemporary review of tourism degrees in the United Kingdom. *Journal of Vocational Education and Training, 53*(4), 501–552.

Canziani, B. F., Sonmez, S., Hsieh, Y. J., & Byrd, E. T. (2012). A learning theory framework for sustainability education in tourism. *Journal of Teaching in Travel & Tourism, 12,* 3–20.

Department of Education, Employment, and Workplace Relations. (2012). *Teaching and learning performance fund.* Retrieved from http://www.deewr.gov.au

Dredge, D., Benckendorff, P., Day, M., Gross, M., Walo, M., Weeks, P., & Whitelaw, P. (2010, February). *Conceptualising the perfect blend in the tourism and hospitality curriculum space.* Paper presented at the Council for Australasian

University Tourism and Hospitality Education Conference, University of South Australia, Adelaide, Australia.

Dredge, D., Benckendorff, P., Day, M., Gross, M. J., Walo, M., Weeks, P., & Whitelaw, P. (2012). The philosophic practitioner and the curriculum space. *Annals of Tourism Research, 39*(4), 2154–2176.

Fallon, W. (2006, November). *The critical turn in teaching hospitality and tourism: Reflections on a Socratic approach.* Paper presented at the Critical Tourism Downunder Workshop, University of Technology Sydney, Kuring-gai, Australia.

Ferraro, C., & Sands, S. (2009, November). *'Greentailing': A key to thriving in recession?* Paper presented at the Australian and New Zealand Marketing Academy, Melbourne, Australia. Retrieved from http://www.duplication.net.au/ ANZMAC09/papers/ANZMAC2009-052.pdf

Fidgeon, P. R. (2010). Tourism education and curriculum design: A time for consolidation and review? *Tourism Management, 31*, 699–723.

Fien, J., & Tilbury, D. (1996). *Learning for a sustainable environment: An agenda for teacher education in Asia and the Pacific.* Bangkok, Thailand: UN Educational, Scientific, and Cultural Organization.

Filho, L. (2000). Dealing with misconceptions on the concept of sustainability. *International Journal of Sustainability in Higher Education, 1*(1), 9–19.

Fullagar, S., & Wilson, E. (2012). Critical pedagogies: A reflexive approach to knowledge creation in tourism and hospitality studies. *Journal of Hospitality and Tourism Management, 19*, e2. Retrieved from http://dx.doi.org/10.1017/ jht.2012.3

Galea, C. (2007). Introduction. In C. Galea (Ed.), *Teaching business sustainability* (pp. 8–15). Sheffield, UK: Greenleaf.

Glasser, H., Calder, W., & Fadeeva, Z. (2005). *Definition: Research in higher education for sustainability.* Halifax, Canada: Halifax Consultation.

Greenspoon, J. S. (2008). *Sustainability in the graduate business curriculum: Implications for business schools* (Unpuplished master's thesis). University of Toronto, Toronto, Canada.

Hallinger, P. (2003). Leading educational change: Reflections on the practice of instructional and transformational leadership. *Cambridge Journal of Education, 33*(3), 329–352.

Harding, R. (1998). Value systems and paradigms. In R. Harding (Ed.), *Environmental decision making: The roles of scientists, engineers and the public* (pp. 61–68). Sydney, Australia: The Federation Press.

Hasan, S. (1993). The greening of business schools. *Journal of Teaching in International Business, 5*(1/2), 9–18.

Inui, Y., Wheeler, D., & Lankford, S. (2006). Rethinking tourism education: What should schools teach? *Journal of Hospitality, Leisure, Sport and Tourism Education, 5*(2), 25–35.

Jafari, J. (2003). Research and scholarship: The basis of tourism education. *Journal of Tourism Studies, 14*(1), 6–16.

Jamal, T. (2004). Virtue ethics and sustainable tourism pedagogy: Phronesis, principles and practice. *Journal of Sustainable Tourism, 12*(6), 530–545.

James, R. (2002). *Academic standards and the assessment of student learning: Some current issues in Australian higher education.* Melbourne, Australia: Centre for the Study of Higher Education, University of Melbourne.

Kearins, K., & Springett, D. (2003). Educating for sustainability: Developing critical skills. *Journal of Management Education, 27*(2), 188–204.

Kvale, S., & Brinkmann, S. (2009). *Interviews: Learning the craft of qualitative research interviewing* (2nd ed.). Thousand Oaks, CA: Sage.

Leihy, P., & Salazar, J. (2011). *Education for sustainability in university curricula: Policies and practice in Victoria.* Melbourne, Australia: Centre for the Study of Higher Education, University of Melbourne.

Leithwood, K., & Jantzi, D. (2005). A review of transformational school leadership research 1996–2005. *Leadership and Policy in Schools, 4*(3), 177–199.

Macquarie University. (2009). *Sustainability in the curriculum project.* Sydney, Australia: Learning and Teaching Centre. Retrieved from http://www.mq.edu.au/ltc/pdfs/039sustincurric.pdf

McKercher, B. (2002). The future of tourism education: An Australian scenario. *Tourism and Hospitality Research, 3*(3), 199–210.

Miller, C., Cardinal, L., & Glick, W. (1997). Retrospective reports in organizational research: A reexamination of recent evidence. *Academy of Management Journal, 40*(1), 189–204.

Munilla, L., Bleicken, L., & Miles, M. (1998). Social responsibility and AACSB accreditation standards: How ISO 14000 can integrate environmental issues into the marketing curriculum. *Marketing Education Review, 8*(3), 57–65.

Nidumolu, R., Prahalad, C. K., & Rangaswami, M. R. (2009, September). Why sustainability is now the key driver of innovation. *Harvard Business Review,* 57–64.

Pitkethly, A., & Prosser, M. (2001). The First Year Experience Project: A model for university-wide change. *Higher Education Research and Development, 20*(2), 185–198.

Seidler, J. (1974). On using informants: A technique for collecting quantitative data and controlling measurement error in organization analysis. *American Sociological Review, 39,* 816–831.

Sheldon, P., Fesenmaier, D., & Tribe, J. (2009). The Tourism Education Futures Initiative. *E-Review of Tourism Research, 7*(3), 39–44.

Southern Cross University. (2011). *Strategic plan 2011–2015.* Lismore, Australia: Author. Retrieved from http://www.scu.edu.au

Springett, D. (2005). Education for sustainability in the business studies curriculum: A call for a critical agenda. *Business Strategy and the Environment, 14,* 146–159.

Stergiou, D., Airey, D., & Riley, M. (2008). Making sense of tourism teaching. *Annals of Tourism Research, 35*(3), 631–649.

Tilbury, D., Crawley, C., & Berry, F. (2004). *Education about and for sustainability in Australian business schools: Stage 1.* Sydney, Australia: Australian Research Institute in Education for Sustainability and Arup Sustainability for the Australian Government Department of the Environment and Heritage. Retrieved from http://www.aries.mq.edu.au/projects/ed_sustainability

Tribe, J. (2002). The philosophic practitioner. *Annals of Tourism Research, 29*(2), 338–357.

UN Educational, Scientific and Cultural Organization. (2012). *Education for sustainable development*. Paris, France: Author. Retrieved from http://unesco. org

von der Heidt, T., & Lamberton, G. (2011). Sustainability in the undergraduate and postgraduate business curriculum of a regional university: A critical perspective. *Journal of Management & Organization, 17*(5), 672–692.

von der Heidt, T., Lamberton, G., Wilson, E., & Morrison, D. (2012, April). *To what extent does the Bachelor of Business curriculum reflect the sustainability paradigm shift? An audit and evaluation of current sustainability embeddedness in curriculum and assessment in the first-year Bachelor of Business in Southern Cross Business School and School of Tourism & Hospitality Management*. Unpublished final report, Southern Cross University, Lismore, Australia.

Weaver, D. (2006). *Sustainable tourism: Theory and practice*. Oxford, UK: Elsevier Butterworth-Heinemann.

Wilson, E. (2010, February). *Practice what you teach: Using critically reflective practice in teaching sustainable tourism planning*. Paper presented at the 20th Annual Conference of the Council for Australian University Tourism and Hospitality Education, Hobart, Australia.

Wilson, E., Harris, C., & Small, J. (2008). Furthering critical approaches in tourism and hospitality studies: Perspectives from Australia and New Zealand. *Journal of Tourism and Hospitality Management, 15*, 15–18.

World Commission on Environment and Development. (1987). *Our common future*. Oxford, UK: Oxford University Press.

TEFI Values in Tourism Education:
A Comparative Analysis

LOREDANA PADUREAN and RICO MAGGI
Faculty of Economics, University of Lugano, Lugano, Switzerland

This article brings empirical evidence to the conceptual framework of tourism values developed by the Tourism Education Future Initiative by exploring the content of the mission statements of 85 graduate programs in tourism around the world as well as the content of 156 posts in international job search engines advertising for positions in tourism related industries. Finally a survey conducted in several international universities, with an in-depth case study applied at the University of Lugano, Switzerland revealed interesting results concerning the values students in tourism programs believe are important for themselves, their universities and the industry.

INTRODUCTION

Higher education in tourism has been the interest of many authors focusing on the nature of education studies (Airey, 2005; Ateljevic, Pritchard, & Morgan, 2007; Ayikoru, Tribe, & Airey, 2009; Dwyer et al., 2007; Hsu, 2005; Pearce, 1993; Ritchie, 1993; Sigala & Baum, 2003; Tribe, 2006a), on the knowledge and the university curriculum development (Gretzel, Jamal, Stronza, & Nepal, 2008; Tribe, 2006b), on the disciplinary dilemma of tourism studies (Echtner & Jamal, 1997), and on the internationalization of tourism education (Jennings, 2001; Mok, 2005).

Loredana Padurean acknowledges the Swiss National Foundation for Research for its support and would like to thank Stefano Maggi and Silvia Ghirelli for their assistance.

Higher education today is expanding globally with rates of change never seen before (Hjalager, 2003). Studies concerned with the global expansion in tourism education identified three main responsible drivers of this phenomenon: a set of structural changes in higher education in general (Ayres, 2006), a perceived need of increasing qualified human resources for tourism industry (Littlejohn & Watson, 2004), and a common perception of tourism as a major source of jobs and careers (Cooper, 1993; Deery & Jago, 2009). Previous literature confirms that the world economic powers are still leading the trend (Airey & Johnson, 1998) but the growth and the welfare in the emerging economies along with implementation of educational policies will be a strong factor of impact on the future distribution of higher education in the world (Maggi & Padurean, 2009).

However, in today's global environment, universities face a severe challenge to remain both attractive to students and an important source of highly skilled graduates for the industry. Literature debates whether the human resources provided by tourism education are matching the real needs of the industry (Goodenough & Page, 1993) and points out that there is a considerable gap between what education providers offer and tourism industry needs. One source of confusion might be the multi-disciplines character of tourism education and the variety of graduate typologies generated by the educational system. Also, literature is reflecting whether the profiles of the tourism employment as they are today may not exist in the coming decades implying again that educational systems need to change radically to meet these challenges (Wallis & Steptoe, 2006).

The community of tourism scholars continued to debate on how tourism education needs to adapt to societal and industry changes and what are the values that should lead the development of the tourism world and therefore that higher education institutions should provide (Antonioli, Cooper, Fesenmaier, Sheldon, & Woeber, 2008). In particular, a number of innovative and experienced educators together with some industry leaders have begun to recognize the importance of values at university and in the workplace and tried to provide a framework for the future of tourism education (TEFI 2007, Vienna, Modul University).

TOURISM EDUCATION FUTURES INITIATIVE (TEFI)

Universities . . . need to fundamentally retool and redesign—not incrementally by adding new courses or simply by putting courses online—but by changing the nature of what is taught and how it is taught. Programs (in tourism) must identify the key values, knowledge, and capabilities that graduates will need to lead positively, responsibly and effectively. (Sheldon et al., 2008)

Understanding the changing environment that future students of tourism and hospitality will enter upon graduation became the main concern of a group of leading tourism educators (Sheldon et al., 2008) therefore in 2007 the Tourism Education Futures Initiative (TEFI) was born. In 2010 over 70 representatives of the leading universities offering study programs in tourism take part to this yearly meetings seeking to provide vision, knowledge, and a framework for tourism education programs to promote global citizenship and optimistic for a better world.

TEFI is organized around a process that is both proactive and action oriented and it represents an important model of interaction. An important output of TEFI is the set of five values-based principles that tourism students should embody upon graduation to become responsible leaders and stewards for the destinations where they work or live. The five value sets are

- Stewardship: sustainability, responsibility and service to the community;
- Knowledge: critical thinking, innovation, creativity, networking;
- Professionalism: leadership, practicality, services, relevance, timeliness, reflexivity, teamwork, and partnerships;
- Ethics: honesty, transparency, authenticity, authentic self; and
- Mutual respect: diversity, inclusion, equity, humility, and collaboration.

These values do not represent only a theoretical framework but also a practical instrument that educators could use to improve the quality of their pedagogy. While the annual summit provides the starting point of discussion, TEFI is organized around working groups which throughout the years seek to develop tools that can be used to affect tourism education.

METHODOLOGY

This article is a response to this initiative and tries to bring empirical evidence to the conceptual framework developed at TEFI using the value set as an analytical tool for identifying: (a) What are the values that tourism education programs are promoting?; (b) What are the main skills, competences, and values that employers of tourism industries are looking for?; and last but not least (c) What are the values the students perceive as important for themselves, the industry, and their academic programs of origin, from the perspective of the TEFI value framework?

For the first question (What are the values that tourism education programs are promoting?), —in order to identify the values that tourism education programs are promoting, we analyzed the content of mission statements of graduate programs around the world. The data set contains

124 graduate programs (post-bachelor) identified online on various search engines and taught in English. Out of the 124 programs, 85 were valid (the rest of 39 were programs providing from the same university, having therefore the same mission, statement, and objectives or were programs were there was not obvious statement of intent).

The second question (What are the main skills, competences, and values that employers of tourism industries are looking for?) investigates the key skills, competencies and values that the employers in tourism are demanding by exploring the content of 156 job ads in international job search engines that were looking for profiles of graduates with either a background in tourism or in tourism related industries. The language of the ads was English but the jobs posted were not necessarily only for Anglo-Saxon countries.

The answer to the third question (What are the values the students perceive as important for themselves, the industry, and their academic programs of origin, from the perspective of the TEFI value framework?) came from an international survey conducted among students in tourism and tourism related programs around the world. A focus group also took place February 16, 2010 with the students of the Master in International Tourism at the University of Lugano, Switzerland.

RESULTS

The first research question investigated the values are promoted by academic programs in tourism around the world where the language of teaching is English. Out of the 85 programs analyzed, 49% are programs of Master of Science, 34% programs of Master in Tourism, 10% MBA, 4% MA, and 3% MPhil. In terms of geographic distribution there is a strong dominance of the Anglo-Saxon market (also given the choice of language).

A codebook was developed for the content analysis (Krippendorff, 1980, 2004) based on the assumption that words and phrases mentioned most often are those reflecting important values in the message. Therefore, the authors started with a quantitative content analysis using as key words the TEFI values (word frequencies and keyword frequencies) and extended to synonyms and homonyms that are close to the given categories.

The content analysis revealed that the programs promote *leadership* (43), *critical thinking* (31), *practicality* (28), *networking* (19), *diversity* (16) *stewardship* (10), and *partnership* (9). We were not able to find enough relevant data on *timeliness, reflexivity* and *relevance*. The value with the highest overall score is *professionalism* followed by *knowledge.* The *ethics* value had the lowest overall score (Figure 1).

The results are not very surprising considering that the majority of the programs are focused on business and management and just a small

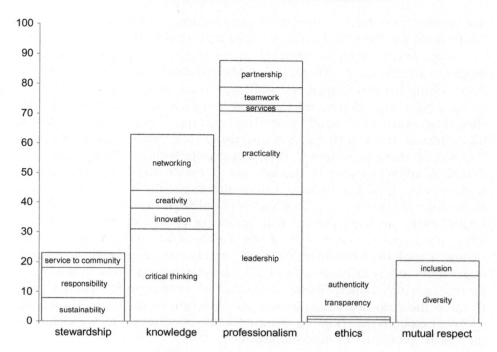

FIGURE 1 Values in tourism education.

minority in specific fields like sustainability, environmental, destination, and so on. However, we have noticed a strong variation in content and format of various mission statements. Some universities tend to declare a mission statement for the whole faculty/department, whereas other universities have mission statements specific to individual degrees and still other degrees lack a proper statement altogether.

The second research question investigated the key skills, competencies, and values that the employers in tourism are demanding. Using the same methodological approach as in the first question, we analyzed the content of 156 ads for management positions from various international websites that target qualified workforce in the area of tourism, travel, leisure (www.careerbuilder.com, www.monster.com, www.leisurejobs.com, www.traveljobsearch.com, and www.jobsearchusa.org). The source countries were again dominated by the Anglo-Saxon countries, given the language of analysis, with 60% of the ads from the United Kingdom and 34% from the United States. The rest of the ads came from Switzerland, France and Belgium (3%), Germany (2%), and Spain (1%). Some job offers contain inadequate or incomplete descriptions, especially as far as requirements are concerned (no requirements at all; "university degree" without further specification, etc.). Work experience seems to be more important than tertiary education in tourism/hospitality industry. Also, some of the positions are not directly connected to tourism industry, although a tourism degree might be useful in fulfilling the job (hence their inclusion).

The content analysis revealed that the industry needs experienced employees most of all. There is a slight paradox here, because they are also looking for young qualified staff, so having both relevant work experience and a high degree education at a young age is a challenge. This should be however a signal for students and universities to try to combine the academic study with relevant internships and other work experiences. The second thing most sought after was people with excellent communication skills given probably by the fact that tourism is a sector of diversity and human interaction. The industry values almost equally leadership, demands *technological* knowledge, is looking for people that value the clients and the organization, are team players with good analytical and negotiation skills. Most jobs require a great deal of travel experience and a high education degree. People with initiative, creativity, multitasking capability, and knowledge of the local environment and other languages, especially in the case of Europe, are also valued. These results can be interesting for new programs rising in the field of tourism as well as for future graduates trying to enter a very competitive market. To resume the industry demands, we elaborated the "ideal" profile of a future employee:

> Highly educated, young and experienced team player that can creatively manage and perfectly communicate with demanding international and local clients and lead in innovative ways a competitive organization.

In 2007, at the first edition in Vienna, TEFI leaders also identified four key capabilities and knowledge areas that graduates entering the world of the future will need but do not currently acquire in their education: destination stewardship skills; political and ethical skills; enhanced human resource skills; and dynamic business skills.

- Destination stewardship skills: management of real and virtual networks, knowledge sharing skills, ability to respect and work with all stakeholders, managing complex adaptive systems, and environmental management skills.
- Political and ethical skills: ethical behavior, demonstration and motivation, integration of basic human values into the workplace, lobbying, and the ability to influence the political process.
- Enhanced human resource skills: team building, effective listening and negotiation, motivation and leadership, working with distributed, virtual project teams, and emotional intelligence.
- Dynamic business skills: flexibility, multi-tasking, critical thinking, optimal use of common sense, innovation/entrepreneurship, communication

skills using new multi-media technologies, cross-cultural competencies, risk identification, estimation and control, and avoiding problems rather than solving them.

We clustered our findings from the ads' content analysis using the same methodology and identified that, as expected, dynamic business skills are most valued followed by enhanced human resource skills (Figure 2). Destination stewardship had almost no relevant results. While arguing that the profile of a future employee should be industry transversal, the lack of interest for destination stewardship when working in such a complex, multi-cultural, and multi-perspective field is a matter of concern. Universities should probably find ways to communicate with the industry the importance of the "softer" skills that are so critical for a sustainable socio-economic development.

The third question asked students in tourism to reflect upon which values they believe are important for the industry, for their own programs, and for themselves. In this step of the research we were interested to find the students' perceptions in relation to the TEFI framework given the fact that

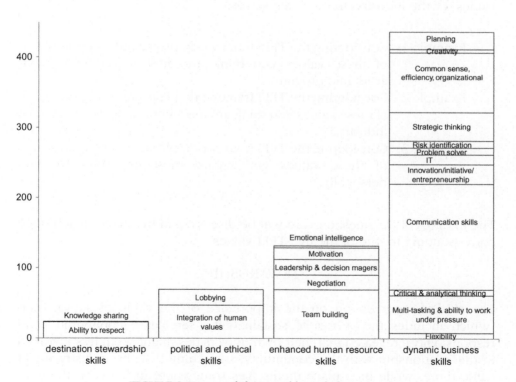

FIGURE 2 Key capabilities and knowledge areas.

they are both a "product" of the academia and a "tool" for the industry. To measure the perceptions of students who are currently studying tourism at university level in universities around the world, an online questionnaire was administered starting October 2008 until April 2009. The questionnaire was distributed to the population of students in tourism with the assistance of tourism academics (via Trinet) and TEFI members that sent out the questionnaire to their own students. There were a total of 198 valid responses out of 318 (female, 78.79%; male, 21.21%). Sixty-three percent of the respondents are bachelor students, 29% are graduate or master students, and the rest are PhD students. The majority (62%) graduated in 2009 or will do in 2010 (26%). The vast majority is convinced that they will pursue a career in tourism after graduation or at least consider it (92%), and almost 52% would consider continuing an academic career (e.g., PhD). The respondents provided from all five continents, with a high response rate coming from Italy, Australia, United Kingdom, United States, Phillipines, Denmark, and Canada. The questionnaire was designed around the TEFI value framework, which was described and explained in the introduction. Divided in three major sections (besides the socio-demographic section), the survey addressed through both closed and open-end questions, the perceived importance of these values in their academic programs as well as the perceived importance of the values for the industry and for themselves.

> Example 1: "Considering the TEFI framework, please reflect upon which of these values you think are most important in your academic program."
> Example 2: "Considering the TEFI framework, please reflect upon which of these values you think are most important for the tourism industry."
> Example 3: "Considering the TEFI framework, please reflect upon which of these values you regard most important for you personally."

The findings of the questionnaire will be discussed in five stages, each stage corresponding to one of the five TEFI values.

STEWARDSHIP

The students' perception on the importance of the value of stewardship (which includes the subset of sustainability, service to community, and responsibility), revealed that their own universities might seem less involved in the relationship with the community, something that the industry might value more, while they place themselves somewhere in between the two, with a stronger interest for responsibility.

KNOWLEDGE

The students' perception on the importance of the value of knowledge, which includes the subset of critical thinking, innovation, creativity and networking, revealed that critical thinking is important for the universities, whereas networking is less whereas for the industry networking stands high. Creativity was the only variable perceived equally important for industry, students, and academia. When it comes to the students, they are again somewhere in the middle of the industry and the academics, with a stronger interest in innovation.

PROFESSIONALISM

The professionalism set, which includes leadership, practicality, services, relevance, timeliness, reflexivity, teamwork, and partnerships, revealed teamwork and relevance as least important for their universities, followed by reflexivity, timeliness, and partnerships. The industry is perceived as very concerned about practicality, relevance, and teamwork. The students perceive as very important for themselves practicality (highest ranking overall), followed by relevance whereas teamwork got the lowest ranking.

ETHICS

The set of ethics, which includes honesty, transparency, authenticity, and authentic self, revealed that their universities do not value transparency and the authentic self but they do value honesty; whereas, the industry is considered more interested in transparency and honesty. The students valued more the authenticity and the authentic self, both highest ranked overall.

MUTUAL RESPECT

The value of mutual respect includes diversity, inclusion, equity, humility, and collaboration. The students belief is that universities are less concerned about collaboration and humility, but much more concerned with diversity and equity. In the students perception the industry is also less concerned with collaboration (the lowest ranked overall) and humility, but might be more interested in equity, diversity, and inclusion. The results are very similar when it comes to what the students are more interested in, with a high ranking of the inclusion, equity, and diversity and very little on collaboration and humility.

In summary, the general perception of the students in tourism is that there is a gap between what the industry needs and the academia provides while they see themselves to be more or less in the middle. They believe that for the industry, the sustainability, creativity, practicality, honesty and transparency, diversity, and equity is much more important and less the community, partnerships, authenticity, collaboration, and humility. For the universities, the perception is that critical thinking, innovation, diversity, and humility are more important than service to the community, teamwork, and transparency. For the students, the innovation, responsibility, practicality and honesty is very important, as well as equity and diversity.

Overall, the students seem to believe that the industry is the champion of stewardship, the academia of mutual respect, and they resonate mostly to the professionalism.

These results are not aligned with the findings of the previous two questions; therefore it made us reflect whether the surveyed students really understood the meaning of the values or whether there is really a misalignment in this triangle. For this purpose we conducted in February 16th, 2010 a 2-hour focus group on the values promoted by TEFI with 41 students of the Master in International Tourism at the University of Lugano, Switzerland (MT-USI) of which 27 from the first year of the master, 11 from the second, and 3 from graduates. After having presented the TEFI's mission and intent, the students were divided in six teams to discuss the TEFI's values and fill up a short questionnaire as a group, trying to find a common agreement. The questions were similar to the survey discussed previously: "(1) Which values do you believe are important for the Universities? (2) Which values do you believe are important for the industry? (3) Which values are more important for you as students in tourism?" The groups' discussions, moderated and recorded by us, were very active and the students reacted positively to the task. However, we have noticed that there was some confusion around the meaning of a few of the values, especially in the case of mutual respect and ethics. The problem was solved with our assistance or in some cases the solution came from the group discussion. The data collected was analyzed and summarized in three steps, each corresponding to the question of research.

Indeed our doubts about the survey findings, especially about the understanding of the values seem to be confirmed as the results of this focus group showed a completely different picture, with almost a perfect alignment between the industry, the academia, and the students. The students believe professionalism to be the most important value for all three variables followed by knowledge. The third place is stewardship for the industry and mutuality for the students and the academia. The last was ethics; however, a long debate started on how and who should teach ethics—family, school, personal education, and so on. Specifically for the first question "Which values do you believe are important for the universities?", the focus group revealed critical thinking, teamwork, and practicality as very important. To the second question "Which values do you believe are important for the industry?", the students agreed on teamwork, followed by responsibility, critical thinking, creativity, and collaboration. The students have indicated as central also innovation, leadership and practicality. For the third question "Which values are more important for you as students in tourism?", they indicated critical teamwork followed by critical thinking, collaboration, and networking. They agreed also on practicality and diversity. The focus group was also asked to critically discuss their program. The results revealed that the MT-USI is a leader of critical thinking, being very strong in creating opportunities for teamwork and students' collaboration as well as diversity, knowledge, and innovation. The main problems of the MT-USI program are in the area of professionalism. The students have criticized the lack of part- nership with the tourism companies that lead to issues on finding internship and job opportunities. They are confused about their possible career paths and would appreciate more guest speakers from the industry and overall more interest in networking and practicality. These observations are critical for the administrators of the program and can become useful guidelines for strategic decisions.

The main observation regarding the survey and the focus group is that in the survey it is possible that the understanding of the values was not obvi- ous. This investigation might be more adequate for a focus group rather than a survey since the values need to be "translated" to the students; therefore we encourage further research interested in the topic to take this method of analysis. We should consider also that this group—even though very international—is not representative of students from other universities. The peer pressure is also a variable to reflect upon when interpreting the data. While an online questionnaire guarantees the anonymity, a focus group confronts them openly; therefore they might choose to provide socially acceptable answers. Further research in other settings might clarify some of these issues.

CONCLUSIONS

This research is based on the five-value framework provided by the TEFI and has tried to give an empirical support to the TEFI values by analyz- ing both (a) supply (tourism academia) and (b) demand (tourism industry). Also, we surveyed students involved in programs that offer degrees in tourism in order to find out their perception on the importance of TEFI values for the industry, academia, and themselves. The content analysis of the academia statements revealed that universities value professional- ism and knowledge, with a strong focus on leadership, practicality, critical thinking, and networking. Diversity, stewardship, and partnerships are also values that the analysis revealed to be important. Looking at the content of the ads for jobs in tourism we found that the industry is mostly looking for experienced, young adults, with great communication skills, capable of multi-tasking in teams' part of international organizations. While most ads didn't specify the discipline of the degree, the majority is looking for highly educated people with strong business skills. This message is important for our future graduates in tourism programs, that have to be aware that the industry is very demanding as well as for the suppliers of programs in tourism that intend to become more competitive on international markets. The survey results indicated that students might feel confused about their positioning in between the academia and the industry, and they perceive a big gap in between the two parties. The findings of the survey reveal that universities where our respondents are coming from value mostly the mutual respect, with a specific interest in innovation, diversity, and humility but might be less interested in the service to the community, teamwork, and transparency. Their responses on the industry conclude that sustainability, creativity, practicality, honesty, transparency, diversity, and equity are important and much less the service to the community, partnerships, authenticity, collaboration, and humility. Students perceive a general gap between what the industry is looking for and the academia provides and they are somewhere in the middle. This situation can be given by where they are in this critical point in their life. The findings from all three questions of research in this article are not aligned. This is a problematic signal. If what the academia provides is not exactly what the industry needs or the students might believe important, there is the time for reflecting upon strategies for programmatic change. Our findings clearly demonstrated barriers but also potential strategies for changing educational processes within the universities.

This research is relevant in the context of the five-value framework provided by the TEFI. Using this structure, we conducted the research only in programs taught in English and we looked only at job ads posted in English. Other languages and cultures might offer different results and further investigation in this direction would certainly be interesting. The bias of the findings could also be given by the set of values used for investigation. While the TEFI values are very relevant, they are representing the beliefs of a relatively small group of experts.

The findings are important for the academic programs that are contemplating strategic transformations, just as much for students in tourism who are preparing to face the demands on the industry. We hope that this article will be the reason for reflection upon translating the core values into action and implementation in order to create a fundamental change in tourism education.

REFERENCES

Airey, D. (2005). United Kingdom. In D. Airey & J. Tribe (Eds.), *An international handbook of tourism education* (pp. 271–282). Oxford, UK: Elsevier.

Airey, D., & Johnson, S. (1998). *The profile of tourism studies degree courses in the UK: 1997/98*. National Liaison Group Guideline No. 7. London, UK: NLG.

Ateljevic, I., Pritchard, A., & Morgan, N. (2007). *The critical turn in tourism studies*. Oxford, UK: Elsevier.

Ayikoru, M., Tribe, J., & Airey, D. (2009). Reading tourism education: Neoliberalism unveiled. *Annals of Tourism Research, 36*(2), 191–221.

Ayres, H. (2006). Career development in tourism and leisure: An exploratory study of the influence of mobility and mentoring. *Journal of Hospitality and Tourism Management, 13*(2), 113–123.

Cooper, C. (1993). An analysis of the relationship between industry and education in travel and tourism. *Teoros International, 1*(1), 65–73.

Deery, M., & Jago, L. (2009). A framework for work–life balance practices: Addressing the needs of the tourism industry. *Tourism and Hospitality Research, 9*(2), 97–108.

Dwyer, L., Edwards, D., Mistilis, N., Scott, N., Cooper, C., & Roman, C. (2007). *Trends underpinning tourism until 2020: An analysis for key drivers for change*. Gold Coast, Qld, Australia: Sustainable Tourism CRC.

Echtner, C. M., & Jamal, T. B. (1997). The disciplinary dilemma of tourism studies. *Annals of Tourism Research, 24*(4), 868–883.

Goodenough, R. A., & Page, S. J. (1993). Planning for tourism education and training in the 1990s: Bridging the gap between industry and education. *Journal of Geography in Higher Education, 17*(1), 57–72.

Gretzel, U., Jamal, T., Stronza, A., & Nepal, S. K. (2008). Teaching international tourism: An interdisciplinary, field-based course. *Journal of Teaching in Travel and Tourism, 8*(2–3), 261–282.

Hjalager, A. (2003). Global tourism careers? Opportunities and dilemmas facing higher education in tourism. *Journal of Hospitality, Leisure, Sport and Tourism Education, 2*(2), 26–38.

Hsu, C. (Ed.). (2005). *Global tourism higher education: Past, present, and future*. New York, NY: The Haworth Hospitality Press.

Jennings, G. R. (2001). Do I or don't I teach them? *Journal of Teaching in Travel and Tourism, 1*(4), 35–52.

Littlejohn, D., & Watson S. (2004). Developing graduate managers for hospitality and tourism. *International Journal of Contemporary Hospitality Management, 16*(7), 408–414.

Maggi, R., & Padurean, L. (2009). Higher tourism education in English: Where and why? *Tourism Review, 64*(1), 48–58.

Mok, K. (2005). Globalization and educational restructuring: University merging and changing governance in China. *Higher Education, 50*, 57–88.

Pearce, L. (1993). Defining tourism study as a specialism: A justification and implications. *Teoros International, 1*, 25–32.

Ritchie, J. (1993). Educating the tourism educators: Guidelines for policy and program development. *Teoros International*, *1*(1), 9–23.

Sigala, M., & Baum, T. (2003). Trends and segues in tourism and hospitality higher education: Visioning the future. *Tourism and Hospitality Research*, *4*(4), 77–86.

Sheldon, P., Fesenmaier, D., Woeber, K., Cooper, C., & Antonioli, M. (2008). Tourism education futures, 2010–2030: Building the capacity to lead. *Journal of Teaching in Travel & Tourism*, *7*(3), 61–68.

Tribe, J. (2003). Editorial: The future of higher education in hospitality, leisure, sport and tourism. *Journal of Hospitality, Leisure, Sport and Tourism Education*, *2*(1), 1–4.

Tribe, J. (2006a). The idea of tourism higher education. *Hospitality Review*, *8*(4), 35–42.

Tribe, J. (2006b). Tourism, knowledge and the curriculum. In D. Airey & J. Tribe (Eds.), *An international handbook of tourism education* (pp. 47–60). Oxford, UK: Elsevier.

Wallis, C., & Steptoe, S. (2006, December 10). How to bring our schools out of the 20th century. *Time*, pp. 50–56.

Valuing Tourism Education 2.0

JANNE LIBURD
University of Southern Denmark, Esbjerg, Denmark

ANNE-METTE HJALAGER
Advance/1, Aarhus, Denmark

INGER-MARIE F. CHRISTENSEN
University of Southern Denmark, Esbjerg, Denmark

This article reports on learning experiences from the INNOTOUR project that aims to raise the quality of tourism education by use of Web 2.0 technology, new pedagogy, and values-based education. The article describes the main areas of the INNOTOUR platform, associated teacher training, and examples of course implementation. A discussion on key challenges sets into perspective handling of formal requirements, which incorporation of Web 2.0 tools and learning poses to participants, and alignment of curricula and exam forms to reflect new teaching methods and the Web 2.0 philosophy. In conclusion, reflections are provided on Web 2.0, the forming of identity and contestation of current university practice.

BACKGROUND

Universities continue to play a key role in the development of society, but they are also faced with significant economic and educational challenges. Looking back at the "good old days", many university employees tend to believe that if budgets were increased, everything would be better. But things are hardly likely to become as they were and there are many reasons for that. Universities are required, amongst other things, to ensure a balance between research and education, undertake ongoing strategic selection, prioritize, and develop their educational disciplines and disseminate knowledge of scientific methods and results as well as "collaborate with the society around them and contribute to development of international cooperation" (Universities Act § 2, 2003). In addition student behavior, attitudes, and future prospects are markedly different from previously (Benkendorff, Moscado, & Pendergast, 2010). Further education is part of a complex web of international competition and collaboration this is highly dependent upon both personal network and explicit strategy. At the same time, there is considerable inertia in terms of merit and career motivation amongst university staff, where teaching is somewhat paradoxically typically regarded as a secondary activity with low status.

There is an urgent need to create new traditions and teaching methods in order to ensure that students as individuals and universities as institutions can contribute critical knowledge about the present and be instrumental in forming the future (Liburd & Hjalager, 2010a, 2010b; Sheldon, Fesenmaier, Woeber, Cooper, & Antonioli, 2008; Tylor, 2009). Despite skepticism, it is therefore necessary to instigate visionary processes, albeit on an experimental basis. A grant from the Danish IT and Telecom Agency's e-learning pool has thus provided the Centre for Tourism, Innovation and Culture at the University of Southern Denmark (SDU) with an opportunity to gain their first experience with an international Web 2.0 platform for tourism education, research and business development.

Since 2003, SDU has offered Bachelor and Master programs specializing in international tourism management. Since its initiation, there has been sufficient but not overwhelming demand. Interest has however increased markedly as a result of collaboration between the University of Ljubliana, Slovenia, the University of Girona, Spain, and SDU in an Erasmus Mundus accredited joint degree, entitled European Master in Tourism Management. This initiative has resulted in greater publicity and manifestation of the international dimension of tourism studies. Even with such offensive strategies, there is no denying that the study and research environment for tourism, in its broadest sense, has only a modest volume. SDU's situation is not atypical. Other universities, both within Denmark and abroad, are burdened in much the same way by the disadvantages of their small scale (Morris, 2008). It is difficult to offer economically viable teaching at the same time as offering a broad range of high quality opportunities (Sheldon et al., 2008). Conversely, this intimate environment has the advantage that productive alliances are formed between staff and students, and between students and local companies. Furthermore, the students appear to be very satisfied with a "tailored" rather than a "mass produced" training.

The INNOTOUR platform addresses this set of privileges and problems. INNOTOUR is a virtual meeting place for students, teachers, researchers, and companies with an interest in tourism and innovation, and who are seeking to enhance their knowledge, products and skills. INNOTOUR is an English language site because tourism as a subject and phenomenon has a large international interface. INNOTOUR is therefore envisaged in an international teaching context and is available both as a tool and as a dynamic collaboration interface with partners at other universities. INNOTOUR is based on Web 2.0: It is interactive and is based upon users creating and developing content. INNOTOUR is therefore an e-learning project, but it also has much broader aims. The objectives of INNOTOUR are therefore:

- to improve the quality and effectiveness of tourism training through use of a broad spectrum of technological tools and teaching methods;
- to involve students and partner companies in the development and spread of advanced educational resources;
- to strengthen international cooperation and share knowledge on innovation in tourism, and to market INNOTOUR as a hub for knowledge creation;
- to assist commercial enterprise and society in tourism related innovation processes by establishing relationships and open dialogue to communicate experiences;
- to promote a creative culture, which tolerates experimentation and error, and thereby encourages students and researchers to go beyond conventional knowledge in the effort to create something original;
- to play an important—and internationally recognized—role within academic tourism research;
- to build mutually beneficial relationships with partners in the third world;
- to provide a testing ground for the SDU's efforts to develop new teaching and learning methods, and cooperation practices; and
- to build bridges between academic skills and campuses.

INNOTOUR has financial and strategic backing from the university management, and the project is also supported by the regional Growth Forum for the South of Denmark, which sees it as a pioneering, regional innovation initiative. Further information about the wider aspects of the project is available on www.INNOTOUR.com. This article focuses exclusively on experiences with the e-learning courses and collaboration between students and teachers. The aim is especially to describe the most important tools in INNOTOUR and their use in an educational context, identifying the results and challenges involved in getting students to work constructively in a Web 2.0 environment on the basis of initial trials. The article concludes by outlining some of the most important perspectives for INNOTOUR in particular and Web 2.0 based learning in general.

INNOTOUR FOR TOURISM STUDENTS

INNOTOUR is built around a common platform for students, teachers, businesses, and researchers. There are subsections for each of these groups. Many of the resources are freely available to everyone, but it is necessary to register as a user in order to comment and upload content. In accordance with INNOTOURs highly integral philosophy of reciprocal interests, differing user groups share resources to a great extent.

Students, for example, may use the innovation case studies as a starting point to try theories, or as inspiration to a project. For companies, the innovation cases are "best practice" scenarios. Researchers can benefit from an overview or make use of illustrative examples in their research publications and teaching. The pages especially for students contain a number of menu items; the pedagogic intent and potential uses are described here.

Innovation Cases

Innovation, creativity, and business are INNOTOURs principal subject areas and are elements within both the humanistic and social science oriented subjects. Continuous innovations in industry, and at destinations, are crucial to economic sustainability and are important parameters in tourists' experiences and potential return visits (Dwyer & Edwards, 2010; Hjalager, 2010). The innovation cases describe concrete innovations in the tourist industry and at tourist destinations. They represent different ways of working with innovation and include examples of product, process, marketing and logistical innovations. The innovation cases are a central feature in INNOTOUR. Cases vary in length, but all are equipped with photos and links to the companies involved. Other relevant sources, such as videos are embedded where available. It is important to note that the cases are not marketing material, but rather have the character of "best innovation practice" or are innovation process experiences within a professional environment.

The innovation cases can be a tool for teachers to set a context or provoke discussion in a teaching situation. Videos can be activated to supplement individual cases, and to create diversity between communication forms.

The user can leave written comments on individual cases. In teaching situations, students can, for example, be asked to make a professional evaluation of a case in relation to a given theory or with inspiration from other examples. Students can analyze a case in a geographical context, take a critical view, and discuss marketing opportunities or consumer reactions, dependent upon the particular educational topic.

It is also possible for students to prepare cases and upload them onto INNOTOUR. Many projects within the course can conclude with presentation of a case on the web. The possibilities are many, although cases do not typically have an "academic" approach. Upload of a case could therefore be part of a project, where the students also work with other written products and presentations.

Academic Resources

This section comprises references to important innovation literature in tourism. It is a supplement to library services for students and teachers. It is possible to search by keywords, author, and so on, and any geographic sites referred to in the articles appear on Google Maps.

There are also opportunities to comment. This can be part of a task set by teachers, so that students make use of these and other sources in a literature search, and at the same time contribute with a cross-reference. It is an accepted and integral part of an academic education that students should learn to use research materials, and, in this respect, INNOTOUR is a shortcut and new pedagogical possibility for teachers and students to do so.

Innovation Tools and Tests

This section is under continual renewal and is available for companies as well as students. There are examples of interactive "innovation ability tests", which are directed toward companies, but which students can also use in their project work. INNOTOURs "risk assessment test" is based on theory and research in business and social economics and it can be used both in the classroom and in connection with problem solving. INNOTOUR has not developed its own set of specific personality tests, instead it links to tests, which map creative abilities and profiles. Such tests generally have a widespread appeal because they combine relevant knowledge with an element of entertainment.

Dilemma Games

Dilemma games are a tool that is particularly relevant in educational contexts. The aim is to consider difficult issues and discuss possible options, either in the classroom or individually. INNOTOUR describes the dilemma and sets out varying options. It is possible to "vote" interactively for the solution that you find most appropriate, and justify its choice in a blog. It is possible to see the suggested dilemma play solutions of others. The dilemma games are primarily suited for Bachelor-level students. In collaboration with INNOTOURs webmaster, students can work on developing new dilemmas, which are subsequently uploaded on INNOTOUR. This suggestion came from one of the teachers at SDU and is consistent with INNOTOURs basic idea of user-created content.

INNOWHEEL

INNOWHEEL is uniquely developed for INNOTOUR. It is a creativity instrument that helps users to move beyond conventional thinking. The user is challenged to think creatively about possible innovations in relation to product, target group, distribution channel, and customer needs in hitherto unseen combinations. User-driven innovation has been the subject of much discussion in Denmark. INNOTOUR aims to summarize available methods and to provide students and businesses with both practical advice, links to cases and theory and thereby generate curiosity and lust for entrepreneurial activity. INNOTOUR introduces many other creative tools in the same way.

Student Blogs

In a small environment, it is important that students network beyond their local area. INNOTOUR brings together tourism students across national borders, and the student blog is an ideal tool for this. It is possible to ask subject-related questions to other students and to raise topics for discussion freely.

Student Forum

This is also a discussion forum, but one where the topics are raised only by the teaching staff. The idea is that discussions run for a limited time (e.g.,in connection with part of a course), and that the topics reflect the themes of the course. To the extent that other universities run parallel courses, as is further described below, the forum can be used as a joint meeting place across borders and cultures. Previous discussions are saved on INNOTOUR when they are closed and will then become possible source material.

Student Wikis

A *wiki* is a "living" document with several contributors at the same time. INNOTOUR is working to introduce wikis as a tool for project groups, where several students can contribute, revise, and further develop a document in a joint iterative process. This is a way of working, with which many "knowledge workers" are already familiar, optimizes preparation of joint documents. It is also a popular way of building and maintaining online resources with different subjects. In this way, the wikis on INNOTOUR help to prepare students for their future career (McLoughlin & Luca, 2002; Parker & Chao, 2007; Richardson, 2006).

Tutorials, Slides, and Streamed Sessions

These three menu items provide opportunities to accumulate educational materials over a period of time which students can use freely. INNOTOUR links to teacher's slides, which are often a good source to gain an overview of a subject matter. Streamed teaching sessions can help to spread knowledge and bring unique skills into teaching and can, for example, offer students an opportunity for a unique repetition before exams. What should be included in the tutorials on INNOTOUR is not yet certain, and this function is currently under development in collaboration with partners at other universities. It is especially these resources on INNOTOUR that represent an opportunity for marked improvement of student access to good teaching resources and to sharing material across international borders between often small, academic tourism environments.

Work and Learn

Students of tourism are often motivated by an inner globetrotter. They know that their own international travel experience and cultural understanding contribute to their knowledge and skill profile, which also make them better professionals in the long term. INNOTOUR wants to promote travel opportunities with a high learning potential, including internship and volunteer work in Denmark and around the world. As such it is also an opportunity for INNOTOURs international partner universities to present their "summer schools" and various forms for exchange visits.

The above is a systematic review of all menu items on the student pages. INNOTOUR is still under development and the menu items are therefore subject to continual revision based upon feedback from colleagues and students who use INNOTOUR as a tool in their teaching.

INNOTOUR FOR TOURISM EDUCATORS

The entire INNOTOUR site is available to educators who teach innovation, business development, creativity, experience design, sustainability, marketing, and so on. There is also a special section dedicated to teachers, which is amongst other things inspired and shaped by project partners. This professional section, which is designed to make the lives of educators both more interesting and easier, contains the following:

Shared Teaching Resources

Development of teaching materials is very time consuming. INNOTOUR provides an opportunity to exchange, share, and learn from one another. Material could, for example, include phrasing of assignments, group exercises, questions relating to tourism innovation, field trips, and course syllabuses. It is about reusing material that works well, so that each individual teacher can provide a more informed content in their teaching.

Best Practice in E-Learning

The intention here is to place special focus on e-learning, and Web 2.0 in particular. It is of basic importance that students are motivated to cooperation and that they learn to use web-based resources and new social media as learning tools. Likewise, e-learning often challenges teachers' practical, pedagogic, and organizational skills. This section of INNOTOUR is under continual development, with opportunities to comment on existing material and upload new references.

Slides and Streamed Sessions

This section is shared with the students and includes both PowerPoint presentations and videos. The streamed teaching sessions are generated by users and by the autumn of 2010 will include contributions from partner universities in Brazil, United States, Switzerland, Austria, and New Zealand, where work on value-based education is carried out under the auspices of the Tourism Education Futures Initiative (Liburd, 2010; Sheldon et al., 2008).

Teachers Wiki

Here it is possible for teachers to learn to work with wikis in tourism education via simple exercises, test versions and an introductory video on the subject. The page can also be used to plan a common, value-based teaching course (Dohn & Johnsen, 2009; Lund & Smørdal, 2006).

Teachers Forum

Communication via e-learning platforms such as INNOTOUR is challenged communicatively and socially by a lack of physical closeness. Here, tourism educators in small, scattered communities will be able to find a virtual "coffee room" with space for discussion of the ideas or thoughts that occupy them personally. The web-editor has the administrative rights, and subjects are started up and closed again after contacting INNOTOURs webmaster.

Creative Commons

INNOTOUR falls into a much debated area concerning copyright. INNOTOUR is built up around the concept of Creative Commons where others are given a license to reuse, modify, and further develop existing material with the acknowledgement of the original version. Another approach is found in Copy left, a license where copyright restrictions are either removed entirely or are modified in new versions against requirements that these rights are maintained in future versions (Berry, 2008). This phenomenon is known from open source software and provides significant new challenges to intellectual property rights (Liburd & Hjalager, 2010a).

Kubus

Kubus is a general, copyrighted model for teaching about innovation. Developed by SDU and Copenhagen Business School it is well suited as tool to support project-oriented courses for tourism students. The model is designed for managing the work of interdisciplinary groups in the early phases of the innovative process. Over time, it is expected that INNOTOUR will link to, or incorporate, more resources of this type.

The close collaboration between the Centre for Tourism, Innovation and Culture, and the e-learning unit at SDU ensures that the INNOTOUR platform is based on the latest developments in web-based teaching and learning, and that the platform is periodically renewed, new tools added, and new teaching methods and pedagogic approaches integrated. The Staff at the e-learning unit test these new tools, in collaboration with staff and students at SDU, to chart and assess how these tools can support and enhance student's learning. Based on such experiments and assessments, scenarios are prepared that can inspire teachers at SDU to make increasing use of e-learning in their teaching. Amongst other initiatives, much effort is focused on web conferences for live online teaching using Adobe Connect.

TEACHER TRAINING

INNOTOUR went live in September 2009 in an alpha version. It was far from finished, and in many sections users were met with a "coming soon" text. We wanted to be open about the development process, and it was important to gain experience in an established learning environment. As described by Dohn and Johnsen (2009), teaching in a Web 2.0 environment is new to most teachers and exploitation of the opportunities in practice necessitates rethinking of content, forms, performance reviews, and much else. In the spring of 2009, teaching staff at SDU completed three training sessions to learn to work with Web 2.0 as a teaching tool in general and INNOTOUR in specific. These training sessions were important eye-openers for teachers, the concept designers, and developers. A number of comments from teachers were directly translated into concrete platform improvements.

These teacher training courses set focus on the important aspects relating to involvement of INNOTOUR in teaching. Use of wikis and blogs in teaching involves more than inclusion of these new tools, it is simultaneously a whole new way of viewing knowledge and learning. Knowledge becomes about processes and activities. Learning is centered on participation. This is in many ways a position that conflicts with the traditional view of education where information is transferred from teachers to students (Dohn & Johnsen, 2009). In addition, teachers had to be equipped to deal with net-based teaching methods and learning, as the available experience base was minimal. A pivotal point in all three training sessions were tasks designed to make teachers familiar with the INNOTOUR tools, and not least to inspire them as to how these tools could be used in their teaching. Materials from the teacher training session can be accessed from INNOTOUR's Teacher & Tutor's area, where they are located under TEFI courses. Courses had the following content:

1. Introduction to social media: Web 2.0 motivating elements and tools, forms for interaction and underlying values. The aim of the first training course was to make teachers familiar with the INNOTOUR platform and its various tools, with a particular focus on blogs and wikis. Through the use of a number of practical assignments, teachers were given a good understanding of the platform, available tools, and not least how these could be incorporated into their teaching. Blogs and wikis are concepts frequently used but far from all of the teaching staff were familiar with these tools and their characteristics. The first training course was designed to remedy that.
2. Design of web 2.0 activities with inspiration from Gilly Salmon's (2002) five-phase model and e-tivities concept: The teacher's role in carrying out Web 2.0 activities. When net-based activities are used in teaching, it is important that an introductory phase is included which gives participants a chance to become familiar with the virtual environment before they begin on educational tasks. This is also the case with Web 2.0

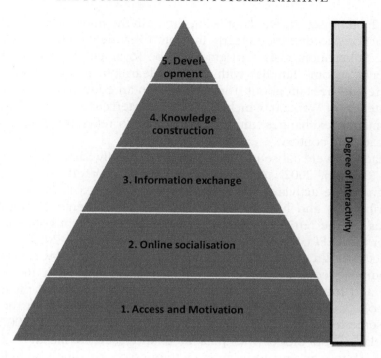

FIGURE 1 Development of e-tivities. Source: Authors, adapted from Salmon (2002).

courses. Many students use social networks such as Facebook, but it is new for them to use Web 2.0 tools in an educational context. The second course was inspired by Gilly Salmon's five-phase model (Salmon, 2002) illustrated in Figure 1.

Salmon's (2002) model offers good advice as to how participants in an asynchronous, web-based course can be introduced to the tools to be applied. Careful teacher moderation allows students to become more familiar with the online study environment and their fellow students while interacting increasingly on vocational topics with other participants. Each of the five stages requires participants to master certain technical skills and each stage calls for different e-moderating skills. The "interactivity bar" running along the right of the figure suggests the intensity of interactivity that can be expected between the participants at each stage. At first, at Stage 1, they interact only with one or two others. After Stage 2, the numbers of others with whom they interact, and the frequency, gradually increases, although Stage 5 often results in a return to more individual pursuits (Salmon, 2002). When designing Web 2.0 activities for students, it is important to orchestrate the students' online interaction and set standards that ensure that a suitable academic level is achieved. This might appear contrary to the free and open participation, which is part of the

Web 2.0 mindset. However, it is important in the initial phase to formulate instructions so that they clearly indicate to students what is expected of them. Subsequent tasks can gradually be formulated more freely as the students become familiar with Web 2.0 learning. Many students will be unsure and hesitant about using Web 2.0 in an educational context. Their private use of Web 2.0, which is often characterized by fast and superficial information exchanges, must be converted to reflective contributions in an academic context.

Teachers were subsequently introduced to Gilly Salmon's e-tivities concept (Salmon, 2002) to give them a simple, but effective template to design online activities that also clearly indicate expectations to student contributions and how to interact with other students. Examples of e-tivities can be retrieved from the INNOTOUR platform's student section under the TEFI courses, "Dr. Liburd: Intro to Tourism—2010."

3. Didactic design of blended learning, web 2.0 courses: How do you design a complete course? The third training course was at a more general level and focused on discussions of how the INNOTOUR platform and its tools could be incorporated into an entire course, from the start of the semester to the final exam. Here Hiim and Hippe's (2007) didactic relationship model was presented and used to illustrate a holistic approach to planning and running a training course, likewise highlighting the theoretical basis for the INNOTOUR learning platform. The desire to involve researchers, teachers, students, and businesses in open, equitable cooperation that aims to create new knowledge suggests a need for a problem-based approach to learning and a constructive understanding of the learning process.

When planning a Web 2.0 course, it is recommended that not only vocational goals are articulated but that goals should also be formulated for the use of the Web 2.0 tools involved. The reason is to make clear to the students which specific goals there are for using the given tools. It is important to emphasize that all of the tools applied serve an educational purpose. This will contribute greatly to students' perceptions of Web 2.0 activities as a meaningful element in their studies, rather than use of the tools being viewed as an end in its own right.

Based on these training sessions, the following examples of goals for inclusion of Web 2.0 tools were listed. The student should be able to:

- take part in individual and collaborative knowledge construction (produce texts themselves and in collaboration with others) via Web 2.0 tools on a virtual platform;
- contribute to discussions on vocational topics from differing perspectives via Web 2.0 tools on a virtual platform;

- build up a virtual network of vocational contacts and make use of them in the educational activities;
- act as a sparring partner for others in virtual, professional networks;
- transfer and make use of knowledge/material in a variety of contexts (use and re-use); and
- apply a critical approach to used and re-used material.

A key issue in working with Web 2.0 in education is how to ensure consistency between the semester activities and evaluation/appraisal; also called *alignment* (Biggs & Tang, 2007). Because Web 2.0 activities implicitly view learning as active participation and knowledge as a process/activity, there is no correlation with traditional final test forms such as individual written assignments or oral examinations. Involvement of Web 2.0 necessitates new thinking in relation to evaluation and assessment (Christensen, 2009). Not only is it important that assessment focuses on the process rather than solely valuing the end result, it is also essential that part of the evaluation procedure becomes the responsibility of the participants. This could be in the form of peer review, for example, based upon comments from fellow students, constructive criticism during the process, and so on. This places significant demands on the established educational system to renew and not least accept the idea that students should have a greater role in evaluating, learning and assessment.

TEACHING EXPERIENCES AND PROGRESSION

That teachers have very different approaches in their own teaching was self-evident, it was therefore quite expectedly very different parts of the INNOTOUR platform that they subsequently chose to use. Examples from three courses by tourism teachers using INNOTOUR are presented below.

Blended Learning in Innovative Event Management

Teaching using the INNOTOUR platform and Web 2.0-learning was conducted by Dr. Janne J. Liburd with a class of 12 master-level tourism students enrolled in the spring of 2009. The semester was devised as a blended learning course on "Innovative Event Management," with intensive work both in workshops of 4–6 hours per week and with an external business partner to collaborate on strategy formulation. Because of technical problems and delays with the INNOTOUR platform, all writing processes were assigned to Blackboard (the university's own closed e-learning platform). The online part of the course was based on Gilly Salmon's (2002) five-phase model and designed as an e-tivity. The result was to positively raise the level of discussion and exchange of topically relevant knowledge toward a collaborative effort that concluded with a jointly written report, where students had sufficient overview to reflect on synergies and make strategic recommendations. The industry partner, Odense Event House, praised the student's efforts and final report highly.

Unfortunately, there proved to be a discrepancy between the results of the learning process and the final, individual exam paper. The following dilemmas were identified by the teacher and students in the subsequent course evaluation:

- Work on the collaborative report was very time consuming. Left less time was left preparing for a written home assignment.
- Very few students were able to re-use their contribution to the joint report in the concluding paper despite the teacher's clear suggestion that they do so. Most failed the course!
- The student's contribution to the entire process varied widely. A single student dropped out and two ended by completing the report on their own initiative.

Teacher and student reflections:

- The exam form and requirements for this particular course did not fit the teaching and learning process well.
- The extent of online activities was not weighted correctly versus classroom teaching.
- Requirements to the process, including the division of roles between students, should have been clearer.
- The teacher's management, meta-communication, and motivation of the students who did not contribute adequately, was insufficient.
- Overall feedback from the students, industry partner, and the teacher was positive in assessment of the entire course, the new work processes and learning methods in many "classrooms."

An E-tivity from the Gastronomy and Tourism Course

The course in Gastronomy and Tourism is offered in the fifth semester of the Bachelor degree in Hotel Management. A small e-tivity designed to test the class of 15 students' response to INNOTOUR cases through blogging features was included in the fall semester of 2009. The task was described by Dr. Anne-Mette Hjalager as follows:

The purpose of the course is, amongst other things, to analyse and discuss the dining out experience and the meal as a symbol of, and a contributor to, identity. This small e-tivitiy will help you to reflect on the dining experience. You will have to lay your own preferences behind you and identity and assess a dining experience through a cultural and social filter.

Step 1: Find the indicated home page on the web. Each of you will be given different websites.

Step 2: If necessary, create an account if you do not have one already.

Step 3: Read the case and observe the pictures or video. If relevant, find more information about the restaurant, for example on the restaurant's own home page.

Step 4: Write a comment. You should use one of the four Bourdieu life styles as a filter, as indicated in the annex text. Imagine that you are representing this particular life style and write a review of the restaurant based on this. It is important that your review is based on solid argumentation of what this restaurant means to you; how it feels in terms of your identity and preferences, and how you would like to see the proprietor develop it in the future. Keep a sober tone; do not criticize without an argumentation. Make your review 200–300 words.

Step 5: Submit your review and see it come up on the home page.

Step 6: Swop to the next home page and read the text and your co-student's contribution. Upload a smaller comment (100 words) imagining that you represent another life style than your co-student.

Step 7: Reflect on this exercise in the class.

Materials: Computer with internet access. Slides from the presentation. Individual task sheets.

The following were highlighted by the students:

- In general, working this way was seen as both fun and challenging.
- A couple of the students felt that it was almost unreasonable to comment on a business that they had not visited.
- It could be difficult to use a "lifestyle" theory, without it becoming a little stereotyped.
- There were technical problems, with one student repeatedly losing her network connection, which caused significant delays.
- YouTube, which was used by some of the students, only has 500 characters available, which was insufficient.
- Some only managed half of the task, and in general, too little time was allowed.
- Some felt uncomfortable about seeing their input published directly on the Internet without necessarily being revised and thoroughly checked.
- Some tried to get around the requirement to use their (real) name in the blog posts.

Reflection by the teacher: Examination of the contributions on the web showed that the exercise was largely solved systematically and as intended. But if the students are to perceive this type of task as an integral and useful part of the course, it must be part of a larger exercise and a related teaching programme.

The "Celebrating Nature" Event

As part of the "Tourism, Culture, and Events" course at the bachelor-level in International Tourism and Leisure Management, 24 students were to develop and organize an event at SDU's campus in Esbjerg. The first phase of the program was described by Dr. Carina Ren as follows:

A "green innovation" theme was pre-selected by the teacher, which many students found difficult to address. INNOTOUR was introduced as a tool to post and discuss existing examples of green events. Under the "Student Forum" section two folders were set up, one entitled *Innovations in Green and CO2-Neutral Tourism* with cases, for example, from the Winter Olympics in Vancouver and the world's first CO2-neutral festival, CO2penhagen. The other folder entitled *Green Event* was designed to allow students to share thoughts, reflections, and ideas about their own, upcoming green event.

One initial hurdle to getting the platform up and running in relation to education and event planning was not technical at all but simply to get students to register. Several students had difficulties simply logging on. As a result, more teaching time was spent on these teething problems than anticipated. Another obstacle to using the platform was that the comments were not passed on to all (at that time the teacher was not aware that it was possible to activate an RSS feed). This meant that everyone had to log on at regular intervals, with the result that the platform was largely discarded. The various groups that the class was divided into according to event tasks during the semester opted to switch communication channels; internally to Blackboard, the university's own educational web portal, and externally to Facebook. In consequence, the opportunity to post cases and brainstorm on them in an open and informal fashion was lost, and relevant documents were not collated and made accessible for ongoing comment.

This first trial was particularly valuable for the teacher, both in uncovering INNOTOURs many opportunities and apparent limitations, as well as the challenges that exist in relation to the framework for a specific subject area and within INNOTOURs own structure.

In general, the challenges from this pilot trial can be summarized as follows:

- That some students are unsure about new media and web-platforms and are not automatically all "super users," as often assumed of this generation.
- That ample time should be set aside for an introduction to the platform, its use, and potential in a learning context
- That automatic "response to all" and RSS feeds should be activated. It is hereby possible to avoid the need to log on and check for any activity.

In coming semesters, use of INNOTOUR will be amplified and extended to SDU's tourism programs. In the Erasmus Mundus master program, the European Master in Tourism Management, which has 34 students enrolled from Thailand, Serbia, Ethiopia, Malaysia, Uganda, Russia, Taiwan, Ukraine, Bangladesh, Bulgaria, Holland, Romania, Slovakia, Croatia, Austria, Ireland, Germany, England, Greece, Spain, and Denmark, INNOTOUR will become a key learning component in the core disciplines, Strategic Communication and Sustainable Tourism Development.

Furthermore, in the fall semester of 2010, tourism students at the bachelor-level at SDU will take part in joint value-based teaching sessions together with tourism students in Brazil, United States, Switzerland, Austria, and New Zealand. All of the lessons address the five core values: ethics, professionalism, mutual respect, knowledge, and stewardship developed by the Tourism Education Futures Initiative (TEFI; see Sheldon, Fesenmaier, & Tribe, 2011). TEFI aims to provide optimism for a better world by providing vision, knowledge, and a framework for tourism education programs to promote global citizenship (Liburd, 2010; Sheldon et al., 2008). The vision of TEFI is therefore not only to reshape tourism education worldwide, but to help the leaders of the tourism industry follow practices that are rooted in these basic values. Aims are pursued through a number of initiatives, which includes collaborative, values-based teaching. Teachers from the above mentioned countries thus contribute with expert knowledge in the various thematic fields, where individual lectures are streamed via Adobe Connect and uploaded onto INNOTOUR together with related value-based student exercises designed to be solved in groups across the six campuses using the blogs, wikis and discussion forums as tools.

There are continued experiments to develop "own pages" for each individual student, "MyINNOTOUR," as a personal learning area (Johnson, Levine, & Smith, 2009). The philosophy behind the personal learning areas is to support individual, academic, and professional learning in a holistic manner. In this way, learning is not limited to individual topics in specific semesters but acts as a personal portfolio for lifelong learning (Mott, 2010). Moreover, in close cooperation with the e-learning unit the Centre for Tourism, Innovation, and Culture will continue to focus on how to create alignment between semester activities where Web 2.0 tools are involved for evaluation or appraisal in the given subjects. Concrete measures include the incorporation of goals for achievement of competencies using the use of Web 2.0 tools as part of the curricula and adoption of a portfolio pedagogic with the aim of emphasizing the procedural aspect, rather than a traditional view of knowledge as an acquired condition (Andrus, 2005; Brown & Adler, 2008).

EXPERIENCES IN CRITICAL PERSPECTIVE

A wealth of e-learning experience exits, but Web 2.0 based learning is by its nature a new phenomenon, and where intensive work to develop forms and didactics is currently underway (Christensen, 2009; Dohn & Johnsen, 2009). Many tasks are still ahead of the INNOTOUR team and other interested tourism teachers around the world.

In general, it is not difficult to get students interested in INNOTOUR. Social media are "their" home turf, and it is natural for them to use related tools (Thomson, 2007). But it is a job to enhance students' motivation to work with INNOTOUR as a serious study activity, and they must be initially motivated by careful moderation of academic activities, as argued in the above. Because of revisions to educational requirements and, in particular, study grant regulations, the current generation of students is relatively focused on academic outcomes. They want clear directives about the syllabus, assignments, and deliveries. Broadly orientated "con amore" reading students appear to be a rarity. In pragmatic terms, an intensified use of INNOTOUR, where students are active contributors, will necessitate substantial changes to study plans, formulation of exercises, and curriculum requirements. It must be clear to students that their use of and contribution to INNOTOUR is a requirement, and that their online efforts are judged similar to other study activities.

Evidently, it is not new for students to collaborate on solving assignments. But once again, experience with INNOTOUR pilot teaching and other forms of Web 2.0-based learning indicates that new behavioral norms are necessary (Sigala, 2007). In relation to blogs and wikis, it is necessary for students to be able to give and receive criticism in a constructive and a future-oriented spirit in order to raise the quality of the joint product. Many are simply too cordial whereas others appear uncomfortable with making their views known. Students continue to look for definite truths about a given problem, which the teacher, as an expert, ought to be able to provide a definitive answer.

The evidence here suggests that successful integration of Web 2.0 in education requires students and teachers to take on radically different roles from the traditional ones. Everyone is a contributor, helping one another to create of a knowledge base, within a given subject area. Everyone helps to improve and update texts in the employed wikis. Everyone contributes with new angles and nuances on a topic in the related blogs. It requires an outgoing personality and courage, which may take time for a student to develop. It is obvious that a certain professional modesty may exist in the first semester of a course. Here it would be an advantage for teachers to act as role models and coach their students through the first Web 2.0 learning activities. Additionally, collaboration with students from other universities, who may be only vaguely familiar from correspondence via mail and Skype, can be difficult to motivate. The realization of creating "TEFI world citizens" in the sense of students committing themselves ethically and professionally to implement, test and develop equitable working relationships beyond the safe limits of their own campus thus lies into the future.

For teachers, it is not just a challenge to make use of INNOTOURs tools, but also to invest the time in developing and adapting learning materials. Traditionally, teachers function as individual "course kings" and there is a legitimate, intensive recycling of own material from one year to the next. Recycling of other's material is limited, and with the exception of textbooks, it is often regarded as illegitimate to copy slides, examples, and other's course material. The INNOTOUR platform is, as mentioned, built around the concept of Creative Commons. Creative Commons is a new way of regulating copyrights and producers of materials can give permission for others to further and adapt their work in a continuous creative process. We urge those creating content on INNOTOUR to give as far-reaching rights as possible to reuse, modify, and remix, based on the view that it will result in better teaching overall.

INNOTOUR is not yet filled with short-cuts to tourism teaching. Experience from the early trials with INNOTOUR has shown that a number of considerations are necessary in order to prepare a thorough e-tivity (Salmon, 2002). The initial investment of time appears to pay off as results can be reused by the teachers themselves and ideally by others, although it continues to be very much against the grain for teachers to openly post slides, tutorials, and streamed material on the web. These materials are often regarded as private property and require a significant shift in thinking and everyday teaching practice. On top of this are speculations about whether the material is of sufficient quality for distribution. Such reflections cannot simply be attributed to intellectual humility, but also to a genuine fear of colleagues' judgments, which ought to incite to greater collegial openness that is not common in current teaching environments, notwithstanding their smallness in size.

Study guides are normally structured to define learning targets, content, and form. If one looks at the curricula for in the International Tourism and Leisure Management, Hotel Management and European Master in Tourism Management programs at SDU, a thorough review is needed to create consistency between learning processes and evaluation of value-based Web 2.0

teaching process. As previously argued, it is important to devote resources to this task. Involvement of the Web 2.0 tools represents, at the same time, adoption of a new learning and knowledge paradigm that conflicts with traditional views of teaching and knowledge. In order to put a Web 2.0 activity into context and for students to experience this as meaningful, it is necessary to rethink evaluation and assessment forms so that they match the new position on learning and knowledge acquisition.

Changes to the study programs for SDU's tourism courses are typically a lengthy process. Suggestions for change are first compiled locally, the legal basis is subsequently centrally processed, then sent for peer consultation after which changes may finally be agreed by the study board albeit only at fixed times of the year. Two years of delay are thus to be anticipated before adjustments can be implemented. The implementation of INNOTOUR puts into focus a number of challenges in relation to the adaptation of curricula, assessment forms, and intellectual property rights. Work with INNOTOUR has clearly demonstrated just how well established these conservative institutional structures are, and how much work is required to renegotiate them. Moreover, the development of new teaching materials and methods is not considered of general academic merit, which is hardly motivating for radical innovation in higher learning institutions.

Technical developments within Web 2.0 occur very fast, and there is thus a significant gap between the cadence of development and that of study course regulation (Alger, 2002). Setting up the INNOTOUR system was initially cumbersome due to extensive technical programming, but this was helped by adaptation to TYPO3. The modular structure of TYPO3 supports flexible content development. Other considerations involve the interface between technique and concept in INNOTOURs interaction with other social media, especially Facebook and Twitter. INNOTOUR has—primarily to create awareness—a profile on Facebook, and key players are now also seeking to promote INNOTOUR through other social media while intentionally staying away from competing as a social networking site.

An important philosophical basis for INNOTOUR is that students, teachers, and business users are co-creators of content on an equitable basis in an open and changing professional space. Some of the major challenges in getting players out onto this new pitch are named above. In contrast to the universities' traditional role as an ivory tower in society, it is transformed into a glass tower that is not protected from outsiders eyes (Carson, 2009). This offensive and extroverted way of working is inevitable in modern tourism, characterized by global, socio-economic movements, technological innovations, and transnational resource flows. This does not imply that Web 2.0 or INNOTOUR should be seen as the only way to prepare students for their future field of practice, but here is an embedded understanding of professionalization, reciprocal relationships and sustainability that goes well beyond a traditional transfer of knowledge, proficiency and skills from teachers to students. Mindful of the digital divide, it is essential to appreciate that the learning environment is markedly enlarged. The teacher is no longer the only one to challenge and assess students, and INNOTOUR is trying to work constructively with the new opportunities and ethical challenges—including assessment of the quality of knowledge produced and represented by the transparency and equality of access.

Extending Giddens's (1991) considerations regarding modernity, the individual finds himself in three axes simultaneously: a market axis, a state institutional axis, and a civil society axis. Individuals are formed and socialized in all of these fields, and they share a knowledge universe with others on the basis of the roles that they play within these axes. But the underlying logic of the three axes also partially conflict with one another. Modern society is characterized by choices between these axes, where navigation comprises both opportunities and risks.

As a student, one is especially caught up in conformity and limits formulated by the state to determine an effective level of citizen education and to ensure dependability in ways that are recognizable to actors in the labor market. What a university can and must concern itself with is clearly articulated. Universities are permeated by traditional reflection and continuous negotiation and cultural development, and for this reason there is also criticism of orthodoxy and development inertia. One could argue that the state-regulated axis is of a place for reflection, intellectual contemplation, aesthetic education, and so on that represents a wide range of traditional academic virtues.

Students are also actors in a market-based space (Iiyoshi et al., 2008) and they are bombarded with rapid, innovative changes and exciting offers. University offerings are a part of a highly competitive market and marketing and branding are needed. To a far greater extent, teachers become performers, orchestrators, and scene setters, who vie for attention with the Web, TV, and street life. Understood in this light, the students' personal "knowledge mix" has validity for the constellation of privatised skills.

The civil society axis consists of joint traditions supporting both the academic and social communities. With a university education follows a history and professional spirit that permeates one's route through the labor market in perpetuity. Regardless of professional competency, a university education is a privilege that obligates to "pay back society," a kind of Hippocratic oath or ethos. The civil society will thereby impose a certain discipline and also incorporate a moral and ethical basis (Hammershoej, 2003).

In modern universities it is easy for students to get confused. Is the student in a shop, where the tuition fees allow for free choice from all shelves, with the right to complain and return? Or is the student amongst friends in a professional environment, which has become far too large to encourage communal solidarity? Or is this a straightjacket, where the system already has plans for the student's future and where the material has been digested and thought through by others (Luhmann, 2006)? It would obviously be too much to expect that INNOTOUR put an end to student confusion and create order, where one can feel somewhat lost. Web 2.0 has an educational potential, even if it often disappears into a "cult of amateurism" in this roaring pioneer period (Keen, 2007). Accordingly, INNOTOUR encourages self-transcending, creative action, and alternative reflexive processes.

Web 2.0 is not just about new technology and new ways to learn. It is also presents users with an opportunity to organize into new professional communities and to be an unbiased cultural actor on the civil society axis. It places great demands on all members of participating groups, where requirements and expectations must be explicated. In many ways, the teacher must act as a guide/mentor/coach and initiate the students in the use of Web 2.0 tools, and not least Web 2.0 learning and interaction forms. In the start-up phase, it is important that the teacher is visible and can provide constructive feedback. By cultivating an environment of creativity, mutual respect, and open knowledge construction, which recognizes and learns from failure, students will learn to act in a Web 2.0 environment.

Giddens's (1991) considerations give optimism for the future. In the change of tourism education in particular, and for further education institutions in general, it is important that the three axes are spanned in a new way, as promoted by INNOTOUR. INNOTOUR encompasses opportunities for immersion: academic sources, many tests and tools, models and theories, a profusion of innovation cases, and the opportunity to play with ideas and creative processes. Expectations and opportunities to build bridges in civil society by development of trans-national cooperation between institutions are also supported by values-based teaching and open access. Finally, with its roots in Web 2.0 tools, learning, and interaction forms, INNOTOUR disturbs the otherwise well-established approach to learning, media, and knowledge, which calls for relentless questioning and a rethinking that can help to bring universities into the 21st century.

REFERENCES

Alger, J. R. (2002). Legal issues in on-line education. *Educause*. Retrieved from http://net.educause.edu/ir/library/pdf/NTW0204.pdf

Andrus, D. C. (2005). The Wiki and the Blog: Toward a complex adaptive intelligence community. *Studies in Intelligence, 49*(3). Retrieved from http://ssrn.com/abstract=755904

Benkendorff, P., Moscado, G., & Pendergast, D. (Eds.). (2010). *Tourism and generation Y*. Wallingford, UK: CABI.

Berry, D. M. (2008). *Copy, rip, burn: The political of Copyleft and Open Source*. London, UK: Pluto Press.

Biggs, J., & Tang, C. (2007). *Teaching for quality learning at university* (3rd ed.). Maidenhead, UK: Open University Press.

Brown, J. S., & Adler, R. P. (2008). Minds on fire: Open education, the long tail, and learning 2.0. *Educause Review, 43*(1), 16–32.

Carson, A. (2009). The unwalled garden: Growth of the OpenCourseware Consotium, 2001–2008. *Open Learning, 24*(1), 23–29.

Christensen, I. F. (2009). How can examination practices reflect the use of collaborative web 2.0 courses? In *Book of Abstracts, Online Educa Berlin 2009* (pp. 334–337). Berlin: 15th International Conference on Technology Supported Learning & Training.

Dohn, N. B., & Johnsen, L. (2009). *E-læring på web 2.0* [E-learning on Web 2.0]. Frederiksberg, Denmark: Samfundslitteratur.

Dwyer, L., & Edwards, D. (2010). Sustainable tourism planning. In J. J. Liburd & D. Edwards (Eds.), *Understanding the sustainable development of tourism* (pp. 19–44). Oxford, UK: Goodfellow.

Giddens, A. (1991). *Modernity and self-identity: Self and society in the late modern age*. Cambridge, UK: Polity.

Hammershoej, L. G. (2003). *Selvdannelse og socialitet* [Self-education and socialization]. København, Denmark: Danmarks Pædagogiske Universitets Forlag.

Hiim, H., & Hippe, E. (2007). *Læring gennem oplevelse, forståelse og handling. En studiebog i didaktik: 2. udgave* [Learning through experiences, understanding and practice. 2nd edition]. København, Denmark: Gyldendal.

Hjalager, A.-M. (2010). Supplier-driven innovations for sustainable tourism. In J. J. Liburd & D. Edwards (Eds.), *Understanding the sustainable development of tourism* (pp. 148–162). Oxford, UK: Goodfellow.

Iiyoshi, T., & Kumar, M. S. V. (Eds.). (2008). *Opening up education: The collective advancement of education through open technology, open content, open knowledge*. Cambridge, MA: MIT Press. Retrieved from http://mitpress.mit.edu/opening_up_education/

Johnson, L., Levine, A., & Smith, R. (2009). *The 2009 horizon report*. Austin, TX: The New Media Consortium. Retrieved from http://www.nmc.org/pdf/2009-Horizon-Report.pdf

Keen, A. (2007). *Cult of the amateur*. London, UK: Nicholas Brealey.

Liburd, J. J. (2010). Sustainable tourism development. In J. J. Liburd & D. Edwards (Eds.), *Understanding the sustainable development of tourism* (pp. 1–18). Oxford, UK: Goodfellow.

Liburd, J. J., & Hjalager, A.-M. (2010a). Changing approaches to education, innovation and research: Student experiences. *Tourism Journal of Hospitality and Tourism Management, 17*, 12–20.

Liburd, J. J., & Hjalager, A.-M. (2010b). *From copyright to Copyleft: Towards tourism education 2.0. The critical turn in tourism studies* (2nd ed.). Amsterdam, The Netherlands: Elsevier. (In review)

Lov nr. 403 om universiteter. 28.5.2003. [Act on Universities (2003)]. Retrieved from http://www.cepes.ro/services/pdf/Denmark.pdf

Luhmann, N. (2006). *Samfundets uddannelsessystem*. København: Hans Reitzel.

Lund, A., & Smørdal, O. (2006). Is there a space for the teacher in a WIKI? *WikiSym '06—Conference Proceedings of the 2006 International Symposium on Wikis* (pp. 37–46). Odense, Denmark: ACM Press.

McLoughlin, C., & Luca, J. (2002). Experiential learning online: The role of asynchronous communication tools. In P. Parker & S. Rebelsky (Eds.), *Proceedings of the World Conference on Educational Multimedia, Hypermedia and Telecommunications* (pp. 1637–1639). Chesapeake, VA: AACE.

Morris, D. (2008). Economies of scale and scope in e-learning. *Studies in Higher Education, 33*(3), 331–343.

Mott, J. (2010). Envisioning the Post-LMS Era: The open learning network. *EDUCAUSE Quarterly, 33*(1). Retrieved from http://www.educause.edu/ EDUCAUSE + Quarterly / EDUCAUSE Quarterly Magazine Volum / Envisioning the PostLMSEraTheOpe/199389

Parker, K. R., & Chao, J. T. (2007). Wiki as a teaching tool. *Interdisciplinary Journal of Knowledge and Learning Objects, 3*. Retrieved from http://ijklo.org/ Volume3/IJKLOv3p057-072Parker284.pdf

Richardson, W. (2006). *Blogs, Wikis, Podcasts and other powerful web tools for classroom.* Thousand Oaks, CA: Corwin Press.

Salmon, G. (2002). *E-tivities: The key to active online learning.* Abingdon, UK: Routledge Falmer.

Sheldon, P., Fesenmaier, D., Woeber, C., Cooper, C., & Antonioli, M. (2008). Tourism education futures, 2010–2030: Building the capacity to lead. *Journal of Travel and Tourism Teaching, 7*(3), 61–68.

Sigala, M. (2007). Integrating Web 2.0 in e-learning environments: A socio-technical approach. *International Journal of Knowledge and Learning, 6*(3), 628–648.

Thomson, J. (2007). Is education 1.0 ready for Web 2.0 students? *Journal of Online Education, 3*(4). Retrieved from http://www.innovateonline.info/ pdf/vol3_issue4/Is_Education_1.0_Ready_for_Web_2.0_Students_.pdf

Tylor, M. C. (2009, April 26). The end of the university as we know it. *New York Times.* Retrieved from http://www.nytimes.com/2009/04/27/ opinion/27taylor.html?_r=1

Using YouTube Videos of Anthropology of Tourism Pioneer Valene Smith's Work and Philosophy to Balance the Tourism Curriculum

LINDA JOYCE FORRISTAL

Drexel University, Philadelphia, Pennsylvania, USA

An analysis of four undergraduate tourism textbooks revealed a content imbalance tipped in favor of economics, or the business of tourism. Based on the concept of a balanced and interdisciplinary pedagogy implied by the Tourism Education Futures Initiative core values of stewardship, mutuality, and knowledge, YouTube videos highlighting the six-decade career and work of cultural anthropologist Valene Smith were introduced into two undergraduate tourism classes. The videos immediately augmented the curriculum with sociocultural content, exposed students to the anthropological foundations of tourism, and furthered an interdisciplinary approach to tourism education. The easily adopted Web 2.0 technology was well received by Net Generation students.

INTRODUCTION

As we move into the second decade of the third millennium, universities are being called to bring about the fundamental changes in education needed to prepare students to be competitive, productive, innovative, and ethical to respond to "significant societal and industry changes" (Sheldon, Fesenmaier, Woeber, Cooper, & Antonioli, 2007). To achieve these goals and to sustain the results, a "shift in tourism education is necessary to respond to global challenges impacting tourism at a fundamental level" (Sheldon, Fesenmaier, and Tribe, 2011).

The five values-based principles of the Tourism Education Futures Initiative (TEFI) are professionalism, stewardship, ethics, mutuality, and knowledge (Barber, 2011; Sheldon et al., 2011; TEFI, 2009). Within these principles, the call for a broad, inclusive, and interdisciplinary approach to tourism education is implied.

TEFI's call for stewardship includes the concepts of sustainability and corporate social responsibility (CSR), both of which embrace the concept of sustainability and a "triple-bottom line" approach. Mirroring the concept of sustainable development (Bramwell & Lane, 1993), the concept of sustainability consistently draws from three pillars: economics (business or financial environment), environmental (physical and natural environment), and sociocultural (cultural and built environment). This "triple-bottom line" model is often visualized as a Venn diagram of three proportional overlapping circles of equal size (Figure 1), which implies that each pillar should be given equal weight or attention when striving for sustainability or well-being in all endeavors and enterprises, including those tied to tourism and its pedagogy. Equal weighting can be equated with *equilibrium*, which is defined as a "state of balance between opposing forces or actions" (Merriam-Webster, 2008, p. 421).

A rising interest in sustainability among tourism academics and advocates for sustainable development (Bramwell & Lane, 1993; Edgell, 2006; Hall & Lew, 2009; Honey, 2008; Weaver, 2006), as well as among well-informed consumers, has inspired the tourism industry to start measuring, monitoring, and reporting on its progress toward sustainability (Cowper-Smith & de Grosbois, 2011; Sheldon & Park, 2011). These CSR reports are often voluntarily posted on corporate Web sites. Although a study of efforts in the airline industry showed a stronger focus on environmental issues than on the social

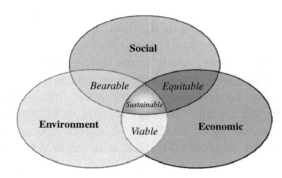

FIGURE 1 The three pillars of sustainability are routinely conceptualized as economic, environment, and social, with social increasingly referred to as the sociocultural aspects.

Source: Wikipedia, copyright free.

or economic dimensions of CSR (Cowper-Smith & de Grosbois), most world-level tourism suppliers and destinations include content related to all three pillars of sustainability. Tourism-related CSR reports include those from air transport and Dow Jones Sustainability Index leader Air France-KLM (2011), cruise ship (water transport) leader Royal Caribbean (2010), accommodations world player InterContinental Hotels Group (IHG, 2011), and the world-level attractions giant Disney (Walt Disney Company, 2011). All include content related to the three pillars of sustainability. "Rising concerns over climate change (environmental), environmental degradation (environmental), and human rights (sociocultural) have stimulated more responsible corporate behaviors (economics), strengthening the CSR–sustainability link" (Sheldon & Park, 2011). In light of this development, it makes sense that tourism curriculum should incorporate cutting-edge insights gleaned from academic tourism research and tourism industry practices by exposing students to content drawn from the academic disciplines that inform the environmental, economic, and sociocultural aspects of tourism.

TEFI's core value of mutuality recognizes mutual respect and inclusion, diversity, and the power of collaboration and cooperation. TEFI's call for mutuality is another strengthening of the argument that students should be guided to explore the various disciplines that underpin the field of tourism. Tourism is intrinsically interdisciplinary and draws elements from numerous academic fields (Echtner & Jamal, 1997; Gunn, 1991; Jamal & Jourdan, 2008). If the "element of travel (tourism) is to be understood, several disciplines and specialties are implied" (Gunn, 1991). In relation to transportation, Gunn listed political science, geography, and engineering as related disciplines. In relation to travel behavior and visitor activities, Gunn mentioned the importance of geography, psychology, sociology, history, archeology, and marketing. Jafari and Brent Ritchie (1981) listed 5 key foundational academic disciplines important to tourism: economics, sociology, psychology, geography, and anthropology. A review of tourism doctoral dissertations found linkages to 15 disciplines (Jafari & Aaser, 1988). Echtner and Jamal explored the contributions of marketing and consumer research, geography, psychology, sociology, and social psychology to tourism studies. Thus, it can be argued that a balanced and future-oriented tourism curriculum embraces a multidisciplinary or an interdisciplinary approach to tourism pedagogy. As such, students should be instilled with respect for not only the business of tourism (i.e., the management and marketing of tourism suppliers, destinations, and attractions) but the impact tourism has on the environment as well as the social dynamics of tourism—areas of academic discourse addressed, but not exclusively, by various fields of science, psychologists, sociologists, and anthropologists.

TEFI's core value of knowledge addresses the need to make students aware of industry concepts, trends, and goals. "Industry concepts" should include a thorough introduction to both the history of the field of tourism, especially its early practitioners and scholars, and emerging concepts, such as pollution prevention, the aforementioned sustainability, and social equity. In relation to the environmental aspects, students should learn about changing attitudes toward nature that arose in the 1960s and 1970s to help launch the environmental movement (Carson, 1962) and that are expressed in today's concern for air, land, and water pollution (Carson & Gore, 1994). These concerns are often discussed in terms of CO_2 and greenhouse gas emissions (with reduction efforts routinely chronicled in CSR reports), global climate change, green tourism, and carbon offsets (Hall & Lew, 2009). In relation to the sociocultural aspects of tourism, students should be exposed to the anthropological underpinnings of tourism and the growing body of work that is shedding light on the importance of host–guest relations, employee well-being, and community outreach (among others) in the tourism industry. Thus, a balanced curriculum should pay homage to the past by exploring the work of seminal environmental and sociocultural figures that shaped tourism, while at the same time exploring the dynamics that shape the experience of the modern-day traveler and the current landscape of the tourism industry.

Web 2.0 in the Classroom

There is increasing evidence of the effectiveness of a multimedia approach to teaching (Berk, 2009), especially among this generation of students who have been dubbed alternatively, and somewhat confusingly, Millennials, Generation Y, Trophy Kids, Digital Natives, or the Net Generation. This article adopted the term *Net Generation* as coined by Tapscott (1997) and adopted by Berk (2010) and abbreviated the term to Net Gens. Net Gens are techno-savvy, visually oriented learners who prefer interactive media (Berk, 2010). To address Net Gen learning characteristics, Berk (2010) recommends matching their generational characteristics with pedagogical strategies that include Web 2.0 technology. Net Gen visual orientation can be addressed and capitalized on by using "graphics, images, and visual representations in your [classroom] presentations, especially *videos from TV, movies, and YouTub*e, with which students can relate" (Berk, 2010, p. 8). This approach is supported by emerging research that supports the concept that "verbal and visual components of a video potentially provide a best fit to the characteristics of this *Net Generation* of students and a valid approach to tap their multiple intelligences and learning style" (Berk, 2009, p. 1). The use of Web 2.0 technology is one of the strategies recommended to "raise the quality of tourism education" (Liburd, Hjalager, & Christensen, 2011, p. 107). Lastly, there is a growing use of YouTube among academics for effective instruction in disciplines ranging from nursing to political science (Snelson, 2011), although hospitality and/or tourism titles were lacking from Snelson's meta-analysis based on academic articles and conference proceedings from 2006 to 2009.

METHODOLOGY

For this research, a balanced curriculum was equated with one that draws equal content from all three areas traditionally used to define sustainability (i.e., economic, sociocultural, and environmental). With the Venn diagram of sustainability visualization as a framework, a meta-analysis of the table of contents (TOCs) of four recent undergraduate tourism textbooks (Goeldner & Ritchie, 2009; Mill & Morrison, 2009; Page, 2009; Walker & Walker, 2011) was undertaken. The goal was to broadly assess within which of the three areas of sustainability each of the chapters from the four tourism textbooks would fall. This was completed by an initial examination of the title and subtitles of chapters in the TOC. Subsequently, if the content of a particular chapter was not clear from the titles, the chapter itself was physically examined to note and record the focus of the material. An Excel spreadsheet for each title was created to record the data. If it was deemed that a particular chapter contained content from more than one of three sustainability areas, the chapter title was added to the associated columns in the table.

RESULTS

The content analysis revealed that among the 65 chapters within the four textbooks, 51 chapters contained economic content, 7 chapters focused primarily on environmental concerns in relation to tourism, and 18 chapters included a majority of content on the sociocultural aspect of tourism (Table 5). An imbalance of content coverage was tipped in favor of economics or the business of tourism (see Tables 1 through 4 and Figure 2).

Because a key stated goal of TEFI is to help bring about fundamental change in tourism education to prepare students for a sustainable future (TEFI, 2009), this author suggests that one of the changes should be to encourage the adoption of balanced tourism curricula, specifically curricula that reflect the complex interrelationships of tourism—focusing not only on the "business" of tourism, but also shedding more light on the importance of the environment as the natural playground of tourism and on host–guest relationships and other sociocultural dynamics.

Although this research revealed the need to add both environmental and sociocultural content to introductory tourism textbooks, a first step should be to attend to the sociocultural lacunae due to the people-oriented host–guest nature of tourism and hospitality. Fundamentally, positive human relationships lie at the heart of tourism (MacCannell, 2009, p. 8). While natural climate and beauty are often judged the most important determinants of the attractiveness of a given region, cultural and social characteristics have been judged second in importance (Ritchie & Zins, 1978). Thus, there is call for the sociocultural side of tourism to be better presented.

TABLE 1 Review of Table of Contents of Goeldner and Ritchie (2009)

Economic	Environmental	Sociocultural
Chapter 1: Tourism in Perspective	Chapter 17: Tourism and the Environment	Chapter 2: Tourism Through the Ages, History
Chapter 3: Career Opportunities		Chapter 9: Motivation for Pleasure Travel
Chapter 4: Organizations		Chapter 10: Culture and International Life's Enrichment
Chapter 5: Passenger Transportation		Chapter 11: Sociology of Tourism
Chapter 6: Hospitality Services		
Chapter 7: Organizations in the Distribution Process		
Chapter 8: Attractions, Entertainment, Recreation, and Other		
Chapter 12: Tourism Components and Supply		
Chapter 13: Measuring and Forecasting Demand		
Chapter 14: Tourism's Economic Impact		
Chapter 15: Tourism Policy		
Chapter 16: Tourism Planning		
Chapter 18: Travel and Tourism Research		
Chapter 19: Tourism Marketing		
Chapter 20: Tourism Future?		

Scholars have tried to make "sociological sense" of tourism for decades (Urry, 1990, p. 7). One of the earliest scholars looking at the sociocultural underpinnings of tourism was cultural anthropologist Valene Smith (Graburn, 2007, pp. 99–100). Smith is credited with organizing the first symposium on the anthropology of tourism at the 1974 meeting of the American Anthropological Association in Mexico City (Nash, 2007), as well as the first international tourism symposium at the 1977 meeting of the Society of Applied Anthropology in Merida, Yucatan, Mexico. She is a founding member and fellow of the prestigious, invitation-only International Academy for the Study of Tourism (see http://www.polyu.edu.hk/htm/iast). Smith's status in the world of the anthropology of tourism was also attested to by the symposium at California State University, Chico (held March 4–5, 2011), entitled "Reflections and New Directions: A Conference on the Anthropology of Tourism in Honor of Valene L. Smith." In one of the tributes gathered by anthropologist Margaret Swain Byrne for her keynote address, tourism scholar John Tribe described Smith as the "wise chief of our academic tribe and pioneer of our academic territories" (Byrne, 2011).

In recent years, Smith has formulated an assessment tool called "The 4Hs of Tourism," which can be used to "pinpoint host assets and liabilities in the

TABLE 2 Review of Table of Contents of Mill and Morrison (2009)

Economic	Environmental	Sociocultural
Chapter 1: The Destination Mix	Chapter 2: Tourism Impacts on the Economy, Society, Culture, and Environment	Chapter 2: Tourism Impacts on the Economy, Society, Culture, and Environment
Chapter 2: Tourism Impacts on the Economy, Society, Culture, and Environment	Chapter 15: The Geography of Travel	Chapter 10: Forces Shaping Tourism
Chapter 3: Tourism Policy and Organizations		Chapter 11: Why Do People Take Vacations?
Chapter 4: Tourism Regulation		Chapter 12: Selecting a Travel Destination
Chapter 5: Tourism Planning		Chapter 13: Travel Purchase
Chapter 6: Tourism Development		Chapter 14: Purposes of Travel
Chapter 7: Tourism Marketing		Chapter 15: The Geography of Travel
Chapter 8: Tourism Promotion		
Chapter 9: The Distribution Mix in Tourism		
Chapter 10: Forces Shaping Tourism		
Chapter 12: Selecting a Travel Destination		
Chapter 13: Travel Purchase		
Chapter 14: Purposes of Travel		
Chapter 15: The Geography of Travel		
Chapter 16: Modes of Travel		

TABLE 3 Review of Table of Contents of Page (2009)

Economic	Environmental	Sociocultural
Chapter 1: Tourism Today: Why Is a Global Phenomenon Embracing All Our Lives?	Chapter 12: Managing the Visitor and Their Impacts	Chapter 2: Tourism: Its Origin, Growth, and Future
Chapter 3: Demand: Why Do People Engage in Tourism?		Chapter 11: The Public Sector and Tourism
Chapter 4: The Supply of Tourism		Chapter 12: Managing the Visitor and Their Impacts
Chapter 5: Surface Transport		Chapter 13: The Future of Tourism. Post-tourism?
Chapter 6: The Aviation Sector		
Chapter 7: Accommodations and Hospitality Services		
Chapter 8: Tour Operating and Travel Retailing		
Chapter 9: Visitor Attractions		
Chapter 10: The Management of Tourism		
Chapter 12: Managing the Visitor and Their Impacts		
Chapter 13: The Future of Tourism. Post-tourism?		

TABLE 4 Review of Table of Contents of Walker and Walker (2011)

Economic	Environmental	Sociocultural
Chapter 1: Introduction to Tourism	Chapter 6: Tourism Planning and Sustainability	Chapter 1: Introduction to Tourism
Chapter 3: Tourism Marketing	Chapter 12: Ecotourism	Chapter 2: Motivation for Leisure Tourism
Chapter 4: Tourism Economics	Chapter 16: Tourism in the Future	Chapter 6: Tourism Planning and Sustainability
Chapter 5: Tourism Policy and Organizations		Chapter 8: Attractions and Entertainment
Chapter 6: Tourism Planning and Sustainability		Chapter 10: Social Aspects of Tourism
Chapter 7: Tourism Research		Chapter 11: Cultural and Heritage Tourism
Chapter 8: Attractions and Entertainment		
Chapter 9: Business Travel: Meetings, Conventions, and Expositions		
Chapter 13: Tourism Distribution Organizations		
Chapter 14: Transportation		
Chapter 15: Lodging and Restaurants		
Chapter 16: Tourism in the Future		

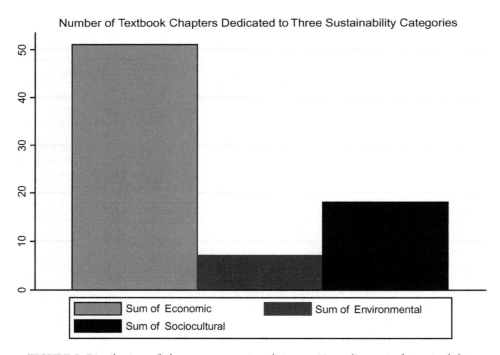

FIGURE 2 Distribution of chapter content in relation to Venn diagram of sustainability.

TABLE 5 Summary of the Content Analysis of Four Tourism Textbooks

Economic	Environmental	Sociocultural
53	7	21

market mix for initial tourism development" (Smith & Brent, 2001, p. 112). Smith's 4Hs are habitat, history, heritage, and handicraft. Habitat "refers to the physical landscape and its tourist attractions" including access, appeal, climate, landscape, and resources (Smith & Brent, 2001, p. 112). History was defined as the "record of contact with *outsiders* (Smith & Brent, 2001, p. 113) and was a useful function to gain insights in "assessing potential conflicts between government and individuals in decision-making" (Smith & Brent, 2001, p. 113). Heritage referred to the analysis "*by the resident population* of the traditional culture in terms of appropriateness for display and manner of display" (Smith & Brent, 2001, p. 113) in various settings such as museums, ceremonies, folk villages, ethnic centers, and festivals. Handicraft was referred to as "heritage crafts." According to Smith, market demand for tourism souvenirs often leads to "heterogenization of tourist art" and the "miniaturization of traditional art forms" and a "proliferation of new styles" (Smith & Brent, 2001, p. 114).

Despite this prestigious career, including several influential tourism-based studies (Smith, 1977, 1989; Smith & Brent, 2001), Smith's work is seldom mentioned in tourism-focused textbooks, either at the undergraduate or graduate level. Some textbooks address the foundational role of anthropology to tourism studies and anthropologists who study tourism (MacCannell, 1976; Nash, 2007), while others do not. A review of the body of the textbooks and their indexes revealed the extent to which Smith's work had been mentioned in the four chosen textbooks. Goeldner and Ritchie (2009, p. 268) mentioned Smith's "categories of tourism" but did not specifically mention her 4Hs or her place as a tourism pioneer. The index of Mill and Morrison (2009) did not include entries about Smith or Smith's work. Because the text was not electronically searchable with either Amazon or Google, a more thorough search of publisher-provided chapter overviews yielded no mention of Smith's contributions to tourism. Mill and Morrison did not mention Smith's work. Page (2009, p. 489) mentions Smith as the author of influential studies (Smith, 1977; Smith & Eadington, 1992), but none of the content of her studies is presented, and neither the 4Hs nor her pioneering status were mentioned. Walker and Walker (2011) do not cite the work of Smith. Thus, two of the four textbooks briefly touch on the foundational role of anthropology to tourism studies (Goeldner & Ritchie, 2009; Page, 2009). However, coverage is minimal.

TABLE 6 Valene Smith Videos Posted on the Duster121 YouTube Channel

Title of Video	Video URL
Overview of the 4Hs of Tourism	http://www.youtube.com/user/duster121#p/u/15/STUYz3tdf9Q
1 Habitat in the 4Hs of Tourism	http://www.youtube.com/user/duster121#p/u/16/SxdYWLNffig
2 Heritage in the 4Hs of Tourism	http://www.youtube.com/user/duster121#p/u/17/GOw9fAp8kOo
3 History in the 4Hs of Tourism	http://www.youtube.com/user/duster121#p/u/18/0eIBIJIT_yg
4 Handicraft in the 4Hs of Tourism	http://www.youtube.com/user/duster121#p/u/22/WnjcEfT68Qo
Early Beginnings: Valene Smith Bio 1	http://www.youtube.com/user/duster121#p/u/19/TQ8VH9xtjOc
First World Trip: Valene Smith Bio 2	http://www.youtube.com/user/duster121#p/u/20/vVZ4UC8PFMI
Daughter & Mom: Valene Smith Bio 3	http://www.youtube.com/user/duster121#p/u/21/C8QFOkt_ei8
Valene Smith's Museum of Anthropology	http://www.youtube.com/user/duster121#p/u/23/D38nsic78QE

In June 2010, Jeanne Rawlings, a videographer based in Chico, CA, posted on YouTube a series of high-quality professional videos commissioned by Smith on her life and work (see Table 6 and http://www.youtube.com/user/duster121). Five of the videos are dedicated to Smith's 4Hs. Additional videos look at the early beginnings of tourism from a cultural, anthropological, and historical perspective; chronicle Smith's world trips (at times with her mother), including the first American Express tour around the world in 1957 for which Smith was the tour guide; and give viewers an introduction to and virtual tour of the Valene L. Smith Museum of Anthropology located at Chico State University. The videos were filmed in Smith's Chico home and on the road, especially in Kotzebue, AK, a village where she conducted her thesis research among the Inupiat Eskimo and to which she has returned many times.

Because it usually takes years to conceive, write, and publish a new textbook or a newer edition of an existing textbook, turning to Web 2.0 technology, specifically YouTube, was thought to be an effective and efficient way to address, at least in part, the curricular imbalance revealed in this research. The videos were also chosen over assigning articles or book chapters penned by Smith due to the engaging quality of the videos.

In fall 2010, the videos of Smith's work and philosophy were shown in two introductory face-to-face tourism courses. Because YouTube videos had also been utilized to support other tourism topics, such as the route of the European Grand Tour, the rapid emergence of tourism in Abu Dhabi, and the role of the Santa Fe Railroad in tourism expansion into the Western United States, this was not a departure. The videos not only provided an infusion of engaging multimedia content into the course but also served to balance the curricula with the addition of interdisciplinary content and an introduction to anthropological foundations of tourism and highlighted the importance of the host–guest relationship. The videos invoked lively classrooms discussions, including a discussion of how "handicrafts" might also be viewed as a form of "heritage." Students were also inspired to see in Smith a role model of lifelong learning and six decades of world exploration. An assessment on the final exam presented students with a tourism scenario to describe in terms of Smith's 4Hs. Seventy-nine percent of the students received the maximum 25 possible points, which was considered an appropriate level of comprehension of the sociocultural content the videos brought to the tourism curricula.

CONCLUSION

As demonstrated through the high exam scores, the use of YouTube videos was an effective pedagogical tool for Net Gens, and their use had a demonstrable positive impact on student learning. The addition of YouTube videos to the curriculum not only engaged techno-savvy and visually oriented students but also was a free and immediate way to get the curriculum more up to date and in harmony with the TEFI values of stewardship, mutuality, and knowledge.

Additionally, the adoption of "new teaching methods and the Web 2.0 philosophy" (Liburd et al., 2011), along with the infusion of interdisciplinarity in the tourism curriculum (Mrnjavac & Pavia, 2011) and "different disciplinary perspectives" (Gretzel, Jamal, Stronza, & Nepal, 2008) afforded by the sociocultural content of the YouTube videos, was in harmony with TEFI's overall future-oriented goals for tourism education.

As one of the earliest pioneers of the anthropology of tourism, showcasing the works of Smith was an appropriate first step, but future additions to classroom instruction and textbooks could include the work of other foundational tourism scholars, including Dean MacCannell and other members of the aforementioned International Academy for the Study of Tourism, especially TEFI cofounders Pauline Sheldon and Daniel Fesenmaier. The work of academics from other supporting disciplines could also be considered.

There is also cause for a panel discussion of tourism industry professional and academics as to whether a proportional Venn diagram (with overlapping circles of equal size and implied weight) is the appropriate visualization for a balanced tourism curriculum and/or how much emphasis on each pillar of sustainability is the right focus to achieve the balance.

REFERENCES

Air France-KLM. (2011). *Together: Open & committed: Corporate social responsibility report, 2010–2011*. Retrieved from http://www.klm.com/csr/en/index.html

Barber, E. (2011). Case study: Integrating TEFI (Tourism Education Futures Initiative) core values into the undergraduate curriculum. *Journal of Teaching in Travel & Tourism, 11*(1), 38–75.

Berk, R. A. (2009). Multimedia teaching with video clips: TV, movies, YouTube, and mtvU in the college classroom. *International Journal of Technology in Teaching and Learning, 5*(1), 1–21.

Berk, R. A. (2010). How do you leverage the latest technologies, including Web 2.0 tools, in your classroom? *International Journal of Technology in Teaching and Learning, 6*(1), 1–13.

Bramwell, B., & Lane, B. (1993). Sustainable tourism: An evolving global approach. *Journal of Sustainable Tourism, 1*(1), 1–5.

Byrne, M. S. (2011, March 4). *Indexing Valene Smith's many contributions to the anthropology of tourism and international tourism studies*. Keynote speech delivered at Reflections and New Directions: A Conference on the Anthropology of Tourism in Honor of Valene L. Smith, Chico State University, Chico, CA.

Carson, R. (1962). *Silent spring*. Boston, MA: Houghton Mifflin.

Carson, R., & Gore, A. (1994). *Silent spring*. Boston, MA: Houghton Mifflin.

Cowper-Smith, A., & de Grosbois, D. (2011). The adoption of corporate social responsibility practices in the airline industry. *Journal of Sustainable Tourism, 19*(1), 59–77.

Echtner, C. M., & Jamal, T. B. (1997). The disciplinary dilemma of tourism studies. *Annals of Tourism Research, 24*(4), 868–883.

Edgell, D. L. (2006). *Managing sustainable tourism: A legacy for the future*. New York, NY: The Haworth Hospitality Press.

Goeldner, C. R., & Ritchie, J. R. B. (2009). *Tourism: Principles, practices, and philosophies* (11th ed.). Hoboken, NJ: John Wiley & Sons.

Graburn, N. (2007). Tourism through the looking glass. In D. Nash (Ed.), *The study of tourism: Anthropological and sociological beginnings* (pp. 93–107). Oxford, UK: Elsevier.

Gretzel, U., Jamal, T., Stronza, A., & Nepal, S. K. (2008). Teaching international tourism: An interdisciplinary, field-based course. *Journal of Teaching in Travel & Tourism, 8*(2/3), 261–282.

Gunn, C. A. (1991, July). *The need for multidisciplinary tourism education*. Paper presented at New Horizons in Tourism and Hospitality Education, Training, and Research, Calgary, AB, Canada.

Hall, C. M., & Lew, A. A. (2009). *Understanding and managing tourism impacts: An integrated approach*. New York, NY: Routledge.

Honey, M. (1998). *Ecotourism and sustainable development: Who owns paradise?* (2nd ed.). Washington, DC: Island Press.

InterContinental Hotels Group. (2011, April). *Corporate responsibility report*. Retrieved from http://www.ihgplc.com/index.asp?pageid=718#ref_cr

Jafari, J., & Aaser, D. (1988). Tourism as the subject of doctoral dissertations. *Annals of Tourism Research, 15*(3), 407–429.

Jafari, J., & Brent Ritchie, J. R. (1981). Toward a framework for tourism education: Problems and prospects. *Annals of Tourism Research, 8*(1), 13–34.

Jamal, T., & Jourdan, D. (2008). Interdisciplinary tourism education. In B. Chandramohan & S. J. Fallows (Eds.), *Interdisciplinary learning and teaching in higher education: Theory and practice* (pp. 105–123). London, UK: Routledge.

Liburd, J., Hjalager, A.-M., & Christensen, I.-M. (2011). Valuing Tourism Education 2.0. *Journal of Teaching in Travel & Tourism, 11*(1), 107–130.

MacCannell, D. (1976). *The tourist: A new theory of the leisure class.* New York, NY: Schocken Books.

MacCannell, D. (2009). *Niche tourism development: Theory and practice—Lesson 1.* Davis, CA: UC Davis Extension.

Merriam-Webster. (2008). *Merriam-Webster's collegiate dictionary* (11th ed.). New York, NY: Encyclopedia Britannica.

Mill, R. C., & Morrison, A. (2009). *The tourism system* (6th ed.). Dubuque, IA: Kendall Hunt Publishing.

Mrnjavac, E., & Pavia, N. (2011, May). *Interdisciplinarity in higher education courses for tourism: The case for Croatia.* Paper presented at the Tourism Education Futures Institute (TEFI) 2011 World Congress, Philadelphia, PA.

Nash, D. (2007). *The study of tourism: Anthropological and sociological beginnings* (1st ed.). Boston, MA: Elsevier Science.

Page, S. J. (2009). *Tourism management: Managing for change.* Oxford, UK: Butterworth-Heinemann.

Ritchie, J. R. B., & Zins, M. (1978). Culture as determinant of the attractiveness of a tourism region. *Annals of Tourism Research, 5*(2), 252–267.

Royal Caribbean. (2010). *2010 stewardship report.* Retrieved from http://www.royalcaribbean.com/ourCompany/environment/rcAndEnvironment.do

Sheldon, P. J., Fesenmaier, D. R., & Tribe, J. (2011). The Tourism Education Futures Initiative (TEFI): Activating change in tourism education. *Journal of Teaching in Travel & Tourism, 11*(1), 2–23.

Sheldon, P. J., Fesenmaier, D., Woeber, K., Cooper, C., & Antonioli, M. (2007). Tourism education futures, 2010–2030: Building the capacity to lead. *Journal of Teaching in Travel & Tourism, 7*(3), 61–68.

Sheldon, P. J., & Park, S.-Y. (2011). An exploratory study of corporate social responsibility in the U.S. travel industry. *Journal of Travel Research, 50*(4), 392–407.

Smith, V. L. (1977). *Hosts and guests: The anthropology of tourism.* Philadelphia, PA: University of Pennsylvania Press.

Smith, V. L. (1989). *Hosts and guests: The anthropology of tourism* (2nd ed.). Philadelphia, PA: University of Pennsylvania Press.

Smith, V. L., & Brent, M. (2001). *Hosts and guests revisited: Tourism issues of the 21st century.* New York, NY: Cognizant Communication Corp.

Smith, V. L., & Eadington, W. R. (Eds.). (1992). *Tourism alternatives: Potentials and problems in the development of tourism.* Philadelphia, PA: University of Pennsylvania Press.

Snelson, C. (2011). YouTube across the disciplines: A review of the literature. *MERLOT Journal of Online Learning and Teaching*, 7(1), 159–169. Retrieved from http://jolt.merlot.org/vol7no1/snelson_0311.htm

Tapscott, D. (2009). *Growing up digital: How the Net Generation is changing your world*. New York, NY: McGraw-Hill.

Tourism Education Futures Initiative. (2009). *A values-based framework for tourism education: Building the capacity to lead* [White paper]. Philadelphia, PA: Temple University. Retrieved from http://www.tourismeducationfutures.org

Urry, J. (1990). *The tourist gaze: Leisure and travel in contemporary societies*. London, UK: Sage Publications.

Walker, J. R., & Walker, J. T. (2011). *Tourism: Concepts and practices*. Upper Saddle River, NJ: Prentice Hall.

Walt Disney Company. (2011). *2010 corporate citizenship report*. Retrieved from http://corporate.disney.go.com/citizenship2010/downloads

Weaver, D. (2006). *Sustainable tourism: Theory and practice*. Burlington, MA: Butterworth-Heinemann.

Environmental Attitudes of Generation Y Students: Foundations for Sustainability Education in Tourism

PIERRE BENCKENDORFF

The University of Queensland, Queensland, Australia

GIANNA MOSCARDO and LAURIE MURPHY

James Cook University, Queensland, Australia

Sustainability is an ongoing theme in the tourism literature and is a growing concern in the wider area of business studies. As a consequence, there has been growing recognition of the need for sustainability education in programs for business and tourism students. The development of such programs needs to be based on a sound understanding of the existing values and attitudes of current students. This article reports a study that explored the environmental attitudes of a sample of Generation Y students in a business and tourism program using the New Environmental Paradigm Scale.

INTRODUCTION

In the last decade, there has been considerable pressure for (Bridges & Wilhelm, 2008; Rundle-Thiele & Wymer, 2010; Stubbs & Cocklin, 2007), and growth in the numbers of, sustainability-related courses in university business programs. Christensen, Peirce, Hartman, Hoffman, and Carrier (2007) reviewed curricula at the top 50 business schools named by *Financial Times* and found in some areas a fivefold increase since 1998 in offerings related to sustainability, with an increasing number of universities making such classes compulsory. This increase reflects a growing recognition that future business leaders will need to have the capacity to address environmental issues because they are likely to be held accountable for the social and environmental impacts of their actions (Dunphy, Griffiths, & Benn, 2007; Fukukawa, Shafer, & Lee, 2007). It also reflects a wider return to the incorporation of values into education at all levels (Moscardo & Murphy, 2011). This shift to the inclusion of sustainability in higher education programs can be seen most clearly in the rise of programs such as the Tourism Education Futures Initiative, which advocates a strong focus on sustainability by identifying stewardship as an important value (Sheldon, Fesenmaier, & Tribe, 2011), and the Principles of Responsible Management Education (2011), a United Nations-supported program aimed at encouraging management and business education activities to incorporate principles from the United Nations Global Compact.

But incorporating sustainability into higher education programs is not an easy task as it requires changes in values and behaviors beyond the classroom (Moscardo & Murphy, 2011). A core principle in constructivist models of learning is that knowledge is created by combining new information with existing understandings through engagement in learning experiences (Scardamalia & Bereiter, 2006). In these learning models, it is important to build educational programs on a sound understanding of existing levels of awareness of, and attitudes toward, the chosen topic (Gordon, 2009). Thus, if it is seen as important to incorporate sustainability into tourism business education, then the development of curricula and the specific learning activities within these curricula need to be designed with some understanding of existing knowledge and attitudes of the students. For example, if existing knowledge of a topic is limited and attitudes toward it are either not well formed or hostile, then it becomes important for learning activities to address gaps in knowledge and incorporate activities that encourage reflection about, and change in, current attitudes. Alternatively, if existing knowledge is extensive and attitudes are positive, then the design of the activities can be focused on extending and applying that knowledge.

This article reports a study focused on this aspect of sustainability education for tourism and business students. The research reported here has a number of aims. Firstly, the analysis will establish whether business and tourism students have a positive environmental worldview using Dunlap and Van Liere's (1978) New Environmental Paradigm (NEP). Secondly, the analysis will contrast the environmental attitudes of the current generational cohort of students, Generation Y, with previous studies examining other generational cohorts. Thirdly, the analysis will examine in more detail the nature of environmental attitudes within the sample looking particularly at differences in responses for different groups within the sample.

THE RISE OF A NEW ENVIRONMENTAL PARADIGM

Although the preservation movement can be traced back to the late 1890s with the formation of the Sierra Club, contemporary concern about the impact of human activities on the natural environment is often associated with the events of the 1960s (Mebratu, 1998). The 1960s followed the growth and prosperity of the postwar "golden years" and culminated in the counterculture and social revolution near the end of the decade. The youth involved in the social aspects of the counterculture movement were tagged as "hippies" and became associated with strong proenvironmental views and leftist ideology. According to Benton (1994), proenvironmental attitudes peaked during the early 1970s and declined moderately through the early 1980s before undergoing a resurgence in the 1990s. According to Forgas and Jolliffe (1994), the decline in the 1970s and early 1980s accompanied a period of economic growth and a rise in materialistic attitudes and conservative politics. In the 1990s, however, growing media coverage of various environmental issues contributed to another rise in environmental concern. In the 2000s, this concern also shifted from a focus on localized environmental issues to global challenges such as climate change (Mazur, 2006).

A number of authors have attempted to measure environmental attitudes during the last 40 years. This work has resulted in several scales, but the NEP framework proposed by Dunlap and Van Liere (1978) is by far the most widely used (Dunlap, 2008). The scale was designed to capture a shift in environmental concern from the dominant view (the environment as the unlimited, bountiful dominion of humans) to a new paradigm (the environment as limited and fragile) as proposed by Dunlap and Van Liere. The original NEP consisted of 12 items designed to measure attitudes toward ecological issues such as humankind's influence on the balance of nature, limits to growth on the human population, and whether humans should have rightful dominion over nature. Stern, Dietz, and Guagnano (1995) have suggested that the NEP Scale primarily measures a type of "folk ecological theory" of primitive beliefs about the Earth and human–environment relations. The original NEP was conceived as a single dimension, although later replications have reported that the items form between two and five dimensions. The scale was revised in 1991 to include 15 items and was renamed the New Ecological Paradigm (NEP). Although both the 12- and 15-item scales continue to be widely used, the revised NEP Scale was designed to improve the original in three main areas: (1) It taps a wider range of facets of an ecological worldview; (2) it offers a balanced set of pro- and anti-NEP items; and (3) it avoids outmoded terminology (Dunlap; Dunlap, Van Liere, Mertig, & Jones, 2000). Several studies have also used an abridged 6-item version of the original scale, while some researchers have also developed versions for use with children (Boeve-de Pauw, Donche, & Van Petegem, 2010; Manoli, Johnson, & Dunlap, 2007).

While subsequent studies employing the NEP Scale have examined differences in environmental attitudes across a range of variables, the general consensus is that younger, well-educated, and politically liberal persons tend to be more concerned about environmental quality than their older, less educated, and politically conservative counterparts (Dunlap et al., 2000). This is consistent with reviews of research into environmental attitudes beyond those using the NEP Scale (Torgler & Garcia-Valiñas, 2007). A broad review of the literature suggests that across a range of variables, age consistently has a strong association with environmental concern. However, the question of whether age differences are the result of life experience, family life-cycle stage, changing social, cultural, and economic conditions, or the influence of important historical events on generational cohorts has not received recent research attention (Torgler & Garcia-Valiñas).

THE ENVIRONMENTAL PARADIGMS OF UNIVERSITY STUDENTS

A number of researchers have examined the environmental attitudes of college and university students. A large early study by Thompson and Gasteiger (1985) is of immediate relevance to the aims of this article. Thompson and Gasteiger analyzed the environmental attitudes of Cornell University students in 1971 (3,414 respondents) and 1981 (3,867 respondents). The study indicated that the preference for an economic or materialistic lifestyle in the early 1980s was associated with less willingness to sacrifice material comforts for the cause of the environment. Following this work, Gigliotti (1992) used a modified NEP Scale to analyze a sample of 1,500 students at Cornell University in 1990 to determine whether they had changed their attitudes. The findings follow the pattern identified by Thompson and Gasteiger, with students in 1990 being more materialistic than the students of 1971 and 1981.

In contrast, a recent study of 932 university students in Spain indicated some concern among students about environmental problems. Some differences in environmental attitudes were also found between 1st-year students and final-year students and between male and female students (Fernández Manzanal, Rodráguez Barreiro, & Carrasquer, 2007). Bechtel, Verdugo, and de Queiroz Pinheiro (1999) used the NEP Scale to collect responses from 505 undergraduates from the United States, Mexico, and Brazil and identified interesting cross-cultural differences in the structure of environmental attitudes. Cross-cultural differences have also been reported in other studies (Rauwald & Moore, 2002; Schultz & Zelezny, 1999; Vikan, Camino, Biaggio, & Nordvik, 2007; Watson & Halse, 2005). One of the largest studies of the environmental attitudes of university students was conducted by Schultz and Zelezny to examine the relationship between values and attitudes. Survey data were obtained from university students in 14 countries, resulting in a sample of 2,160 respondents. While there were some clear distinctions between students from different countries, a regression analysis revealed a consistent pattern of findings across countries, with clear links between values and environmental attitudes.

A number of studies have examined the influence of sociodemographic variables on responses. A study of 365 college students in the United States found that males were slightly more likely than females to express environmental concern (MacDonald & Hara, 1994). Blaikie (1992) compared two Australian samples of university students and residents and found that the two samples were similar but that females exhibited stronger proenvironmental views. An evaluation of attitudes by age revealed a curvilinear relationship with a peak in proenvironmental attitudes between the ages of 30 and 40 years. Blaikie argued that these findings suggest that aging and cohort influences had produced a middle-aged cohort with the strongest commitment to the environment but that there is evidence that this commitment also extended back to the younger cohort (25 to 34 years old). Despite these observations, Blaikie did not actually attempt to directly compare generational cohorts of the same age as proposed by Moscardo and Benckendorff (2010).

Several authors have also examined the environmental attitudes of business students; however, specific studies focused on tourism students do not appear in the literature. Shetzer, Stackman, and Moore (1991) administered the NEP Scale to 237 undergraduate business students and found that the attitudes of the sample were strongly proenvironmental. No comparisons were made with other groups, so it is not known whether their sample of business students exhibited stronger or weaker proenvironmental attitudes than students studying in other disciplines.

Earlier work by Wysor (1983) compared the environmental perceptions and attitudes of environmental studies students and business students and reported that environmental studies students scored significantly higher on an environmental attitudes questionnaire. Likewise, Synodinos (1990) compared the environmental knowledge and attitudes of marketing and business students with environmental psychology students as well as with college students and members of the public from the early 1970s. Although Synodinos did not use the NEP Scale, he reported that business students were less environmentally conscious than the other groups of respondents. Benton (1994) used the Environmental Attitude and Knowledge Scale developed by Maloney, Ward, & Braucht (1975) to compare the environmental attitudes of business students to nonbusiness students. He found that although business students did not necessarily know any less about environmental issues, they were less likely to have proenvironmental views. A cross-cultural comparison of the environmental attitudes of business students by Benton and Funkhouser (1994) yielded similar conclusions.

Hodgkinson and Innes (2001) examined the environmental attitudes and ecological beliefs of 1st-year university students in different disciplines to explore whether students studying disciplines traditionally associated with economic rationalism (i.e., commerce and business studies) and with social and political conservatism (i.e., law) would be less likely to be proenvironment compared with students in more liberal disciplines. The findings suggested that although most university students hold positive attitudes toward the environment, different disciplines do attract students of a particular attitudinal orientation. Sociology, biology, and environmental studies students consistently displayed stronger positive beliefs and attitudes toward the environment than students in law, commerce, and computer studies.

GENERATIONAL COHORT THEORY

Although the literature review thus far suggests that, overall, current university students are likely to have proenvironmental attitudes, it also suggests caution in making assumptions with considerable variations in attitudes also found within the student samples. The review also suggests that age effects may be complex and related to both life-cycle stage and generational cohort with little attention paid to date to the latter concept. The concept of generational cohorts is not new and has a long history in the social sciences. Mannheim introduced the concept in the 1920s, and it has subsequently been used in sociology, psychology, and related areas such as political science (Braungart & Braungart, 1986; Elder, 1975, 1994; Mannheim, 1952; Ryder, 1965; Whittier, 1997). Generations or generational cohorts can be defined as "proposed groups of individuals who are born during the same time period and who experienced similar external events during their formative or coming-of-age years (i.e., late adolescent and early adulthood years)" (Noble & Schewe, 2003, p. 979). Formative events include the attitudes and behavior of parents as well as memorable events and shared experiences. It is argued that these shared formative experiences influence the worldview, behaviors, and values of an entire age cohort throughout their lifespan (Lyons, Duxbury, & Higgins, 2005; Mannheim). These formative experiences are significant because they help to shape specific preferences, beliefs, and psychographic tendencies. They influence how individuals from a particular cohort feel about sustainability, what their attitudes are, and how they might behave to satisfy their values and desires (Gursoy, Maier, & Chi, 2007).

Despite a lengthy history of use in sociology and psychology, generational cohorts can be difficult to study. Formative experiences that help to define a generation are not uniform across cultures and places. Moore (2005), for example, has noted some differences between American members of Generation Y and their Chinese counterpart, Generation *Ku*, but observes that the influence of American culture in the media is resulting in a global generation of members who are more alike than previous generations. It can also be difficult to distinguish between the influence of generational cohorts and life-cycle stage (McCrindle, 2009). It is common to claim that a certain generation shares a set of characteristics by simply comparing the different generations at one point in time. But the generations differ not only in age but also in terms of their life-cycle stages. Corvi, Bigi, and Ng (2007) further argue that one of the major challenges in deciphering the characteristics of a generational cohort is determining exactly what formative events or social conditions define each generation. Finally, it could be argued that generations are similar to cultures and that the study of Generation Y is a type of cross-cultural research suggesting that particular care needs to be taken in the construction of research methodologies and that one needs to explicitly recognize differences in values between those being researched and those doing the research (Moscardo & Benckendorff, 2010).

Generation Y has been heralded as the next big generation, a potentially powerful group that has the sheer numbers to transform society both as consumers and producers of goods and services. The majority of definitions of Generation Y include individuals born between 1977 and 1995, although some have argued that the generation extends until 2000 (Donnison, 2007). There are two challenges in defining this generation—the lack of a clear defining set of circumstances or formative event and a trend toward extended adolescence and young adulthood (Moscardo & Benckendorff, 2010). It has been claimed the current global financial crisis is a defining event for people currently aged between 12 and 30 years old (McQueen, 2010). Regardless of how the generation is defined, it is generally agreed that the second part of this generation is currently moving into higher education, and within the next decade, members of this generation will become the leaders, managers, and consumers of tourism experiences. A number of untested and often contradictory claims have been made about the characteristics of members of Generation Y and the specific mechanisms and early-life experiences that have shaped these characteristics (Moscardo & Benckendorff). Of particular interest to the present discussion are claims made about their values in relation to sustainability: that this is a green cohort, and that, like many other claimed characteristics, their environmental concerns are the result of not only their values but the parenting styles of their parents, who are predominantly baby boomers and whose own youth is strongly associated with the rise of the environmental movement.

Firstly, there are claims that this is a generation particularly concerned with environmental and social justice issues and that is therefore especially interested in sustainability practices in a range of areas (Burns, Reid, Toncar, Anderson, & Wells, 2008; Hanks, Odom, Roedl, & Blevis, 2008). Previous research has indicated that tourism and business students who are members of Generation Y are generally concerned about the environment and the potential for environmental problems to affect their future aspirations (Moscardo, Murphy, & Benckendorff, 2011). Many of the student samples reviewed earlier also include members of Generation Y, but with the exception of the work done by Thompson and Gasteiger (1985), Gigliotti (1992), and Synodinos (1990), very few recent studies have examined whether environmental attitudes have changed across generational cohorts. These earlier studies are all based on the attitudes of Generation X and previous generations. Even fewer studies have specifically focused on the environmental attitudes of business and tourism students. These students are of interest because they will be the future custodians, planners, policymakers, and managers of the tourism industry. Studies that have focused on business students have often not used the NEP to evaluate environmental attitudes. When the NEP has been used, the data have not been reported in sufficient detail to allow for meaningful subsequent comparisons. These problems make the task of tracking changes in business students' environmental attitudes across several generations somewhat challenging.

Secondly, there are numerous claims about the role of baby boomer parents in shaping the values and attitudes of Generation Y (Sheahan, 2005). But many of the claims assume a link, and often the results of this proposed baby boomer parenting style are contradictory and conflicting (Moscardo & Benckendorff, 2010). Although it has been suggested that this is an important explanatory mechanism, little detailed research has been published that directly links baby boomer parents to the attitudes and behaviors of their children.

Finally, it is also important to critically examine untested assumptions about the uniformity of Generation Y characteristics. Differences have been noted between cultures, social class, and educational level (Terjesen, Vinnicombe, & Freeman, 2007). Gender in particular has been highlighted as a variable mediating Generation Y responses in a number of areas (Burns et al., 2008; Quintal, Phau, & Sims, 2009; Terjesen et al.). Given that gender has also been associated with differences in environmental attitudes in general (Torgler & Garcia-Valiñas, 2007), this may be an important variable to examine in studies of Generation Y attitudes.

The following study seeks to address some of these shortcomings by surveying a sample of Generation Y students studying business and tourism. The article will examine the environmental attitudes of these students using Dunlap and Van Liere's (1978) NEP Scale. The analysis will contrast the NEP responses of Generation Y students with previous studies examining other generational cohorts. The article will also explore gender differences in environmental attitudes. Finally, the article will explore the age of students' parents to determine whether they may have influenced the environmental attitudes of their children.

METHODOLOGY

The data presented in this article were collected from a sample of undergraduate business and tourism students in a regional Australian university.

TABLE 1 Profile of Respondents

Characteristics	N	Percentage	Characteristics	N	Percentage
Gender			Living with parents	34	34%
Female	63	63%			
Male	37	37%	*Age groups* (mean = 21.8)		
			19 to 20	25	25%
Birthplace			21 to 22	53	53%
Australia	80	82%	23 to 25	16	16%
International	18	18%	Older than 25	6	6%
Data collection			Age of mother (mean)	49.4	
2008	47	36%	Age of father (mean)	51.6	
2009	84	64%			

Dunlap and Van Liere's (1978) original 12-item scale was used to allow for comparison with earlier studies. The sample consisted of 139 business and tourism students studying an undergraduate business research methods course in 2008 and 2009. In this subject, the issues and claims associated with Generation Y as consumers, employees, and future managers provided a focal point to illustrate the development of a research study. The data collected from students were used in statistics tutorials to provide real and relevant data on which to demonstrate the use of the Statistical Package for the Social Sciences for data analysis. The origin and development of the questionnaire items were explained after students completed the survey—not before; however, they had been introduced to the idea of somewhat unsubstantiated claims about Generation Y being more concerned about environmental issues. Screening of the data identified eight students who did not meet the definition of Generation Y adopted for this study (born 1977 through 1995), and these respondents were excluded from further analysis. Table 1 provides a profile of respondents. The majority of the sample was aged between 19 and 22 years old, making this a group that is in the latter part of the generation. Given the recent occurrence of events such as the global financial crisis, it may be that this group could differ from those that have preceded them. But the age profile is a good match to that used in earlier studies and so allows for a better comparison across the time series.

RESULTS AND DISCUSSION

The initial analysis provides an overview of the environmental attitudes of the sample based on the NEP Scale (see Table 2). Four of the 12 items were reverse-coded to maintain the directionality of the items so that a higher value indicates greater support for the environment. The statements that were reversed have also been reworded to their proenvironmental form to

TABLE 2 Descriptives and Factor Analysis of NEP Items

Statement (1 = strongly disagree to 5 = strongly agree)	N	Factor Loadings	% Agree	Mean	SD
Factor 1: Ecocentric (EV = 3.51; % Var = 29.22; α = .74)	126	—	—	3.73	0.67
1. We are approaching the limit of the number of people the Earth can support.	126	0.76	40.5	3.29	1.04
2. The Earth is like a spaceship with only limited room and resources.	126	0.70	77.0	3.89	1.01
3. The balance of nature is very delicate and easily upset.	124	0.63	78.2	3.94	0.86
4. When humans interfere with nature, it often produces disastrous consequences.	126	0.60	58.8	3.49	1.04
5. Mankind is severely abusing the environment.	124	0.58	82.3	4.06	0.89
Factor 2: Balanced Growth (EV = 1.46; % Var = 12.18; α = .59)	126	—	—	3.73	0.69
6. To maintain a healthy economy, we will have to develop a "steady state" economy where industrial growth is controlled.	126	0.76	72.2	3.76	0.85
7. There are limits to growth beyond which our industrialized society cannot expand.	124	0.72	50.0	3.37	1.00
8. Humans must live in harmony with nature to survive.	125	0.60	82.4	4.05	1.02
Factor 3: Anthropocentric (EV = 1.32; % Var = 10.96; α = .63)	126	—	—	3.69	0.75
9. Humans *do not* have the right to modify the natural environment.*	126	0.69	55.6	3.40	1.19
10. Humankind was *not* created to rule over the rest of nature.*	126	0.65	69.9	3.75	1.19
11. Plants and animals *do not* exist primarily to be used by humans.*	126	0.63	77.8	3.95	0.98
12. Humans need *to* adapt to the natural environment because they *cannot* remake it to suit their needs.*	125	0.62	65.6	3.65	1.10
NEP Score	126	—	—	3.72	0.53

*Reverse coded.

assist with interpretation of the results. Following the advice of Dunlap et al. (2000), the data were subjected to a principal components analysis using varimax rotation to explore the dimensions underlying students' responses. The analysis revealed three factors that explained 52.4% of the total variance. These factors are shown in Table 2 along with their factor loadings, eigenvalues, and Cronbach's alpha. Titles have been suggested for each of the three factors based on themes from the literature. An aggregate mean was calculated based on the values of individual items within each factor.

An overall NEP score has also been calculated by averaging the values for all scales across all respondents.

The results indicate strong and consistent proenvironmental views across all three factors. There is particularly strong recognition from students that mankind is severely abusing the environment and that humans will need to live in harmony with the environment to survive. This finding provides some support for claims that Generation Y is a green and environmentally conscious cohort.

Cross-Generational Comparisons

To compare the views of respondents in this study to other samples, an extensive search of the literature was conducted to identify similar studies using students. This search highlighted a number of challenges. Firstly, while a number of previous studies have applied the NEP to a student sample, surprisingly few studies provide detailed descriptive information such as means for individual items. Only studies that reported comparative descriptive data are included in the analysis below. The analysis presented in Table 3 includes a larger number of studies that have reported overall means for the NEP construct, while the second analysis shown in Table 4 includes a much smaller sample of studies that have provided means for individual scale items. Secondly, while some studies employed the original 12-item NEP scale, others have used the revised 15-item scale and a smaller number of studies have used an abridged 6-item version of the 12-item scale. Only scale items that align with the original 12 statements have been included in Table 4. Thirdly, authors have used various scales to measure respondent's attitudes, including scales of 4 points, 5 points, 7 points, and 10 points. To deal with this last challenge, the means from these studies were recalculated along a 5-point scale using a simple linear model.

The analysis presented in Table 3 shows a range of studies focused on the environmental attitudes of university students arranged in chronological order. During the past 30 years, 21 studies have resulted in a sample of more than 10,000 respondents. The overall mean across all of these studies is 3.76, but studies range from 3.24 to 4.11. The standard deviations indicate that some samples are relatively homogenous, while others show more variability. It is clear that there is a great deal of diversity in the sample sizes and number of scale items that have been used. It is useful to note the cultural background of various samples, as well as the gender mix and disciplinary background of students. Although the average age of respondents is fairly consistent, there are some samples that have focused on postgraduate students. A number of authors have found that these sociodemographic variables influence the outcomes of NEP responses. The data indicate that the current study is well positioned around the middle of the various sample means. Based on this analysis, it does not appear that Generation Y students

TABLE 3 Comparison of Current Study and Past Samples

Study	Country	Discipline	n	Gender (% male)	Mean Age	Scale Length	Mean NEP	SD NEP
Blaikie (1992)	Australia	Mixed	390	53	21	6	3.96	—
Furman & Erdur (1995)	Turkey	Mixed	144	49	—	12	3.83	0.45
Thapa (1999)	United States	Mixed	540	55	21	15	3.48	—
Schultz & Zelezny (1999)	Argentina	Social Sciences	54	41	24	15	3.83	0.45
	Canada	Social Sciences	96	28	23	15	4.11	0.40
	Colombia	Social Sciences	149	20	24	15	4.01	0.40
	Costa Rica	Social Sciences	213	36	26	15	4.08	0.45
	Dominican Republic	Social Sciences	121	44	21	15	3.75	0.37
	El Salvador	Social Sciences	194	36	26	15	3.69	0.45
	Ecuador	Social Sciences	201	47	28	15	3.93	0.43
	Mexico	Social Sciences	65	63	37	15	3.88	0.40
	Panama	Social Sciences	100	32	24	15	3.94	0.36
	Peru	Social Sciences	224	30	24	15	3.89	0.41
	Paraguay	Social Sciences	200	40	25	15	3.75	0.38
	Spain	Social Sciences	104	36	23	15	3.83	0.45
	United States	Social Sciences	245	29	21	15	3.67	0.53
	Venezuela	Social sciences	194	41	25	15	3.91	0.39
Hodgkinson & Innes (2001)	Australia	Mixed	391	40	21	12	4.05	0.63
Amérigo & Gonzalez (2001)	Spain	Mixed	165	31	21	15	3.58	0.42
Rauwald & Moore (2002)	Dominican Republic	Mixed	273	43	19	6	3.61	—
	Trinidad	Mixed	228	43	21	6	3.83	—
	United States	Psychology	257	26	18	6	3.78	—
Cordano, Welcomer, & Scherer (2003)	United States	Business	149	50	23	12	3.66	0.54
Cooper, Poe, & Bateman (2004)	United Kingdom	Environmental Science	200	—	—	15	3.88	—
Liu & Sibley (2004)	New Zealand	Mixed	1,924	51	—	8	3.88	0.74

(Continued)

TABLE 3 (Continued)

Study	Country	Discipline	n	Gender (% male)	Mean Age	Scale Length	Mean NEP	SD NEP
Schultz, Shriver, Tabanico, & Khazian (2004)	New Zealand	Mixed	224	—	—	6	3.8	0.66
	United States	Psychology	160	—	—	15	3.57	0.46
Kaiser, Hübner, & Bogner (2005)	Germany	Maths, Biology	468	17	23	15	4.08	0.45
Pahl, Harris, Todd, & Rutter (2005)	United Kingdom	Mixed	45	50	21	15	3.31	—
Schultz et al. (2005)	Brazil	Social Sciences	208	27	27	15	3.55	0.36
	Czech Republic	Social Sciences	113	34	24	15	3.8	0.42
	Germany	Social Sciences	120	25	26	15	4.02	0.34
	India	Social Sciences	210	34	20	15	3.5	0.40
	New Zealand	Social Sciences	217	33	25	15	3.74	0.44
	Russia	Social Sciences	120	84	18	15	3.64	0.40
Watson & Halse (2005)	Australia	Education	211	13	22	12	3.99	0.47
	Indonesia	Education	225	14	21	12	3.71	0.47
	Maldives	Education	199	20	21	12	3.44	0.40
Kortenkamp & Moore (2006)	United States	Psychology	112	29	19	15	3.57	0.58
Milfont, Duckitt, & Cameron (2006)	New Zealand	—	455	30	20	15	3.51	0.48
Shafer (2006)	United States	Master's of Business Administration	302	57	34	15	3.24	0.77
Vikan et al. (2007)	Norway/Brazil	Mixed	120	50	23	15	3.7	—
Shephard et al. (2009)	New Zealand	Mixed	539	31.5	—	15	3.52	1.06
Current Study (2011)	Australia	Business	126	37	22	12	3.73	0.53

Note. Adapted from Milfont and Duckitt (2010).

TABLE 4 Comparison of Individual NEP Items for Current Study and Available Past Samples

Authors	Dunlap & Van Liere (1978)	Blaikie (1992)	Thapa (1999)	Cooper et al. (2004)	Shafer (2006)	Vikan et al. (2007)	Shephard et al. (2009)	Current Study (2011)	Student Mean	SD
Sample	Community	Student	Student	Student	Student	Student	Student	Student		
Sample Size	806	390	540	200	302	120	539	139		
Country	United States	Australia	United States	United Kingdom	United States	Norway/ Brazil	New Zealand	Australia		
1. We are approaching the limit of the number of people the Earth can support.	3.67	—	3.39	3.94	3.15	3.10	3.48	3.29	3.39	0.30
2. The Earth is like a spaceship with only limited room and resources.	3.95	—	3.41	3.68	3.49	3.51	3.43	3.89	3.57	0.18
3. The balance of nature is very delicate and easily upset.	3.91	4.35	3.68	4.06	2.19	4.20	3.90	3.94	3.76	0.73
4. When humans interfere with nature, it often produces disastrous consequences.	3.71	3.94	3.68	4.10	3.62	3.75	3.71	3.49	3.76	0.20
5. Mankind is severely abusing the environment.	3.81	—	3.89	4.43	3.99	4.37	3.94	4.06	4.11	0.23
6. To maintain a healthy economy, we will have to develop a "steady state" economy where industrial growth is controlled.	3.47	—	—	—	—	—	—	3.76	—	—

(*Continued*)

TABLE 4 (Continued)

Authors	Dunlap & Van Liere (1978)	Blaikie (1992)	Thapa (1999)	Cooper et al. (2004)	Shafer (2006)	Vikan et al. (2007)	Shephard et al. (2009)	Current Study (2011)	Student Mean	SD
Sample	Community	Student	Student	Student	Student	Student	Student	Student		
Sample Size	806	390	540	200	302	120	539	139		
Country	United States	Australia	United States	United Kingdom	United States	Norway/ Brazil	New Zealand	Australia		
7. There are limits to growth beyond which our industrialized society cannot expand.	3.59	—	—	—	—	—	—	3.37	—	—
8. Humans must live in harmony with nature to survive.	4.36	4.43	—	—	—	—	—	4.05	4.24	0.27
9. Humans *do not* have the right to modify the natural environment.*	3.35	3.21	3.14	3.99	2.98	3.27	3.27	3.40	3.32	0.32
10. Humankind was *not* created to rule over the rest of nature.*	3.17	—	—	—	—	—	—	3.75	—	—
11. Plants and animals *do not* exist primarily to be used by humans.*	3.41	4.01	—	—	—	—	—	3.95	3.98	0.04
12. Humans need *to* adapt to the natural environment because they *cannot* remake it to suit their needs.*	4.00	3.82	—	—	—	—	—	3.65	3.74	0.12
NEP Mean	3.70	3.96	3.53	4.03	3.24	3.70	3.62	3.72	3.69	0.27

*Reverse coded.

Note. Dunlap and Van Liere's (1978) original study employed a 4-point scale. The means from this study were redistributed along a 5-point scale using a simple linear model.

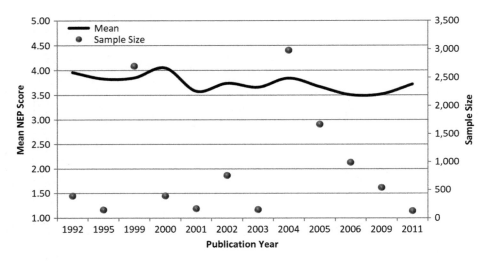

FIGURE 1 NEP Scale mean scores and total sample sizes by year of publication.

are any less or more disposed toward a positive environmental worldview than previous generations. To highlight this pattern of results, the samples and means for each year were combined and plotted on the chart shown in Figure 1. The figure indicates that in spite of the range of cultural backgrounds, gender distributions, and sample sizes, the mean NEP score has remained relatively stable between 1992 and 2011. This time period includes students who were members of Generation X (1990s) as well as Generation Y (2000s).

The next step of the analysis was to examine individual NEP Scale items to explore whether there have been major shifts in the attitudes of students during the last 20 years. This analysis is limited to only six studies, which provided full descriptive data suitable for comparison with the current study. For benchmarking purposes, Dunlap and Van Liere's (1978) original study is also included, although this work was based on a community sample. The analysis is presented in Table 4. Missing data are due to the use of different scales by authors. The current study again compares well with the range of student studies conducted between 1992 and 2009. While the publication date for Blaikie's study was 1992, the data were actually collected in 1989. Most university students at this time would have been members of Generation X. Thapa's study in 1999 captures the "cuspers," late Gen Xers and early Gen Ys. Shafer's (2006) study was focused on master's of business administration students and provides a good comparative sample for mature baby boomers and Generation Xers. The remainder of the studies conducted during the 2000s covers mostly Generation Y students.

Figure 2 provides a visual summary of the data to more fully understand the key patterns and to contrast the current study more clearly with

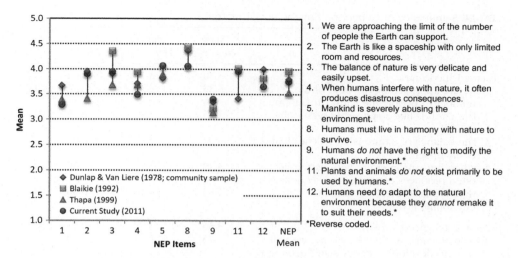

FIGURE 2 Comparison of current study with past generational cohorts.

the earlier work of Blaikie (1992) and Thapa (1999). It is clear from this figure that the environmental attitudes of the current Generation Y sample are not dramatically different to other generational cohorts. There are several possible interpretations for these patterns. Firstly, it could be that proenvironmental attitudes are most strongly linked to life-cycle stage and educational level and that this is an enduring pattern across cohorts. This raises questions about changes in environmental attitudes across life-cycle stages. Alternatively, it could be that a certain level of proenvironmental concern has become embedded in our cultural consciousness, making it difficult to measure and detect significant changes.

Intragenerational Analyses

The analysis now returns to the current study to further explore gender differences. An independent *t*-test indicates a number of significant differences between male and female students. The scores for female students are consistently higher for items that were significant, indicating stronger proenvironmental attitudes. There was also a significant difference between the overall NEP score for males and females (Table 5). The difference between males and females is particularly noticeable for the anthropocentric factor. These results are not entirely unexpected. Gender differences in environmental attitudes have been researched extensively, and although there are some inconsistencies (cf. Milfont & Duckitt, 2010), research during the last decade suggests that females are more likely to express proenvironmental attitudes than males (Casey & Scott, 2006; Shephard, Mann, Smith, & Deaker, 2009; Zelezny, Chua, & Aldrich, 2000).

TABLE 5 Influence of Gender on Environmental Attitudes

	Male (n = 37)	Female (n = 63)	t-score	Sig.
Factor 1: Ecocentric	3.70	3.78	−0.62	0.54
1. We are approaching the limit of the number of people the Earth can support.	3.38	3.30	0.37	0.71
2. The Earth is like a spaceship with only limited room and resources.	3.95	3.83	0.55	0.58
3. The balance of nature is very delicate and easily upset.	3.94	3.95	−0.04	0.97
4. When humans interfere with nature, it often produces disastrous consequences.	3.19	3.71	−2.50	0.01
5. Mankind is severely abusing the environment.	4.03	4.13	−0.56	0.58
Factor 2: Balanced Growth	3.56	3.78	−1.50	0.14
6. To maintain a healthy economy, we will have to develop a "steady state" economy where industrial growth is controlled.	3.73	3.71	0.09	0.93
7. There are limits to growth beyond which our industrialized society cannot expand.	3.06	3.66	−3.02	0.00
8. Humans must live in harmony with nature to survive.	3.86	3.98	−0.53	0.60
Factor 3: Anthropocentric	3.43	3.91	−3.26	0.00
9. Humans *do not* have the right to modify the natural environment.*	3.08	3.73	−2.82	0.01
10. Humankind was *not* created to rule over the rest of nature.*	3.62	3.90	−1.16	0.25
11. Plants and animals *do not* exist primarily to be used by humans.*	3.68	4.11	−2.12	0.04
12. Humans need *to* adapt to the natural environment because they *cannot* remake it to suit their needs.*	3.32	3.89	−2.56	0.01
NEP Score	3.57	3.83	−2.26	0.03

*Reverse coded.

The final analysis was based on the notion in generational cohort theory that generations are shaped by events that occurred during their formative years. Parents play an important role in these formative years, and parental style and attitudes are believed to influence the attitudes of their children. To explore this idea, the analysis presented in Table 6 examined Generation Y students' environmental attitudes based on the birth year of their parents. Mothers and fathers were divided into two groups using 1960 as the dividing year. This date was selected because the literature suggests that the 1960s were an important decade in the development of the environmental movement. It is likely that parents born before 1960 would have been old enough during the 1960s and 1970s to appreciate many of the events that were occurring around them. Parents born after the 1960s would not yet have been in their teens when key events related to the counterculture

TABLE 6 Influence of Parental Age on Environmental Attitudes

	Mother's Birth Year				Father's Birth Year			
	<1960 (n = 52)	>1960 (n = 43)	t-score	Sig.	<1960 (n = 64)	>1960 (n = 31)	t-score	Sig.
Factor 1: Ecocentric	3.92	3.62	2.29	0.02	3.85	3.59	1.75	0.08
1. We are approaching the limit of the number of people the Earth can support.	3.63	3.07	2.87	0.01	3.55	3.00	2.57	0.01
2. The Earth is like a spaceship with only limited room and resources.	4.06	3.74	1.52	0.13	4.02	3.65	1.63	0.11
3. The balance of nature is very delicate and easily upset.	4.16	3.76	2.33	0.02	4.09	3.66	2.34	0.02
4. When humans interfere with nature, it often produces disastrous consequences.	3.62	3.49	0.60	0.55	3.52	3.55	−0.14	0.89
5. Mankind is severely abusing the environment.	4.14	4.02	0.62	0.54	4.06	4.10	−0.17	0.87
Factor 2: Balanced Growth	3.81	3.60	1.45	0.15	3.76	3.61	0.89	0.38
6. To maintain a healthy economy, we will have to develop a "steady state" economy where industrial growth is controlled.	3.79	3.65	0.76	0.45	3.72	3.74	−0.12	0.91
7. There are limits to growth beyond which our industrialized society cannot expand.	3.57	3.31	1.25	0.21	3.56	3.16	1.85	0.07
8. Humans must live in harmony with nature to survive.	4.08	3.84	1.07	0.29	3.98	3.94	0.21	0.84
Factor 3: Anthropocentric	3.85	3.60	1.59	0.12	3.76	3.68	0.50	0.62
9. Humans do not have the right to modify the natural environment.*	3.56	3.49	0.29	0.77	3.42	3.68	−1.00	0.32
10. Humankind was not created to rule over the rest of nature.*	3.98	3.56	1.76	0.08	3.94	3.58	1.41	0.16
11. Plants and animals do not exist primarily to be used by humans.*	4.12	3.74	1.84	0.07	4.03	3.74	1.33	0.19
12. Humans need to adapt to the natural environment because they cannot remake it to suit their needs.*	3.73	3.60	0.53	0.60	3.65	3.71	−0.24	0.81
NEP Score	3.87	3.61	2.36	0.02	3.80	3.62	1.39	0.17

and the social revolution occurred. As a result, these two groups of parents, although both classed as baby boomers, may have exhibited different attitudes and parental styles that may have impacted their Generation Y children. A t-test was conducted to explore differences based on the birth year of both mothers and fathers.

Although the results are not dramatic, they do highlight some significant contrasts. The overall pattern of results suggests that students raised by parents born before 1960 were more likely to exhibit proenvironmental views. These differences were, however, only statistically significant at the $p < .05$ level for items that made up the ecocentric factor. In the case of mothers, the differences are sufficient to influence the overall NEP score. Although these results offer a somewhat simplistic attempt at identifying the influence of parents on their children, the significant differences warrant further investigation.

IMPLICATIONS AND CONCLUSIONS

The results of this study can be seen as having implications in three main areas—for research into environmental attitudes, for our understanding of Generation Y as a the main cohort among current university students, and for the development of effective sustainability education for tourism. The present study used the NEP Scale because it has been the most commonly used measurement of environmental attitudes in the last 30 years and so the only scale that allows for cross-generational analyses. It has been criticized, however, especially in terms of its continuing relevance. Lalonde and Jackson (2002) argued that public awareness of, and attitudes toward, environmental issues have become much more sophisticated in the 30 years since the original NEP Scale was developed and that the scale's items are so broad that they tell us little about these more complex attitudes. In addition, it could be argued that with a growing awareness of environmental issues, responses to the scale have become more influenced by social desirability biases (Wise, 2010). If these two criticisms are valid, this would make it difficult to detect changes in attitudes over time and in particular cohort differences. Certainly high proenvironmental attitudes across all samples, consistent with a social desirability bias, make it difficult to detect significant changes, and this could explain some of the cross-generational results in the present study. This would suggest that further research is needed into the environmental attitudes of current students using a wider range of more complex measures. Despite the potential limitations of the NEP Scale as a measurement tool, the results of the present study offer a number of implications for our understanding of Generation Y as a cohort. Firstly, the significant differences in environmental attitudes associated with gender confirm the importance of recognizing heterogeneity within the generation and the dangers of assuming that claimed characteristics are uniform. Secondly, the lack of difference in student population responses to the NEP Scale over time also alerts us to the possibility that attributes of today's students could be more to do with their life cycle or developmental stage than their cohort. It is important that research into generational cohorts is designed so that this important distinction can be detected. Further, if it is a life-cycle or developmental stage, then it becomes important to understand how environmental attitudes may change during the course of life. Finally, the present study provides some preliminary evidence that parental values and behaviors may be important variables influencing Generation Y. Although this finding has been suggested in the existing Generation Y literature, this is one of the first empirical studies to demonstrate a link.

Finally, and of most importance to the present article, are the implications of the research for sustainability education. As noted in the Introduction, in a constructivist approach to learning, it is important to develop educational experiences that build upon existing knowledge and that take existing values and attitudes into account. In the present case, the pattern of results suggests that in general, tourism students are likely to be open to discussions and activities around the environmental dimensions of sustainability. In most tourism classes, there is likely to be a preexisting level of environmental awareness and support for an environmental rather than economic paradigm. Additionally, the data revealed generally low standard deviations suggesting there was a reasonable level of consensus around these attitudes within the group. This consensus can provide additional support for sustainability activities in the classroom as not only are individuals supportive, but it is also likely that they know that their views are shared among others. In the theory of planned behavior, this level of social support is important in enhancing the link between attitudes and behavioral intentions and between behavioral intentions and actual behaviors (Fielding, McDonald, & Louis, 2008).

But within this overall pattern of results, the present sample did have lower scores on items related to limits to growth and the extent to which humans should adapt to the environment rather than changing the environment. In this particular sample, the students are part of a larger business program and it may be that a business disciplinary orientation supports a progrowth perspective. What cannot be determined from this study is whether the individuals choose business to fit their preexisting attitudes or whether their experience of more general business and tourism education contributes to these attitudes. In either case, it is important to review all aspects of a curriculum to ensure that there is consistency in the way sustainability is addressed.

In conclusion, this study provides preliminary evidence that tourism students are likely to be receptive to educational programs on the environmental dimensions of sustainability. But such programs will need to be integrated throughout a curriculum as having sustainability, as a separate component is unlikely to encourage changes in attitudes toward things like growth and human adaptation of environments. Finally, the study provides baseline data for evaluating the effectiveness of future environmental sustainability activities and experiences in subsequent classes with these students.

REFERENCES

Amérigo, M., & Gonzalez, A. (2001). Los valores y las creencias medioambientales en relación con las decisiones sobre dilemas ecológicos [The relationship of values and environmental beliefs to decisions about ecological dilemmas]. *Estudios de Psicología, 22*, 65–73.

Bechtel, R. B., Verdugo, V. C., & de Queiroz Pinheiro, J. (1999). Environmental belief systems. *Journal of Cross-Cultural Psychology, 30*(1), 122–128.

Benton, R. (1994). Environmental knowledge and attitudes of undergraduate business students compared to nonbusiness students. *Business & Society, 33*(2), 191–211.

Benton, R., & Funkhouser, G. R. (1994). Environmental attitudes and knowledge: An international comparison among business students. *Journal of Managerial Issues, 6*(3), 366–381.

Blaikie, N. W. H. (1992). The nature and origins of ecological world views: An Australian study. *Social Science Quarterly, 73*(1), 144–165.

Boeve-de Pauw, J., Donche, V., & Van Petegem, P. (2010). Adolescents' environmental worldview and personality: An explorative study. *Journal of Environmental Psychology, 31*(2), 109–117.

Braungart, R., & Braungart, M. (1986). Life-course and generational politics. *Annual Review of Sociology, 12*(1), 205–231.

Bridges, C. M., & Wilhelm, W. B. (2008). Going beyond green: The "why and how" of integrating sustainability into the marketing curriculum. *Journal of Marketing Education, 30*(1), 33–46.

Burns, D. J., Reid, J., Toncar, M., Anderson, C., & Wells, C. (2008). The effect of gender on the motivation of members of Generation Y college students to volunteer. *Journal of Nonprofit & Public Sector Marketing, 19*(1), 99–118.

Casey, P. J., & Scott, K. (2006). Environmental concern and behavior in an Australian sample within an ecocentric-anthropocentric framework. *Australian Journal of Psychology, 58*(2), 57–67.

Christensen, L. J., Peirce, E., Hartman, L. P., Hoffman, W. M., & Carrier, J. (2007). Ethics, CSR, and sustainability education in the Financial Times Top 50 global business schools: Baseline data and future research directions. *Journal of Business Ethics, 73*(4), 347–368.

Cooper, P., Poe, G. L., & Bateman, I. J. (2004). The structure of motivation for contingent values: A case study of lake water quality improvement. *Ecological Economics, 50*(1/2), 69–82.

Cordano, M., Welcomer, S. A., & Scherer, R. F. (2003). An analysis of the predictive validity of the New Ecological Paradigm Scale. *The Journal of Environmental Education, 34*(3), 22–28.

Corvi, E., Bigi, A., & Ng, G. (2007, December). *The European Millennials versus the U.S. Millennials: Similarities and differences.* Paper presented at the International Business Research Conference, Sydney, Australia.

Donnison, S. (2007). Unpacking the Millennials: A cautionary tale for teacher education. *Australian Journal of Teacher Education, 32*(3), 1–13.

Dunlap, R. E. (2008). The New Environmental Paradigm Scale: From marginality to worldwide use. *The Journal of Environmental Education, 40*(1), 3–18.

Dunlap, R. E., & Van Liere, K. D. (1978). The 'New Environmental Paradigm': A proposed measuring instrument and preliminary results. *Journal of Environmental Education, 9,* 10–19.

Dunlap, R. E., Van Liere, K. D., Mertig, A. G., & Jones, R. E. (2000). Measuring endorsement of the New Ecological Paradigm: A revised NEP scale. *Journal of Social Issues, 56*(3), 425–442.

Dunphy, D., Griffiths, A., & Benn, S. (2007). *Organizational change for corporate sustainability* (2nd ed.). London, UK: Routledge.

Elder, G. (1975). Age differentiation and the life course. *Annual Review of Sociology, 1*(1), 165–190.

Elder, G. (1994). Time, human agency, and social change: Perspectives on the life course. *Social Psychology Quarterly, 57*(1), 4–15.

Fernández Manzanal, R., Rodríguez Barreiro, L., & Carrasquer, J. (2007). Evaluation of environmental attitudes: Analysis and results of a scale applied to university students. *Science Education, 91*(6), 988–1009.

Fielding, K. S., McDonald, R., & Louis, W. R. (2008). Theory of planned behavior, identity, and intentions to engage in environmental activism. *Journal of Environmental Psychology, 29*(2), 318–326.

Forgas, J. P., & Jolliffe, C. D. (1994). How conservative are Greenies? Environmental attitudes, conservation, and traditional morality among university students. *Australian Journal of Psychology, 46*(3), 123–130.

Fukukawa, K., Shafer, W. E., & Lee, G. M. (2007). Values and attitudes toward social and environmental accountability: A study of MBA students. *Journal of Business Ethics, 71*(4), 381–394.

Furman, A., & Erdur, O. (1995). Environmental attitudes among Bogazici university students: Testing the 'environmentalist' hypothesis. *Review of Social, Economic, and Administrative Studies, 9,* 109–122.

Gigliotti, L. M. (1992). Environmental attitudes: 20 years of change? *Journal of Environmental Education, 24*(1), 15–26.

Gordon, M. (2009). Toward a pragmatic discourse of constructivism: Reflections on lessons from practice. *Educational Studies, 45,* 39–58.

Gursoy, D., Maier, T., & Chi, C. (2007). Generational differences: An examination of work values and generational gaps in the hospitality workforce. *International Journal of Hospitality Management, 27,* 448–458.

Hanks, K., Odom, W., Roedl, D., & Blevis, E. (2008, April). *Sustainable Millennials: Attitudes toward sustainability and the material effects of interactive technologies.* Paper presented at the 26th Annual SIGCHI Conference on Human Factors in Computing Systems, Florence, Italy. Retrieved from http://dx.doi.org/10.1145/1357054.1357111

Hodgkinson, S. P., & Innes, J. M. (2001). The attitudinal influence of career orientation in 1st-year university students: Environmental attitudes as a function of degree choice. *The Journal of Environmental Education*, *32*(3), 37–40.

Kaiser, F. G., Hübner, G., & Bogner, F. X. (2005). Contrasting the theory of planned behavior with the value belief norm model in explaining conservation behavior. *Journal of Applied Social Psychology*, *35*(10), 2150–2170.

Kortenkamp, K. V., & Moore, C. F. (2006). Time, uncertainty, and individual differences in decisions to cooperate in resource dilemmas. *Personality and Social Psychology Bulletin*, *32*(5), 603.

Lalonde, R., & Jackson, E. L. (2002). The New Environmental Paradigm Scale: Has it outlived its usefulness? *Journal of Environmental Education*, *33*(4), 28–36.

Liu, J. H., & Sibley, C. G. (2004). Attitudes and behavior in social space: Public good interventions based on shared representations and environmental influences. *Journal of Environmental Psychology*, *24*(3), 373–384.

Lyons, S., Duxbury, L., & Higgins, C. (2005). An empirical assessment of generational difference in work-related values. *Human Resources Management*, *26*, 62–71.

MacDonald, W. L., & Hara, N. (1994). Gender differences in environmental concern among college students. *Sex Roles*, *31*(5), 369–374.

Maloney, M. P., Ward, M. P., & Braucht, G. N. (1975). Psychology inaction: A revised scale for the measurement of ecological attitudes and knowledge. *American Psychologist*, *30*, 787–790.

Mannheim, K. (1952). The problem of generations. In K. Mannheim & P. Kecskemeti (Eds.), *Essays on the sociology of knowledge* (pp. 276–322). London, UK: Routledge & Kegan Paul.

Manoli, C. C., Johnson, B., & Dunlap, R. E. (2007). Assessing children's environmental worldviews: Modifying and validating the New Ecological Paradigm Scale for use with children. *The Journal of Environmental Education*, *38*(4), 3–13.

Mazur, A. (2006). Risk perception and news coverage across nations. *Risk Management*, *8*, 149–174.

McCrindle, M. (2009). *Seriously cool: Marketing, communicating, and engaging with the diverse generations*. Retrieved from http://www.mccrindle.com.au

McQueen, S. (2010). *The 'new' rules of engagement*. New York, NY: Morgan James Publishing.

Mebratu, D. (1998). Sustainability and sustainable development: Historical and conceptual review. *Environmental Impact and Assessment Review*, *18*, 493–520.

Milfont, T. L., & Duckitt, J. (2010). The Environmental Attitudes Inventory: A valid and reliable measure to assess the structure of environmental attitudes. *Journal of Environmental Psychology*, *30*(1), 80–94.

Milfont, T. L., Duckitt, J., & Cameron, L. D. (2006). A cross-cultural study of environmental motive concerns and their implications for proenvironmental behavior. *Environment and Behavior*, *38*(6), 745–767.

Moore, R. (2005). Generation Ku: Individualism and China's millennial youth. *Ethnology*, *44*(4), 357–376.

Moscardo, G., & Benckendorff, P. (2010). Myth busting: Generation Y and travel. In P. Benckendorff, G. Moscardo, & D. Pendergast (Eds.), *Tourism and Generation Y* (pp. 16–26). Oxfordshire, UK: CAB International.

Moscardo, G., & Murphy, L. (2011). Towards values education in tourism: The challenge of measuring the values. *Journal of Teaching in Tourism and Travel*, *11*(1), 76–93.

Moscardo, G., Murphy, L., & Benckendorff, P. (2011). Generation Y and travel futures. In I. Yeoman, C. H. C. Hsu, K. A. Smith, & S. Watson (Eds.), *Tourism and demography* (pp. 87–99). Woodeaton, Oxford, UK: Goodfellow Publishers.

Noble, S., & Schewe, C. (2003). Cohort segmentation: An exploration of its validity. *Journal of Business Research*, *56*(12), 979–987.

Pahl, S., Harris, P., Todd, H. A., & Rutter, D. (2005). Comparative optimism for environmental risks. *Journal of Environmental Psychology*, *25*(1), 1–11.

Principles of Responsible Management Education. (2011). *The principles for responsible management education*. Retrieved from http://www.unprme.org/the-6-principles/index.php

Quintal, V., Phau, I., & Sims, D. (2009, November–December). *Exploring gender differences in Generation Y's purchase intentions of prototypical and me-too brands*. Paper presented at the Australian and New Zealand Marketing Academy Conference 2009, Melbourne, Australia.

Rauwald, K. S., & Moore, C. F. (2002). Environmental attitudes as predictors of policy support across three countries. *Environment and Behavior*, *34*(6), 709–739.

Rundle-Thiele, S. R., & Wymer, W. (2010). Stand-alone ethics, social responsibility, and sustainability course requirements. *Journal of Marketing Education*, *32*(1), 5–12.

Ryder, N. (1965). The cohort as a concept in the study of social change. *American Sociological Review*, *30*, 843–861.

Scardamalia, M., & Bereiter, C. (2006). Knowledge building: Theory, pedagogy, and technology. In K. Sawyer (Ed.), *Cambridge handbook of the learning sciences* (pp. 97–118). New York, NY: Cambridge University Press.

Schultz, P., Gouveia, V. V., Cameron, L. D., Tankha, G., Schmuck, P., & Frank, M. (2005). Values and their relationship to environmental concern and conservation behavior. *Journal of Cross-Cultural Psychology*, *36*(4), 457–475.

Schultz, P., Shriver, C., Tabanico, J. J., & Khazian, A. M. (2004). Implicit connections with nature. *Journal of Environmental Psychology*, *24*(1), 31–42.

Schultz, P., & Zelezny, L. (1999). Values as predictors of environmental attitudes: Evidence for consistency across 14 countries. *Journal of Environmental Psychology*, *19*(3), 255–265.

Shafer, W. E. (2006). Social paradigms and attitudes toward environmental accountability. *Journal of Business Ethics*, *65*(2), 121–147.

Sheahan, P. (2005). *Generation Y: Surviving (and thriving) with Generation Y at work*. Melbourne, Australia: Hardie Grant.

Sheldon, P. J., Fesenmaier, D. R., & Tribe, J. (2011). The Tourism Education Futures Initiative (TEFI): Activating change in tourism education. *Journal of Teaching in Travel & Tourism*, *11*(1), 2–23.

Shephard, K., Mann, S., Smith, N., & Deaker, L. (2009). Benchmarking the environmental values and attitudes of students in New Zealand's postcompulsory education. *Environmental Education Research*, *15*(5), 571–587.

Shetzer, L., Stackman, R. W., & Moore, L. F. (1991). Business-environment attitudes and the New Environmental Paradigm. *Journal of Environmental Education*, *22*(4), 14–21.

Stern, P. C., Dietz, T., & Guagnano, G. A. (1995). The New Ecological Paradigm in social-psychological context. *Environment and Behavior, 27*(6), 723–743.

Stubbs, W., & Cocklin, C. (2007). Teaching sustainability to business students: Shifting mindsets. *International Journal of Sustainability in Higher Education, 9*(3), 206–221.

Synodinos, N. E. (1990). Environmental attitudes and knowledge: A comparison of marketing and business students with other groups. *Journal of Business Research, 20*(2), 161–170.

Terjesen, S., Vinnicombe, S., & Freeman, C. (2007). Attracting Generation Y graduates: Organizational attributes, likelihood to apply, and sex differences. *Career Development International, 12*(6), 504–522.

Thapa, B. (1999). Environmentalism: The relation of environmental attitudes and environmentally responsible behaviors among undergraduate students. *Bulletin of Science, Technology, & Society, 19*(5), 426–438.

Thompson, J. C., & Gasteiger, E. L. (1985). Environmental attitude survey of university students 1971 versus 1981. *Journal of Environmental Education, 17*(1), 13–22.

Torgler, B., & Garcia-Valiñas, M. A. (2007). The determinants of individuals' attitudes towards preventing environmental damage. *Ecological Economics, 63*, 536–552.

Vikan, A., Camino, C., Biaggio, A., & Nordvik, H. (2007). Endorsement of the new ecological paradigm. *Environment and Behavior, 39*(2), 217–228.

Watson, K., & Halse, C. M. (2005). Environmental attitudes of preservice teachers: A conceptual and methodological dilemma in cross-cultural data collection. *Asia-Pacific Education Review, 6*(1), 59–71.

Whittier, N. (1997). Political generations, microcohorts, and the transformation of social movements. *American Sociological Review, 62*(5), 760–778.

Wise, P. (2010). *An improved approach to community segmentation as the foundation for environmental behavioral change communication.* Sydney, Australia: Ipsos-Eureka Social Research Institute. Retrieved from http://www.ipsos.com.au/IESRI/lib/IpsosEureka_EnvironmentalSegmentation.pdf

Wysor, M. S. (1983). Comparing college students' environmental perceptions and attitudes. *Environment and Behavior, 15*(5), 615–645.

Zelezny, L. C., Chua, P. P., & Aldrich, C. (2000). New ways of thinking about environmentalism: Elaborating on gender differences in environmentalism. *Journal of Social Issues, 56*(3), 443–457.

Future Higher Education in Tourism Studies and the Labor Market: Gender Perspectives on Expectations and Experiences

CARLOS COSTA, INÊS CARVALHO, SANDRA
CAÇADOR, and ZÉLIA BREDA
University of Aveiro, Aveiro, Portugal

Although women prevail among tourism graduates in Portugal, men earn higher salaries and fill most top-level positions in the tourism sector. This study diagnoses disparities between male and female tourism graduates in the following domains: areas of activity, positions, and salary. Expectations of students are compared to the real situation of tourism graduates. Data from a survey covering all Portuguese higher education institutions with tourism degrees were used. It is concluded that male graduates have more favorable situations in employment than female graduates do and that the reality in the labor market is far from corresponding to enrolled students' expectations.

This article results from a research project being carried out on gender issues in the tourism sector. The authors would like to thank the support provided by the Portuguese Foundation for Science and Technology and the Commission for Citizenship and Gender Equality, as well as the cofinancing of the European Union through the National Strategic Reference Framework, European Regional Development Fund, and the Operational Program for Competitiveness Factors. The authors would also like to thank Statistics Portugal (Instituto Nacional de Estatística) for providing part of the data, which were essential for the conduction of this research.

INTRODUCTION

Tourism is a great contributor to the generation of employment in Portugal. According to the World Travel & Tourism Council (2011), tourism is responsible for 18.4% of Portuguese employment. This is due to the fact that tourism is a labor-intensive sector, crucial for the Portuguese economy. However, the nature and conditions of the employment generated often reinforce inequalities and reproduce social stratification. Hence, tourism should not be regarded as a "panacea" for job creation (Jordan, 1997).

Although the majority of tourism workers have low levels of education (Costa, Carvalho, & Breda, 2011; Santos & Varejão, 2006), there is an increasing number of holders of higher education degrees in tourism studies. However, it is observed that despite women being the majority of such degree holders, men hold upper-management and decision-making positions more often than women do, besides earning better salaries (European Commission, 2004; Purcell, 1997). This situation raises not only ethical issues but also economic, because it suggests that human resources with better education and training are being undervalued and underutilized.

The aim of this article is to analyze the employment situation of tourism higher education graduates in Portugal in terms of levels of education, fields of activity, leadership positions, and salaries. Gender differences in these variables are examined, and the expectations concerning the labor market of students enrolled in tourism higher education are compared to the actual situation of graduates.

In the first section, literature on gender issues in education and employment, particularly in the tourism field, is reviewed, taking into account both the Portuguese and the international contexts. The impact on employment of having a higher education degree in tourism is studied, as is Portugal's profile in terms of gender and employment.

In the following section, the methodology adopted in the presented study is put forward. The data used stem from a survey carried out in Portugal within an ongoing research project and were used to examine the employment expectations and employment conditions of tourism students and graduates, respectively. Predictive Analytics Software (PASW) was used to perform the univariate and bivariate statistical analyses. Microdata from the Employment Survey, which is carried out by Statistics Portugal (Instituto Nacional de Estatísticsa [INE]), are also used. These data are used to establish some comparisons between the sample used in the study, namely tourism graduates, and workers from all economic fields.

Not only are disparities between female and male graduates analyzed, but the expectations of tourism students are also compared with the real employment situations of graduates in the same field of study. Moreover, INE data allow for comparisons between tourism graduates and workers in the overall economy in Portugal. The need to rethink tourism higher education in Portugal is advocated.

GENDER PATTERNS IN TOURISM HIGHER EDUCATION AND EMPLOYMENT

Women are increasingly better educated than men. Worldwide, there are more young women than men enrolled in tertiary education, except in sub-Saharan Africa, Southern Asia, and Oceania (United Nations, 2009). In the European Union (EU), the percentage of women in tertiary education has also surpassed that of men (Eurostat, 2011), because women account for 55.3% of students at this level. In Portugal, this tendency is also observable, given that 53.5% of higher education graduates are female (Eurostat, 2011) and 52.1% of doctoral scholarships awarded by the Portuguese Foundation for Science and Technology (2011) are granted to women.

However, prevailing gender stereotypes still shape male and female choices concerning the fields of study preferred. In the EU, women represent only 37.5% of students pursuing science, mathematics, and computing degrees and 24.8% of those pursuing engineering, manufacturing, and construction degrees (Eurostat, 2011). In Portugal, the majority of male enrollments in higher education programs are in the fields of engineering, manufacturing, and construction, whereas female enrollments prevail in the fields of health and social protection, education and social sciences, commerce, and law. Tourism studies are one of these female-dominated areas (Gabinete de Planeamento, Estratégia, Avaliação e Relações Internacionais – Ministério da Ciência, Tecnologia e Ensino Superior, 2009).

Despite women's improvements in the field of education, there is still a long path to follow if the same progress is to be seen in the employment field. Female unemployment rates are still higher than male rates (Eurostat, 2010; Ferreira, 2007); women are more represented in precarious and part-time jobs than men (Donlevy & Silvera, 2007; Parrett, n.d.; Sinclair, 1997b); and women tend to earn lower salaries and fill lower positions in the occupational hierarchy (Hemmati, 2000; Parrett; Ranftl, 2006). The main causes underlying gender inequalities pointed out in the literature are the splitting of tasks between men and women, gender stereotypes, practices embedded within corporate culture, structural characteristics of companies, and the fact that, though apparently gender-neutral, companies and society itself reproduce gender (Bruni, Gherardi, & Poggio, 2004; Commission of the European Communities, 2009; Guerreiro & Pereira, 2006; Jordan, 1997; Parrett; Purcell, 1997).

In the particular case of Portugal, it distinguishes itself among the other Southern European countries due to its high rate of female employment, around 65% (Guerreiro & Pereira, 2007). Moreover, there is a particularly high participation of women in full-time employment, namely of working mothers (76%), as compared with most EU countries (60% on average; Eurostat, 2005). In Portugal, there is a general agreement that both spouses should contribute to the family budget. This prevalence is partly justified by the fact that it is necessary for both partners to work in most cases, so that they can reach decent income levels (Torres, Silva, Monteiro, & Cabrita, 2005), because salaries in Portugal are below the EU average. However, in what concerns the gender pay gap, as well as the horizontal and vertical segregation of employment, Portugal does not differ from the other EU countries, because employment is segregated along gender lines and women earn significantly lower salaries compared with men as well (Santos & Varejão, 2006; Torres et al.).

Nonetheless, as argued by Scott (1997), women's higher education raises their expectations and leads them to aspire for jobs that suit their qualifications. However, some authors point out that there are differences between the expectations of young men and women concerning the labor market. Blau and Ferber (1991) point out that young women tend to expect similar starting salaries but anticipate lower earnings in subsequent years.

As far as the tourism sector is concerned, gender research has been published in areas such as employment (Moore & Wen, 2009; Sinclair, 1997a); women's empowerment (Hemmati, 2000; Swain, 1993); and analysis of tourism development within a gender-aware framework (Kinnaird & Hall, 1996).

As to the relationship between education, gender, and tourism employment, most studies devoted to this topic adopt an econometrical approach (Bañuls & Casado-Díaz, 2010; Thrane, 2008, 2010; Vartiainen, 2002). Bañuls and Casado-Díaz unveiled that in the Spanish context, returns to education (i.e., the increase in salary associated with an additional year of study) are higher for men (8.39%) than for women (3.13%). The gap in returns to education between young male workers (7.7%) and young female workers (1.9%) is particularly remarkable. According to Vartiainen, women with good educational qualifications in well-remunerated occupations in Finland lag behind their male counterparts endowed with similar characteristics. Hence, these studies suggest that possessing higher levels of education does not necessarily lead to gender equality in the labor market.

In fact, Purcell (1997) stated that despite the female penetration of career occupations that might result from the increasing presence of women in higher education, female graduates are still less likely than their male counterparts to have a career leading to mainstream management, because "initial inequalities of access are reinforced by subsequent early career moves" (p. 52). In this author's opinion, it is more common for female graduates to have had negative experiences during their supervised work experience year and less common for them to obtain the kind of job they want. In addition, they have more difficulties than male graduates in finding jobs that offer them intrinsic satisfaction and good career prospects, as well as "'professional" salaries with accompanying fringe benefits (Purcell, p. 50).

Unfairness is more likely to occur 3 or 4 years after graduation than right after its completion (Trickey, 2009). In the United Kingdom, after this relatively short period, there is already a sharp pay gap, of £2,000, between the median pay of male and female full-time workers (Trickey, 2009). Gender inequalities in employment occur across most economic sectors, and tourism is one of the sectors where these inequalities persist. This sector has a sharp vertical segregation, despite the fact that the majority of tourism workers are women (European Commission, 2004; Hemmati, 2000; Parrett, n.d.).

In the Portuguese context, research on gender issues in the tourism sector has been conducted only by a few authors (Costa et al., 2011; Reis, 2000; Santos & Varejão, 2006), but there is evidence of sharp inequalities in this sector. Even though 60.1% of tourism workers are female, male workers occupy most top-level and best-paid positions (Costa et al.). Moreover, this sector has one of the widest gender pay gaps, given that women earn 26.3% less than men (Costa et al.).

Particularly underresearched is the relationship between education, gender, and tourism employment in Portugal. The situation of male and female tourism graduates in the labor market has not been studied yet, nor have the expectations of female and male Portuguese students concerning employment. Therefore, in the following sections, the main results of a study carried out in Portugal in this field will be presented and discussed.

DATA AND METHODOLOGY

This study aims to analyze the employment situation of tourism graduates, as well as the expectations of students enrolled in these degrees concerning the labor market. The empirical study underlying the present research was based on two surveys, one directed at male and female graduates in tourism studies, and the other targeting male and female students enrolled in higher education degrees in this field. The aim of targeting both enrolled students and graduates was to compare the actual employment situation of those already graduated with the expectations toward the labor market of those who were still pursuing their studies. The surveys were launched online.

The degrees taken into account for the present study were those included in the National Classification of Fields of Education and Training under the subareas "Hospitality" and "Tourism and Leisure." All Portuguese institutions with these higher education degrees were contacted and asked for the databases with the contacts of all current and former students. Because some institutions did not provide their databases, the coordinators of tourism degrees in each institution were asked to forward the link leading to the Web version of the surveys to their current and former students.

Several e-mails were sent to the coordinators until a satisfactory number of responses was obtained from each institution. From the beginning of December 2010 to mid-March 2011, 3,017 respondents participated in the study (1,692 graduates and 1,325 enrolled students). After a consistency analysis, 2,989 surveys were considered valid (1,688 from graduates and from 1,301 enrolled students).

Microdata from the Employment Survey (INE, 2009) were analyzed. It provides a background for the situation of Portuguese workers in general, against which data obtained in the empirical study are compared. These data also provide information on workers employed in some of the main tourism subsectors (accommodation, food and beverage, and travel agencies and tour operators), thus allowing for comparisons between tourism workers, regardless of their levels of education, and tourism graduates. The software PASW was used for the univariate and bivariate statistical analysis of the data provided both by the survey underlying this research and by INE's Employment Survey.

GRADUATES AND ENROLLED STUDENTS IN TOURISM HIGHER EDUCATION IN PORTUGAL

In this section, after a broad characterization of the sample in terms of gender composition, levels of education, and percentage of employed individuals, several domains are analyzed concerning graduates' employment and enrolled students' expectations on employment—namely, fields of activity, leadership positions, and salaries. Gender comparisons are established, as are comparisons between students and graduates. INE's Employment Survey data from 2009 are used so that the results from our empirical study can be contrasted with those derived from this data set, which encompasses both workers in the economy as a whole and, more specifically, workers from the subsectors of accommodation, food and beverage, and travel agencies, tour operators, and tour guides.

Gender Composition, Levels of Education, and Employment Rates

It is estimated that there are 19,082 tourism graduates in Portugal, from the academic year 1986–1987 until the academic year 2008–2009. There are 8,395 students enrolled in tourism degrees in 2009–2010. Hence, the sample obtained in the empirical study, 3,017 individuals, corresponds to more than 10% of the population.

The graduates and the enrolled students' samples have a similar gender distribution: 31.6% of the graduates are men and 68.4% are women, whereas 32% of the students are men and 68% are women (Figure 1).

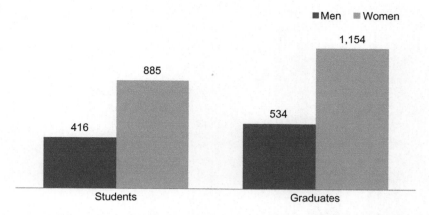

FIGURE 1 Number of individuals surveyed by type of survey and gender.

About 95% of the enrolled students are attending a *Licenciatura*,[1] whereas about 3% are attending a master's program and only about 1% are attending postgraduate and doctorate programs. Female students outnumber male students in all these levels of education. Concerning the graduates' sample, men are also outnumbered by women in all levels of education. However, a higher concentration of female graduates can be seen in the lower levels of education (bachelor's and *Licenciatura*), while male graduates are more likely than their female counterparts to be holders of higher degrees (postgraduate, master's, and doctorate). Men account for about half of the doctorate subsample, even though they represent less than a third of all the graduates (Figure 2).

Employment rates were 74.4% for male graduates and 75.1% for female graduates. It is observed that the higher the levels of education are, the higher the percentage of those employed tends to be (Figure 3).

Apart from tourism degrees, the respondents also possess nontourism degrees: *Licenciaturas* (4.2% of women and 3.9% of men) and postgraduate (2.9% of women and 4.1% of men).

Fields of Activity: Preferences and Expectations Versus Reality

The fields where enrolled students would rather work are travel agencies and tour operators, accommodation, recreation and leisure services, and national tourism organizations (Figure 4). The least-chosen areas are transportation and rent-a-car. Some of these areas are mostly preferred by male students (e.g., food and beverage, transportation, deconcentrated organs

---

[1]   *Licenciaturas* were traditionally 5-year degrees, but their length was reduced to 3 years with the recent introduction of the Bologna process.

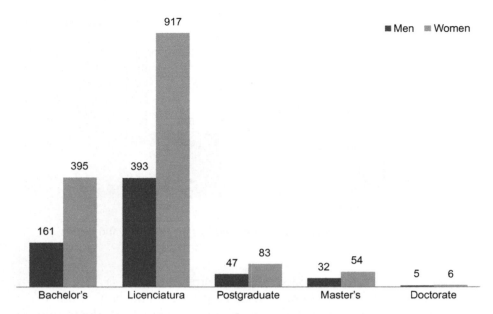

FIGURE 2 Number of individuals surveyed by level of education and gender.

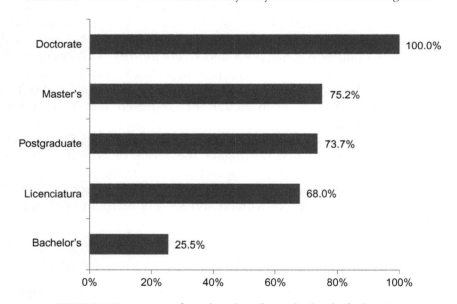

FIGURE 3 Percentage of employed graduates by level of education.

of central government, and development agencies), while other fields are mostly preferred by female students (e.g., travel agencies and tour operators, as well as recreation and leisure services).

Concerning the areas where most graduates work, it is surprising to observe that 28.4% of those employed are working outside the tourism

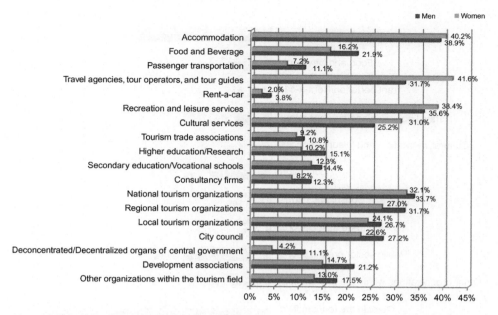

FIGURE 4 Fields of activity in the tourism sector preferred by enrolled students, by gender.

sector (Figure 5). If the salaries by field of activity are analyzed, it can be concluded that the salaries of these graduates are lower than the salaries of those graduates employed within the tourism field. Whereas those working in the tourism field earn about €600 (US$788.70) to €899 (US$1,181.74), those working outside the tourism field only earn slightly above the Portuguese minimum salary between €475 (US$624.39) and €599 (US$787.39). This hints at difficulties in finding a job within the tourism sector and at either a saturation of the labor market or a lack of recognition of tourism degrees, because working outside the tourism sector does not seem to be a voluntary choice for these graduates, given that salaries are particularly low.

Of those who are employed in tourism, the majority work in accommodation. Other significant areas are travel agencies and tour operators, as well as education and public sector organizations.

Among those who live outside Portugal, the percentage of nontourism workers is much lower than that for the general sample (15.6%). This subgroup of graduates also earns salaries below the average for graduates living abroad (29% lower). Thus, these data suggest that working outside the tourism sector might not have been a voluntary choice for these graduates either and that they might have been pushed to that due to constraints to find a job in the tourism field. Nonetheless, the size of the sample ($N = 42$) limits the conclusions that can be drawn.

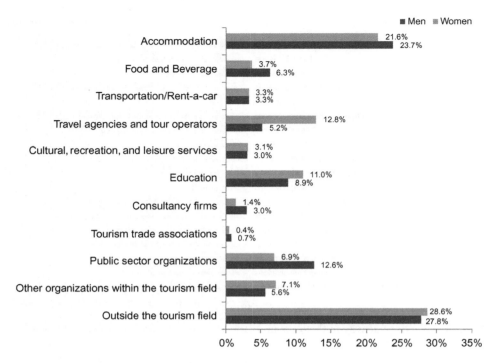

FIGURE 5 Tourism graduates employed by field of activity and gender.

Part-Time and Full-Time Employment

It was analyzed whether the respondents worked full time or part time, and in the cases where they worked part time, the reasons were examined. The majority of respondents work full time; nonetheless the gender disparity is remarkable, given that while 8% of men work part time, 33% of women do so. According to the literature, part-time work implies several disadvantages. Besides salaries being lower, the conditions of the work itself tend to be worse and there are more obstacles to career progression (European Commission, 2004).

The main reason pointed out by enrolled students for working part time is being engaged in studying or training (89.5% of male and 76.2% of female students), whereas graduates mostly mentioned not having found a full-time job (72.8% of male and 53.4% of female graduates). Hence, part-time work cannot be said to be a "real" choice.

If INE's Employment Survey is analyzed, some differences can be observed. According to that survey, it is women who, in greater proportion, mention that they work part time because they did not find a full-time job (47% of women vs. 33% of men working in the tourism sector), whereas it is men who more commonly mention study or training (30% of men vs. 9% of women). Personal reasons have a much greater importance in the decision to work part time in the INE database (24% of women, 20% of men), as compared with the database of this empirical study (only 1.4% of women and 0% of men).

Additionally, the students were asked if they planned to work part or full time after finishing their degree: 10.4% of male and 8.9% of female students mentioned a preference for part-time work. Thus, it suggests that the gap observed between male and female respondents concerning part-time work is not related to a female preference for such type of work but by other kinds of factors, namely those related with the labor market or with study/ training. The great majority of these respondents state that they would like to work this way to have time for themselves or more free time. However, there is a significant gender difference, because this is the most important reason for 65.8% of women, but only for 55% of men. The second most common reason is to continue studying or training. A greater proportion of women chose this option (27.4% of women vs. 22.5% of men). The most striking gender differences are among those who mentioned the conciliation with other projects or activities as the main reason for wanting to work part time (15% of male vs. 0% of female respondents), as well as among those who mentioned taking care of children (8.2% of women but only 0.7% of men).

Leadership Positions

There are more female than male tourism graduates in leadership positions. However, given the fact that more women than men were interviewed, the percentage of leaders within each gender should be used to compare the proportion of women and men in leadership positions. In this case, it can be concluded that the proportion of men in leadership positions almost doubles that of women: Whereas 29.4% of male graduates hold leadership positions, only 14.8% of female graduates do so (Figure 6).

There are also more male than female respondents among those who are not leaders but would like to hold such positions: 82.7% of men compared with 74.8% of women. Nonetheless, the gender gap concerning the willingness to have a leadership position is not as wide as the gender gap in the occupation of leadership positions (Figure 6).

The proportion of respondents with leadership positions is higher than that in INE's Employment Survey. According to this survey, 29.4% of male graduates and 14.8% of female graduates working in the tourism sector hold leadership positions, as compared with 25.5% of male and 11.7% of female respondents in the tourism subsample of the Employment Survey. This might be explained by the fact that the sample under analysis in the present study is only composed by individuals with a higher education degree, which might predispose them to fill higher-level positions within companies. In addition, it can be observed that both in the sample used for this study and in the

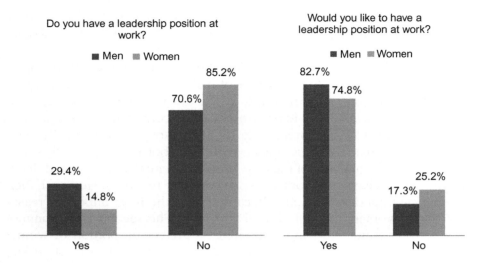

FIGURE 6 Tourism graduates by occupation of leadership positions and willingness to occupy leadership positions.

tourism subsample of INE's Employment Survey, there is a higher proportion of individuals with leadership positions than in the general sample of the Employment Survey (3.8% of all men and 1.8% of all women). The fact that there is a greater amount of small-sized companies in the tourism sector (Gabinete de Estratégia e Planeamento, 2007) might account for the higher proportion of leadership roles.

Among enrolled students, those who state that they would like to be in leadership represent a higher proportion of respondents than in the graduates subsample (5.3% higher for male students and 3.3% higher for female students).

Expected and Real Salaries

To analyze pay, monthly salaries were used. The majority of graduates, both male and female, earn between €600 (US$788.70) and €899 (US$1,181.74) per month. However, while women prevail in all salary categories below €900 (US$1,183.05), men prevail in all the salary categories above this amount. Female graduates are 3 times more represented than male graduates in salary levels below €474 (US$623.07), while the latter are 3 times more represented than the former above the €2,500 (US$3,286.25) to €2,999 (US$3,942.19) level and 10 times more above the €3,000 (US$3,943.50) level. Furthermore, male respondents' median salaries are higher than female respondents' median salaries: €900 (US$1,183.05) to €1,199 (US$1,576.09) and €600 (US$788.70) to €899 (US$1,181.74), respectively. The differences between the average wages of

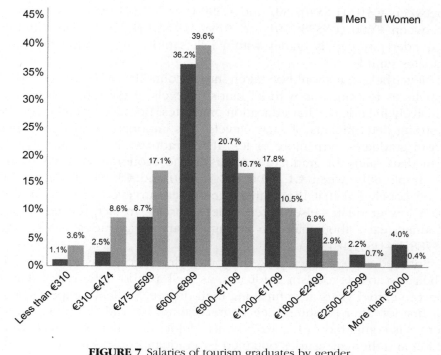

FIGURE 7 Salaries of tourism graduates by gender.

female and male graduates are significant, $t(348,02) = 6,59$, $p < .001$, $r = .33$, 95% CI [226.72;419.75], and show that female graduates earn, on average, between €227 (US$298.39) and €420 (US$552.09) less than male graduates (Figure 7).

The average monthly salary of tourism graduates living outside Portugal is €1,726 (US$2,268.83), which is much higher than the average salary for graduates living in Portugal (€960.23 [US$1,262.22]). This suggests that these graduates have more favorable situations in employment. However, pay inequalities persist even among these graduates. For example, 91.7% of male graduates earn more than €1,200 (US$1,577.40), as compared with only 60.9% of female graduates. The average net monthly salary of male graduates ($M = $ €2,019.79 [US$2,655.01]; $SE = 270.23$) is higher than that of female graduates ($M = $ €1,572.72 [US$2,067.34]; $SE = 184.43$). This corresponds to a 22% gender pay gap,[2] which is slightly lower than that for the overall sample (26%).

If these results are compared to INE data, it can be concluded that in that data set, female salaries are lower (albeit male salaries are not), both in the economy as a whole and in the tourism sector. The median female salary

---

[2]   The gender pay gap is the difference between male and female earnings expressed as a percentage of male earnings.

is between €310 (US$407.50) and €599 (US$787.39), whereas for men, it is between €600 (US$788.70) and €899 (US$1,181.74). It seems thus that the gender pay gap is higher within INE sample than within the tourism graduates sample.

Nevertheless, it should be taken into account that whereas the INE data set includes respondents with all kinds of levels of education, our data set exclusively includes higher education graduates. Because levels of education are strong determinants of salary levels, it is important to analyze whether tourism graduates earn more or less than graduates in general. Given that the median salary of graduate workers in the economy as a whole in the INE sample is between €1,200 (US$1,577.40) and €1,799 (US$2,364.79), it can be concluded that the tourism graduates surveyed in our study earn well below graduates elsewhere in the economy. In fact, female graduates in tourism earn about half the average salary of a graduate (€600–€899 [US$788.70–US$1,181.74]).

Enrolled students were asked about their expectations regarding salary in their first job as tourism graduates, as well as about the salary that they expect to earn 5 years after finishing their degree. Students' expectations for their first job after finishing their degree cannot be said to be unrealistic, if Figure 8 is compared to Figure 7, which depict the salaries expected in the first job and the real salaries obtained by graduates, respectively.

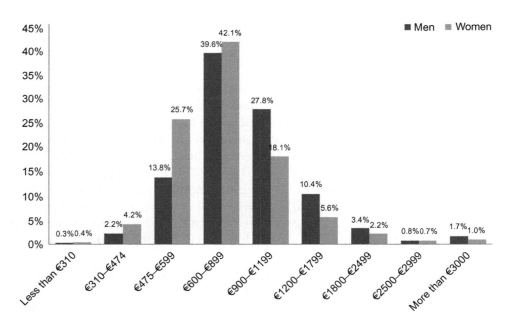

FIGURE 8 Salaries expected by tourism students in the first job after finishing their degrees.

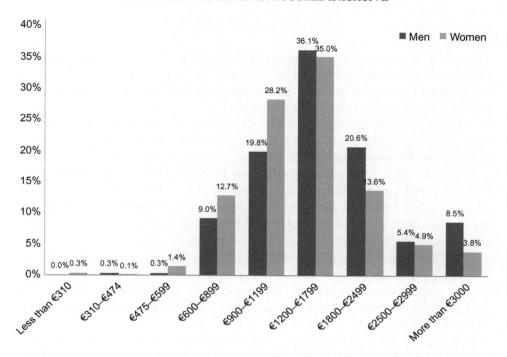

FIGURE 9 Salaries expected by tourism students 5 years after finishing their degrees.

However, students expect a significant raise in their salaries 5 years after finishing their degree (Figure 9). Only 0.6% of male and 1.8% of female students expect to earn less than €599 (US$787.39) at that stage. However, a significant proportion of graduates earn salaries below this level: 12.3% of men and 29.3% of women. This hints at a broad gap between students' expectations and reality.

Whereas the mode for the actual salary that graduates are receiving is €600 (US$788.70) to €899 (US$1,181.74), the mode concerning expectations of students is much higher, €1,200 (US$1,577.40) to €1,799 (US$2,364.79). Concerning expectations, male students prevail in all the salary levels above €1,200 (US$1,577.40), while female students predominate in the lower levels. Particularly in the salary level above €3,000 (US$3,943.50), there is a very wide gap between expectations and reality, particularly for female students: Those who expect such salaries are almost 10 times more than those who actually earn such salaries. The expectations of enrolled students are thus highly unrealistic. It can also be concluded that although female students' expectations are lower than male students' expectations, women's expectations are still further from reality than men's expectations.

DISCUSSION OF RESULTS

This study aimed to examine gender differences in the employment situation of graduates in tourism studies in Portugal, as well as to compare the real employment situation of these graduates with the expectations of students enrolled in the same field of education.

It was concluded that nowadays, women prevail in higher education and, more specifically, in tourism higher education. Despite that, several inequalities between men and women persist in the labor market (e.g., gender pay gap, lack of representation of women in upper-management positions, etc.). Even though higher education has the potential to raise the expectations of women and lead them to search for jobs that suit their qualifications, several studies demonstrate that having higher levels of education does not lead to equality between male and female salaries.

In Portugal, women outnumber men in higher education, and the tourism field is no exception. Gender inequalities in the employment situation of male and female tourism graduates were examined. In addition, the expectations of students were compared to data concerning the employment of tourism graduates.

It was found that a strikingly high percentage of tourism graduates are working outside the tourism field. This suggests that the labor market is failing to meet the expectations of students, either because it is saturated or because the skills earned by tourism graduates are not adequately recognized and valued by the labor market.

The field of activity preferred by tourism students is hospitality, and it is indeed in this tourism subsector that most graduates are employed. Although recreation and leisure services is one of the areas preferred by students, it only employs a low proportion of graduates. Concerning public sector organizations (national, regional, and local tourism organizations, as well as city councils and deconcentrated/decentralized organs of central government), these also gather the preference of a significant number of students. Yet, these organizations do not absorb a great percentage of tourism graduates either.

The proportion of tourism graduates in leadership positions is high if a comparison is established with data from the INE Employment Survey. This might be due to a higher presence of small-sized businesses in the tourism sector. There is a significant gender gap in the fulfillment of leadership roles; however, this gap does not seem to be justifiable by the gender gap in the preference for these positions. Even though more men than women aim to be leaders, the disparity between men and women's willingness to have such a role is not nearly as high as the disparity observed between the actual number of male and female leaders. This suggests that it is either due to the labor market or other kinds of constraints that the gap in upper management is observable.

Salaries earned by tourism graduates are low, particularly if these are compared to those of the graduates in general who were surveyed by INE. There is also a gender gap in expectations, because women expect lower salaries than men do. Nevertheless, the real gender gap in salaries is much wider than the gender gap in expectations. Moreover, students' expectations concerning salaries 5 years after finishing a degree exceed by far the salaries earned by graduates.

The data suggest that graduates living abroad have better jobs than the ones who live in Portugal, because they have much higher salaries. However, the gender pay gap is maintained, albeit being slightly narrower.

It can thus be concluded that there is a significant gender gap, particularly in leadership positions and salaries, not justifiable by differences in expectations. In addition, salaries earned by graduates are much lower than what students expect, and what is more, a very large proportion of graduates fail to find a job within the tourism field. Tourism students' expectations are likely to be thwarted once they reach the labor market.

LIMITATIONS OF THE STUDY

The present study has some limitations, namely the fact that the data are not longitudinal. It implies that when we claim that the jobs obtained by graduates may not match students' expectations, we are not comparing expectations and outcomes for the same individuals. Nonetheless, we believe that it is possible to assert that students have unrealistic expectations toward salaries and that most of them will probably be frustrated when trying to enter the labor market. This seems particularly likely if one considers the vast number of tourism degrees in Portugal (81), as well as the current economic and social crisis in the country, which is leading to a growing number of unemployed graduates in several fields.

Another limitation of the study is the fact that the sample was mostly collected through e-mail contact. It was thus difficult to reach graduates who finished their degrees a longer time ago, because universities and professors do not have any records of their e-mail addresses or graduates have changed e-mail accounts in the meantime. As a consequence, the sample for this study is very young, even among graduates, which might to some extent account for the low salaries obtained. Still, it should be borne in mind that tourism higher education in Portugal only started in 1987 and that it was not until a few years ago that the number of degrees underwent a sharp increase.

One should be cautious concerning the application of these results to other contexts. On the one hand, there are some findings that diverge from those of other authors. For example, McKercher, Williams, and Coghlan (1995) pointed out that tourism workers earn salaries above the average within 3 years of graduation, whereas our data suggest that salaries for tourism graduates are much lower than those of other graduates. Finally, whereas O'Leary and Deegan (2005) mentioned that the tourism sector in Ireland has difficulties in retaining and attracting "high caliber staff," our results hint that the tourism labor market has difficulties in absorbing this highly skilled workforce.

On the other hand, many of our findings are consistent with those of other studies, namely the following: Female students and graduates in tourism outnumber their male counterparts (McKercher et al., 1995; Waryszak, 2002, cited in King, McKercher, & Waryszak, 2003); salaries earned in the tourism industry are below the average of other sectors (O'Leary & Deegan, 2005); female tourism graduates earn less than male tourism graduates (Bañuls & Casado-Díaz, 2010; Barros & Santos, 2007; McKercher et al.; O'Leary & Deegan); and women have more difficulties than men in entering the labor market (McKercher et al.) and have lower expectations (Purcell, 1997). Thus, rather than extending to other contexts these conclusions, this article aims to contribute to the widening of the debate concerning the questions raised in this research.

FUTURE ISSUES FOR TOURISM HIGHER EDUCATION

Even though this study presented a somewhat negative view of the career paths of tourism graduates in Portugal, it does not intend to end on a pessimistic note. Action has to be devised and undertaken to reverse the trends observed.

It is necessary to rethink tourism higher education. Nowadays, tourism programs still rely on simple transmission of factual knowledge, which soon after graduation becomes obsolete. Given the rapid pace of change in our current societies, it is increasingly important to provide students with solid values and competencies that allow them to find a place for themselves in the tourism sector (Sheldon, Fesenmaier, & Tribe, 2011).

According to Sheldon et al. (2011), the core values to be transmitted to students are ethics, professionalism, knowledge, stewardship, and mutuality. These values were defined by the participants in the Tourism Education Futures Initiative (TEFI) to provide a new framework for tourism education programs.

The full integration of TEFI principles in tourism higher education curricula would contribute to a more gender-balanced labor market in the tourism sector, because TEFI principles aim to help the leaders of the future to follow practices rooted in basic values. In addition, these principles provide students with "the foundation to meet the multitude of uncertainties of the future" (Sheldon et al., 2011, p. 8), such as the difficulties in entering the labor market. Hence, the integration of *ethics* in tourism programs contributes to the deconstruction of prevailing gender stereotypes and changes in the dominant practices of recruitment and promotion toward more formalized and ethical-based practices; *knowledge* stimulates the critical thinking necessary for reading beyond the stereotypes; *stewardship* makes future leaders more responsible and gender aware; *professionalism* endows students with the creativity, proactivity, and leadership skills necessary to overcome the barriers they might face in the labor market; and *mutual respect* provides the future tourism leaders and actors with "self-awareness of structural inequalities, open-mindedness, empowerment, and ability to revisit one's cultural understanding of the world" (Sheldon et al., 2011, p. 17), which are essential to reach more gender-just societies.

Not only are the above-mentioned values essential if our aim is to provide the tourism sector with responsible and gender-aware leaders, but it is also necessary to diagnose the evolution of the trends analyzed in this study and to compare the results obtained for Portuguese tourism graduates with those obtained in different contexts.

REFERENCES

Bañuls, A. L., & Casado-Díaz, J. M. (2010). Rewards to education in the tourism sector: One step ahead. *Tourism Economics, 16*(1), 11–23.

Barros, C. P., & Santos, C. M. (2007). The economic return on education for hotel managers. *International Journal of Tourism Research, 9*(2), 103–113.

Blau, F., & Ferber, M. (1991). Career plans and expectations of young women and men: The earnings gap and labor force participation. *The Journal of Human Resources, 26*(4), 581–607.

Bruni, A., Gherardi, S., & Poggio, B. (2004). Entrepreneur mentality, gender, and the study of women entrepreneurs. *Journal of Organizational Change Management, 17*(3), 256–268.

Commission of the European Communities. (2009). *Report from the Commission to the Council, the European Parliament, the European Economic and Social Committee, and the Committee of the Regions: Equality between women and men—2009*. Brussels, Belgium: Commission of the European Communities.

Costa, C., Carvalho, I., & Breda, Z. (2011). Gender inequalities in tourism employment: The Portuguese case. *Revista Turismo & Desenvolvimento, 15*, 37–52.

Donlevy, V., & Silvera, R. (2007). *Implementing gender equality in enterprises: Report on best practices and tools in Europe*. Retrieved from http://ec.europa.eu/employment_social/equal/data/document/0801_gender_twinning_en.pdf

European Commission. (2004). *Guia EQUAL sobre a integração da perspectiva de género* [EQUAL guide on gender mainstreaming]. European Commission.

Eurostat. (2005, April 12). Reconciling work and family life in the EU25 in 2003: Employment rates lower and part-time rates higher for women with children; higher employment rates for men with children. *Eurostat News Release, 49*.

Eurostat. (2010). *Unemployment rate by gender*. Retrieved from http://epp.eurostat.ec.europa.eu/tgm/refreshTableAction.do?tab=table&plugin=1&pcode=tsiem110&language=en

Eurostat. (2011). *Share of women among tertiary students*. Retrieved from http://epp.eurostat.ec.europa.eu/tgm/download.do?tab=table&plugin=1& language=en&pcode=tps00063

Ferreira, A. (2007). Women in the service sector: Historical background and inequalities. *Campus Social: Revista Lusófona de Ciências Sociais, 3/4*, 259–268.

Foundation for Science and Technology. (2011). *PhD scholarships awarded by sex, 1994–2009*. Foundation for Science and Technology–Scholarships for advanced training. Retrieved from http://alfa.fct.mctes.pt/estatisticas/bolsas

Guerreiro, M. D., & Pereira, I. (2006). *Social responsibility of enterprises, equality and work-life balance: Experiences of the prize equality is quality*. Lisbon, Portugal: Commission for Equality in Labor and Employment.

Guerreiro, M. D., & Pereira, I. (2007). Women's occupational patterns and work–family arrangements: Do national and organizational policies matter? In R. Crompton, S. Lewis, & C. Lyonette (Eds.), *Women, men, work, and family in Europe* (pp. 190–209). New York, NY: Palgrave Macmillan.

Hemmati, M. (2000). Women's employment and participation in tourism. *Sustainable Travel & Tourism, 5*(1), 17–20.

Jordan, F. (1997). An occupational hazard? Sex segregation in tourism employment. *Tourism Management, 18*(8), 525–534.

King, B., McKercher, B., & Waryszak, R. (2003). A comparative study of hospitality and tourism graduates in Australia and Hong Kong. *International Journal of Tourism Research, 5*(6), 409–420.

Kinnaird, V., & Hall, D. (1996). Understanding tourism processes: A gender-aware framework. *Tourism Management, 17*(2), 95–102.

McKercher, B., Williams, A., & Coghlan, I. (1995). Career progress of recent tourism graduates. *Tourism Management, 16*(7), 541–549.

Moore, S., & Wen, J. J. (2009). Tourism employment in China: A look at gender equity, equality, and responsibility. *Journal of Human Resources in Hospitality & Tourism, 8*(1), 32–42.

Office for Planning, Strategy, Evaluation, and International Relations (GPEARI) – Ministry for Science, Technology, and Higher Education. (2009). *Estatísticas*. Retrieved from http://www.gpeari.mctes.pt/archive/doc/Tabelas_e_Anexos_ Diplomados_no_Ensino_Superior_2000-2001_a_2008-2009.xls

Office for Strategy and Planning. (2007). *Quadros de Pessoal 2007*. Lisbon, Portugal: Office for Strategy and Planning, Ministry of Labour and Social Solidarity.

O'Leary, S., & Deegan, J. (2005). Career progression of Irish tourism and hospitality management graduates. *International Journal of Contemporary Hospitality Management, 17*(5), 421–432.

Parrett, L. (n.d.). *Women in tourism employment: A guided tour of the Greenwich experience* [Research report]. London, UK: London Thames Gateway Forum Equality, Access & Participation.

Purcell, K. (1997). Women's employment in UK tourism: Gender roles and labor markets. In M. T. Sinclair (Ed.), *Gender, work, and tourism* (pp. 35–59). London, UK: Routledge.

Ranftl, E. (2006). *Equal pay for equal work and work of equal value: Guide to legal provisions governing equal pay and nondiscriminatory job evaluation*. Vienna, Austria: Federal Ministry of Health and Women.

Reis, H. (2000). Female entrepreneurship: Strategies and paths of women in travel agencies in the Algarve (Unpublished master's thesis). Universidade Aberta, Lisbon, Portugal.

Santos, L. D., & Varejão, J. (2006). Employment, pay, and discrimination in the tourism industry [Electronic version]. *FEP Working Papers, 205*.

Scott, J. (1997). Chances and choices: Women and tourism in Northern Cyprus. In M. T. Sinclair (Ed.), *Gender, work, and tourism* (pp. 60–90). London, UK: Routledge.

Sheldon, P. J., Fesenmaier, D. R., & Tribe, J. (2011). The Tourism Education Futures Initiative (TEFI): Activating change in tourism education. *Journal of Teaching in Travel & Tourism, 11*(1), 2–23.

Sinclair, M. T. (Ed.). (1997a). *Gender, work, and tourism*. London, UK: Routledge.

Sinclair, M. T. (1997b). Issues and theories of gender and work in tourism. In M. T. Sinclair (Ed.), *Gender, work, and tourism* (pp. 1–15). London, UK: Routledge.

Statistics Portugal. (2009). *Tourism statistics*. Lisbon, Portugal: Author.

Swain, M. B. (1993). Women producers of ethnic arts. *Annals of Tourism Research, 20*(1), 32–51.

Thrane, C. (2008). Earnings differentiation in the tourism industry: Gender, human capital, and sociodemographic effects. *Tourism Management, 29*, 514–524.

Thrane, C. (2010). Education and earnings in the tourism industry: The role of sheepskin effects. *Tourism Economics, 16*(3), 549–563.

Torres, A. C., Silva, F., Monteiro, T. L., & Cabrita, M. (2005). Men and women between family and work. Lisbon, Portugal: Commission for Equality in Labor and Employment.

Trickey, G. (2009). *Equal opportunities: Women*. Retrieved from http://www. prospects.ac.uk/equal_opportunities_women.htm

United Nations. (2009). *The millennium development goals report 2009*. New York, NY: Author.

Vartiainen, J. (2002). Gender wage differentials in the Finnish labor market. *Labor Institute for Economic Research: Discussion Papers, 179*.

World Travel & Tourism Council. (2011). *Travel and tourism economic impact 2011—Portugal*. Retrieved from http://www.wttc.org/site_media/uploads/downloads/portugal.pdf

Real Stories About Real Women: Communicating Role Models for Female Tourism Students

ULRIKE GRETZEL

University of Wollongong, Wollongong, Australia

GILLIAN BOWSER

Colorado State University, Fort Collins, Colorado, USA

This article identifies the lack of role models as an important factor that discourages women from taking on leadership roles in tourism communities, government agencies, companies, and academia. Based on discussions of the current literature on role models and the importance of stories, the article presents case studies of initiatives that use social media to collect and share the stories of female role models. The article then discusses opportunities to replicate such initiatives within the tourism education context to provide female students and educators with opportunities to identify with and be encouraged by the real stories of real female tourism leaders.

We cannot solve global problems using half of the world's brain power.

(Monika Devikka, as cited in Phelan, 2012)

INTRODUCTION

Understanding tourism requires a gendered perspective as all tourism activities and processes emerge from a gendered society and affect genders in different ways (Apostolopoulos, Sönmez, & Timothy, 2001; Byrne Swain, 1995; Kinnaird & Hall, 1994). Gender refers to ". . . a system of culturally constructed identities, expressed in ideologies of masculinity and femininity, interacting with socially structured relationships in divisions of labor and leisure, sexuality, and power between women and men" (Byrne Swain, 1995, pp. 258–259). Gender stereotypes and gender-discriminating practices embedded in society are transferred to and reproduced within tourism education and the tourism industry. This leads to great gender inequalities in tourism employment (Costa, Carvalho, Cacador, & Breda, 2012). Although gender and tourism have been discussed to some extent in the tourism literature (Sinclair, 1997), policy related to tourism and especially tourism education is still to a large extent gender-blind (Ferguson, 2009). The Tourism Education Futures Initiative (TEFI) 2011 meeting in Philadelphia, PA, started discussions on viewing tourism education through a gender lens, but no concrete efforts were initiated in response to the gender-related panel discussions. This article seeks to rekindle the interest in a gender-equal future for tourism and suggests a concrete project as a step toward mobilizing greater gender awareness in tourism education and toward supporting leadership development in women. In support of the project idea, it presents case studies of initiatives that aim(ed) to foster gender equality through role models who portray "real women" instead of models or celebrities and used social media extensively to mobilize interest and participation in the projects.

FEMALE LEADERSHIP IN TOURISM

The tourism industry seems to be a particularly important sector for women and provides a wide range of income-generation opportunities for women, especially in developing regions (UN Women, 2011). There are also clear leadership opportunities for women in tourism. Women are almost twice as likely to be employers in tourism compared with other sectors, and women account for one in five tourism ministers worldwide, which is more than in any other branch of government (UN Women, 2011). However, like in other sectors, there is a significant horizontal and vertical gender segregation of the labor market in tourism, with certain types of professions (e.g., chambermaids), lower-level jobs, and occupations with few career development opportunities being dominated by women (Costa, Carvalho, & Breda, 2011; Earthsummit2002.org, 2002). Only one in five tourism board chief executive officers are women, and only 23% of tourism industry associations have a female chairperson (UN World Tourism Organization [UNWTO], 2011). The

UNWTO report also stresses that although the proportion of women graduates in all fields of education is increasing, there is still a shortage of women teaching at the tertiary level.

King, McKercher, and Waryszak (2003) illustrate that in many Western countries, women make up a majority of tourism and hospitality student cohorts, but about half of these students never enter the industry and those who do mostly occupy lower-level positions. Hjalager (2003) shows that female tourism students are less ambitious compared with male students and that they aim mostly for middle-management positions and consider a significantly narrower range of career opportunities. It is also worth noting that none of the female students in the sample considered embarking on an academic career path. Hjalager concludes that perceived career prospects and attitudes toward work life in the tourism industry are highly influenced by traditional gender patterns, with female students being less adventurous and less keen to work in large organizations. Similarly, Costa et al. (2012) report that female tourism students in Portugal are less likely to indicate that they would like to take on a leadership position compared with their male counterparts, and they also have lower salary expectations.

Only 14% of FTSE 100 directorships are held by women, and women are also significantly less likely to hold senior management positions in these organizations (Garcea, Linley, Mazurkiewicz, & Bailey, 2012). Rice (2012b) specifically looks at the lack of women in academic careers and points out that women see academic careers as more all-consuming, solitary, and unnecessarily competitive compared with how men see them. Women also perceive great sacrifice as a prerequisite for success in academia. They are further told that they will have more problems simply because they are women. All these factors discourage them from pursuing respective career options. Pritchard, Morgan, Ateljevic, and Harris (2007) report that ". . . structural gender inequalities remain depressingly intact in the world's higher education academies" (p. 3), indicating that female doctoral graduates are more likely to pursue careers in the more family-friendly private sector, and those females who pursue academic careers are less likely to have tenure than are their male colleagues. Lack of female leadership is very visible in the tourism academy with only six women listed among the leading tourism scholars (Zhao & Ritchie, 2007) and only eight out of 70 fellows of the International Academy for the Study of Tourism being women.

Therefore, although tourism programs around the world attract a large number of female students, these female students often lack role models in leadership positions in industry, academia, government, and communities. This is especially true for women of underrepresented groups, as they have an even smaller likelihood of being represented in leadership positions. The UN Environment and Development UK Committee stresses that sharing of experiences and networking among women are critical in supporting women in their pursuit of leadership roles in tourism (Earthsummit2002.org,

2002). This article reflects on the importance of role models and opportunities to take advantage of new media to collect and widely communicate stories about female leaders in tourism to inspire more women to consider leadership roles in the tourism industry, tourism-related government bodies, nongovernmental organizations, and academia.

LEADERSHIP FOR TRANSFORMATION

Management focuses on keeping current systems functioning, while leadership is essentially about producing change. Leadership for transformation as a concept refers to leadership that brings about fundamental changes to systems. It is therefore a broader concept than traditional transformational leadership, which concentrates on unleashing potential and instigating changes in followers (Bass, 1985). Ackoff (1999) explains systemic transformation as follows: "A system is transformed when the type of system it is thought to be is changed" (p. 25). Accordingly, leadership for transformation is leadership that can produce and mobilize a vision of a transformed system. Isaksen and Tidd (2006) stress that leadership for transformation requires integration of leadership, management, creativity, and innovation, and they emphasize that it is not exclusive to higher levels in organizational structures but, rather, happens across functions and levels. They also point out that leadership for transformation requires recognition of the full spectrum of talent in the entire employee population. Yet, focusing on female talent and leadership development can be an organizational taboo (Garcea et al., 2012).

Female Leaders as Change Agents

Female leaders are seen as instrumental for ending gender inequalities in the workplace as gender gaps are wider and there is a stronger male representation among organizational managers and supervisors (Hultin & Szulkin, 2003). The explanations for this phenomenon cited in the literature include in-group preference and stereotyping as well as out-group exclusion (Gorman, 2005). Therefore, female leaders are often conceptualized as change agents necessary to break the vicious cycle of male leaders cultivating male-dominated organizational structures and cultures. For such change to happen, it is important that women reach the highest levels of leadership in organizations. However, women generally report lower confidence in regard to their careers (Garcea et al., 2012), and women are selected less often as leaders than is suggested by their past performance due to the general overconfidence of males in their representation (Reuben, Rey-Biel, Sapienza, & Zingales, 2012). Further, leaders are typically seen as possessing qualities that are stereotypically masculine (e.g., assertiveness, rationality). This creates problems for female leaders who need to fulfill a leader role while at the same time needing to balance their gender role (Kark, Waismel-Manor, & Shamir, 2012). However, transformational leadership and leadership for transformation are often associated with feminine values such as caring and compassion, which might actually provide women with an advantage (Eagly & Carli, 2003).

A recent study by Stainback and Kwon (2012) revealed that only having women in higher levels of organizational power actually leads to lower levels of sex segregation, while a large percentage of women in supervisory positions is associated with higher levels of sex segregation. Ely (1994) suggests that social identity theory is the key to understanding whether female leaders will actually make a difference in the workplace. She found that women in firms with few senior-level female leaders were less likely to perceive female leaders as role models and found less support in relationships with them because they see them as women who had to give up their identity as women to reach these high ranks. The research therefore suggests that being able to be seen as a role model is critical in motivating other women to follow suit but that not all female leaders are automatically seen as role models, suggesting that it is possible and desirable for women to reach high-level leadership positions.

Importance of Role Models

A role model is a person whose behavior in a particular role is imitated by others (Merriam Webster Online Dictionary, 2012a). Role models are looked up to and revered and provide concrete examples for others to follow. Role models positively influence aspirations and self-perceptions by means of social comparison processes (Hoyt & Simon, 2011). They serve an essential function in socialization processes. Consequently, role models have important impacts on career choices (Wright, Wong, & Newill, 1997) and are seen as critical in inspiring future leaders (Gibson & Cordova, 1999). Cheryan, Siy, Vichayapai, Drury, and Kim (2011, p. 661) point out that "interacting with one member of a field, even briefly, can shape students' beliefs about their potential for success in that field." Therefore, creating opportunities for exposure to role models is important in shaping the career aspirations of current students, especially when they are female. Women tend to underestimate their potential for success, but their expectations can be modified if exposed to role models they can identify with (Rice, 2012a).

Existing research has looked at how characteristics of role models moderate their positive impacts on aspirations. Women can have male role models, but the sex of an authority model can matter under some circumstances (Geis, Boston, & Hoffman, 1985). Lockwood (2006) showed that women are more inspired by female career role models who demonstrate that gender barriers can be overcome. Similarly, Cheryan et al. (2011)

revealed through experimental research that the most important criterion for positive influence is whether the role model embodies stereotypes that are seen as congruent with the female gender role. For example, successful female professors are often perceived by female doctoral students as displaying masculine characteristics, such as aggression and competiveness, and they are often childless, thus confirming negative stereotypes rather than challenging them (Rice, 2012b). Women who display such stereotypical characteristics are not likely to serve as an inspiration for women who would like to pursue a similar career. In brief, women see themselves as outsiders and are influenced when they perceive that outsiders can make it (Rice, 2012a).

Rios, Stewart, and Winter (2010) found that female students benefit greatly from a curriculum that features female exemplars in terms of identification with female leaders and changes in perceptions of career opportunities. Unfortunately, female role models are hard to find in top leadership positions due to negative stereotypes and discrimination against women in the leadership domain (Eagly & Carli, 2007). Beaman, Duflo, Pande, and Topalova (2012) found that quotas can help in that the resulting exposure to female leadership raises aspirations and educational attainment for girls in villages with female council leaders.

However, role models can only inspire and provoke self-enhancement when their success seems achievable (Lockwood & Kunda, 1997). Hoyt and Simon (2011) suggest that perceiving success to be attainable is particularly important for women who have to perform in a negatively stereotyped leadership domain. Top-level female leaders are likely seen as exceptions to the rule (Dasgupta & Asgari, 2004). A review of research that deals with the relationship between stereotypes, gender, and effectiveness of role models is provided by Betz and Sekaquaptewa (2012) and further illustrates its complexity. Research by Hoyt and Simon demonstrates that the critical characteristic is not how far removed the leadership level is, but how able women are to identify with these female role models. As such, same-sex role models can be more effective, but they have to involve "real" women whose accomplishments are seen as replicable.

Importantly, as opposed to mentors and sponsors, direct interaction with a role model is not necessary for impacts (Gibson & Cordova, 1999). This opens up opportunities as to who could serve as a role model that should be seized. If the number of potential role models is small, sharing their stories across a wide population of female students becomes essential.

THE POWER OF STORIES AS A COMMUNICATION MEDIUM

Stories represent powerful means of communicating knowledge (Schank & Abelson, 1995), and they are generally seen as an essential structure for human meaning-making (Bruner, 2002). They are perceived as more persuasive than other text genres (Padgett & Allen, 1997) because the specific structure of stories influences the way in which they are processed. According to Packer and Jordon (2001), stories allow the human mind to "collapse boundaries of space and time, drawing attention to previously undetected connections, creating links between disparate ideas and elements" (p. 174). Some researchers claim that this is the case because the structure of stories resembles the associative way the human mind stores knowledge (Schank & Abelson, 1995). They are also inherently entertaining (Brewer, 1988), which makes it easier to pay attention to them and fosters recall. Slater and Rouner (2002) further indicate that a student's absorption in a narrative and response to characters in a narrative enhances persuasive effects and reduces counterarguing for contexts in which the content of the story is counterattitudinal, while also limiting the influence of topic involvement. Stories are especially useful in situations of uncertainty and ambiguity (Fleming, 2001). According to Rossiter (2002), stories encourage deep involvement of the learner, and this involvement stimulates empathic response. She explains that the details and vivid imagery communicated through stories foster both cognitive appreciation and affective response to the experience of another person and are therefore especially useful for situations where identification with a role model is desirable.

The importance and persuasive power of stories has been recognized in various fields, including leadership (Fleming, 2001; Parkin, 2004). Shamir, Dayan-Horesh, and Adler (2005) propose that a leader's life story can be an important source of influence and that the meaning(s) it communicates can help enact leadership roles. Neuhauser (1993) stresses the importance of stories as management tools due to their believability based on perceived authenticity and credibility. Storytelling has also been identified as an important means of constructing social bonds (Kraus, 2006), which is a critical issue in building mentoring relationships. Driscoll and McKee (2006) recognize storytelling by leaders as a vital component of authentic transformational leadership.

New technologies such as social media make it increasingly possible to collect rich multimedia stories and distribute them. The Merriam Webster Online Dictionary (2012b) defines social media as forms of electronic communication (e.g., Web sites for social networking and microblogging) through which users create online communities to share information, ideas, personal messages, and other content (e.g., photos and videos). Web 2.0 as a technological platform, but also as a philosophy regarding control over content, provides important opportunities for information to be exchanged. Content in the social media space is to a large extent created by consumers for consumers. It is typically based on real experiences by real people, which contributes to the high credibility and perceived authenticity of social media messages. The emergence of social media also created a culture of putting the self constantly on display and revealing intimate details of one's life story. Therefore, social media is a critical means of social identity construction and portrayal. Importantly, social media encourages social interactions, which means that contents can be jointly created and easily shared, therefore allowing information to quickly spread through social networks. The narrative quality of social media and its resulting persuasive communication potential has been researched in the context of travelers sharing their tourism experiences (Gretzel, Fesenmaier, Lee, & Tussyadiah, 2011), but it has yet to be explored in the context of tourism education and leadership in tourism.

Case Studies of Stories by Real Women

The following describes cases in which social media in conjunction with consumer-generated stories was successfully used to expose a wide audience to role models based on "real women"; therefore, they can be seen as instrumental in understanding how these different domains can be effectively combined (Stake, 1995). Companies have already taken advantage of the opportunity to elicit authentic consumption stories using social media (see the Dove campaign for real beauty, http://web.archive. org/web/20070712074051/http://www.campaignforrealbeauty.ca/supports. asp?url=supports.asp&section=campaign&id=1560), thereby creating very persuasive campaigns with powerful message contents. Instead of using highly idealized and photo-brushed models, these stories portray women with whom others can easily identify. They therefore present role models in positions that are seen as not only desirable but also achievable. The Dove campaign was recognized with two Grand Prix Cannes Advertising Awards in 2007. One of its explicit goals was to encourage women to participate in the discussion by casting votes and posting comments on the campaign Web site. It led to the development of the Dove Self-Esteem Fund with the goal of educating girls and women about a wider definition of beauty (http://www.dove.us/Social-Mission/campaign-for-real-beauty. aspx). The Web site further reveals that in 2010, the Dove Movement for Self-Esteem was founded to provide women with opportunities to mentor the next generation. The movement has resulted in the development of self-esteem building, educational programs, and activities, which have reached seven million girls so far.

The question is if and how social media can be used to elicit stories to inspire women to become female leaders in the same way they inspired them to use Dove products. An example of how social media can be used to mobilize leaders among women is "1 Million Women," a not-for-profit organization that uses social media to engage women in climate-change actions (http://www.1millionwomen.com.au). Its goal is to encourage women to actively reduce CO_2 emissions in their own lives and to create a powerful network of women ambassadors for climate change. Like Dove, the campaign uses the faces and stories of real women to inspire others to engage in leadership efforts. Again, social media is employed to capture and share the stories of those women who have dedicated themselves to playing a leadership role in the effort. 1 Million Women has grown into one of the largest nonpolitical women's organizations in Australia. It is one of the largest members-based environmental groups, with nearly 80,000 members, more than 36,000 members on Facebook, and about 9,000 women and girls having attended one of its events (http://www.newsmaker.com. au/news/20596). Australian Prime Minister Julia Gillard backed one of its recent campaigns called Recipe for Change (http://www.1millionwomen. com.au), which involved encouraging women across Australia to host a get-together of women to discuss ways in which women can save the Earth. As a result of the campaign, thousands of Australian women got together to exchange ideas about how to save energy and reduce waste (http:// recipeforchange.1millionwomen.com.au).

Other examples can be extracted from the efforts of the Global Women Scholars Network (GWSN; for more information, see http://globalwomenscholars.wordpress.com) funded by the U.S. National Science Foundation to cultivate leadership among women in sustainability-related sciences (http://nsf.gov/awardsearch/showAward.do? AwardNumber=1140182). The GWSN is a network of female scholars and scholars interested in gender issues pertaining to sustainability research, recognizing that climate change affects women in different ways and that a female perspective is needed in solving global sustainability problems. As a research collaborative network, it is charged with connecting these scholars on a global scale to change the face of climate change and sustainability research. Mentoring is a key aspect of GWSN's activities, and the importance of providing role models and support to female scholars is recognized. Although the network actively hosts workshops to co-locate scholars in physical space, it quickly realized that inspiration and role modeling are required on a more global scale to trigger change. It therefore initiated a project to collect stories of female role models to acknowledge them and to make their insights available to women around the world interested in tackling climate change and sustainability problems. The initiative aims to celebrate transformational leaders and potentially encourage a new generation of female students to pursue leadership roles who would otherwise not have identified with such opportunities.

Starting with a small group of female leaders organized under the umbrella of Climate Wise Women (http://climatewisewomen.org/?page_id= 12), the GWSN initiative seeks to create rich and convincing portrayals of the important role women play in guiding climate-change efforts in communities, industry, government, and academia. One of the Climate Wise Women is Ursula Rakova, who is leading the Carteret Islands evacuation efforts. Her story has been captured through a traditional documentary called "Sun Come Up" and has been told and retold through various YouTube videos and blog entries available online (http://journeytothesinkinglands. wordpress.com). Additional stories were collected from women who were instrumental in driving gender issues forward within the UN climate change summits during the Rio+20 Climate Change Summit in 2012. A small selection of stories is available through the GWSN YouTube channel (http://www. youtube.com/globalwomenscholars). All of these stories stress the importance of mentoring and role models as well as networking women to encourage potential female leaders. Recognizing the viral nature of social media and its potential to foster interactive dialogue, these initial stories will act as seeds for a wider social media campaign that will ask women across the globe to describe their leadership efforts in this domain and will encourage others to actively comment on them. The literature review clearly showed the importance of portraying role models with different characteristics. The social media-based campaign democratizes the process of identifying role models and allows women from different backgrounds to be included. Thus, the stories will feature very high-level, formal leaders as well as women who enact leadership at community levels. In all cases, the emphasis is on letting the women speak with their own voices, telling very personal stories rather than presenting official biographies. A specific focus will be placed on women in academia to increase retention of women in higher education programs and in academic and research-related jobs. Due to the nature of the social media used for the project, there will even be opportunities for interactive dialogues as the women who are portrayed in the stories can respond to comments made by others.

Implications for the Future of Tourism Education

The question raised in this article is how efforts similar to the GWSN initiative could be implemented within the tourism education community. The introduction clearly outlined a need for more female leaders in all areas of tourism. Taking advantage of storytelling and social media, persuasive portraits of female role models could be created to inspire female tourism students to become the future generation of academic, government, and industry leaders. Following the TEFI spirit of global reach, such stories could be made available on the TEFI Web site and on its social media pages to share role models across geographical boundaries. The success of the initiative would depend on a distributed social effort of collecting stories at the local level and sharing them with the global tourism community. This would ensure diversity in the stories told and greater access to role models beyond geographic and institutional boundaries. Social media tools provide the technological basis for this to happen.

An important aspect of such an initiative would be to find ways in which such stories could be effectively integrated into existing curricula and courses as well as recruiting efforts for tourism education programs. Given the insights derived from the literature and the case studies, the authenticity of the stories and the ability of tourism students and/or junior tourism academics to identify with them have to be ensured. The education literature suggests that the stories could be used to support autobiographical writing activities that allow students to reflect on their own life experiences and how they relate to the role-model stories (Birren & Deutchmann, 1991). Another question to be addressed is how to measure the effectiveness of such an initiative beyond immediate inspiration by the stories. Although reflections by current female leaders on the importance of role models in their own career choices can provide some insights, ultimately, longitudinal studies will be needed to measure the long-term effects of exposure to role-model stories.

Overall, such an effort would contribute to greater gender awareness within the TEFI community and beyond and would constitute a concrete follow-up from the discussions in Philadelphia and now Milan, Italy. TEFI's new vision statement ("To be the leading, forward-looking network that inspires, informs and supports tourism educators and students to passionately and courageously transform the world for the better") clearly calls for not only transformational leadership but also transformational learning with the end-goal being transformation of the system that currently discourages women to take on leadership roles. If TEFI played a central role in the collection and distribution of these stories, it could use the initiative to further increase its impact and add another concrete project to its portfolio of already existing initiatives. The key is that it would actively engage a great number of tourism scholars and would foster links with the industry. The project would also direct more attention to the topic of female leadership in tourism, which so far has been largely ignored by tourism educators and researchers.

REFERENCES

Ackoff, R. L. (1999). Transformational leadership. *Strategy & Leadership*, *27*(1), 20–25.

Apostolopoulos, Y., Sönmez, S., & Timothy, D. J. (Eds.). (2001). *Women as producers and consumers of tourism in developing regions*. Westport, CT: Praeger.

Bass, B. M. (1985). *Leadership and performance beyond expectations*. New York, NY: Free Press.

Beaman, L., Duflo, E., Pande, R., & Topalova, P. (2012). Female leadership raises aspirations and educational attainment for girls: A policy experiment in India. *Science*, *335*, 582–586.

Betz, D. E., & Sekaquaptewa, D. (2012). My fair physicist? Feminine math and science role models demotivate young girls. *Social Psychological and Personality Science*, *3*(6), 738–746.

Birren, J. E., & Deutchmann, D. E. (1991). *Guiding autobiography groups for older adults*. Baltimore, MD: Johns Hopkins University Press.

Brewer, W. F. (1988). Imagery and text genre. *Text, 8*, 431–439.

Bruner, J. (2002). *Making stories*. New York, NY: Farrar, Strauss, and Giroux.

Byrne Swain, M. (1995). Gender in tourism. *Annals of Tourism Research, 22*(2), 247–266.

Cheryan, S., Siy, J. O., Vichayapai, M., Drury, B. J., & Kim, S. (2011). Do female and male role models who embody STEM stereotypes hinder women's anticipated success in STEM? *Social Psychological and Personality Science, 2*(6), 656–664.

Costa, C., Carvalho, I., & Breda, Z. (2011). Gender inequalities in tourism employment: The Portuguese case. *Revista Turismo & Desenvolvimento, 15*, 37–52.

Costa, C., Carvalho, I., Cacador, S., & Breda, Z. (2012). Future higher education in tourism studies and the labor market: Gender perspectives on expectations and experiences. *Journal of Teaching in Travel & Tourism, 12*, 70–90.

Dasgupta, N., & Asgari, S. (2004). Seeing is believing: Exposure to counterstereotypic women leaders and its effect on automatic gender stereotyping. *Journal of Experimental Social Psychology, 40*, 642–658.

Driscoll, C., & McKee, M. (2006). Restorying a culture of ethical and spiritual values: A role of leader storytelling. *Journal of Business Ethics, 73*, 205–217.

Eagly, A. H., & Carli, L. L. (2003). The female leadership advantage: An evaluation of the evidence. *The Leadership Quarterly, 14*, 807–832.

Eagly, A. H., & Carli, L. L. (2007). Women and the labyrinth of leadership. *Harvard Business Review, 85*, 62–71.

Earthsummit2002.org. (2002). *Gender & tourism: Women's employment and participation in tourism* (Summary of the UNED-UK's project report). Retrieved from http://www.earthsummit2002.org/toolkits/women/current/gendertourismrep.html

Ely, R. J. (1994). The effects of organizational demographics and social identity on relationships among professional women. *Administrative Science Quarterly, 39*(2), 203–238.

Ferguson, L. (2009). *Analysing the gender dimensions of tourism as a development strategy* (Working paper). Retrieved from http://eprints.ucm.es/10237/1/PP_03-09.pdf

Fleming, D. (2001). Narrative leadership: Using the power of stories. *Strategy & Leadership, 29*(4), 34–36.

Garcea, N., Linley, A., Mazurkiewicz, K., & Bailey, T. (2012). Future female talent development. *Strategic HR Review, 11*(4), 199–204.

Geis, F. L., Boston, M. B., & Hoffman, N. (1985). Sex of authority role models and achievement by men and women: Leadership performance and recognition. *Journal of Personality and Social Psychology, 49*(3), 636–653.

Gibson, D. E., & Cordova, D. I. (1999). Women's and men's role models: The importance of exemplars. In A. J. Murrell, F. J. Crosby, & R. J. Ely (Eds.), *Mentoring dilemmas: Development relationships within multicultural organizations* (pp. 115–134). Mahwah, NJ: Lawrence Erlbaum.

Gorman, E. H. (2005). Gender stereotypes, same-gender preferences, and organizational variation in the hiring of women: Evidence from law firms. *American Sociological Review, 70*(4), 702–728.

Gretzel, U., Fesenmaier, D. R., Lee, Y.-J., & Tussyadiah, I. (2011). Narrating travel experiences: The role of new media. In R. Sharpley & P. Stone (Eds.),

Tourist experiences: Contemporary perspectives (pp. 171–182). New York, NY: Routledge.

Hjalager, A. (2003). Global tourism careers? Opportunities and dilemmas facing higher education in tourism. *Journal of Hospitality, Leisure, Sport & Tourism Education, 2*(2), 26–38.

Hoyt, C. L., & Simon, S. (2011). Female leaders: Injurious or inspiring role models for women? *Psychology of Women Quarterly, 35*(1), 143–157.

Hultin, M., & Szulkin, R. (2003). Mechanisms of inequality: Unequal access to organizational power and the gender wage gap. *European Sociological Review, 19*(2), 143–159.

Isaksen, S. G., & Tidd, J. (2006). *Meeting the innovation challenge: Leadership for transformation and growth*. Chichester, UK: John Wiley & Sons.

Kark, R., Waismel-Manor, R., & Shamir, B. (2012). Does valuing androgyny and femininity lead to a female advantage? The relationship between gender-role, transformational leadership and identification. *The Leadership Quarterly, 23*, 620–640.

King, B., McKercher, B., & Waryszak, R. (2003). A comparative study of hospitality and tourism graduates in Australia and Hong Kong. *International Journal of Tourism Research, 5*, 409–420.

Kinnaird, V., & Hall, D. (1994). *Tourism: A gender analysis*. Chichester, UK: John Wiley & Sons.

Kraus, W. (2006). The narrative negotiation of identity and belonging. *Narrative Inquiry, 16*(1), 103–111.

Lockwood, P. (2006). 'Someone like me can be successful': Do college students need same-gender role models? *Psychology of Women Quarterly, 30*, 36–46.

Lockwood, P., & Kunda, Z. (1997). Superstars and me: Predicting the impact of role models on the self. *Journal of Personality and Social Psychology, 73*(1), 91–103.

Merriam Webster Online Dictionary. (2012a). *Role model*. Retrieved from http://www.merriam-webster.com/dictionary/role%20model

Merriam Webster Online Dictionary. (2012b). *Social media*. Retrieved from http://www.merriam-webster.com/dictionary/social%20media

Neuhauser, P. C. (1993). *Corporate legends and love: The power of storytelling as a management tool*. New York, NY: McGraw-Hill.

Packer, R. K., & Jordan, K. (2001). *Multimedia: From Wagner to virtual reality*. New York, NY: W. W. Norton.

Padgett, D., & Allen, D. (1997). Communicating experiences: A narrative approach to creating service brand image. *Journal of Advertising, 26*(4), 49–62.

Parkin, M. (2004). *Tales for change: Using storytelling to develop people and organisations*. London, UK: Kogan Page.

Phelan, D. (2012, February 29). Gender in Cancun: WEDO & case studies [Web log post]. Retrieved from http://women-rio20.ning.com/m/blogpost?id=6430845%3ABlogPost%3A9130

Pritchard, A., Morgan, N., Ateljevic, I., & Harris, C. (2007). Tourism, gender, embodiment and experience. In A. Pritchard, N. Morgan, I. Ateljevic, & C. Harris (Eds.), *Tourism and gender: Embodiment, sensuality, and experience* (pp. 1–12). Cambridge, MA: CABI.

Reuben, E., Rey-Biel, P., Sapienza, P., & Zingales, L. (2012). The emergence of male leadership in competitive environments. *Journal of Economic Behavior & Organization, 83*, 111–117.

Rice, C. (2012a). *Why not just any old role model will do: What early career men and women need*. Retrieved from http://curt-rice.com/2012/01/13/why-not-just-any-old-role-model-will-do-what-early-career-men-and-women-need

Rice, C. (2012b). Why women leave academia and why universities should be worried. *The Guardian*. Retrieved from http://www.guardian.co.uk/higher-education-network/blog/2012/may/24/why-women-leave-academia

Rios, S., Stewart, A. J., & Winter, D. G. (2010). 'Thinking she could be the next President': Why identifying with the curriculum matters. *Psychology of Women Quarterly, 34*, 328–338.

Rossiter, M. (2002). *Narrative and stories in adult teaching and learning* (ERIC Document Reproduction Service No. 241). Retrieved from http://calpro-online.org/eric/docs/dig241.pdf

Schank, R. C., & Abelson, R. P. (1995). Knowledge and memory: The real story. In R. S. Wyer (Ed.), *Advances in social cognition* (Vol. 8, pp. 1–85). Hillsdale, NJ: Lawrence Erlbaum.

Shamir, B., Dayan-Horesh, H., & Adler, D. (2005). Leading by biography: Towards a life-story approach to the study of leadership. *Leadership, 1*(1), 13–29.

Sinclair, M. T. (1997). Issues and theories of gender and work in tourism. In M. T. Sinclair (Ed.), *Gender, work and tourism* (pp. 1–14). London, UK: Routledge.

Slater, M. D., & Rouner, D. (2002). Entertainment-education and elaboration likelihood: Understanding the processing of narrative persuasion. *Communication Theory, 12*(2), 173–191.

Stainback, K., & Kwon, S. (2012). Female leaders, organizational power, and sex segregation. *The Annals of the American Academy of Political and Social Science, 639*, 217–235.

Stake, R. E. (1995). *The art of case study research*. Thousand Oaks, CA: Sage.

UN Women. (2011). *Tourism a vehicle for gender equality and women's empowerment*. Retrieved from http://www.unwomen.org

UN World Tourism Organization. (2011). *Global report on women in tourism 2010*. Retrieved from http://unwto.org

Wright, S., Wong, A., & Newill, C. (1997). The impact of role models on medical students. *Journal of General Internal Medicine, 12*, 53–56.

Zhao, W., & Ritchie, J. R. B. (2007). An investigation of academic leadership in tourism research: 1985–2004. *Tourism Management, 28*(2), 476–490.

Case Study: Integrating TEFI (Tourism Education Futures Initiative) Core Values into the Undergraduate Curriculum

ELIZABETH BARBER

Temple University, Philadelphia, Pennsylvania, USA

This case study explains the implementation of the five core values defined by the Tourism Education Futures Initiative (TEFI) into an undergraduate program in tourism and hospitality management. The case study creates a model for writing learning objectives, creating instructional modules, and defining assessment tools. Learning objectives were written for each core value and integrated into each class within the curriculum. The bases of the learning objectives, as well as the appropriate type of instructional modules, were extracted from the core values' descriptions. Assessment tools were created to evaluate student learning. The goal of this case study is to present a model that describes how the TEFI set of defined core values might be integrated into a tourism and hospitality management curriculum.

INTRODUCTION

When considering the impact of higher education on a person, one often tries to take into consideration a myriad of experiences a student may have encountered. Is it the social life, is it the dorm life, the faculty, the classes, the classroom? Just what is it that we can say held the most value to a student upon graduation? While all of these things seem very important, one might worry that these factors will soon become distant memories, while a graduate moves away from school and into the next phase of his or her life. The desire to have a lifelong impact on a student was part of the motivation of the School of Tourism and Hospitality Management (STHM) at Temple University to implement a specific set of learning outcomes into the undergraduate curriculum. The bases of the learning objectives were extracted from the core values defined by the Tourism Education Futures Initiative (TEFI; Sheldon, Fesenmaier, & Tribe, 2009). With our profound commitment to providing students with the knowledge and skills necessary to be future leaders in the tourism and hospitality industry, the school carefully crafted a vision and mission statement that reflects our core values, many of which are similar to the TEFI core values. The purpose of the case study was to integrate a comprehensive set of learning objectives, which matched the values of the school, and to assess the impact of values-based education. This belief was taken into careful consideration as the learning objectives were written. The goal of this case study is to present a model that describes how a set of defined core values might be integrated into a tourism and hospitality management (THM) program using the process as described by Temple University's STHM for the pilot, and steps others may follow worldwide.

BACKGROUND

As highlighted in the previous section, the seeds of TEFI are based upon the general recognition that higher education and, more particularly, tourism and hospitality education must change in order to meet the various challenges. Additionally, it was recognized that many people (including academicians, teachers, industry professionals, and government leaders) throughout the world have voiced their concerns regarding the future. Led by these voices, a number of innovators concerned about the future of tourism and hospitality education met in Vienna, Austria in 2007 to discuss the status of tourism and hospitality education and to assess the degree to which there was an agreement concerning the need to develop alternative models for tourism and hospitality education. During this meeting, a process emerged that provided a framework for the growth and development of TEFI. That is, TEFI is largely organized around a process that is both proactive and action oriented, focusing on translating the core values articulated by the membership to implementation so that there can be a fundamental change in tourism and hospitality education (Sheldon et al., 2009).

The TEFI process includes two important action settings: (a) an Annual Summit, which brings together innovators from around the world to consider issues related to tourism and hospitality education; and (b) Working Groups, which throughout the year seek to develop tools that can be used to affect tourism and hospitality education (Sheldon et al., 2009). The Annual Summit is generally comprised of 30–40 leading scholars and industry professionals and includes both lectures and breakout groups. The lectures are conducted to stimulate thinking and to challenge the status quo. For example, in the First Summit, Dr. Jim Dator, a leading futurist from the University of Hawaii, challenged the TEFI members to develop scenarios of future worlds and then to propose possible solutions/responses to these scenarios. In the Second Summit (2008), Dr. John Tribe articulated a vision of hope—an Academy of Hope—for the future of society and tourism education, in particular. But, he also challenged the group to take personal responsibility in shaping this future world. Dr. Gianna Moscardo presented a lecture focusing on the learning styles of the next generation, arguing that how we teach is just as important as what we teach. And, Scott Meis, former director of research for the Tourism Industry Association of Canada, demonstrated quite conclusively that the industry need for qualified employees will become even more critical over the next decade. The Third Summit (2009) focused on barriers to change within the university (as discussed by Dr. Thomas Bieger of the University of St. Gallen) and strategies for programmatic change (as exemplified by lectures by Drs. Irena Ateljevic, Simon Wong, Loredana Padurean, and Betsy Barber). These presentations clearly demonstrated barriers and potential strategies for changing educational processes within the university; they also highlighted a number of conflicts within higher education in realizing the changes. The fourth summit in San Sebastian, Spain (April 2010) focused primarily on the challenges and opportunities for the future. This meeting also prepared the groundwork for the fifth summit, which is to be held in Philadelphia, Pennsylvania, calling for the World Congress, May 2011.

The second pillar of the TEFI process is the Working Group. For each of the Summits, Working Groups have been organized to provide essential energy and direction so as to result in concrete action-oriented tools that can be used by TEFI. For example, prior to the first TEFI summit, a Working Group identified a core set of readings that established a foundation—a common language and set of ideas and ideals—for discussion. In addition, the Working Group conducted a pre-meeting survey of participants regarding key knowledge and skill sets needed for the tourism graduate of the future. Three different Working Groups emerged from the first Summit, focusing on defining TEFI values, identifying case studies in the values-based education, and assessing programmatic changes through outcome-based education. Each of the Working Groups developed working papers and presentations, which were then presented and discussed at the TEFI 2009. And finally, as the result of the Third Summit, a series of Working Groups have been developed so as to create more concrete tools for supporting TEFI. These Working Groups include the following activities: (a) developing a White Paper that outlines/documents the progress made by TEFI members (which can be found at www.tourismeducationsummit.com; http://www.quovadis.

wu-wien.ac.at/drupal/files/White%20Paper%20May22_0.pdf); (b) proposing a Faculty Code of Ethics; (c) developing an outreach pilot program to universities worldwide; and (d) developing a values inventory that may be used as part of program assessment.

TEFI VALUES

An important outcome of the TEFI process is a set of five values-based principles that tourism and hospitality students should embody upon so that they will become responsible leaders and stewards for the destinations where they work or live (see Figure 1 in the lead article of this special issue). The five values are (a) ethics, (b) stewardship, (c) knowledge, (d) professionalism, and (e) mutuality, and are portrayed as interlocking value principles because of the interconnectedness of the value sets and their permeability. It is envisioned by TEFI members that educators can use subsets of the five value principles to integrate into their courses as appropriate. The specifics of how to incorporate them are left to the educator.

A more thorough definition of the values can be found in the lead article. For the purposes of this article, the definitions were briefly described for the purposes of context of writing learning objectives.

Ethics

Ethical behavior means striving for actions that are deemed "good" based on principles and values of honesty. We need to recognize that good actions do not occur in a vacuum but are derived from specific value systems that further require understanding and respect for actions based on authenticity and authentic self (Sheldon et al., 2009).

Stewardship

Stewardship involves the activity one performs when getting involved in sustainability, responsibility, and service to the community. Sustainability requires managing resources and the impacts of tourism for future generations. Linked to sustainability is the idea of responsibility. Sustainability can only be achieved if individuals and organizations acknowledge their responsibilities and act accordingly. If all stakeholders are to take responsibility for the future of the planet in tourism, empowerment of those who are currently powerless is necessary, as is the restraint of power of other groups. Finally, service to the community is one way that stakeholders can demonstrate their commitment to taking responsibility (Sheldon et al., 2009).

Knowledge

Knowledge can be described as (a) expertise and skills acquired by a person through experience or education, the theoretical or practical understanding of a subject; (b) what is known in a particular field; facts and information; or (c) awareness or familiarity gained by experience of a fact or situation. Knowledge is created through processes of selecting, connecting, and reflecting. Knowledge is always already predicated by existing knowledge, which means that knowledge involves interpretation and contextualization. In due course, the knowledge of others should be recognized and existing knowledge that may be taken for granted should be challenged (Sheldon et al., 2009).

Professionalism

It has been defined as the ability to align personal and organizational conduct with ethical and professional behavior. *Professionalism* is defined as incorporating leadership, a practical approach (practicality), attention to services, concern for the relevance and timeliness of evidence, reflexivity, teamwork and partnership building skills, and proactively (Sheldon et al., 2009).

Mutuality

Within the TEFI framework mutual respect had been initially defined as mutual respect, inclusive of diversity, inclusion, equity, humility, and collaboration. *Mutual respect* is seen as a value grounded in human relationships that requires attitudinal developments that are evolving, dynamic, and involve acceptance, self-awareness of structural inequalities, open-mindedness, empowerment, and ability to revisit one's cultural understanding of the world. *Mutuality* is a process that is evolving and dynamic, emphasizing that achieving mutual respect is a long-term and even life-long learning process that can be developed at different levels, starting from the individual to the society and global levels. Mutuality is about developing respectful relationships between self and people through sharing and understanding values and attitudes. It involves open discussions and appreciation of diverse opinions (Sheldon et al., 2009).

TEMPLE UNIVERSITY STHM CASE STUDY

First, the five core values were carefully reviewed and placed in specific courses. As each specific core value was embedded into courses, special attention was made to make sure that each core value is found in more than one course. The chart in Appendix A shows how each of the values were individually integrated into the existing courses. It also shows how the value can progress through the curriculum, from freshman to senior level courses (1000–4000), as well as from core courses, through the major courses, and into the elective courses. By charting the values in this manner, it visually shows how the core values can be built upon through the learning process. The values were attached to courses based on prior knowledge of what the content of the class was, plus the appropriateness of the value being taught in the specific course.

The next step was to write learning objectives for each of the core values. The learning objectives were written following Bloom's Taxonomy of Learning (Bloom, Engelhart, Furst, Hill, & Krathwohl, 1956; Marzano & Kendall, 2007). The taxonomy builds in level of complexity of cognitive processing and includes knowledge, comprehension, application, analysis, synthesis, and evaluation. Each level is designed to possess defining characteristics that are expected to match the desirable level of learning. Action verbs are selected based on the level of the desirable learning (see Appendix B). For example, the lower level of Bloom's Taxonomy calls for the types of learning objectives and action verbs in the categories of knowledge and comprehension, such as "define, describe, and list." This pattern can be seen as the course level increases, the level of Bloom's learning objectives move up from knowledge and comprehension through the highest level of learning objectives to synthesis and evaluation. The action verbs are expected to result in a higher level of learning or a higher level of understanding. For example, a learning objective in the level of knowledge states that a student is expected to "define the term networking." A faculty member might then ask if the written definition was correct. At a higher level, a student might be asked to "compare appropriate networking vs. inappropriate networking behaviors." The student could be asked to view video and select scenarios of appropriate networking. This would require a higher level of understanding, based on the theory of learning supported by Bloom.

Airasian (1994) described how Ralph Tyler (1949) influenced Bloom's development of the taxonomy. This explanation shows the relationship between the writing of an objective in a way that requires the assessment of a behavior that signals the understanding of knowledge. It was Tyler who first noted a relationship between instruction and learning. The evolution of Bloom's taxonomy took Tyler's initial notion of achievement tests being the best way to assess learning, to allowing for a hierarchy of learning assessment based on deeper understanding than recall.

Mager (1962) explained that a well-written learning objective should have three elements. The first element is performance. An objective always says what the learner is expected to do; the objective sometimes describes the product or the result of the doing. The second element is conditions. An objective always describes the important conditions under which the performance is to occur. And finally, criterion: An objective should describe the criterion of acceptable performance by describing how well the learner must perform in order to be acceptable. While this case study wrote learning objectives using the action verb showing what action needs to take place to evaluate the performance and examples of the conditions under which the learning objective will be evaluated, it does not include the criterion to evaluate acceptable performance. The faculty was asked to complete this for the implementation of the core values exercise for STHM.

After the objectives were written they were shared with the faculty, who teach the courses, for final approval. The whole curriculum, with the embedded learning objectives, was presented to the faculty, who collectively reviewed the appropriateness of the value placement. This process occurred during a school retreat. Although the objectives had been written prior to the retreat, the whole faculty was involved in the modifications and implementation of the integration. The entire set of courses for the Tourism and Hospitality Management major, with defined learning objectives, is found in Appendix C. Just as a reminder, this listing does not include the content learning objectives established for each class. This just shows the core value learning objectives.

Assessment tool examples were developed at this time. Most assessment activities are done through course embedded assessments. Examples of appropriate assessment tools have been diagrammed (see Appendix D). The assessments (assignments) have been carefully designed to follow the progression of Bloom's Taxonomy, so that what a freshman course might have as an appropriate assignment could be to write a reaction paper, where as a senior class would be asked to create a company policy or code of conduct.

Lastly, the evaluation of the individual course outcomes of the learning objectives was imbedded in the Student Feedback Form (SFF). This is a course and instructor evaluation tool that is required in every class at the end of each semester. Students were asked how they perceived their learning or their attitude and behavioral change because of the instruction within the class of the specific core values. Examples of student responses to assessment questions can be found in Appendix E. Results have been collected each semester, 2009–2010. This information has been used to either verify behavioral and attitudinal outcomes that show positive growth in the students' understanding and appreciation of the core values, or the faculty member will be asked to modify the teaching and learning activities. It will be important to show positive conclusions. Faculty members are responsible for establishing the baseline and formation for each student in their course and calculating the semester end results. These results will be used as a formative evaluation barometer. Out of 18 full-time faculty, 17 faculty have participated in this project. To get their "buy-in" on the project did not seem difficult. In general, they all saw the pedagogical value in moving the curriculum and the student experience in this direction.

STHM students are required to complete two internships. The greatest depth of assessment information has been collected in the final semester of the students' program and with the completion of the senior internship and senior project. This is completed in the final semester, where a student engages in an internship in an organization for 600 hours. Within the internship the student is required to establish individual goals, and write monthly assessments of goal attainment. The students' university supervisor has been instructed to assist the student in identifying core value type goals, along with the typical work-related goals. With more of a qualitative approach, this will allow us to analyze the students' attitudes and beliefs. In addition, the site supervisor is required to complete a midterm and final evaluation of the student's performance. The site supervisors' evaluation tool is directly related to the core values. Supervisors are asked to complete a checklist (Likert scale) where the student is evaluated on various attributes of professionalism, knowledge, stewardship, mutuality, and ethics. This allows us to assess student behaviors based on external feedback. These two evaluations will allow us to complete a method of summative evaluation and use self declaration and external feedback to verify internal practices. As the project continues, this is the current status of gathering data.

SUMMARY

The implementation of the TEFI core values into the undergraduate curriculum for STHM has been through a series of steps. In spring and summer 2009, the core values were defined and charted to reflect insertion of the core values throughout the entire academic program; freshman through senior level; core, major, and elective courses, as well as the senior internship for external verification of student learning. In fall and spring 2009–2010, all tourism and hospitality management courses inserted learning objectives related to the appropriate core values' education. Assessment of behavioral and attitudinal impact of students' reaction to the core values has occurred through the fall and spring 2009–2010 academic year. Summer, fall, and spring 2010–2011 senior internship assessments will be collected and analyzed (along with the continuation of the course embedded project). This is an on-going program for STHM; however this case study serves as an attempt to create a model for other undergraduate programs to incorporate the same program. Hopefully, other academic institutions will join in this effort.

REFERENCES

Airasian, P. W. (1994). The impact of the taxonomy on testing and evaluation. In L. W. Anderson & L. A. Sosniak (Eds.), *Bloom's taxonomy: A forty-year retrospective: Ninety-third yearbook of the National Society for the Study of Education* (pp. 82–102). Chicago, IL: University of Chicago Press.

Bloom, B. S., Engelhart, M. D., Furst, E. J., Hill, W. H., & Krathwohl, D. R. (Eds.). (1956). *Taxonomy of educational objectives: The classification of educational goals. Handbook I: Cognitive domain.* New York, NY: David McKay.

Mager, R. (1962). *Preparing instructional objectives.* Palo Alto, CA: Fearon.

Marzano, R. J., & Kendall, J. S. (2007). *The new taxonomy of educational objectives* (2nd ed.). Thousand Oaks, CA: Corwin Press.

Sheldon, P., Fesenmaier, D. R., & Tribe, J. (2009). A values-based framework for tourism education: Building capacity to lead. *Tourism Education Futures Initiative.* Retrieved from http://www.tourismeducationfutures.org/related-reading-material

Tyler, R. W. (1949). *Basic principles of curriculum and instruction.* Chicago, IL: University of Chicago Press.

APPENDIX A: TEMPLE UNIVERSITY THM CURRICULUM AND CORE VALUES' OBJECTIVES

	CORE								MAJOR						ELECTIVES						
Course numbers	1112	1113	1114	2112	2114	3111	3196	4112	*1311*	*3311*	*3313*	*3323*	*4312*	*4433 / 2212*	**3425**	**3328**	**3324**	**3320**	**3327**	**3330**	**3321**
Core values																					
Professionalism																					
Leadership			X					X	*X*					*XX*	**X**		**X**				
Practical approach	X										*X*		*X*		**X**						**X**
Services	X	X													**X**		**X**		**X**		**X**
Teamwork						X	X	X	*X*						**X**		**X**				**X**
Relevance		X		X					*X*	*X*	*X*	*X*						**X**	**X**	**X**	**X**
Partnerships		X								*X*			*X*	*XX*	**X**						**X**
Timeliness	X									*X*								**X**	**X**	**X**	**X**
Reflexivity								X						*XX*			**X**			**X**	**X**
Stewardship																					
Sustainability									*X*	*X*	*X*	*X*		*XX*	**X**		**X**		**X**		**X**
Responsibility		X				X			*X*			*X*		*XX*	**X**	**X**	**X**	**X**		**X**	**X**
Service to community	X			X	X	X									**X**		**X**				**X**
Ethics																					
Honesty	X		X			X			*X*	*X*		*X*		*XX*		**X**					
Transparency	X		X			X				*X*		*X*							**X**		
Authenticity	X		X			X						*X*		*XX*							
Authentic self	X		X			X															
Mutual respect																					
Diversity					X						*X*								**X**		
Inclusion		X			X						*X*	*X*					**X**		**X**		**X**
Equity					X							*X*					**X**				
Humility					X				*X*												
Cooperation						X	X	X	*X*		*X*						**X**				**X**
Knowledge																					
Critical thinking				X		X			*X*	*X*		*X*		*XX*			**X**	**X**	**X**	**X**	**X**
Innovation				X		X				*X*			*X*		**X**			**X**	**X**	**X**	**X**
Creativity				X		X									**X**						
Networking skills	X							X							**X**		**X**				

Notes. THM Core = normal font; THM Major = italic font; THM Electives = bold.

APPENDIX B: BLOOMS TAXONOMY—KNOWLEDGE, COMPREHENSION, APPLICATION, ANALYSIS, SYNTHESIS, EVALUATION

Bloom recommended that the learning objectives always started with:

Upon conclusion of the learning unit students will be able to: (then fill in the action verb)

Course level	Bloom Taxonomy	Action verbs
Freshman 1000's	Knowledge	Attend, choose, complete, define, describe, differentiate, distinguish, identify, imitate, indicate, label, list, match, name, recall, recognize, select
	Comprehension	Arrange, categorize, cite, classify, compile, conduct, defend, demonstrate, determine, diagram, differentiate, explain, extrapolate, formulate, generalize, give example, illustrate, in own words, infer interpret, itemize, locate, organize, paraphrase, predict, prepare, relate, rephrase, summarize, translate, update
Sophomore 2000's	Application	Apply, calculate, change, choose, classify, compute, construct, develop, discover, employ, generalize, manipulate, modify, organize, predict, prepare, produce, restructure, show, solve, use
Junior 3000's	Analysis	Analyze, appraise, breakdown, categorize, combine, compare, conclude, contrast, criticize, deduce, defend, detect, diagram, differentiate, distinguish, evaluate, formulate, generate, identify, illustrate, induce, infer, outline, paraphrase, plan, point out, present, question, relate, separate
Senior 4000's	Synthesis	Alter, change, compile, create, derive, discuss, document, expand, explain, generalize, modify, originate, propose, rearrange, reconstruct, reorganize, revise, rewrite, summarize, systemize, tell, write
	Evaluation	Appraise, argue, assess, compare, conclude, consider, contrast, critique, decide, discriminate, interpret, judge, justify, recommend, standardize, validate

APPENDIX C: SCHOOL OF TOURISM AND HOSPITALITY MANAGEMENT CORE

THM 1112: Career Seminar (1 semester hour [s.h.])

This course is designed to expose new students to academic and professional development through a series of lectures from industry leaders, exposure to student professional organizations (SPOs), explanation and practice on writing criteria within STHM, and resume development. In addition, students will register in e-Recruiting through the Center for Student Professional Development (CSPD). Other areas of discussion will involve advising practices, e-mail etiquette, professional attire, and public speaking. Values addressed include:

PROFESSIONALISM
Practical Approach
Services
Timeliness

STEWARDNESS
Service to the Community

ETHICS
Honesty
Transparency
Authenticity
Authentic Self

KNOWLEDGE
Networking Skills

Upon conclusion of this course students will be able to:

1. Define professionalism
2. Demonstrate stewardship
3. Distinguish appropriate stewardship
4. Describe ethics
5. Illustrate knowledge of networking

Assignments include exams and quizzes, reaction papers, interviews, and conference attendance.

THM 1113: Foundation of Leisure (3 s.h.)

This course is an introduction to the nature, scope, and significance of leisure. The course will address the history, conceptual foundations, and socio-cultural dimensions of play, recreation, sport, tourism, hospitality, and leisure; the significance of play, recreation, sport, tourism, hospitality, and leisure in contemporary society and throughout the life span; the interrelationship between leisure behavior and the natural environment; the motivational basis for play, recreation, sport, tourism, hospitality, and leisure behavior; concepts of time, work, and leisure; leisure around the world; patterns of leisure involvement; and the issues, trends, challenges, and the future of leisure. Values addressed include:

PROFESSIONALISM
Services
Relevance
Partnerships

STEWARDSHIP
Responsibility

MUTUAL RESPECT
Inclusion

Upon conclusion of this course students will be able to:

1. Summarize the history of professionalism inclusive of the service industry, relevance of the services, and the importance of partnerships.
2. Recognize the value of stewardship and their individual responsibility.
3. Defend the concept of mutual respect and inclusion.

Assignments include exams and quizzes, position papers, and reaction papers.

THM 1114: Leadership (3 s.h.)

This course introduces the core critical concepts in tourism, hospitality, sport, and recreation organizational and servant leadership. Theoretical, philosophical, and applied leadership concepts are introduced to cultivate leadership qualities and skills within each participant for application in a variety of different managerial settings. A wide range of contemporary leadership challenges and opportunities are analyzed to promote ethical decision making among future leaders in tourism, hospitality, sport, and recreation. Values addressed include:

PROFESSIONALISM
Leadership

ETHICS
Honesty
Transparency
Authenticity
Authentic Self

Upon conclusion of this course students will be able to:

1. Define leadership and give examples of leaders in the industry.
2. Differentiate between ethical and non-ethical behavior.
3. Formulate an opinion of what it means to be transparent and authentic.

4. Give an example of experiencing an encounter when a person was presumed to be their authentic self (or not).

Assignments include exams and quizzes, role playing, position paper, and case study.

THM 2112: Sophomore Research Seminar (2 s.h.)

This course is designed to expose students to research methods and search capabilities. Students will be exposed to literature searches using Paley Library Publications and online databases. Students will be expected to prepare a thesis topic and write a literature review supporting the related theory. In addition, students will be exposed to strategies for Internet searching for industry issues, expected to formulate an opinion, and write a paper based on a synthesis of the information. Values addressed include:

PROFESSIONALISM
Relevance

KNOWLEDGE
Critical Thinking
Innovation
Creativity

Upon conclusion of this course students will be able to:

1. Distinguish relevant research and give examples of the contribution research made the tourism industry.
2. Interpret research (critical thinking) by paraphrasing the implications of published research.
3. Generate a researchable topic (innovation and creativity) and conduct a literature review to support the topic.

Assignments include literature review, annotated bibliography, and research proposal.

2114: Leisure and Tourism in a Diverse Society (3 s.h.)

This course emphasizes leisure, sport, recreation, tourism, and hospitality services for a multi-cultural, multi-racial, multi-ethnic society, as well as for persons with disabilities. As the course explores the significance of play, recreation, and leisure throughout the life span, it will focus on the impact of leisure delivery systems on diverse populations within our society.

Implications of personal biases will be a thread throughout the course. Values addressed include:

STEWARDSHIP
Service to the Community

MUTUAL RESPECT
Diversity
Inclusion
Equity
Humility

Upon conclusion of this course students will be able to:

1. Demonstrate service to the community by organizing a service project.
2. Prepare a statement on Mutual Respect including the terms diversity and inclusion.
3. Formulate a policy on equity (inclusive of persons with disabilities) for your business.
4. Write a reaction paper on how you felt when role playing a disability.

Assignments include event planning, reaction papers, policy development and role playing.

3111: Program and Special Event Planning (3 s.h.)

This course presents a sequential model of the program and event planning process with particular focus upon the role of the servant leader. The course includes a strong theoretical foundation, formulation of philosophy and goals; needs assessment; selection and design of special program and/or one-time event elements; implementation; and evaluation. Different program and special event formats, including fairs, family reunions, festivals, recreation events, sporting events, meetings, conferences, social events, and grand openings, with different levels of leadership involvement will be discussed. Values addressed include:

PROFESSIONALISM
Teamwork

STEWARDSHIP
Service to the Community

MUTUAL RESPECT
Cooperation

Upon conclusion of this course students will be able to:

1. Identify a community need, develop a special event with a team and produce the event in the community.
2. Organize a productive team.

Assignments include event planning and team building.

THM 3196: Research Methodology (3 s.h.)

Prerequisite: Sophomore Research Seminar (THM 2112), and successful completion of Core QA and QB requirements. Warning: Failure to comply with prerequisite(s) may result in the de-enrollment of your courses.

This course will examine ways that research helps solve practical industry problems in hospitality, recreation, sports, and tourism. Topics will include problem identification, the logic of research, research designs, information search strategies, questionnaire development, and statistical analysis. Written and oral communication skills, as well as the use of data analysis software, will be stressed. Values addressed include:

PROFESSIONALISM
Teamwork

MUTUAL RESPECT
Collaboration

KNOWLEDGE
Critical Thinking
Innovation
Creativity

Upon conclusion of this course students will be able to:

1. Write a proposal to conduct research (critical thinking, innovation, and creativity).
2. Identify and critically evaluate literature (both practical and academic) that provides the foundation for research.
3. Critique a survey focusing on the various aspects of survey design and concept evaluation.
4. With a team, conduct a study which includes sampling, survey design, data collection, analysis and interpretation.
5. With a team, present in both written and oral formats the results of a research project.

Assignments include exams and quizzes, research proposal, research paper, and presentation.

THM 4112: Senior Professional Development (3 s.h.)

(Prerequisite: Successful completion of Internship I (THM 3185) and Research Methodology (THM 3196), and senior standing. Strongly recommended: Public Speaking (STOC 1111 [0065]). Warning: Failure to comply with prerequisite(s) may result in the de-enrollment of your courses.

The purpose of this class is to expose the students to a model of organizational structure in the sport, recreation, tourism, hospitality, and leisure services profession through simulated experiences. The class is designed with a president, departments, and staff roles. These roles are designed to represent the interactions that take place with various constituencies needed to enhance sport, recreation, tourism, and hospitality education and opportunities. Values addressed include:

PROFESSIONALISM
Leadership
Teamwork
Reflexivity

STEWARDSHIP
Responsibility
Service to the Community

ETHICS
Honesty
Transparency
Authenticity
Authentic Self

MUTUAL RESPECT
Collaboration

KNOWLEDGE
Networking

Upon conclusion of this course students will be able to:

1. Critique of group (class) dynamics on professionalism.
2. Evaluate the quality of stewardship.
3. Illustrate and formulate ethical behavior.
4. Illustrate and formulate appropriate networking skills.

5. Illustrate and show mutual respect.
6. Reflect on undergraduate experience.
7. Explain the TEFI core values.

Assignments include role playing, team building, conference attendance, reaction papers, and event planning.

MAJOR – TOURISM AND HOSPITALITY MANAGEMENT

THM 1311: Introduction to Tourism and Hospitality (3 s.h.)

The nature, scope and significance of the total field of tourism and hospitality; history and development, philosophies and theories, analysis of trends, issues and challenges. Values addressed include:

PROFESSIONALISM
Relevance
Partnerships

STEWARDSHIP
Sustainability

Upon conclusion of this course students will be able to:

1. Describe how the tourism industry must position itself as relevant to the economic, political and, social infrastructure of the community.
2. Describe the partnerships that exist in a typical tourism destination and explain the importance of the partnerships.
3. Illustrate the dimension of sustainability in the tourism industry.

Assignments include position paper, reaction paper, and case study.

THM 3311: Organization Management in Tourism and Hospitality (3 s.h.)

This course provides the knowledge required to formulate and manage effectively the resources in a tourism or hospitality operation. Human resource administration will be the main focus; managerial history, organizational needs, job designs, recruitment process, hiring/firing process, discipline and grievance procedures, motivation and performance appraisals are examples of topics. Team learning approach and environment are highly emphasized. Values addressed include:

PROFESSIONALISM
Leadership
Teamwork
Relevance
Timeliness

STEWARDSHIP
Sustainability
Responsibility

ETHICS
Honesty

MUTUAL RESPECT
Humility
Cooperation

KNOWLEDGE
Critical Thinking
Innovation

Upon conclusion of this course students will be able to:

1. Compare and contrast a current business with a hypothetical future business
2. Formulate an innovative future business concept, inclusive of issues related to sustainability and social responsibility
3. Apply leadership and ethical skills within a team
4. Create a collaborative environment throughout the semester with your assigned team.
5. Document the team experience and describe the various dynamics of the team.

Assignments include case study, team building, role playing, reaction paper, and business plan.

THM 3313: Financial Issues in Tourism and Hospitality (3 s.h.)

Prerequisite: ACCT 2101 (0001) and ECON 1101 (C051). Warning: Failure to comply with prerequisite(s) may result in the de-enrollment of your courses.

This course is designed to provide students with knowledge of the fundamental concepts and tools that represent the core of financial management. The course will particularly emphasize the financial function and issues in a hospitality organization and will provide the student with applications of financial concepts in the context of hospitality financial management. Values addressed include:

PROFESSIONALISM
Practical Approach
Relevance

STEWARDSHIP
Sustainability

ETHICS
Honesty
Transparency

KNOWLEDGE
Critical Thinking

Upon conclusion of this course students will be able to:

1. Construct a financial statement for a profitable and sustainable business.
2. Critique the financial statements from an authentic business and contrast various projections for growth, from practical to audacious.
3. Write a corporate policy on financial management, inclusive of honesty and penalties for being dishonest.
4. Write a memo to stockholders describing the financial health of your business.

Assignments include business plan, critique, policy writing, and business memo.

THM 3323: International Tourism (3 s.h.)

The course concentrates on international issues for tourism activities. Problems and characteristics specific to the international aspect of the tourism industry will be examined. By the end of the course, students will develop a comprehensive understanding of the international tourism system. Special readings from the current literature will form an integral part of this course. Students will also improve their knowledge of world geography through the exploration of developed and potential tourist areas. Values addressed include:

PROFESSIONALISM
Relevance
Partnerships

STEWARDSHIP
Sustainability
Responsibility

MUTUAL RESPECT
Diversity
Inclusion
Cooperation

Upon conclusion of this course students will be able to:

1. Illustrate the relevance of the tourism industry and the global importance.
2. Propose a policy on sustainability and responsibility.
3. Identify and describe examples of collaboration and partnership in tourism in a global perspective.
4. Critique tourism in an emerging market.

Assignments include term papers, policy development, and reaction paper.

THM 4312: Legal Issues: Tourism and Hospitality (3 s.h.)

A comprehensive overview of laws and regulatory agencies governing the tourism and hospitality industry. Legal implications of civil laws, areas of tort and contract will be discussed, along with the law and legal relationships that exist in the business context. Hospitality law, especially when dealing with customers and business contracts, will be the main focus. Issues will be discussed from the points of view of innkeepers, restaurateurs, travel agents, and event planners. Attention will be given to labor relations laws, the Americans with Disabilities Act, risk management, zoning, and unions. Values addressed include:

PROFESSIONALISM
Practical Approach

ETHICS
Honesty
Transparency
Authenticity

MUTUAL RESPECT
Inclusion
Equity

KNOWLEDGE
Critical Thinking
Innovation

Upon conclusion of this course students will be able to:

1. Explain professionalism and legal ethics.
2. Write a position paper of business ethics.
3. Explain the laws for Affirmative Action and Equal Employment Opportunity (EEOC).
4. Explain the NAACP Report Card.
5. Defend or prosecute a specific civil case brought before the US court system.

Assignments include exams and quizzes, position paper, term paper, critique, and case analysis.

THM 4321: Capstone-Hospitality Management Systems or THM 4322 – Capstone-Designing Tourism Experiences

4321: HOSPITALITY MANAGEMENT SYSTEMS (3 s.h.)

Co-Requisite: Senior Professional Development Seminar (THM 4112).

The hospitality organization's use a variety of information technologies to facilitate various business activities such as reservation, marketing, operations, and management, with a direct impact on revenues and market share. A perfect synergy between information systems and the hospitality industry requires decision-makers to not only understand the functionalities of advanced systems, but also be able to successfully interpret systems' analyses for their current management practices (e.g., yield management). Using an advanced lodging management system as an effective instructional tool, this course focuses on the fundamentals of management systems within the today's hospitality organizations in general and lodging operations in particular. Students will be exposed to industry examples, in-depth discussions, and simulation projects about how to strategically integrate system applications such as property management, reservation management, sales and marketing management, point of sales systems, and meeting space rentals, etc. within a hotel setting, as well as their impacts on organizations and the industry as a whole. Values addressed include:

4322: DESIGNING TOURISM EXPERIENCES (3 s.h.)

Co-Requisite: Senior Professional Development Seminar (THM 4112).

This course presents an overview of the process of designing effective tourism hardware (attractions, etc.) and software (programs, special events, etc.). Students will learn how to define effective tourism experiences that add value to the visitor experience and how to measure and evaluate these experiences using both qualitative and quantitative methods. Furthermore, students will learn customer experience marketing and management principles to promote affinity and loyalty among tourism consumer groups. Values addressed include:

PROFESSIONALISM
Leadership
Partnerships
Reflexivity

STEWARDSHIP
Sustainability
Responsibility

ETHICS
Honesty
Authenticity

KNOWLEDGE
Critical Thinking

Upon conclusion of this course students will be able to:

1. Compare and contrast professionalism as a required skill to possess in the tourism and hospitality industry.
2. Compare and contrast stewardship required of the tourism and hospitality community.
3. Compare and contrast ethical behavior required in the tourism and hospitality industry.
4. Assess the Core Values curriculum provided in the tourism and hospitality management degree program.

Assignments include simulations, position papers, and reaction papers.

ELECTIVES - TOURISM AND HOSPITALITY MANAGEMENT

THM 3425: Event Management: History, Theory, and Best Practices (3 s.h.)

This course provides an in-depth and comprehensive analysis of the global events industry. Topics will include the feasibility, viability, and sustainability of the event process; the strategic planning, business development, marketing, human resource management, finance and budgeting, event creation and event orchestration, communications, and career development aspects of event leaders. The course will also include Third Wave event leadership thinking and trace the development of the field from process, to outcomes, to sustainability. Values addressed include:

PROFESSIONALISM
Leadership
Practicality
Services
Teamwork
Partnerships

STEWARDSHIP
Sustainability
Responsibility
Service to the Community

KNOWLEDGE
Innovation
Creativity
Networking

Upon conclusion of this course students will be able to:

1. Demonstrate a leadership role in an assigned team to produce an event with an industry partner where community needs have been analyzed and an event designed to meet one or more of those needs.
2. Prepare a sustainable event policy for an event enterprise.
3. Use the BHAG theory and design an event for the 25th anniversary of STHM (2023).
4. Produce the STHM Networking event.

Assignments include event design, event production, and policy writing.

THM 3328: Gaming and Casino Management (3 s.h.)

This course is an overview of the role gambling plays in today's society. The course's goal is to provide students with the background necessary to understand the gaming industry and its relationship to tourism, hospitality, recreation, and sports. Topics include the evolution of legal gaming, its management and regulation, the structure of the various gaming industries, and key terminology. Analysis of participation patterns and impacts of gambling, both positive and negative, on society will be addressed. An introduction to game rules and basic concepts from probability and statistics necessary to understand gambling operations will be discussed. Values addressed include:

STEWARDSHIP
Responsibility

ETHICS
Honesty

Upon conclusion of this course students will be able to:

1. Defend gaming as a leisure activity.
2. Prepare a social responsibility policy for a casino.
3. Describe ethical issues in the gaming industry.

Assignments include term paper, policy writing, and position paper.

THM 3324: Hospitality Operations (3 s.h.)

Hospitality Operations will focus on an integration and application of planning, implementation, operation, and maintenance of accommodations, including hotels, motels, and resorts. The physical aspects, capital investments, layout, and design will be included with the operational component. The course will also provide students with guided learning and hands-on experience in using a property management system. Values addressed include:

PROFESSIONALISM
Leadership
Services
Teamwork

STEWARDSHIP
Sustainability
Responsibility
Service to the Community

MUTUAL RESPECT
Inclusion
Equity
Collaboration

KNOWLEDGE
Critical Thinking
Networking

Upon conclusion of this course students will be able to:

1. Describe leadership role models in the hospitality industry.
2. Write a social responsibility policy for a hotel.
3. Describe a model for a "green" hotel, and give examples of companies who are doing it well.
4. Write an affirmative action policy for a hotel.
5. Illustrate the process of hotel planning and development.

Assignments include exams and quizzes, hotel design project, business plan, and position papers.

THM 3320: Special Topics: Hospitality Management (3 s.h.)

This course is designed to provide students with an in-depth analysis of the current issues facing hospitality management. The course will address some of the major issues currently facing tourism and hospitality managers in the areas of advertising, public relations, information technology, and management systems. The course will build on the competencies students have already developed in their earlier courses, which introduced them to the basics of marketing, management, and finance. Given their working knowledge, students will be called upon in class to identify potential solutions to current issues. Values addressed include:

PROFESSIONALISM
Relevance
Timeliness
Reflexivity

STEWARDSHIP
Responsibility

KNOWLEDGE
Critical Thinking
Innovation

Upon conclusion of this course students will be able to:

1. Generate realistic concepts about future trends in the hospitality industry.
2. Describe relevance and timeliness about trends and the product life cycle.
3. Defend a position about the evolution of the hospitality industry- past to present to future.

Assignments include position paper, term paper, and presentations.

THM 3327: Advanced Destination Marketing Systems (3 s.h.)

Destination marketing has changed dramatically as the result of increasing competition and environmental change. This course takes a system approach and is designed to extend students' knowledge and experience in marketing to tourism and hospitality by first understanding the nature of competition within the tourism industry; second, by understanding the role of information technology; and third, by developing extensive analytical skills. Values addressed include:

PROFESSIONALISM
Services
Relevance
Timeliness

STEWARDSHIP
Sustainability

ETHICS
Transparency

MUTUALITY
Diversity
Inclusion

KNOWLEDGE
Critical Thinking
Innovation

Upon conclusion of this course students will be able to:

1. Give examples of current marketing campaigns where generation differences are used appropriately.
2. Describe concepts related to ethical marketing.
3. Create a marketing campaign to enhance a destinations image for diversity and inclusiveness.
4. Analyze the appropriateness of a comprehensive marketing plan.

Assignments include exams and quizzes, case studies, position paper, and marketing plan.

THM 3330: Special Topics: Destination and Event Management (3 s.h.)

Discussion of concepts, theories and issues relevant to the development of special interest tourism such as ecotourism, rural tourism, ethnic tourism, adventure tourism, sports tourism, health tourism, farm and ranch tourism, arts tourism, cultural heritage tourism, casino tourism, urban tourism, peace tourism, nature tourism and educational tourism. Examination of the development of tourism based on cultural, historic and natural resources. The role of historic preservation, the arts, and the humanities to the tourism industry will be explored, as well as the unlimited opportunities for future growth. Values addressed include:

PROFESSIONALISM
Relevance
Timeliness
Reflexivity

STEWARDSHIP
Responsibility

KNOWLEDGE
Critical Thinking
Innovation

Upon conclusion of this course students will be able to:

1. Generate realistic concepts about future trends in the hospitality industry.
2. Describe relevance and timeliness about trends and the product life cycle.
3. Defend a position about the evolution of the hospitality industry past to present to future.

Assignments include position paper and term paper.

THM 3321 – Tourism Planning and Development (3 s.h.)

An analysis of the socioeconomic planning process involved in developing tourism destinations in global, community, metropolitan, urban, and rural settings. Emphasis will be on policy and product development, regeneration and enhancement of facilities and services to meet the needs of tourists. Includes the adjustment process involved in integrating tourism into a developing economy, and the project management skills inherent in steering a development from inception to fruition. Extensive use is made of concepts from sociology, economics, political science, and business disciplines. Special readings from the current literature, case studies, guest speakers, and video cases will form an integral part of this course. Values addressed include:

PROFESSIONALISM
Practical Approach
Services
Teamwork
Relevance
Timeliness
Partnerships
Reflexivity

STEWARDSHIP
Sustainability
Responsibility
Service to the Community

MUTUAL RESPECT
Inclusion
Cooperation

KNOWLEDGE
Critical Thinking
Innovation

Upon conclusion of this course students will be able to:

1. Describe the importance of teamwork and partnerships in tourism planning.
2. Describe the importance of relevance and timeliness of the tourism industry to respond to global issues.
3. Create a tourism policy that describes responsibility and sustainability to the community and includes economic, social, political, and environmental impacts.
4. Define the term inclusion as it relates to a tourism destination.
5. Analyze a tourism destination and evaluate its successes and failures.

Assignments include exams and quizzes, position paper, policy writing, and case study.

THM 3185, 4185, and 4191(Not included in the chart): Internship Requirements

3185: INTERNSHIP I (3 S.H.)

Prerequisite: C- or better in all THM 1000- and 2000-level courses. Warning: Failure to comply with prerequisite(s) may result in the de-enrollment of your courses.

Students will be assigned to an industry agency to complete 180 hours of professional experience. The agency will be selected through cooperation between the student, the School Internship Coordinator and an agency supervisor.

4185: INTERNSHIP II (10 TO 12 S.H.)

Prerequisite: C- or better in all THM courses. Warning: Failure to comply with prerequisite(s) may result in the de-enrollment of your courses. Co-Requisite: THM 4191 (0381).

After having completed the student's last semester of classes, and taken in conjunction with THM 4191 (0381). The student must complete 600 hours with an industry agency.
Note: The requirements of this experience are addressed in the School's senior internship manual (which is distributed in THM 4112 [0370]).

4191: SENIOR PROJECT (3 S.H.)

Prerequisite: C- or better in all THM courses. Warning: Failure to comply with prerequisite(s) may result in the de-enrollment of your courses. Co-Requisite: THM 4185 (0380).

The culminating written project agreed upon by the University and agency supervisors.

Experiential education is a key to summative assessment of student learning. While the insertion of learning objectives into individual courses in a curriculum allows for a base assessment (or formative evaluation), the most comprehensive assessment models require an overall evaluation tool or summative evaluation. STHM has chosen the internship component of the students' experience to formulate a measurement tool to evaluate learning. Observation from the internship supervisor is the main form of evaluation. Students receive a midterm and final evaluation from the site supervisor. Obviously this evaluation includes the students' work performance, but it also includes some of the core values. The supervisor is asked to rate the students' behaviors and attitudes. Professionalism, ethics, mutual respect, and knowledge are heavily covered in this evaluation.

APPENDIX D: COURSE EMBEDDED ASSESSMENT

CORE Values: Based on Tourism Education Futures Initiative (TEFI)

COURSE INTEGRATED PLAN

Core Value:

Professionalism: incorporating leadership, a practical approach, attention to services, concern for the relevance and timeliness of evidence, reflexivity, teamwork and partnership building skills.

Bloom's Taxonomy: the measures of Bloom's Taxonomy cut across all levels of classes; perhaps in different levels of intensity.

Knowledge	Comprehension	Application	Analysis	Synthesis	Evaluation
•Define, Describe, Recall, Identify, List, Recognize	•Explain, Classify, Interpret, Summarize, Give Examples	•Apply, Generalize, Develop, Criticize, Modify, Organize	•Analyze, Appraise, Compare, Criticize, Outline, Paraphrase	•Change, Create, Compile, Modify, Revise, Summarize	•Assess, Judge, Recommend, Validate, Compare/Contrast
Define for Value · Awareness of service in industry; · Aware of elements of professionalism in industry; and · Understanding about groups teamwork, and partnerships.	· Understand about differences among organizations; · Understand about the mission/goals/purpose of organizations or teams; and · Understand they can join teams, build networks.	· Join an organization; or · Join a team in the classroom setting; · Perceive group dynamics; and · Classify leadership styles.	· As a member of the organization (or team); able to think critically of the work of the organization; · Begin to reflect on what could be improved; and · Analyze group dynamics.	· Reflect on the purpose or work of the team or organization; · Submit change or innovative ideas; and · Display leadership characteristics.	· Become a change agent; · Become a decision maker (executive member) of the organization; and · Provide input into setting priorities.
Assignments · Test and quiz knowledge and purpose of organizations.	· Video critique · Personal statement of leadership · Role play and Case studies	· Team building exercises	· Industry Interviews · SWOT Analysis	· Business Plans; Marketing Plans; strategic Plans · Team project (course specific) · Socratic teaching method	· Reflection of college experience · Conference Attendance

Core Value:

Stewardship: including the concepts of sustainability, responsibility and service to community.

Bloom's Taxonomy: the measures of Bloom's Taxonomy cut across all levels of classes; perhaps in different levels of intensity.

Knowledge	Comprehension	Application	Analysis	Synthesis	Evaluation
•Define, Describe, Identify, List, Recall, Recognize	•Explain, Classify, Interpret, Summarize, Give Examples	•Apply, Generalize, Develop, Criticize, Modify, Organize	•Analyze, Appraise, Compare, Criticize, Outline, Paraphrase	•Change, Create, Compile, Modify, Revise, Summarize	•Assess, Judge, Recommend, Validate, Compare/Contrast

Define for Value

Knowledge	Comprehension	Application	Analysis	Synthesis	Evaluation
· Awareness of stewardness; · Aware of professional and individual responsibility for organizations in industry; and · Understanding corporate social responsibility.	· Understand about differences among organizations – good practices vs. minimal effort; and · Understanding about the mission/goals/purpose of organizations or teams.	· Select an organization to use as role model; or · Join a team in the classroom setting.	· As a member of the organization (or team), student is able to think critically of the stewardship of the organization; and · Begin to reflect on what could be improved.	· Reflect and the purpose of the team or organizations' sustainability and responsibility; · Discuss sustainability options for organization; and · Outline policy on corporate social responsibility.	· Become a change agent; · Become a decision maker (executive member) of the organization; and · Provide input into setting priorities.

Assignments

Knowledge	Comprehension	Application	Analysis	Synthesis	Evaluation
· Test and quiz knowledge and purpose of organizations.	· Review event footprint · Role play and simulation · Review company websites for "green Initiatives"	· Compare and contrast company policies · Case study · Industry Interviews on community service · Research paper	· Event Volunteerism and Analysis · Organize Service Learning	· Business Plans; strategic Plans · Policy analysis · Execute a community event	· Write company policy · Conference Attendance

Core Value:

Ethics: honesty, transparency, authenticity, authentic self.

Bloom's Taxonomy: The measures of Bloom's Taxonomy cut across all levels of classes; perhaps in different levels of intensity.

Knowledge	Comprehension	Application	Analysis	Synthesis	Evaluation
•Define, Describe, Identify, List, Recall, Recognize	•Explain, Classify, Interpret, Summarize, Give Examples	•Apply, Generalize, Develop, Criticize, Modify, Organize	•Analyze, Appraise, Compare, Criticize, Outline, Paraphrase	•Change, Create, Compile, Summarize, Modify, Revise	•Assess, Conclude, Judge, Recommend, Validate

Define for Value

Knowledge	Comprehension	Application	Analysis	Synthesis	Evaluation
· Awareness of industry ethical issues; · Aware of professional organizations and codes of conduct and · Describe ethics and ethical behavior.	· Understand about differences among organizations ethical issues; · Understanding about the mission/goals/codes of ethics; and · Understand self awareness and authenticity.	· Join an organization; · Apply ethical standards in work setting; and · Illustrate ethical behavior	· As a member of the organization able to think critically of the work of the organization; and · Begin to reflect on what could be improved.	· Reflect on the purpose or work of the team or organization; · Create a code of conduct or vise a company's policies on ethics; and · Compare and contrast ethical issues.	· Become a change agent; · Become a decision maker (executive member) of the organization; and · Provide input into setting priorities.

Assignments

· Test and quiz knowledge and purpose of organizations.
· Video critique
· Review current events
· Role play and Case studies
· Oral presentation
· Reaction paper
· Industry interviews
· Review mission statements, codes of ethics, and standards of conduct
· SWOT Analysis
· Business Plans; Corporate social responsibility Plans;
· Socratic teaching method
· Write a Code of Ethics
· Conference Attendance

Core Value:

Mutuality: recognition of diversity, inclusion, equity, humility, and a commitment to cooperation.

Bloom's Taxonomy: the measures of Bloom's Taxonomy cut across all levels of classes; perhaps in different levels of intensity.

Knowledge	Comprehension	Application	Analysis	Synthesis	Evaluation
• Define, Describe, Identify, List, Recall, Recognize	• Explain, Classify, Interpret, Summarize, Give Examples	• Apply, Generalize, Develop, Criticize, Modify, Organize	• Analyze, Apprraise, Compare, Criticize, Outline, Paraphrase	• Change, Create, Compile, Summarize, Modify, Revise	• Assess, Conclude, Judge, Recommend, Validate
Define for Value					
• Awareness of mutual respect and inclusion;	• Understand about differences among people;	• Collaboration as a management style;	• As a member of the organization (or team), think critically of the work of the organization; and	• Reflect on related issues;	• Become a change agent;
• Aware of professional organization in industry; and	• Understanding about the mission/goals/purpose of organizations related to diversity; and	• Display humility;		• Illustrate and formulate mutual respect policies;	• Become a decision maker (executive member) of the organization; and
• Understanding about group dynamics.	• Understanding of building networks.	• Mentorship program and integration; and	• They begin to reflect on what could be improved.	• Create policies on tolerance; and	• Provide input into setting priorities.
		• Join an organization (or team) serving an underrepresented group.		• Present position statement.	
Assignments					
• Test and quiz knowledge and purpose of organizations.	• Understand knowledge and purpose of organizations.	• Role play and Case studies	• Review HR policies	• Prepare a statement on Mutual Respect	• Write a policy on equity
	• Video critique	• Team building exercises	• Reaction paper	• Socratic teaching method	• Conference Attendance
	• Interview protected class	• Self Awareness	• Sensitivity assessment	• Service project	• Study abroad
		• Service learning	• Sensitivity training		

Core Value:
Knowledge: emphasis on critical thinking skills, innovation, creativity, and networking skills.
Bloom's Taxonomy: the measures of Bloom's Taxonomy cut across all levels of classes; perhaps in different levels of intensity.

Knowledge	Comprehension	Application	Analysis	Synthesis	Evaluation
• Define, Describe, Identify, List, Recall, Recognize	• Explain, Classify, Interpret, Summarize, Give Examples	• Apply, Generalize, Develop, Criticize, Modify, Organize	• Analyze, Appraise, Compare, Criticize, Outline, Paraphrase	• Change, Create, Compile, Summarize, Modify, Revise	• Assess, Conclude, Judge, Recommend, Validate

Define for Value

Knowledge	Comprehension	Application	Analysis	Synthesis	Evaluation
· Awareness of industry concepts; · Aware of professional issues; and · Understanding about industry concepts .	· Understand about differences among organizations; · Understanding about the mission/goals/purpose of organizations or teams; and · Understanding they can join teams, build networks.	· Generate researchable topics (innovation and creativity); Interpret critical issues	· As a member of the organization (or team), student is able to think critically of the work of the organization. · They begin to reflect on what could be improved.	· Reflect and modify; critical thinking and innovation.	· Become a change agent; · Become a decision maker (executive member) of the organization; and · Provide input into setting priorities.

Assignments

· Test and quiz knowledge and purpose of organizations.
· Video critique
· Annotated bibliography
· Role play and case studies
· Literature review
· Team building exercises
· Industry Interviews
· SWOT Analysis
· Research proposals
· Business Plans; marketing plans; strategic plans
· Conduct a survey
· Socratic teaching method
· Conduct research project and present findings
· Conference Attendance

APPENDIX E: SAMPLE STUDENT RESPONSES TO ASSESSMENT QUESTIONS

Professionalism

- *Because of this course, I appreciate the importance of teamwork and partnerships.*
- *This course contributed to my understanding of professionalism as it relates to the industries.*
- *This course challenged me to think more strategically in terms of the future of the industry.*
- *This course increased my understanding of the importance of building a professional network.*
- *This course improved my comfort level with networking.*
- *This course contributed to my understanding of finance as it relates to the broader local, state and national economies.*
- *This course contributed to my understanding of professionalism as it relates to managerial tasks, such as problem solving.*
- *This course contributed to my understanding of professionalism as it relates to the services provided in the industries.*
- *Because of this course, I understand that research is a critical aspect on today's work environment.*
- *This course contributed to my understanding of research as a part of professionalism.*
- *I have learned to work as a part of a team through the research project, in this course.*
- *This course contributed to my understanding of what it means to be a professional in the field.*
- *This course contributed to my understanding of professionalism as it relates to managerial tasks such as working with employees and working as a team member.*
- *Because of this course I appreciate the importance of relevance, timeliness, and reflexivity.*
- *This course has contributed to my understanding of professionalism as it was related to "leadership."*
- *Because of this course I appreciate the importance of research.*

Stewardship

- *I have a greater understanding of the importance of my responsibility of sustainability, because of this course.*
- *This course contributed to my knowledge of stewardship and the responsibilities our industry has to protect the natural environment.*
- *This course helped me to understand social responsibility with the industry.*

- *This course contributed to my understanding of how financial decisions made by an organization impacts the public.*
- *This course contributed to my knowledge of stewardship within the industry.*
- *I feel more compelled to volunteer within my community, because of what I learned in this course.*
- *This course has made me feel more compelled to volunteer within my community.*
- *Because of this course, I have a greater understanding of the importance of my responsibility towards the industry.*

Ethics

- *This course contributed to my understanding and appreciation of ethics within the industry.*
- *This course contributed to my understanding and appreciation of current and ethics within the industry.*
- *This course contributed to my understanding of ethics within the industry, including the importance and awareness of such issues.*
- *Because of this course, I feel I will be better prepared to deal with ethical issues within the industry*
- *Because of this course, I feel better prepared to deal with ethical issues in my career.*
- *This course encouraged me to be open to ethical positions that are not similar to my own.*
- *This course contributed to my understanding and appreciation of ethics in research.*
- *I have an understanding of ethical issues related to research, because of this course.*
- *Because of this course, I have a better understanding of the ethical financial practices in the profession.*
- *Because of this course, I have an understanding of ethical issues related to research such as using human subjects.*
- *This discussion about IRB (Institutional Review Board) contributed to my understanding and appreciation of ethical issues involved in the design and execution of research in academia.*

Mutuality

- *This course contributed to my ability to appreciate individual differences*
- *This course contributed to my ability to appreciate individual differences, I am more culturally sensitive.*
- *This course contributed to my ability to appreciate individual differences and be more culturally sensitive.*

- *Because of this course, I have become more knowledgeable of issues related to diversity and inclusion.*
- *This course helped me become more knowledgeable of the issues related to diversity and inclusions.*
- *Because of this course, I have become more knowledgeable of issues related to humility.*
- *This course contributed to my understanding of cooperation with other people.*

Knowledge

- *This course has helped me improve my critical thinking skills.*
- *This course has helped me improve my critical thinking skills from a management prospective.*
- *This course challenged me to think more amount innovation and the future of the industry.*
- *This course challenged me to think more amount innovation and the future of the industry as compared to focusing solely on today's issues.*
- *This course helped me be better prepared for the real world.*
- *This course challenged me to think more about research.*
- *This course helped me improve my research skills.*
- *This course has helped me to understand current issues facing professionals in the field.*
- *This course required me to "think outside the box."*
- *The test items in this class required me to apply my theoretical knowledge rather than defining theories.*
- *This course has given me greater knowledge about what is currently happening in the industry.*
- *The projects facilitated an opportunity to experience the challenges and benefits of teamwork and partnerships; as such it better prepared me for a career in the industry where teamwork is a fundamental component.*

Teaching Based on TEFI Values: A Case Study

ULRIKE GRETZEL

Texas A&M University, College Station, Texas, USA, and Institute for Innovation in Business and Social Research, University of Wollongong, Wollongong, New South Wales, Australia

ANNICA ISACSSON

Laurea University of Applied Sciences, Kerava, Finland

DAVID MATARRITA

Texas A&M University, College Station, Texas, USA

ELINA WAINIO

Laurea University of Applied Sciences, Kerava, Finland

The case study presented in this article illustrates an example of value-based teaching in the context of sustainable tourism. Specifically, the five TEFI core values of mutuality, stewardship, knowledge, ethics and professionalism were integrated in an innovative learning environment that involved students from two universities in Finland and the United States who built a collaborative knowledge base via Facebook, worked on group reports, and produced a video reflecting on their learning experience. The article discusses the structure of the learning experiment and some of its outcomes while reflecting on the importance of value-based teaching in tourism.

INTRODUCTION

TEFI, the Tourism Education Future Initiatives, was created with the background and rationale that there is an urgent need for tourism education to fundamentally re-tool and re-design approaches—not incrementally by adding new courses or simply by putting courses online—but by changing the nature of what is taught and how it is taught. New ways of acting and thinking, educating and sharing, building competencies, teaching skills and knowledge are called for in a fast-changing, technology-dependent world with a global labor force and imminent threats to natural environments and the livelihoods of communities. These pressures and the increasing need for responsible stewardship in the context of tourism were hence the basic fundaments of the TEFI initiative (Sheldon, Fesenmaier, & Tribe, 2009). Based on the assumption that tourism education has to respond to current and future trends in systematic ways, a new paradigm labeled *value-based tourism education* (Sheldon & Fesenmaier, 2009) was initiated. TEFI members identified values as critical in addressing the challenges faced by tourism education in the present and the future. Therefore, the goal of previous TEFI meetings was to create a framework for value-based tourism curricula that will be globally relevant and effective in creating responsible future tourism leaders (Sheldon, Fesenmaier, Woeber, Cooper, & Antonioli, 2008).

The first challenge as defined by TEFI is the avoidance of unthinking reproduction, that is, to encourage and teach students not to fit in passively to the world that exists (Minogue, 1973). Giving insufficient attention to questions of desirable ends was a second identified challenge meaning that we can, are, and should all be responsible for the world that we create. Leadership is the third one that is being identified by TEFI as an important factor in value-based education. The fourth challenge deals with sustainability and is neatly captured by Giddens' Paradox (Giddens, 2009). This is the paradox of climate change where Giddens noted that because we are not currently unduly affected by the outcomes of climate change we fail to act. But when we are finally pressed into action by its consequences it will be too late to do anything about them. The fifth TEFI challenge deals with consensus and the sixth one with the urge and promotion of lifelong learning since trends, capacities, and competences for working life challenges in 2020–2030 cannot fully be estimated nor anticipated by research or education in 2010.

At the TEFI summit of 2009 in Lugano, Switzerland new ideas on education were discussed in the context of the value-based framework. To further the discussion and also to put some of the principles into practice, two participating faculty members decided that Texas A&M University in the United States and Laurea University of Applied Sciences in Finland would pursue an experiment related to value-based teaching involving students from both countries. Two courses taught at the two institutions, both dealing with global perspectives and sustainability in tourism, were selected as the environments in which the experiment was to be implemented. This article presents a case study of the learning/teaching experiment and reflects on implications for value-based, collaborative teaching in tourism.

BACKGROUND

Value-Based Teaching

Values are enduring beliefs that certain modes of conduct or certain end states are personally or socially preferable over others and form the supporting roots for the tree of knowledge that curricula try to nurture in students (Rodriguez & Frechtling, 2008). Teaching is always influenced by values (Veugelers, 2000), but in contrast to other forms of education, value-based education makes the underlying values transparent and emphasizes the transfer of values (Lickona, 1991). Also, value-based teaching is focused on the moral and character development of students and assumes that the learned values provide the foundation for professional practice when students assume leadership roles in their professional fields (Fahrenwald et al., 2005). As such, it requires purposeful integration of values in the curriculum. Consequently, value-based education implies not only the transfer of knowledge and the development of skills but also the development of values (Veugelers, 2000). Further, value-based education is different from the critical thinking education paradigm in that critical thinking focused education tries to develop skills to analyze values, while value-based education implies explicit ideas about the values that are necessary for students (Veugelers, 2000). These values link a certain career field to society (Rodriguez & Frechtling, 2008). Rodriguez and Frechtling (2008) also emphasized that "a curriculum grounded in a reflective, stabilizing value system may be the best strategy against the disorienting effects of environmental change and for achieving desired futures" (p. 4). Especially in a dynamic field like tourism, values are important in providing the foundation for ethical decision-making in the absence of environmental stability (Sheldon et al., 2008).

The TEFI Values-Based Education Framework

Recognizing that values are an important component of future-directed tourism education, TEFI acknowledges and promotes five core values, namely stewardship, mutuality, ethics, professionalism, and knowledge (Sheldon et al., 2009). It, thus, strongly endorses meaningful education that goes beyond the simple transfer of knowledge and skills. Figure 1 in the lead article of this special issue illustrates the various dimensions of the core values and the overlap of the value bubbles, signifying that the values are interdependent. *Stewardship* refers to an engagement with the world and stresses the connection between our actions today and their consequences in the future. It encompasses sustainability, responsibility and service to communities. *Mutuality* integrates diversity, equity, inclusion, humility, and collaboration. It is conceptualized as "a value grounded in human relationships that requires attitudinal developments that are evolving, dynamic and involve acceptance, self-awareness of structural inequalities, open-mindedness, empowerment, and ability to revisit one'[s] cultural understanding of the world" (Sheldon & Fesenmaier, 2009, p. 21). *Ethics* involves among other things honesty and transparency. It is fundamentally concerned with distinguishing between right and wrong behaviors and having the ability to judge questionable behaviors. It also involves the recognition of the existence of differences in moral systems that guide behaviors. Ethics is further concerned with defining and promoting authenticity. *Professionalism* is defined as "incorporating leadership, a practical approach (practicality), attention to services, concern for the relevance and timeliness of evidence, reflexivity, teamwork and partnership building skills, and proactivity" (Sheldon & Fesenmaier, 2009, p. 18). It not only refers to skills, competencies, or standards associated with it but also to an attitude that reflects all these dimensions and fundamentally influences behavior. Last but not least, the knowledge value stresses that knowledge does not only refer to specific contents but that it emerges from value-driven creation and dissemination processes. As such, the knowledge value addresses questions related to creativity, critical thinking, networking, and innovation.

Implied in the framework is the notion that these values are especially important in tourism and, consequently, in the education of future tourism leaders. A fundamental assumption of the TEFI values-based framework is that it is not enough to teach these values as content areas in existing courses based on traditional classroom settings. Rather, it calls for innovative ways in which these values can be integrated into curricula, teaching methods, and the design of learning environments.

Teaching Sustainable Tourism

Sustainable tourism as a subject area has been integrated in many tourism curricula around the world. However, there is an ever greater recognition that sustainable tourism education has to be value-based. Sustainability is a value dimension in the TEFI values framework as described above. In addition, Jennings, Kensbock, and Kachel (2010) have recently pointed out that tourism education should not only be "about" but also "for" sustainability, suggesting that sustainability education requires value development in students. Leaders with strong core values are seen as fundamental to the "necessary revolution" toward sustainability in business described by Senge, Smith, Kruschwitz, Laur, and Schley (2008). Also, sustainability is a complex, highly political subject that makes intellectual engagement with values a must (Rodriguez & Frechtling, 2008).

Value-based education in general, and in particular in the context of teaching sustainable tourism, requires active student-driven learning (Fogarty, 2005). Jennings et al. (2010) described the importance of changing student learning engagements in order to teach "for" sustainability. The complexity of the subject further calls for collaborative teaching approaches as discussed by Gretzel, Jamal, Stronza, and Nepal (2008) who taught an interdisciplinary, field-based course on sustainability in the context of international tourism. The following case study presents a teaching experiment that sought to implement value-based teaching in the context of sustainable tourism, taking into account that the nature of the subject as well as the principles of value-based teaching call for active, self-directed student learning.

CASE STUDY

In the spring of 2010, students from Texas A&M University in the United States were offered the chance to participate in an elective course titled "Sustainability and International Tourism." The purpose of the course was an introduction to International Tourism with the focus on sustainability in the context of tourism planning, management, marketing and impacts. The course was co-taught by Ulrike Gretzel and David Matarrita, two Assistant Professors from the Department of Recreation, Park, and Tourism Sciences. The students were 10 advanced undergraduate and 2 graduate students from various departments including communication, manufacturing engineering, and recreation, park, and tourism sciences. At the same time a similar study unit titled Global and Local Perspectives was being taught at Laurea University of Applied Sciences in Finland. This course was taught by Principal Lecturer Annica Isacsson and Senior Lecturer Elina Wainio. The 19 Laurea students were all in their first year of tourism studies. As part of a class-project, the Texas A&M University and Laurea University of Applied Sciences students collaborated to study sustainability in various countries including Australia, Mauritius, New Zealand, and the Amazon. The destinations were selected by the students based on their interests. Facebook was used as a tool for sharing research and communicating about the project. For this purpose, a private Facebook group was established that allowed students to freely post and comment on other postings (Figure 1). All four faculty members had administrative rights to the group.

Learning Engagements

The core learning activity involved students collecting information about sustainability. As part of the exercise, the students posted on the Facebook group's wall the research they found including government web sites, news articles and YouTube videos on sustainability. Thus, rather than presenting the students with knowledge, they were encouraged to actively create and share knowledge. They also interacted through individual group discussion boards about issues specific to their assigned countries. The project

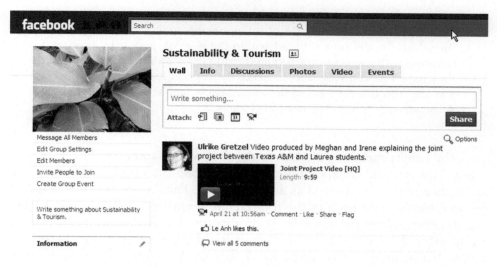

FIGURE 1 Facebook group established for the course.

culminated in the students writing a 10-page paper report based on findings related to government activity, policies and actions, definitions, local action, etc., in the destinations they chose. Moreover, a video on the joint project was produced by two students for the purpose of demonstration, evaluation, and reflection. All students contributed to the video with ideas and actual commentary included in the video.

Although very limited, the faculty members provided some structure and seeded some of the discussions in order to initiate the student participation. As part of this initial structure, the faculty members agreed upon the following readings for the course:

- Ehmer, P., & Heymann, E. (2008). *Climate change and tourism: Where will the journey lead?* Report by Deutsche Bank Research. Frankfurt, Germany.
- Hardy, A., Beeton, R. J. S., & Pearson, L. (2002). Sustainable tourism: An overview of the concept and its position in relation to conceptualisations of tourism. *Journal of Sustainable Tourism, 10*(6), 475–496.
- Forsyth, T. (n.d.). *Sustainable tourism.* Retrieved from http://www.fathom.com/course/21701788/index.html

Over a four-week period (February 1–February 28), students engaged in joint discussions on the Facebook group. The posting rules were defined as follows:

Every student needs to post at least once a week. Posts can be any of the following: Links to newspaper articles, Websites or YouTube videos, photos, references to journal articles or book chapters, etc. related to sustainability and tourism. Every student needs to at least start one new thread on the discussion board within the 4 week period by posting a question with respect to the required readings or additional readings that they have found. Every student needs to respond to posts at least twice a week. You can respond to the same post twice. Your post has to be a substantial response (e.g. not just "I agree).

The faculty members monitored the discussions and provided additional input. This ensured collaboration not only among students but also between students and faculty, as well as among faculty. Faculty members divided up responsibilities with each of the four faculty members monitoring and grading the discussions for a week. They also provided guidance with respect to the overall format and content structure of the reports. Students formed teams that included both Laurea and Texas A&M students. There were three teams with eight members and one team with seven students. The team formation process started with a decision on what country/region the students wanted to study. They then assigned themselves to teams based on their interest, with the limitation that all groups had to be similar in size. As a team the students were required to submit a written report, 10–15 pages, 12 pt font Times New Roman, double-spaced, with a title page including the team members' names, pages numbered, and a bibliography included at the end. In their group report, the students needed to address the following issues/questions:

1. Define sustainable tourism. Use different sources, viewpoints and references.
2. What sustainability issues do you find to be the most pressing for the destination and/or geographical area?
3. What is the role of the government in promoting sustainability in the area?
4. What challenges might be encountered when implementing sustainability in the area/destination?
5. What actions do you recommend in order to make tourism at the destination more sustainable?
6. How should these strategies and/or actions be implemented and by whom?

Value Integration

The following describes how the five TEFI core values were integrated into overall course structures and the specific learning activities:

MUTUALITY

The students in the courses were diverse not only in terms of the country they were studying in but also in terms of their ethnical background (ranging from Vietnamese to Hispanic), their study majors, their age, the stage in their university careers (first year students to graduate students, gender and their prior knowledge of sustainability issues. They had to learn to respect differences in study habits, time differences, communication preferences, technology access, etc. and actively look for common grounds that would allow them to work together. Inclusion was practiced by forming teams that included students from both universities. All students were graded based on the same grading principles, making sure that students felt they were equal partners in the learning engagements. Facebook was selected as the communication platform as it allowed for the kind of collaborative learning the instructors wanted to facilitate. Students could not only post and see what others posted but could also respond to posts and engage in discussions.

STEWARDSHIP

Rather than presenting the students with pre-processed knowledge about sustainability, it was left to the students to define sustainability and to take responsibility for their own learning. The materials collected by the students will be made available to the wider research and teaching community through posting the links on the INNOTOUR platform (Liburd & Hjalager, 2010).

KNOWLEDGE

Through their postings, the students created a collaborative knowledge base. They were actively engaged in building the knowledge instead of being mere consumers of it. They also had to critically reflect on what postings were appropriate and what information was actually credible. In addition, they discussed postings made by others, engaging them into yet another level of critical thinking. Through the group reports, they then had to integrate the knowledge into a document. The video they created also allowed them to reflect on what they had learned as well as the processes they engaged in.

ETHICS

The group report required them to adequately cite sources they had used. The group project also forced students to make sure everyone contributed. Further, they needed to acknowledge and negotiate differences in value systems that existed in the two university cultures the project spanned.

PROFESSIONALISM

While the faculty members provided some basic structure, the students were mostly left on their own in terms of structuring the engagements with their counterparts in the other country. They had to be pro-active in making contacts and establishing the ground rules for their teams. They also had to work out the practicalities of writing a report together with people they had never met, had very different backgrounds, and resided in a different time zone. Timeliness of their work was critical as they had to take into account that it would take longer to accomplish things given the structural barriers to collaboration they were facing. The two students producing the video had to take on leadership in that effort, which required them to coordinate interview questions and schedule meetings with the different student groups outside of regular class times.

Learning Outcomes

POSTINGS

The project involved 38 members (22 from Finland and 16 from Texas). These members all actively contributed to the Facebook group. A total of 111 postings were counted within discussion groups, in addition to 147 links, 39 photos, YouTube videos, newspaper articles, and so on. The contents were not only extremely interesting and current, but also a lot more engaging than the typical textbook or class lecture. The knowledge and resource repository resulting from the project can serve as a valuable source for others interested in the topic.

Finnish students seemed to be inclined to post on the front wall whereas the American students often used the discussions boards created for the purpose. Some postings were found more interesting or enhanced discussions and commenting more than others. The YouTube videos combining speech, audio effects, and moving pictures were the most popular postings and brought the most discussion. This often seems to be the case in Facebook. All students did the minimum amount of work; however, one Finnish student and one American student did three times the requested amount of postings. Although Facebook is assumed to be a commonly used tool among students, not all students were active Facebook users at the beginning of the course. One Finnish student used a false ID to protect identity and ensure anonymity whereas another Finnish student refused to engage in Facebook entirely because of privacy concerns and ended up helping produce the course video instead. The option of taking on a leadership role in the video project was only offered to those students who had expressed strong reservations regarding the use of Facebook. The students were generally encouraging and gave positive remarks and/or constructive comments on their peers' postings. A few times we had to remind our students to post to keep the project going. An example of a posting is presented in the appendix.

GROUP REPORTS

The four mixed Finnish and American student groups worked on group reports for Australia, Mauritius, New Zealand, and the Amazon. The deadline for the group project reports was the end of March, one month after the Facebook discussions on sustainability. The four groups produced their reports on time but encountered many obstacles on the way, ranging from language difficulties to different expectations as to how the report should be written. In the end, the faculty members decided to grade the Finnish students and the American students separately as the differences in writing level were too drastic. This was possible as the students, rather than truly collaborating on every aspect of the report, had clearly divided different sections of the report among themselves, as is unfortunately often the case with group projects.

VIDEO

The students produced a 10-minute video about their experience. The end product was a quite professionally edited summary of the background, the learning activities, newly gained knowledge about sustainability efforts at the four destinations, and reflections on their learning. The students were rather critical of their own efforts when it came to postings and working on the group project and pointed out the many problems they had in making things work. However, they also expressed great excitement about the idea and seem to really appreciate having been exposed to a different form of learning environment. They further commented on the ability of Facebook to support some forms of communication but not others. The video also allowed them to see each other and get to know each other beyond the Facebook profile pictures as an originally planned joint virtual meeting had to be canceled due to scheduling difficulties.

DISCUSSION AND CONCLUSIONS

Rodriguez and Frechtling (2008) pointed out that it is important to evaluate value-based teaching in terms of the students' demonstrated ability to apply the values. While we did not formally assess if and to what extent the students applied the values, the conversations with students during the process, as well as the outcomes of the learning experiment illustrate that they at least had to actively engage with the values and that they were able to critically reflect on them. To our surprise, the students wanted a lot more guidance than what we were willing to give them, implying that leadership and pro-activity were especially challenging to them. The fact that in the end the grading of the group reports was split also suggests that some barriers in terms of differences in university cultures could not be overcome in a short period of time. However, overall the experiment was successful and has led to discussions on future collaboration opportunities and potentially a joint degree program involving the two tourism programs in Finland and in the United States.

Liburd and Hjalager (2010) called for the use of interactive technologies to facilitate dynamic, interdisciplinary, international learning experiences in tourism. We were able to use Facebook as a platform to engage the students in such a learning experience. However, while most students embrace Facebook in their lives, others were very reluctant to use it. In addition, the comments presented in the student video hint at students being very aware of some of the limitations of Facebook when it comes to organizing teamwork. We think that a joint virtual meeting at the beginning of the course and an introduction to available collaborative technologies could have helped the students in better organizing their group work and also in fostering deeper personal connections. The posting exercise was mentioned as being very successful in providing a very diverse and engaging pool of resources but not very personal and, thus, not effective in helping students get to know each other.

Overall, we think that the case study presents a successful example of how TEFI core values can support the creation of an innovative learning environment that affects students beyond expanding their knowledge base of a subject area. As future leaders in a profession that is inherently international and collaborative, the students were exposed to values that will hopefully guide their future decision-making. However, the experiment showed that isolated efforts are not enough to break down barriers and that a lot more could have been achieved if the effort had continued across an entire curriculum as proposed by Rodriguez and Frechtling (2008). By sharing our experiences as faculty members who created and taught within it we hope we can contribute to building grounded theory and consolidated practice that can enhance tourism education (Liburd & Hjalager, 2010).

REFERENCES

Fahrenwald, N. L., Bassett, S. D., Tschetter, L., Carson, P. P., White, L., & Winterboer, V. J. (2005). Teaching core nursing values. *Journal of Professional Nursing*, *21*(1), 46–51.

Fogarty, T. J. (2005). Learning in business ethics courses: Initial ideas about content and assessment. In K. Martell & T. Calderon (Eds.), *Assessment of student learning in business schools: Best practices each step of the way* (pp. 92–109). Tallahassee, FL: The Association of Institutional Research.

Giddens, A. (2009). *The politics of climate change*. Cambridge, UK: Polity Press.

Gretzel, U., Jamal, T., Stronza, A., & Nepal, S. K. (2008). Teaching international tourism: An interdisciplinary, field-based course. *Journal of Teaching in Travel & Tourism*, *8*(2/3), 261–282.

Jennings, G., Kensbock, S., & Kachel, U. (2010). Enhancing 'Education *About* and *For* Sustainability' in a tourism studies enterprise management course: An action research approach. *Journal of Teaching in Travel & Tourism*, *10*(2), 163–191.

Liburd, J., & Hjalager, A. (2010). Changing approaches towards open education, innovation and research in tourism. *Journal of Hospitality and Tourism Management*, *17*(1), 12–20.

Lickona, T. (1991). *Educating for character: How our schools can teach respect and responsibility*. New York, NY: Bantam Books.

Minogue, K. (1973). *The concept of a university*. London, UK: Weidenfeld and Nicolson.

Rodriguez, P. B., & Frechtling, D. C. (2008). *Minding the roots: Incorporating values-based learning in distance tourism and hospitality management masters curricula*. Paper presented at the Annual Conference of the International Society of Travel and Tourism Educators, September 30–October 2, 2008, Dublin, Ireland.

Senge, P., Smith, B., Kruschwitz, N., Laur, J., & Schley, S. (2008). *The necessary revolution: How individuals and organizations are working together to create a sustainable world*. New York, NY: Doubleday.

Sheldon, P., & Fesenmaier, D. R. (2009). *A values-based framework for tourism education: Building the capacity to lead*. Retrieved from http://quovadis.wu-wien.ac.at/drupal/files/White%20Paper%20May22_0.pdf

Sheldon, P., Fesenmaier, D. R., & Tribe, J. (2009). The Tourism Education Futures Initiative. *E-Review of Tourism Research*, *7*(3), 39–44.

Sheldon, P., Fesenmaier, D., Woeber, K., Cooper, C., & Antonioli, M. (2008). Tourism education futures, 2010–2030: Building the capacity to lead. *Journal of Teaching in Travel & Tourism*, *7*(3), 61–68.

Veugelers, W. (2000). Different ways of teaching values. *Educational Review*, *52*(1), 37–46.

APPENDIX: EXAMPLE OF POST AND RELATED COMMENTS

Posting by vietnamese female student at Laurea (Finland):

Western Australia enjoys eco-tourism boom
http://www.youtube.com/watch?v=4SSyZcdAW7E&feature=related

With more than 12,000 km of pristine coastline and so many unique natural landscapes and ecosystems, it´s no wonder that many tourism operators are introducing sustainable principles to ensure Western Australias (WA) precious assets are protected.

2 persons liked this posting and 9 students commented upon it

1. **Female Finnish Student**: There is no hotel or restaurant. Tourists live in tents. That's what I like about it :)
2. **Male Finnish student**: O ya live nature and feel nature.......
3. **Female Finnish student**: that's a real nature friendly option for a holiday, seems that they use solar panels to get electricity which indicates their efforts to be ecological also when it comes to energy acquiring.
4. **Female Finnish student**: I think that other countries should take an example of this kind of tourism (maybe some have already). The tents looked really nice! I wish I could take some time off in an environment like that :)
5. **Female American student**: I think this is a great idea to create tourism with sustainability in mind, I think they could take this further by making some of the amenities more marketable and enjoyable to those travelers who are not completely eco-minded.
6. **Female American student**: I do realize though who this destination is aimed at attracting, and it is not those who are not interested in eco tourism, but they could possibly get more visitors by making some changes.
7. **Female American student**: Great example! I love that tourists are encouraged to stay in tents, and it appears that they are taking many sustainable practices into account (i.e. use of solar panels). Placing tourists in this raw environment just might inspire them to stop and enjoy the natural environment - possibly even engage in more sustainable practices!
8. **Male American student**: I like the idea they had come up, which is good for both the environment and also for the tourist where they can have a great time without a much effect to the nature. This is what the tourism should be all over the world.
9. **Male American student**: I have mixed feelings about this. I agree with A. that the purpose of the eco-resort is to attract and it is a business, but the logistical issues are never discussed here. This is where the line becomes blurred between what is eco friendly and what is sustainable. There was not much discussed about sustainable practices but more emphasis placed on the mitigation of impacts to the environment by the resort.

Integrating Students in Innovative Research and Development-Projects: Case Pompeli

ANNICA ISACSSON

Laurea University of Applied Sciences, Helsinki, Finland

Case Pompeli was introduced at the Helsinki airport's extended international terminal in December 2009 and draws on the assumption that in order for tourism communication and user experiences to be interesting, multiple senses should be activated and aroused. Case Pompeli is a multidisciplinary and multisensory project developed at Laurea University of Applied Sciences (Laurea) Kerava unit involving students, working life representatives, and lecturers from different fields of study (i.e. business information technology, tourism and business management). Hence, while videos are playing, the colors, sounds, scents, and wind effects change accordingly, to support content and to arouse interest towards Finland. There are many studies showing that congruent multisensory stimuli can have a positive impact on sales, behavior, brand perception, mood, emotions, interaction, and ambience. This article discusses and shows through Case Pompeli's different development and research phases how students are integrated in a multisensory tourism market research and development-project applying Laurea University of Applied Science's pedagogical model addressing TEFI values.

INTRODUCTION

TEFI (Tourism Education Future Initiatives) was created with the background and rationale that there is an urge and need for tourism education and research to fundamentally re-tool and re-design—not incrementally by adding new courses, or simply by putting courses online—but by changing the nature of what is taught and how it is taught. Skills and knowledge sets must thus be redefined, structure and assumptions need to be questioned, and old ways of doing things must be transcended. A new paradigm labeled value-based tourism education (Sheldon & Fesenmaier, 2009) was initiated.

Knowledge was identified as one TEFI-core value and manifests itself in both explicit and tacit formats. TEFI-knowledge is understood as ceaselessly incomplete and defined as information connecting to existing knowledge, created through processes of selecting, connecting, and reflecting, involving interpretation and contextualization. The knowledge creation process addresses foremost creativity, critical thinking, and networking for change and innovation through complex cognitive processes of perception, reasoning, learning, communication, association and application (Sheldon & Fesenmaier, 2009)

Pompeli is a six square meter large multisensory space and system in which six videos (content), lighting system with colors, six scents (scent machine), remote control, design, a touch screen (integrated computer), and wind machine are combined and integrated. It is a multisensory innovation created at Laurea University of Applied Sciences, at our Kerava unit, in collaboration with lecturers and assistants, numerous partners and students representing Business Information Technology, Tourism and our Peer to Peer Business Management (P2P) study programs. The P2P-program is completely project-based, aimed at entrepreneurial students, executed without regular teaching. The project was financed by Tekes (the Finnish Funding Agency for Technology and Innovation), Laurea University of Applied Sciences (Laurea), Finavia (the airport administrator), and Greater Helsinki Promotion and Culminatum.

One idea of this Pompeli (kiosque) labeled R&D&I (research & development & innovation) project was to integrate students in an authentic project. Students thus investigated, among other things, different techniques and technologies for the purpose of developing a 6 m2 space in which, for example, Asian transit passengers could experience destinations and atmospheres by multiple senses. Students also studied the commercialization aspects related to Pompeli, in addition to usability and user experience interviews at the airport. The new extended non-Schengen terminal in which Pompeli was to be placed was developed on the argument that the shortest route to Asia goes via Helsinki and is thus the transit area of many Asian transit passengers travelling via Helsinki.

The aim and target of the project was to relate learning with research and co-developing, as Laurea's pedagogical model implies (Kallioinen, 2008), while creating a service innovation platform for potential commercializing purposes by integrating congruent content and multisensory technology in one space; that is, by combining moving pictures, sounds, scents, wind, lighting, touching surface, and design in new ways. The students thus learned about theory on usability, user driven innovation, multisensory marketing, research methodology, and research processes while pursuing this project in collaboration with partners and peers, lecturers and industrial partners.

The Finnish airport administrator, Finavia, was our primary partner in the Pompeli research project. Their interest to be involved was to differentiate themselves from other airports and to promote Lapland (airports) among transit passengers.

The use of multiple senses and applied technology, its impact on tourism, and users has not been studied extensively. This article, however, focuses primarily on the university and student/lecturer involvement in a working life integrated R&D&I project.

LEARNING BY DEVELOPING

In Laurea University of Applied Sciences's *Pedagogical Strategy* (2007) it is stated that Laurea's pedagogical model, Learning by Developing (LbD); that is, development-based learning builds upon authenticity, partnership, creativity, experience, and research. LbD builds on collaboration with "real life partners", authentic needs, and problems. The objective of this pragmatic pedagogical model and approach to teaching and learning is co-developing and co-learning, between and among lecturers, students, stakeholders, and working life partners. This is achieved through systematic approaches and the proposed outcome is new practices, know/how, and knowledge, for all.

Learning by developing is based on authenticity, partnership, experiencing, creativity, and an investigative approach. In Case Pompeli, they intertwine. *Authenticity* refers to the fact that the project is an authentic, working life-based project. In this case, the airport administrator Finavia was our lead partner. Their contribution and input, interest, and support was crucial and presented itself as feedback, collaboration, access to, and space at the airport. *Partnership* refers to collaboration, competence-sharing, and learning together. It also means sharing and agreeing on different roles. In Case Pompeli, Senior Lecturer (JL) introduced Pompeli and software design as a working method and case in one of his Business Information Technology (BIT) study units in Spring 2009 for a group of second year BIT-students. The learning objective for the students was to learn to apply open coding and software design in practice. Fourteen students and one lecturer thus worked on the Pompeli open source and software design in practice, in different roles for about 8 hours per week during Spring 2009. The responsible teacher and his R&D&I assistant worked almost full days on Pompeli software, in order to find and combine technology, design the space, share knowledge and ideas, collect feedback, motivate students to work further and beyond normal study expectations, behavior, etcetera; however, students were seen as partners and developers and took on some responsibilities on their own (i.e. an active and responsible role for their own learning and developing as the LbD model emphasizes and implies). It was, for example, one active student who connected our project group with an appropriate scent company. The students showed enthusiasm for the innovative parts of the project, some being more interested than others, but it was mainly the responsible teacher (JL), who drilled his brain at free time figuring out how to code videos with lighting and coloring technology, how to proceed and deal with the freezing machine, what screen to use, which design to apply, and so on. In the oral and written student feedback some students clearly stated that they do not value or identify it as learning or co-developing to examine, evaluate, and compare tools, computers, and screens with one another. These parts went beyond software design in their opinion and study unit descriptions in their minds. Hence, LbD, at least as executed in this case, beyond regular class boundaries, requires a great deal of flexibility and responsibility of students and planning of lecturers in order for the methodology to be successful. Retrospectively, Case Pompeli would have been more appropriate for senior students participating in open project work environments or labs than for students participating in regular study units.

The investigative approach in the LbD model refers to a research-based and critical way of working which in practice means applying research-based information in scientific studies. The investigative approach is, goes without saying, always closely tied to the development project. Furthermore, creativity is seen as a resource for the development project.

Some lecturers see development projects (Raji, 2007) from the point of view of study units, some from the students' learning, some from the lecturer's job, and some from the progress of the development project. This last kind of participant has the most creativity (Raji, 2007), and indicates clearly what Pompeli was developed upon.

In the LbD-action model students are thus given the possibility, at an early stage of their studies, to be part of an innovation system through development projects. Learning by developing relates to actions carried out together. Through collaboration problem-based skills are developed and new knowledge is created. According to the model, the development project processes contain continuous evaluations of one's own learning through reflection, diaries and discussions, of what has been collectively learnt, of progress and generation of new knowledge. The acquired competence is identified as knowledge-, skill-, and value-related or experiential (cf. Raji, 2003, pp. 43–47). The students who participated learned the objectives as stated in the learning objectives when assessed at the end through regular exams. The aim of each development project is to achieve change. Results are shared in forms of research reports and, possibly also through commercializations, which was one purpose, aim, and target of the Pompeli project from its commencement (i.e., to make it commercially attractive, interesting and viable).

MULTISENSORY MARKETING

Scent marketing has been applied by coffee shops and bakeries for decades. Research conducted by Maureen Morrin and Jean-Charles Chebat (2005) showed that a subtle use of lemon increased store sales by 63%. The use of scent is also argued to have an effect and impact on our sense of time; that is, scented areas enhance the feeling of timelessness (Spangenberg, Crowley, & Henderson, 1996). Lindstrom (2005) has shown that our mood is enhanced by 40% in pleasantly scented surroundings. In order for stimuli to be effective and pleasant though, it has to be compatible and congruent with space, purpose, and content (e.g., Mattila & Wirtz, 2001; Morrin & Chebat, 2005; Spangenberg et al., 2005). Lindstrom's research (2009) showed that a picture, when combined with a compatible scent, is better perceived and memorized. Moreover, Martin Osterberg (2008) argued that scent can have a strong impact on ambience, mood, and behavior, but in order for it to be effective, it has to be clearly linked to the service, situation, or space. In the Bitner (1992) service scape model it is assumed that the optimal combination of temperature, lighting, sounds, music, and scent have an impact on customer behavior. Multisensory marketing can hence be described as the cumulative activation of senses; that is, when one is stimulated, the next one is aroused which in its turn activates the next etc. (Lindstrom, 2005).

Lindstrom (2005) has shown that for customers to whom the visual sense is dominating, they base their decisions on how things look. The auditory consumers on the other hand use their hearing sense to process information and base their decisions on what they hear, whereas kinesthetic/tactile learners use their taste, scent, and touching senses to process information and base decisions upon.

There are thus studies related to social interaction, consumer behavior, brand marketing, and so on, showing that pleasantly and subtly odored areas increase the usage of slot-machines (Hirsch, 1995), that ambient scent has a positive effect on social interactions (Zemke & Shoemaker, 2006), that queuing is perceived as less stressful in scented areas (McDonnell, 2002), and so on. There are also studies showing a positive correlation between the usage of scent and the increase of sales (see, e.g., Morrin & Chebat, 2005; Spangenberg et al., 1996), but not many studies showing the impact and effect that the combination of multiple senses have on tourism marketing, usage, or behavior.

FIGURE 1 Pompeli launched at the airport (December 11, 2009).

Hence, it will be interesting to examine how a multisensory space where Finnish tourism is demonstrated by arousing multiple senses, launched at the new, non-Schengen terminal at Helsinki airport on December 11, 2009 (see Figure 1), in collaboration with students, airport staff, and lecturers will effect Asian transit passengers views on Finland. First, we will though present student research related to Pompeli commercialization prospects, yet another LbD integrative effort.

POMPELI GOES BUSINESS AND STUDENT INTEGRATION

Pompeli goes business was introduced as a case in a Tourism study unit called *Productifying and Quality in Tourism* conducted by Principal Lecturer (AI) during Fall 2009 among third-year tourism students. A management team of three students was elected among our international tourism students and their tasks were primarily to interview technical and some commercial experts in order to find out about Pompeli's business potential (e.g., experts view and interest for a lighter version, other type of applications etc). Moreover, the management team's task was to compile data and make a complete report of peer tourism students' expert-interviews among event-, fair-, media-, marketing- and tourism experts related to the identification of new contexts and surroundings for Pompeli and for the prospect of a lighter/mobile version of Pompeli.

EXPERTS INTERVIEWED BY STUDENTS

The project management team held several meetings and discussions with our in-house Pompeli experts (students and lecturers) about Pompeli's technical issues and business potentiality. In addition, feedback regarding the business potentiality was also gathered from experts outside Laurea through personal interviews both by the project management team as well as by peer students.

Discussions led by the project management team members were thus held with among others, (a) Laurea in-house experts; (b) the Curator of the National Museum of Science and Technology in Stockholm, who has produced 4D multisensory films; (c) a researcher at the Swedish Institute of Computer Science; (d) two Swedish brand- and marketing experts at a consultant company specialized in public installations at airports; and (e) two professors at the Royal Institute of Technology in Stockholm. All experts were carefully selected and defined as experts due to their vast experience and know-how in this or related fields. The Pompeli project was demonstrated to experts through project webpage, pictures, and videos.

Laurea in-house Pompeli experts stated that mobility, weight, and cost were the most important requirement to meet for Pompeli to be commercially viable. One idea that came up during the discussions was that all of the equipment could be packed into two safe and durable aluminum cases, light enough for one or two persons to carry. The equipments mentioned for a light version included a laptop, scent machine, wind machine, lighting, video projector or small screen, surround sound system, five speakers, subwoofer, amplifier, electrical system, distributors, and wiring in addition to the aluminum cases. One question raised by Laurea in-house experts was if a light version can present all the same multisensory effects as a larger version can? The overall challenges mentioned were related to cost, space, weight, easiness in use, safety (overheating), maintenance and warranty, supported audio, scent and video formats, electricity, air conditioning, and overall operational quality. The development costs of a prototype version of micro Pompeli, was evaluated to be expensive.

One of the Swedish experts mentioned Morton Heilig, a thought-leader in Virtual Reality who already in 1960, developed a game called *Sensorama*. The game gave the player the experience of riding a motorcycle on the streets of Brooklyn. The player felt the wind on his face, the vibration of the motorcycle seat, a 3D view, and even the smells of the city. In general, the Swedish experts valued the idea of creating a multisensory environment for the purpose of promoting Finland among transit passengers at Helsinki-Vantaa airport as good. In addition, Pompeli was termed innovative, informative, and experiential; that is, a positive effort in relaying messages and experiences of Finland for the purpose of marketing. Similarly, the

Swedish experts wanted to know about the hardware and software used, also from the point of view of on human computer interface (i.e., how do people react to such a device)? Two experts thought that the reason for placing Pompeli at the airport, however, was to prevent boredom among passengers, which effectively was and had been one of the airport's aims in this project. Moreover, it was suggested that a micro-device could lack authentic multisensory feeling even for a small group of users due to its compact size.

Hence, all the Swedish experts expressed collectively that a macro Pompeli, such as created for the airport, would have higher business potential. The interest group for the device suggested were airports, cinema and interactive media, medical science, educational purposes, shopping malls, exhibition, fair trade and museums, cruise ships, and public places.

At the same time, peer students at the tourism degree program interviewed experts in Finland, representing different sectors (i.e., media, fair, event and tourism). The aim of their interviews was to get better insight about commercialization and business potential of a multisensory device in different target markets. The research approach was qualitative and conducted through semi-structured interviews. The first interviewee, a Recycling Event Manager mentioned that such a device could be used in his recycling event to create an experience about the lifespan of consumables—beginning with the creation process and ending with the smells of a landfill. Similarly, the interviewee mentioned that renting the device was a better option for his business and that he would like to test it before making any decisions. The interviewee also mentioned that the name Pompeli gave a cheap impression and suggested a new innovative name.

The two Art Event interviewees were fascinated by the idea of Pompeli as they did not have any previous personal experiences of similar products but had heard of the use of senses such as touch, hearing, and sight in marketing. The combination of aroma was a new concept for them. The interviewees mentioned that the lighter version may lack the feeling of authenticity and experience when used for marketing purposes. They also felt that Pompeli would be too expensive for their budget and that a desktop version could not cater mass large audiences. The Art Event interviewees also stated that Pompeli could be more desirable if one could order the videos and scents and not have to produce them oneself which could be both difficult and expensive. The interviewees recommended that the name Pompeli wasn't suitable and should be changed especially if marketed to foreign customers.

The Tourism Journalist at a daily newspaper interviewee mentioned that the sounds in the Pompeli videos were excellent, but that the content in the videos were missing a bit of romanticism and she also proposed the use of subtitles for some videos. When asked about the word *Pompeli* the interviewee mentioned that it was a bit awkward, but for foreigners it could be easy to remember and suggested that the idea of a multisensory platform could be used at airports around the world to promote Finland. The idea of a lighter, portable Pompeli for international trades and other marketing occasions was considered to be practical and she suggested that, for example, in Japan the machine could make a remarkable difference in the promotion of Finland.

The Media Agency interviewee's reaction toward Pompeli-project was positive and he considered it to be a good business idea. The design of the Pompeli was not so good in his opinion because of the "swans". He pointed out that the structure is too much focused on the inside. He thought that it would be good if there were attractions also on the outside walls. If the portable Pompeli was light and easy to build and deconstruct like trade fair pop-ups then it would have great potentiality according to the media-interviewee. Outer design could have elements of water, pine trees, and sauna-walls. It was also mentioned that Pompeli could be used in railway and bus stations as well as in hotels, museums, cruisers, and all kinds of places where there are lot of tourists. The interviewee mentioned that he travels a lot and would like to see such a device in other airports around the world.

Another Media Representative interviewee considered the idea to be brilliant, but she didn't like the name and suggested that it should be called something modern, striking, and more sophisticated than Pompeli as it means "shack" in Finnish. New innovative ideas she shared was to use famous Finnish paintings, our national epic, nature, birds, trees, and grass in the content. She suggested that the portable version could be used also for other purposes than marketing (e.g., for wellness purposes).

Hence, many proposals related to the design and attractiveness in addition to content, name and additional contexts, surroundings, and use for Pompeli were suggested by experts interviewed by students. Student learning was Pompeli and LbD-integrated, related to qualitative methods and multisensory marketing and generally perceived interesting. The approach was authentic and partnership-based as they did the interviews with potential partners. It was also research-based as the students designed the interview forms themselves. The analysis was presented in thick descriptions, both orally in class and in written reports. Some student groups taped and transcribed interviews word by word while others took notes. There were roles and responsibilities involved as the international tourism students formed the management group and different expert groups were appointed by them to different student groups. Hence LbD was experienced and operated also from that perspective. In addition, the study unit and learning was perceived creative as the students were given some freedom in their approach and methodology.

USABILITY AND USER EXPERIENCES AMONG ASIAN TRANSIT-PASSENGERS

When Pompeli had been at the airport for 6–8 weeks usability and user experience research was conducted in February 2010 by our first-year tourism students together with older peer students; that is, in collaboration with our in-house Pompeli project experts and project team manager. Our first-year students' involvement was part of their Tourism as Cultural Phenomenon study unit. Their involvement, worth two ects (study points) consisted of learning of the project by participation, learning of basic usability (Figure 2) and ethnographic methods as part of qualitative research and applied practices, conducting interviews and observation at the airport in addition to analyzing results and presenting them in oral and written forms guided by teachers.

The aim of this study was to find out about usability and user experiences in the authentic environment. The approach was qualitative and interviews were conducted through semi-structured interview forms using two sets of questions and an observation sheet. The study was operated by students as individual or pair interviews. The interview questions contained open-ended questions allowing interviewees to share their personal views about Pompeli. The target group for the interviews was Asian transit passengers at the airport, but if not available, also others participated. The first set of interview questions, specifically designed for Asians, were divided into three categories comprising (a) the overall appearance and expectation, (b) user interface and interaction, and (c) purpose, perception (change) and the before and after experience. The second set of interview

FIGURE 2 Usability testing conducted by students.

questions were based on multisensory elements/effects inside Pompeli, use, and experience. The questions dealt with the following: favorite video, use of smell elements combined with other effects, essence of each video displayed, the usability of Pompeli and questions related to change in level of curiosity among users and perception about Finland (pre/post Pompeli experience). Interviewees were randomly selected among visitors, if empty, transit passengers were invited to participate.

The aim of the observation was to make observation of users—that is, users' body language and expressions, perception, positioning, operability, and interaction. A student interviewer mentioned that, "As the smells appeared many leaned forward to enjoy them more." No body movement or strong facial expressions, however, were revealed by users (Asian passengers) during their Pompeli experiences whether single or in a group. The transit passengers, particularly Asian tourists (e.g., Japanese) didn't all feel comfortable entering Pompeli and some termed it to be "too technical and unattractive."

Interviewees shared their personal opinions in this regard by suggesting colorful pictures of Finland on the outer walls of Pompeli or painting the walls with landscapes representing Finland. The presence of numerous advertisements in the areas was considered more eye-catching compared to Pompeli. The functions inside Pompeli were described as "easy to use," while a young Japanese interviewee commented on the smell ("nice smell of coffee") whereas a Japanese respondent wanted to know if "There are videos of Moomin and sauna?"

Interviewees mentioned the system to be fun, entertaining, easy to grasp, and interesting. There appeared, however, to be some confusion among transit passengers whether there was a Pompeli entering cost. A student interviewer mentioned that, "Two out of three participants reported that they would tell others about the experience afterwards and they also said that it left a positive impression of Finland." The outside of Pompeli is now being redesigned (see Figure 3) as a result of the student interview-findings. Consequently, Pompeli content will gradually be changed.

Pompeli was not identified as a multi-sensory marketing platform from the outside, and users were not able to say what the appearance of Pompeli is or what it does. Having experienced it they all understood the purpose of it. Users did find it easy to use but were hesitant to enter. The upper part of the system is visible and looks very technical in some opinions, strange to a few, even a bit scary to some. Videos displayed in Pompeli were considered interesting and funny but didn't generate memorable experience as they didn't change interviewees' perception of Finland. However, the videos titled "Helsinki Our Fresh Capital" aroused interest among interviewees to visit the White Church and some recalled personal memories of Lapland having watched the video entitled "Memories of Lapland & Chocolate." Sample comments are provided in Figure 4.

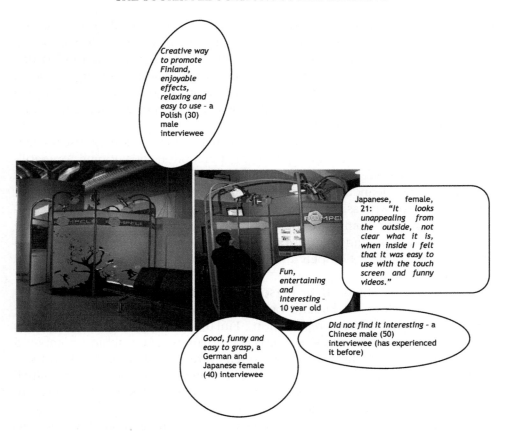

FIGURE 3 Pompeli's new outer design and user comments.

In this case and study unit the students learned about qualitative research methods; that is, interviewing techniques and observations. They were able to be in an authentic environment conducting working life relevant research among transit passengers at the airport. The students were guided by senior peer students and experts on usability testing and research. They experienced authenticity, partnership, creativity, and took an investigative approach in their studies.

STUDENT LEARNING

Students learned through planning and by coordinating interviewing activities, through analyzing and presenting findings and by collecting and concluding research processes in reports that the management team collected into one. Out of Laurea's model authenticity and partnership was fulfilled by thrusting students with potential future partners and transit

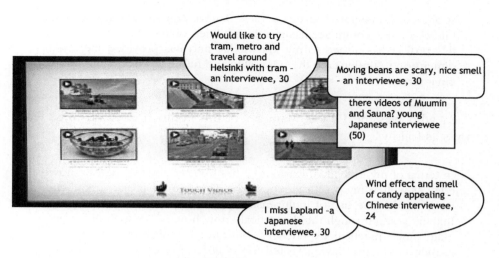

FIGURE 4 User comments.

passenger users. The students experienced different roles and responsibilities within these two study units. Creativity was allowed if not encouraged and research was ensured as the students, in collaboration with senior peers and lecturers, learned about qualitative methods in practice while pursuing authentic research. Student learning and knowledge- processes as defined by Sheldon and Feisenmaier (2009) involved connections to existing knowledge and knowledge was created through processes of selecting, connecting and reflecting, involving both interpretation and contextualization, identifiable in the quotes below.

During the process of working in the project, S., as a project management team member, learned how the use of multiple senses can create an experience for the user. In her evaluation she shares the following information:

> I participated in many classroom sessions and presentations done by students studying at the Tourism degree program. It provided me with new understanding and has broadened my knowledge regarding the use of the device and its effectiveness in conveying different messages to the users. The various research, visits, and interview sessions with numerous experts regarding the effectiveness of Pompeli, the gathering of information, and the work with compiling the final report which we based on common findings has enhanced my different competences such as time management, communication, as well as research and development skills. The ideas and comments given by the experts motivated us to do more research and get better insight regarding the commercialization of Pompeli. Being part of the project which I believe was

successfully integrated in our studies, I have learned about the possibilities of the commercialization possibilities of the device. All in all,
this project has added to my knowledge and has provided me a new
dimension to understand the possibility and future of creating an unique
environment.

E., who was the Project Manager of the Pompeli goes business team,
reports as follows:

> In terms of my individual learning, it has boosted my theoretical knowl-
> edge as well as my practical experience. Through the project I got better
> insight about the use of multisensory platform for marketing purposes.
> Initially going through the theoretical know-how of Pompeli didn't gen-
> erate much practical experiences, but after having participated in the
> usability tests and having visited the multisensory environment I could
> better define the environment. Through classroom sessions and presenta-
> tions, readings of gathered information and reports, conducting research
> and holding discussions, attending conferences and through visits, it
> provided me a lot of information and know-how of the multisensory
> platform. As part of the learning phase it offered me an exposure to
> different tasks and events contributing to my own learning and helped
> me when preparing the report. In addition, the comments made by the
> experts motivated me and my team to look at the device from different
> perspective (e.g., destination, climate change issues, medical topics, etc.).

> Through the project I have developed team management skills. Being
> a project manager meant managing ones team and also communicating
> with other teams involved in the project, delegating tasks to different
> teams, keeping track of the progress and making sure that the given
> tasks are completed within the deadlines. In addition, it also involved
> conducting research, studies of theories, meeting with in-house experts
> and experts from different institutions, partaking in classroom sessions,
> conducting interviews and discussions, sharing information and gaining
> knowledge.

> All in all, the project availed me with the opportunity to be part of
> a team having to undertake different tasks and to communicate with
> different groups comprising technical experts, Finnish degree students,
> project management team and other stakeholders in achieving the given
> goal and fulfilling my own expectation within the learning phase.

CONCLUSIONS

The acquired competence, as identified in the LbD-model, are knowledge-
related, skill-related, value-related, or experiential (cf. Raij, 2003, pp. 43–47).
The aim of each development project is to achieve change. The development

project ends in the form of research reports and possibly also through commercialization; but the learning process continues, offering new competence for the learners to share in new development projects.

The TEFI-knowledge creation processes (Sheldon & Fesenmaier, 2009) involves elements of creativity, critical thinking, and networking. In case Pompeli, the outcome was a novelty, an innovation within the field of tourism marketing communication. The knowledge creation process involved experts, stakeholders, lecturers, and students. The project challenged existing views. It involved creativity and critical thinking questioning previous assumptions on what can be achieved and how knowledge is created. The project and knowledge formation enhanced and required networking involving expert-views and visits in two countries.

This article shows how students can be integrated into working-life centric authentic R&D&I and LbD-based research projects in practice. The model works and learning is achieved, but it demands extensive input in forms of planning, monitoring, coaching, feedback, and evaluation of the responsible teachers.

During the eight months that Pompeli has been at the airport more than 55,000 Pompeli video clicks have taken place, its outer walls have been redesigned and extensive collaboration with some of the interviewed European experts has been established. In addition, demand and interest for Pompeli has been raised at conferences and seminars and during numerous visits with press and stakeholders at the airport.

To conduct such a vast cross-scientific project in collaboration with students is challenging as study units end, student motivation varies, and the outcome is non-predictable. However to be able to motivate staff, teachers, and students to work toward a common goal by learning by developing methodology (i.e., team-based collaborative process-work) is rewarding and requires strong managerial skills and support.

REFERENCES

Hirsch, A. R. (1995). Effects of ambient odors on slot machine usage in a Las Vegas casino. *Psychology and Marketing, 12*(7), 585–594.

Kallioinen, O. (Ed.). (2008). *Oppiminen Learning by Developing toimintamallissa* [Learning through Learning by Developing model]. Vantaa, Finland: Laurea Publications. (University publication A.61)

Lindstrom, M. (2005). *Brand sense: How to build powerful brands through touch, taste, smell, sight & sound*. New York, NY: Free Press.

Lindstrom, M. (2009). *Buyology*. Helsinki, Finland: Talentum.

McDonnell, J. (2002). *Sensorial marketing for those who can wait no longer. Proceedings of the first International Conference of Sensorial Marketing*. Nice, France: The Academy French Marketing and Columbia University.

Morrin, M., & Chebat, J.-C. (2005). Person-place congruency: The interactive effects of shopper style and atmospherics on consumer expenditures. *Journal of Service Research, 8*(2), 181–191.

Pedagogical strategy. (2007). Retrieved from www.laurea.fi

Raji, K. (2003). Osaamisen tuottaminen ammattikorkeakoulun päämääränä [The creation of knowledge the aim of Universities of Applied Sciences]. In H. Kotila (Ed.), *Ammattikorkeakoulupedagogiikka* (pp. 42–58). Vaasa, Finland: Edita.

Raji, K. (2007). *Learning by Developing*. Vantaa, Finland: Laurea Publications. (University publication A58)

Sheldon, P., & Fesenmaier, D. (2009). *A value-based framework for tourism education: Building the capacity to lead*. Retrieved from http://www.tourismeducation.at

Spangenberg, E. R., Crowley, A. Y., & Henderson, P. W. (1996). Improving the store environment: Do olfactory cues affect evaluations and behaviors? *Journal of Marketing, 60*, 67–80.

Zemke, D. M. V., & Shoemaker, S. (2006). Scent across a crowded room: Exploring the effect of ambient scent on social interactions. *International Journal of Hospitality Management, 12*, 1–14.

The Influence of Gender and Education-Related Variables on Career Development: The Case of Portuguese and Brazilian Tourism Graduates

CARLOS COSTA, SANDRA CAÇADOR, INÊS CARVALHO,
ZÉLIA BREDA, and RUI COSTA

University of Aveiro, Aveiro, Portugal

This study examines the influence of higher education-related variables on the career paths of tourism graduates in Portugal and Brazil, while taking into account gender differences. It analyzes whether the geographical location of the educational institution, the educational subsystem, and the level of academic degree influence the graduate outcomes of Portuguese and Brazilian tourism graduates in terms of employment rates, salary levels, and entrepreneurial profile. Data provide empirical evidence that pursuing a tourism postgraduate degree provides access to better conditions in the labor market and attenuates gender inequalities. In addition, the geographical location and the educational subsystem are important factors to consider when selecting a Portuguese higher institution in the tourism field.

This article results from a research project on gender issues in the tourism sector, which is entitled "Does Gender Equality Have a Say in the Boost of Innovative Forms of Economic Growth? Reviving the Economy Through Networks and Internationalisation in the Tourism Sector" (PTDC/CS-SOC/119524/2010). The authors would like to acknowledge the support provided by the Portuguese Foundation for Science and Technology, as well as the cofinancing of the European Union through the National Strategic Reference Framework, European Regional Development Fund, and the Operational Program for Competitiveness Factors.

INTRODUCTION

Tourism stands out as an important sector for many national economies and is a relevant employment generator. In fact, tourism contributes to 9.1% of the world gross domestic product (GDP) and 8.3% of all the employment created, and it has been forecasted that it will continue to grow in the future (World Travel & Tourism Council [WTTC], 2012). In Portugal, tourism accounts for 15.2% of the Portuguese GDP and for 17.8% of employment[1] (WTTC, 2011b). In Brazil, the contribution of this sector to the economy is more attenuated and corresponds to 8.6% of the GDP and 7.8% of the employment created (WTTC, 2011a).

Tourism is a female-dominated sector in most countries (Amaro, 2007; Costa, Carvalho, & Breda, 2011a; Parrett, n.d.). It is an industry characterized by a predominance of low salaries, as well as unsociable working hours, such as working during holidays, nights, and weekends, which complicates work–family balance (O'Leary & Deegan, 2005; Parrett, n.d.; Ramb, 2008). The tourism sector also has many part-time jobs that are mostly filled by women. This sector is also characterized by vertical and horizontal segregation, and the female tourism workers are more likely to be found in low-paid, low-qualified, and low-status jobs compared with their male counterparts (Hemmati, 2000; Jordan, 1997; Kinnaird & Hall, 1996; Parrett, n.d.; Santos & Varejão, 2006).

The employment situation of tourism graduates has been diagnosed in the Portuguese context by Costa, Carvalho, Caçador, and Breda (2012a, 2012b), who concluded that there are not only remarkable gaps between men and women, but also that graduates, in general, have difficulties in finding a tourism job and earn low salaries.

Despite the increase in women's participation in tourism higher education (United Nations, 2009), a proportional growth in women's presence in top-level positions has not been observed yet (Zhong & Couch, 2007). In fact, most of the highly qualified individuals are women, particularly if tourism graduates are considered both in Portugal (Gabinete de Planeamento, Estratégia, Avaliação e Relações Internacionais-Ministério da Ciência, Tecnologia e Ensino Superior, 2011) and in Brazil (Instituto Nacional de Estutos e Pesquisas Educacionais Anísio Teixeira [INEP], 2011). However, strong gender inequalities prevail even among these individuals, and these inequalities hinder the development of women's full potential in the labor market. Therefore, women have lower probability of engaging in leadership positions as they occupy low-level and middle-level positions in their organizations and are, generally, less entrepreneurial and more subjected to constraints to develop their own employment (Costa et al., 2012b).

---

[1]   The measure of employment used is the broadest, including direct and indirect effects via the supply chain of travel and tourism spending.

One might think that a relevant and considerable section of the qualified human resources available is thus being underutilized by the labor market. This scenario is even more alarming if one realizes that the future transformational leaders are being left behind as, according to several studies, women are more likely to reveal a transformational leadership style (Bass & Avolio, 1994, cited in Camps Del Valle, Pérez Santiago, & Martínez Lugo, 2010; Druskat, 1994; Eagly & Johnson, 1990). Eagly and Johnson (1990) suggest that women have a greater tendency to adopt a more democratic or participative style, whereas men are more willing to adopt a more autocratic or directive style. Druskat (1994) also found that women leaders exhibit significantly more transformational behaviors (valuing relationships, collaboration, and communication) compared with men leaders, while men leaders exhibit significantly more transactional behaviors compared to women leaders.

Only the leaders who possess the fundamental elements of transformational leadership, designated by Bass (1985, cited in Slater & Martinez, 2000), namely charisma and inspiration, intellectual stimulation, and individual consideration, will be able to implement necessary organizational changes (Slater & Martinez, 2000). This situation should be addressed by educators as they "set the groundwork for change. The future generation of hospitality [and tourism] managers is in today's classroom, and educators need to take advantage of the opportunity to influence tomorrow's organizational policies and practices" (Brownell, 1998, p. 119).

Furthermore, in times of crisis and pronounced social and economic changes, doubts concerning the returns of higher education in tourism could arise, namely concerning the cost–benefit of pursuing postgraduate degrees. Thus, the question addressed by this study is whether pursuing a postgraduate degree leads to access to better conditions in the labor market and attenuates gender inequalities. Moreover, the influence of the geographical location of the educational institution on the career advancement of tourism graduates also remains unanalyzed. The aim of this article is to explore the influence of higher education-related variables in the professional situation of tourism graduates in Portugal and Brazil, in terms of employment, salaries, and entrepreneurial profile. We also examine, for the Portuguese sample, gender differences in these variables according to the geographical location and the level of the academic degree completed.

In the first section, literature on higher education and the professional situation of graduates is reviewed, particularly concerning the tourism field. Gendered patterns in employment and career-making are highlighted, namely regarding the Portuguese and the Brazilian contexts.

In the following section, the methodology underlying the empirical study is presented. Data were collected through an online questionnaire distributed to both the Portuguese and Brazilian tourism graduates, within the research project Gentour.[2] The software Statistical Package for the Social Sciences Statistics (Version 19) was used to perform the statistical analyses. The results are presented and discussed in the next sections. The article starts with the presentation of the results that concern the influence of pursuing postgraduate degrees on several variables, namely employment rates, wages, and entrepreneurial profile, among Portuguese and Brazilian graduates. Throughout the article, the influence of gender on higher education is analyzed. Then, the influence of other education-related variables is analyzed, namely the type of degree and geographical location of the educational institution. Only the Portuguese sample could be considered in these analyses, given the optimum number of obtained answers and the existence of a significant number of respondents in each region, which allows for this kind of analysis.

Based on the characteristics and patterns of higher education degrees, the need to rethink the tourism higher education supply is advocated to rewrite the current cultural and social models, which are unsustainable in the present and future economic and social reality.

HIGHER EDUCATION IN TOURISM, GENDER, AND EMPLOYMENT OUTCOMES: AN OVERVIEW

In the European Union, women account for 55.3% of tertiary education students (Eurostat, 2011). This trend can also be observed in Portugal and in Brazil, because 53.5% (Eurostat, 2011) and 60.9% (INEP, 2011) of higher education graduates are women, respectively. The increasing participation of women in higher education can be explained by their perception that holding a degree is particularly important, because it reduces men's advantage in the labor market (Viayna & Izquierdo, cited in Esteban, 2004). Moreover, the "educational lever" (Crompton & Anderson, 1992) can be regarded as a predictor of women's behavior (Fagan & O'Reilly, 1998), because highly qualified women are more likely to maintain their involvement in the labor market during motherhood than are women with no such level of education (Crompton et al., 1990; Dale & Egerton, 1995; Dex, 1985; McRae, 1991; Rubery et al., 1995; Spain & Bianch, 1996—all cited in Fagan & O'Reilly, 1998).

---

[2]   The Project Gentour "Towards the Improvement of Women's Skills in the Tourism Sector—Profiting From the Vertical Mobility for Ethic and Economic Purposes" was conducted at the University of Aveiro, in the Research Unit GOVCOPP (Governance, Competitiveness, and Public Policies), under the scientific coordination of Professor Carlos Costa. It was funded by the Portuguese Foundation for Science and Technology and the Commission for Citizenship and Gender Equality, and it was cofunded by the European Union, through the National Strategic Reference Framework, the European Regional Development Fund, and the Operational Program for Competitiveness Factors.

Despite the increasing participation of women in higher education and in the labor market, gender inequalities persist. According to the *Global Gender Gap Index* (Hausmann, Tyson, & Zahidi, 2011), which measures gender equality based on several global indicators, Portugal occupied the 35th and Brazil occupied the 82nd position in the world gender equality ranking in 2011. The first position of this ranking was occupied by Iceland, followed by Norway, Finland, and Sweden.

Gender inequalities among tourism graduates in Portugal were diagnosed within the framework of the Gentour Project. The main conclusions obtained allow for the analysis of gender inequalities among tourism graduates across many aspects (Carvalho, Costa, & Breda, 2011; Costa et al., 2011a, 2012a, 2012b). Firstly, there is a wide pay gap between male and female tourism graduates (16.8%), with the average salary for men being €1,068.63 (US$1,403.00), while the average salary for women is €889.59 ($1,167.94; Costa et al., 2012a). Salaries earned by tourism graduates are low, particularly if these are compared to those of graduates in general, who earn between €1,200 and €1,799 ($1,575.48 and $2,361.91; Costa et al., 2011a). According to Escária (2006), some degrees might have lost some of their importance in terms of raising graduate salaries, which might be the case for tourism degrees.

Despite the fact that women expect lower salaries than men, the real gender gap in salaries is much wider than the gender gap in expectations. There is also a large gap between the salaries expected by students and the ones actually earned by graduates, which are much lower (Costa et al., 2012a). Vertical segregation is also sharp, as can be observed by the significant gender gap in the fulfillment of leadership roles; however, this gap does not seem to be justifiable by the gender gap in the preference for these positions. Even though more men than women aim to be leaders, the disparity between the willingness of men and women to have such a role is not nearly as high as the disparity observed in the actual number of male and female leaders (Costa et al., 2012a). This suggests that it is either due to the labor market or other kinds of constraints that make the gap in upper-management observable.

Moreover, it was concluded that tourism graduates have difficulties in joining the labor market; thus, many of them are employed outside the tourism sector (26.8%), with salaries 9.9% below the average. Women are more likely to be in that situation. A high rate of unemployed individuals is also observed (24.9%). This suggests that the labor market is failing to meet the expectations of students, either because it is saturated or because the skills acquired by tourism graduates are not adequately recognized and valued by the labor market, as suggested by Petrova and Mason (2004). The data suggest that graduates living abroad have better jobs than do the ones who live in Portugal, because they earn much higher salaries (€1,573.03

[$2,065.23]). However, the gender pay gap is even wider among those who are abroad (20.1%).

Another important conclusion is that having children has a much greater impact on the careers and choices of women than it does on those of men. If women with children are compared to childless women, it can be concluded that having children makes women less willing to become entrepreneurs (decrease from 75.8% to 62.6%), while this tendency is attenuated for men (from 76.8% to 70.4%; Carvalho et al., 2011). The proportion of women who express the desire to hold leadership positions decreases from 76.7% of childless women to 67.2% of women with children. In contrast, this tendency is reversed for men, because those who desire to be leaders increase from 79.3% to 90.9% when they have children.

Concerning graduate entrepreneurship, it was concluded that the proportion of male entrepreneurs (21.4%) is more than double that of female entrepreneurs (10.0%). Opportunity entrepreneurs[3] accounted for the vast majority of individuals in both groups (Costa et al., 2012b), thus surpassing the percentage of opportunity entrepreneurs mentioned in other studies, which may be due to the high level of education of the sample. In addition, opportunity entrepreneurs have salaries (€940.33 [$1,234.56]) that are above average for tourism graduates, while necessity entrepreneurs have salaries that are below average; however, the gender pay gap is wider among the former (22.2%) than among the latter (9.3%). It is also observed that the rise in the level of education is associated with the sharp decrease in the rates of necessity entrepreneurship for women. Despite the gap between men and women concerning business creation, there was no statistically significant association between gender and the desire to start one's own business. On the other hand, having children had a statistically significant negative impact on women's desire to start a new business.

This Gentour Project was also expanded to Brazil. Thus, it is possible not only to analyze gender inequalities between male and female tourism graduates in Brazil, but also to establish a comparison between these graduates and those surveyed in Portugal. It was concluded that the gender gap that tourism graduates face in Brazil is narrower than that in Portugal in terms of employability and presence in top-management or leadership positions. However, the gender pay gap is wider for Brazilian tourism graduates (29.7%; Costa, Carvalho, & Breda, 2011b). This study showed that the gender pay gap is particularly wide among the youngest graduates (31.7%) and

---

[3]   "Necessity entrepreneurship" (push) and "opportunity entrepreneurship" (pull) are concepts extensively used in the *Global Entrepreneurship Monitor* and were first introduced by Reynolds, Camp, Bygrave, Autio, and Hay (2002). Whereas the lack of employment or suitable employment opportunities underlies "necessity entrepreneurship," the desire to benefit from business and market opportunities underlies "opportunity entrepreneurship" (Nova Fórum & Sociedade Portuguesa de Inovação, 2004).

among top managers (38%), thus suggesting a situation of strong inequalities, which are intensified with career development.

According to human capital theorists, more education leads to higher salaries and better jobs (Becker, 1962; Mincer, 1958; Thrane, 2008). Thus, gender inequalities would be due to women possessing less human capital (i.e., education, work experience, need for more frequent career breaks, etc.). However, several studies, which adopted an econometrical approach, concluded that the gender pay gap prevails even when controlling for human capital variables (Bañuls & Casado-Díaz, 2010; Thrane, 2008, 2010; Vartiainen, 2002). The unexplained proportion of the wage gap could be attributed to discrimination, even though caution is required when reaching these conclusions, because the unexplained gap may also be attributed to variables not included in the model. Hence, these studies suggest that having higher levels of education does not necessarily ensure gender equality in the labor market. Other studies also point out that pursuing postgraduate degrees may lead to overqualification, instead of leading to better chances of finding a more rewarding job, regardless of whether one is a man or a woman (Elias et al., 1994; Higher Education Funding Council for England, 1996; both cited in Pitcher & Purcell, 1998).

Therefore, interesting issues arise: What is the advantage of pursuing a postgraduate degree in tourism? Does tourism in higher education play an important role concerning gender issues? Does the geographical location of the educational institution influence the career development of tourism graduates in Portugal? These questions will be addressed in the following sections and analyzed in the context of empirical data.

METHODOLOGY

The empirical study underlying the present research was based on a survey applied to tourism graduates in Portugal and Brazil. The survey analyzed the influence of higher education-related variables in the professional situation of tourism graduates in both countries, as well as identified gendered patterns of employment. The survey was carried out from December 2010 to March 2011 in Portugal, and from May 2011 to November 2011 in Brazil. The Portuguese sample consisted of 1,419 graduates, including 990 women (69.8%) and 429 men (30.2%), and the Brazilian sample consisted of 421 graduates, including 312 women (74.1%) and 109 men (25.9%). A convenience sampling technique was used in both cases. In the Portuguese case, contact was established with professors and researchers of all Portuguese institutions with tourism higher education degrees. In Brazil, the consultants of the Gentour Project had the responsibility of disseminating the survey through their wider network of contacts.

The tourism degrees taken into account for the present study were those included under the subareas of "Hospitality" and "Tourism and Leisure," in the Portuguese National Classification of Fields of Education and Training, as well as those identified by the Brazilian Ministry of Education. The instrument used for data collection was an online questionnaire, which covered a wide range of areas. It concerned not only education and employment, but also other areas, such as perceptions of discrimination and work–family balance. The software IBM Statistical Package for the Social Sciences Statistics (Version 19) was used for the quantitative data analysis. Univariate, bivariate, and multivariate statistical techniques were applied, through exploratory and inferential methods, and a 5% significance level was adopted.

FINDINGS

Pursuing Postgraduate Degrees

In this section, it is analyzed whether pursuing postgraduate degrees improves the outcomes of graduates in the labor market, namely in terms of employment rates, salaries, and entrepreneurship. It is also examined whether engaging in further education has any consequences in terms of reducing gender inequalities. According to Tomlinson (2008, p. 49), "students perceive their academic qualifications as having a declining role in shaping their employment outcomes in what is perceived to be a congested and competitive graduate labour market." Moreover, there is currently a profound economic and social crisis in Portugal, which is severely affecting recent graduates and curtailing their employment options. Therefore, it is increasingly questioned whether investing in further education actually contributes to better outcomes in the labor market.

However, the data obtained suggest that a postgraduate degree still provides a return in respect to job opportunities. Unemployment rates tend to be lower among postgraduates than they are among graduates. Thus, there is a positive and statistically significant association between the level of academic degree of the Portuguese respondents and the proportion of employed individuals, $\chi^2(4) = 11.401, p = .022.$[4]

The unemployment rate observed among Brazilian tourism graduates (18.8%) is lower compared with that observed among Portuguese respondents (24.9%). This was expected because the average unemployment rate in Brazil in the fourth trimester of 2011 was significantly lower (5.7%) than the average unemployment rate in Portugal (13.8%) in the same period (Organization for Economic Cooperation and Development, 2012). This positive effect of postgraduate degrees on the employment rate was once again

---

[4]   The chi-square test (χ^2) is presented with its associated degrees of freedom (value specified in brackets) and the significance value (p).

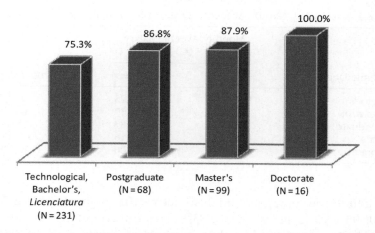

FIGURE 1 Employment rate by academic degree of Brazilian respondents.

observed among Brazilian respondents, $\chi^2(5) = 16.683$, $p = .005$, as we can see in Figure 1. Thus, data suggest that the unemployment rate decreases with the increase in the academic specialization of tourism graduates.

The level of academic degree also seems to have an influence on the rise of the average monthly salary for tourism graduates, given that there is a positive correlation[5] between the monthly average salary and the academic degree of both Portuguese ($r_S = .225$, $p < .001$) and Brazilian respondents ($r_S = .481$, $p < .001$). In fact, the analysis of the average monthly salary of the Portuguese respondents by academic degree revealed statistically significant differences, $\chi_{KW}^2(4) = 81.610$, $p < .001$.[6] The Games-Howell[7] multiple comparison test showed that the monthly average salary of those with postgraduate degrees is statistically significantly different from the average salary of those with the lowest levels of higher education degrees, namely technological, bachelor's, and *Licenciatura*. It can also be observed that women's salaries are lower in most of the academic degrees. As shown in Table 1, the gender pay gap[8] among Portuguese respondents tends to decrease with higher academic degrees.

Regarding the results for Brazil, it is necessary to acknowledge some wider results concerning the Brazilian sample. The monthly average salary of Brazilian respondents is 3,019.49 *reais* ($1,519.23; $M = 3,019.49$; $SE = 133.87$; 95% CI [2,756.18, 3,282.79]), or 5 times higher than the national minimum

---

[5]   A Spearman correlation (r_S) was applied.

[6]   The Kruskal-Wallis Test (χ_{KW}^2) is presented with its associated degrees of freedom (value specified in brackets) and the significance value (p).

[7]   The post-hoc test chosen was the Games-Howell Test as there were unequal sample sizes and unequal variances.

[8]   As defined in Costa et al. (2012a), the gender pay gap is the difference between male and female earnings expressed as a percentage of male earnings.

TABLE 1 Gender Pay Gap by Academic Degree of Portuguese Tourism Graduates

Academic Degree	Monthly Average Salary (€)		Gender Pay Gap
	Men	Women	
Bachelor's	1,198.93	951.25	20.7%
Licenciatura	997.21	829.57	16.8%
Postgraduate	1,268.36	1,057.83	16.6%
Master's	1,194.78	1,307.18	−9.4%
Doctorate	2,350.00	2,025.00	13.8%

wage. A gender-disaggregated analysis shows that women ($M = 2,728.24$; $SE = 143.50$; 95% CI [2,445.65, 3,010.83]) earn, on average, from 500 to 1,800 *reais* ($251.57 to $905.66) less than men ($M = 3,883.19$; $SE = 300.27$; 95% CI [3,286.27, 4,480.11]). These wage differences are statistically significant, $t(127.544) = -3.470$, $p = .001$, and correspond to a 29.7% gender pay gap.

As stated before, the positive correlation between academic degree and salary is also verified among Brazilian respondents, where those with first degrees are more represented in the lowest salary categories, in clear contrast with postgraduates, whose presence is more accentuated in the highest salary ranks. These differences are statistically significant, $\chi_{KW}^2(3) = 88.722$, $p < .001$, as the Games-Howell multiple comparison test confirmed that the monthly average salary is statistically significantly different for each and every level of academic degree considered.

Although women are always the lowest wage earners within each academic degree, the gender pay gap for Brazilian respondents nonetheless decreased sharply in the highest levels of education (Table 2). Thus, data suggest that gender gaps are less pervasive among those with the highest levels of education.

There is a statistically significant association between the academic degree obtained by the Portuguese tourism graduates and the creation of their own business or employment, $\chi^2(4) = 25.330$, $p < .001$. These results suggest that entrepreneurship grows with the increase in the level of education (Figure 2). Costa et al. (2012b) showed that the statistically significant

TABLE 2 Gender Pay Gap by Academic Degree of Brazilian Tourism Graduates

Academic Degree	Monthly Average Salary (R$)		Gender Pay Gap
	Men	Women	
Technological, Bachelor's, or *Licenciatura*	2,722.36	1,920.81	29.4%
Postgraduate	3,683.82	2,857.14	22.4%
Master's	4,703.00	3,980.71	15.4%
Doctorate	7,608.33	7,449.25	2.1%

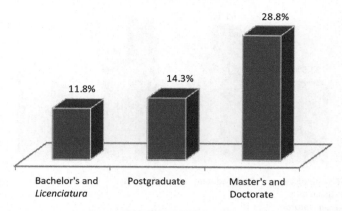

FIGURE 2 Entrepreneurship by academic degree of Portuguese tourism graduates.

association between these variables only occurs among female graduates, whereas no such statistically significant association exists for male graduates. However, it was observed that the higher the level of education, the more likely men were to have started their own business or employment, rising from 19.6% among men with a bachelor's degree or a *Licenciatura* to 30.0% among men with a master's degree or a doctorate.

Although the relation between entrepreneurship and the academic degree is not as linear among Brazilian respondents, the statistically significant association between these variables is again confirmed, $\chi^2(5) = 43.944$, $p < .001$. The proportion of entrepreneurs among respondents with first degrees (technological, bachelor's, or *Licenciatura*; 16.2%) is significantly lower than that observed among the postgraduates (Figure 3).

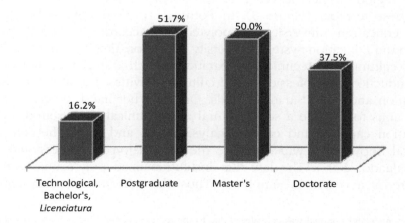

FIGURE 3 Entrepreneurship by academic degree of Brazilian tourism graduates.

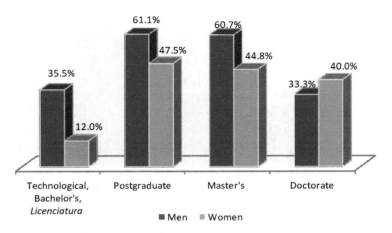

FIGURE 4 Entrepreneurship by gender and academic degree of Brazilian tourism graduates.

If data are disaggregated by gender, one can see that the gender gap in entrepreneurship decreases among postgraduates. While among first-degree holders, the proportion of male graduates (35.5%) is more than double that of female graduates (12%), this disparity decreased among those with higher academic degrees. Moreover, the proportion of women entrepreneurs exceeded the proportion of men among doctorates (40.0% vs. 33.3%, respectively; Figure 4).

Educational Subsystem

It is in the North and Center regions of Portugal[9] that tourism higher education programs are mostly concentrated: 16 higher education institutions are located in the Center, 15 are located in the North, and 9 are in the Lisbon region, while the other 12 are spread throughout the rest of the Portuguese territory (Figure 5). In Portugal, there are two subsystems of higher education: university and polytechnic. According to the Portuguese Law on the Education System, university education aims to provide solid scientific, cultural, and technical preparation, which is important not only for the conduction of professional and cultural activities, but also for fostering innovation and critical analysis skills. On the other hand, polytechnic education aims to provide a solid cultural and technical background, develop innovation capacity and critical analysis skills, and teach theoretical and practical knowledge, which enable the conduction of professional activities (Salgado, 2007). The law that institutionalized polytechnic education conferred it a vocational emphasis. Thus, this educational subsystem aims

---

[9]   Only mainland Portugal was considered due to the reduced number of responses obtained from the autonomous regions of Madeira and Azores.

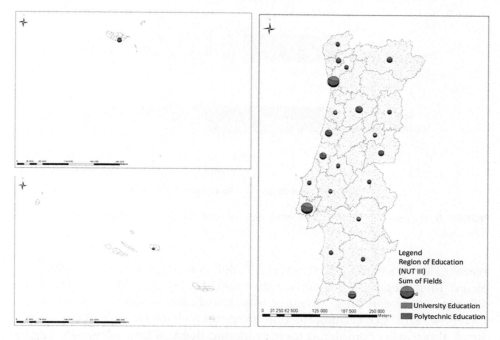

FIGURE 5 Higher education programs on tourism in Portugal, according to the educational subsystem (color figure available online).

to match the needs of the productive system, in contrast with the more conceptual and theoretical characteristics conveyed by university education (Arroteia, 1996, cited in Salgado, 2007).

Almost 60% of tourism higher education programs are provided by polytechnic institutions, while the remaining 40% are administered by universities. This is consistent with the results observed, given that three out of four Portuguese respondents completed their academic degrees at a polytechnic institute. The analysis of the employment rate, according to the educational subsystem of the Portuguese tourism graduates,[10] reveals that tourism graduates who complete their higher education in universities have a higher employment rate (77.6%) than do those who complete their academic degree in polytechnic institutions (73.6%). This association between the employment rate and the educational subsystem is marginally statistically significant, $\chi^2(1) = 2.556$, $p = .062$.

The type of educational subsystem also has a significant statistical association with the monthly average salary and with entrepreneurship. Thus, those who obtained their academic degrees in polytechnic institutions earned, on

---

[10] In this analysis, only the graduates with an academic degree below the doctorate category were considered. The purpose was to homogenize the data, because polytechnic institutions do not offer doctorate degrees.

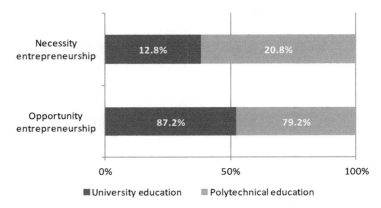

FIGURE 6 Reasons why Portuguese graduates created their own employment, by type of education.

average, lower salaries (€881.30 [$1,157.06]) compared with those who completed their degrees in a university (€963.08 [$1,264.43]), and the wage difference between these two groups is statistically significant, $t(641.514) = 2.529, p = .012$. Concerning the entrepreneurial characteristics of the respondents, those who completed their academic degrees in a university engage more in entrepreneurship (15.6%), as compared with those who completed their degrees in a polytechnic institution (10.5%). If we analyze the motivations underlying the decision to create their own employment, it can be seen that although opportunity-related reasons are most frequently pointed out by both graduate groups, necessity-related reasons are comparatively more highlighted by the group of respondents from polytechnic institutions, as compared with those who attended universities. In fact, a higher proportion of polytechnic graduates worked in business due to *unemployment or to help the family* (Figure 6).

Geographical Location of the Educational Institution

An exploratory cluster analysis[11] was performed to identify regional similarities between the salaries of tourism graduates and to simultaneously understand whether the geographical location of the educational institution influences the career development of Portuguese tourism graduates.

First, a hierarchical cluster analysis was applied using Ward's method and the Euclidean distance as dissimilarity measure. The dendrogram (Figure 7) depicts the three resulting clusters. According to the R-square

---

[11]   The outcome of the cluster analysis presented here resulted from a comparison between the several cluster analyses performed. Because there was a different number of answers by geographical location, several cluster analyses were performed to compare and analyze the resemblances. This cluster analysis encompassed only data concerning graduates employed in full-time jobs.

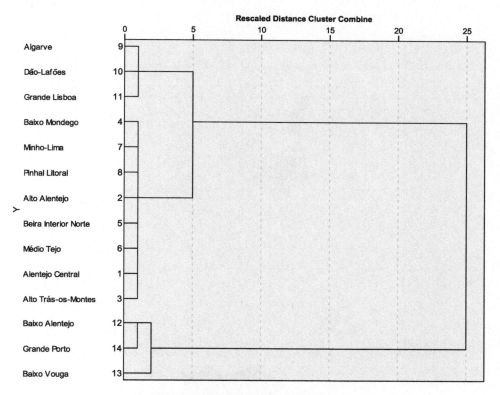

FIGURE 7 Dendrogram using Ward linkage.

criterion, this was the optimum number of clusters to retain, given that they explained a satisfactory proportion of the variance (higher than 80%). The assignment of regions to one of the three identified clusters was further refined by the nonhierarchical k-means method.

Cluster I is mostly formed by regions from the interior of Portugal (Figure 8). The monthly average salary in this region is the lowest (€778.89 [$1,022.61]). The 16.6% gender pay gap is similar to that observed among the general Portuguese sample. The highest gender pay gap is detected in Cluster II (23.1%), which has a monthly average salary of €917.97 ($1,205.20). Cluster III gathers the best conditions concerning both wage (€1,115.87 [$1,465.03]) and gender equality (14.5%; Table 3). In fact, this is the only cluster of regions in which women's average salary exceeds €1,000 ($1,312.90).

Another relevant fact is that the regions in Cluster III (Baixo Alentejo, Baixo Vouga, and Grande Porto) remained isolated in the same cluster in all the cluster analyses performed, thus suggesting that the characteristics of these regions are substantially different from all the others.

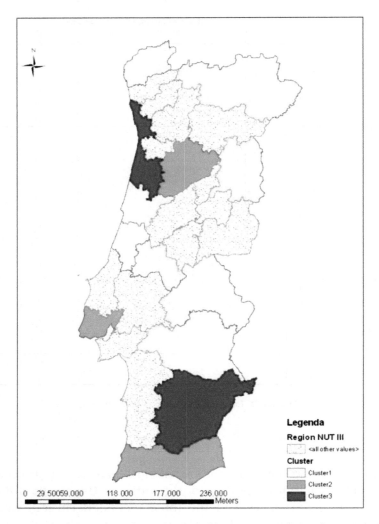

FIGURE 8 Regional clusters based on the monthly average salary of Portuguese tourism graduates according to the region of education (analysis of 14 Nomenclaturas das Unidades Territoriais para fins estatístico [NUT] III regions) (color figure available online).

TABLE 3 Monthly Average Salary and Gender Pay Gap by Cluster

Cluster	Monthly Average Salary (€)	Monthly Average Salary by Gender (€)		Gender Pay Gap (%)
		Men	Women	
I	778.89	875.26	729.60	16.6
II	917.97	1,079.63	830.67	23.1
III	1,115.87	1,231.25	1,052.93	14.5

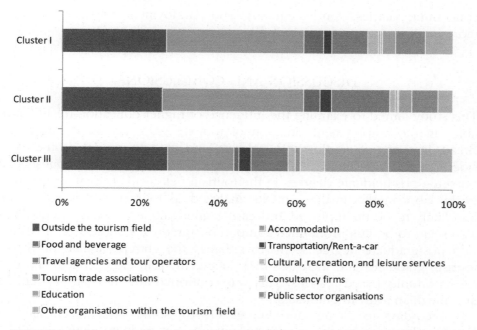

FIGURE 9 Fields of activity of the Portuguese graduates according to cluster allocation.

The higher salary levels obtained by those who graduated in the regions in Cluster III (Baixo Alentejo, Baixo Vouga, and Grande Porto) might be justified by the different pattern of employment in these regions, namely concerning the major fields of activity. In fact, the fields of activity associated with better pay conditions, namely education and consultancy firms, are the ones that prevail in Cluster III, comparatively to the other clusters, in which fields of activity associated with lower wages are more represented, such as accommodation and food and beverage (Figure 9). This suggests that some higher education institutions are training graduates more suited to work in fields like education or planning, while others are preparing a skilled labor force to work in other fields of activity that are traditionally less well paid.

Cluster I has the lowest employment rate (72.1%), followed by Cluster II (74.9%) and Cluster III (79.2%). These differences, verified between the employment rates in the three clusters, are marginally statistically significant, $\chi^2(2) = 5.351$, $p = .069$. The regions of education in Cluster III are those in which a higher proportion of entrepreneurs are concentrated. In fact, the proportion of graduates within Cluster III, who created their own employment (20.1%) is more than double the proportion of entrepreneurs within Cluster II (9.6%) and Cluster I (8.3%), and these differences are statistically significant, $\chi^2(2) = 25.088$, $p < .001$.

Thus, data suggest that graduates who completed their academic degrees in the regions of education allocated to Cluster III (Baixo Alentejo, Baixo Vouga, and Grande Porto) have better employment conditions concerning salaries, gender equality, and employment rates, as well as a more marked entrepreneurial profile.

DISCUSSION AND CONCLUSIONS

This study aimed to examine the influence of higher education-related variables in the employment situation of tourism graduates in Portugal and Brazil, in terms of employment, salaries, and entrepreneurial profile, considering gender differences. The empirical evidence presented suggests that pursuing postgraduate degrees in the tourism field leads to better outcomes in the labor market in the contexts analyzed, as tourism postgraduates are less likely to be unemployed and earn higher salaries. Gender inequalities also seem to be less pronounced among postgraduates. Moreover, investing in a postgraduate degree seems to enhance the entrepreneurial profile of tourism graduates and increases their engagement in entrepreneurship due to opportunity-based reasons. This was confirmed among both Portuguese and Brazilian tourism graduates.

According to Pitcher and Purcell (1998), some students enrolled in higher education studies prefer to pursue postgraduate degrees in the hope of raising their qualifications and general employability, rather than specifically targeting vocational or professional routes. However, Compton-Edwards (1997, cited in Pitcher & Purcell, 1998) raised an important issue concerning the overqualification of the labor force, which may render graduates less attractive to some employers. This suggests that the strategy of pursuing postgraduate degrees for achieving better professional situations may turn out to be unsustainable in the long term. However, the data from our study do not seem to support this stance.

Portuguese tourism graduates who completed their academic degrees in the university educational subsystem, which is characterized by a more conceptual and theoretical approach, revealed better employment conditions compared to those who concluded their higher education studies in polytechnic institutions, which have a more vocational approach.

Currently, polytechnic institutions offer, in general, the same academic degrees as those offered at university institutions, with the exception of the doctoral degrees that can only be conferred by universities. This could explain the differences observed between graduates from these two subsystems. Pitcher and Purcell (1998) highlighted the influence of employers' tripartite model of higher education institutions, classifying them into "milk round elite," "other traditional universities," and "new universities," and concluding that "the traditional 'graduate labour market' persists where 'traditional' students from established universities continue to have reasonable job opportunities after gaining a degree" (Pitcher & Purcell, 1998, p. 198). This is consistent with our findings, as tourism graduates from universities show lower unemployment rates, higher salaries, and higher entrepreneurialism, suggesting that these individuals face fewer obstacles in the labor market.

This study also revealed an association between the geographical location of the educational institution and the monthly average salary of Portuguese tourism graduates. After applying the cluster analysis technique, it was found that there were differences in the salaries and the entrepreneurial profile of tourism graduates according to the regions of education, which were grouped in three clusters. Employment rates and the gender pay gap also differed between the clusters. In addition, a group of regions of education stood out, verifying that their graduates have comparatively better employment situations and a lower gender pay gap.

According to Petrova and Mason (2004), the industry is not convinced of the benefits of tourism degrees or of hiring tourism graduates. However, our results suggest that students stemming from different institutions are having different employment outcomes in the labor market. Such an analysis had not been done before in the contexts analyzed, and we urge that further research is carried out to analyze in more detail the reasons for the discrepancies observed. If most of the tourism education supply is concentrated in the polytechnics, but the employment outcomes of those who graduate from these institutions tend to be worse, perhaps the tourism education system should be rethought. However, we consider that this study only provides some hints that should be analyzed in detail in future research.

We strongly believe that our data should motivate tourism higher education institutions to consider the issues addressed in this article so that the role of tourism higher education can be rethought. The transformative potential of the educators and the leaders of higher education institutions is required to design a path for tourism higher education that brings benefits for the careers of those who want to be involved in the tourism industry, while answering the needs of the labor market. This is particularly urgent in a context of crisis, such as what is currently being experienced in Portugal.

Limitations

The present study has some limitations. The major limitation underlying this empirical study concerns the sampling technique applied, as it does not allow for the generalization of our findings. Both the Portuguese sample and the Brazilian sample were mostly collected through e-mail contact. As a result, it was difficult to reach those graduates who completed their degrees a longer time ago. Thus, the respondents were very young, and results should be interpreted cautiously.

Another important limitation is due to the specificity of some of the education-related variables used in this study, which were only applied in the Portuguese context, which thus made comparison with Brazil impossible.

REFERENCES

Amaro, M. N. (2007). *A mulher e o mercado de trabalho do turiso* [The woman and the tourism labor market]. Retrieved from http://www.alesfe.org.br/v2/materia/materiatoda.asp?numeromateria=196

Bañuls, A. L., & Casado-Díaz, J. M. (2010). Rewards to education in the tourism sector: One step ahead. *Tourism Economics*, *16*(1), 11–23.

Becker, G. S. (1962). Investment in human capital: A theoretical analysis. *Journal of Political Economy*, *70*(5), 9–49.

Brownell, J. (1998). Striking a balance: The future of work and family issues in the hospitality industry. *Marriage & Family Review*, *28*(1), 109–123.

Camps Del Valle, V., Pérez Santiago, J. A., & Martínez Lugo, M. E. (2010). Comparación por género de los estilos de liderazgo en una muestra de gerenciales en Puerto Rico [Gender comparison of the leadership styles in a sample of managers in Puerto Rico]. *Puerto Rican Journal of Psychology*, *21*, 113–132.

Carvalho, I., Costa, C., & Breda, Z. (2011). Work–family unbalance in the Portuguese tourism sector: Strategies for a better life and improved upward mobility. In A. F. Eriksson (Ed.), *Equality, growth and sustainability: Do they mix?* (Linköping Electronic Conference Proceedings No. 5, pp. 183–193). Linköping, Sweden: Linköping University Electronic Press.

Costa, C., Carvalho, I., & Breda, Z. (2011a). Gender inequalities in tourism employment: The Portuguese case. *Revista Turismo & Desenvolvimento*, *15*, 37–52.

Costa, C., Carvalho, I., & Breda, Z. (2011b). Igualdade de género e responsabilidade social das empresas de turismo [Gender equality and social responsibility of tourism companies]. In M. A. N. Costa, M. J. Santos, F. M. Seabra, & F. Jorge (Eds.), *Responsabilildade social: Uma visão ibero-americana* (pp. 211–234). Lisbon, Portugal: Editora Almedina.

Costa, C., Carvalho, I., Caçador, S., & Breda, Z. (2012a). Future higher education in tourism studies and the labor market: Gender perspectives on expectations and experiences. *Journal of Teaching in Travel & Tourism*, *12*, 70–90.

Costa, C., Carvalho, I., Caçador, S., & Breda, Z. (2012b). Gender and entrepreneurship in tourism: An analysis of tourism graduates' entrepreneurial profile. *Revista Turismo & Desenvolvimento*, *17/18*(2), 623–635.

Crompton, R., & Anderson, K. (1992). Gendered jobs and social change. *British Journal of Management*, *3*, 53–59.

Druskat, V. U. (1994). Gender and leadership style: Transformational and transactional leadership in the Roman Catholic Church. *Leadership Quarterly*, *5*, 99–119.

Eagly, A. H., & Johnson, B. T. (1990). Gender and leadership style: A meta-analysis. *Psychological Bulletin*, *108*, 233–256.

Escária, V. (2006). *Percursos de inserção no mercado de trabalho dos diplomados do ensino superior* [Pathways of integration of higher education graduates in the labor market]. Lisbon, Portugal: Direção-geral de Estudos, Estatísticas e Planeamento/Ministério do Trabalho e da Segurança Social.

Esteban, P. G. (2004). As mulheres na ciência: Perda de capital humano e tecto de cristal [Women in science: Human capital loss and glass ceiling]. In E. Figueira

& L. Rainha (Eds.), *Qualificação e género: O papel das competências-chave* (pp. 71–90). Évora, Portugal: Academus, Consultoria, Formação e Investigação.

Eurostat. (2011). *Employment and unemployment (Labour Force Survey)*. Retrieved from http://epp.eurostat.ec.europa.eu/portal/page/portal/employment_unemployment_lfs/data/main_tables

Fagan, C., & O'Reilly, J. (1998). Conceptualising part-time work: The value of an integrated comparative perspective. In J. O'Reilly & C. Fagan (Eds.), *Part-time prospects: An international comparison of part-time work in Europe, North-America and the Pacific Rim* (pp. 1–31). London, UK: Routledge.

Gabinete de Planeamento, Estratégia, Avaliação e Relações Internacionais-Ministério da Ciência, Tecnologia e Ensino Superior. (2011). *Estatísticas* [Statistics]. Retrieved from http://www.gpeari.mctes.pt/?idc=103

Hausmann, R., Tyson, L. D., & Zahidi, S. (2011). *The global gender gap report 2011*. Geneva, Switzerland: World Economic Forum.

Hemmati, M. (2000). Women's employment and participation in tourism. *Sustainable Travel & Tourism*, *5*(1), 17–20.

Instituto Nacional de Estutos e Pesquisas Educacionais Anísio Teixeira. (2011). *Censo da Educação Superior 2010—Divulgação dos principais resultados do Censo da Educação Superior 2010* [Higher Education Census 2010—Dissemination of the main results of the Higher Education Census 2010]. Retrieved from http://portal.mec.gov.br/index.php?option=com_content&view=article&id=17212

Jordan, F. (1997). An occupational hazard? Sex segregation in tourism employment. *Tourism Management*, *18*(8), 525–534.

Kinnaird, V., & Hall, D. (1996). Understanding tourism processes: A gender-aware framework. *Tourism Management*, *17*(2), 95–102.

Mincer, J. (1958). Investment in human capital and personal income distribution. *The Journal of Political Economy*, *66*(4), 281–302.

Nova Fórum & Sociedade Portuguesa de Inovação. (2004). *The global entrepreneurship monitor 2004—Portuguese executive report*. London, UK: Global Entrepreneurship Monitor.

O'Leary, S., & Deegan, J. (2005). Career progression of Irish tourism and hospitality management graduates. *International Journal of Contemporary Hospitality Management*, *17*(5), 421–432.

Organization for Economic Cooperation and Development. (2012). *Labour force statistics (MEI): Survey based unemployment rates and levels*. Retrieved from http://stats.oecd.org/Index.aspx?QueryId=36499

Parrett, L. (n.d.). *Women in tourism employment: A guided tour of the Greenwich experience—research report*. London, UK: London Thames Gateway Forum Equality, Access, & Participation.

Petrova, P., & Mason, P. (2004). The value of tourism degrees: A Luton-based case study. *Education + Training*, *46*(3), 153–161.

Pitcher, J., & Purcell, K. (1998). Diverse expectations and access to opportunities: Is there a graduate labour market? *Higher Education Quarterly*, *52*(2), 179–203.

Ramb, F. (2008). *Employment gender gap in the EU is narrowing: Labour market trends 2000–2007*. Luxembourg, Luxembourg: Office for Official Publications of the European Communities.

Reynolds, P. D., Camp, S. M., Bygrave, W. D., Autio, E., & Hay, M. (2002). *Global Entrepreneurship Monitor 2001 executive report*. London, UK: Babson College and London Business School.

Salgado, M. A. B. (2007). *Educação e organização curricular em turismo no ensino superior português* (Unpublished doctoral dissertation). Universidade de Aveiro, Aveiro, Portugal.

Santos, L. D., & Varejão, J. (2006). *Employment, pay and discrimination in the tourism industry* (FEP Working Papers 205). Porto, Portugal: University of Porto.

Slater, C. L., & Martinez, B. J. (2000). Transformational leadership in the planning of a doctoral program. *The Educational Forum, 64*(4), 308–316.

Thrane, C. (2008). Earnings differentiation in the tourism industry: Gender, human capital and socio-demographic effects. *Tourism Management, 29*(3), 514–524.

Thrane, C. (2010). Education and earnings in the tourism industry—the role of sheepskin effects. *Tourism Economics, 16*(3), 549–563.

Tomlinson, M. (2008). 'The degree is not enough': Students' perceptions of the role of higher education credentials for graduate work and employability. *British Journal of Sociology of Education, 29*(1), 49–61.

United Nations. (2009). *The millennium development goals report 2009*. New York, NY: Author.

Vartiainen, J. (2002). *Gender wage differentials in the Finnish labour market*. Retrieved from http://www.tasa-arvo.fi/c/document_library/get_file?folderId=243322&name=DLFE-8772.pdf

World Travel & Tourism Council. (2011a). *Travel and tourism economic impact 2011—Brazil*. London, UK: Author.

World Travel & Tourism Council. (2011b). *Travel and tourism economic impact 2011—Portugal*. London, UK: Author.

World Travel & Tourism Council. (2012). *Travel and tourism economic impact 2011—world*. London, UK: Author.

Zhong, Y. G., & Couch, S. (2007). Hospitality students' perceptions of facilitators and constraints affecting women's career advancement in the hospitality industry. *Family and Consumer Sciences Research Journal, 35*(4), 357–373.

Tourism-Oriented Educational Leadership in the Dominican Republic: The Key to Change

MONTSERRAT IGLESIAS XAMANÍ, DAVID PEGUERO MANZANARES
and GLORIA SANMARTÍN ANTOLÍN
University of Barcelona, Barcelona, Spain

Educational leadership as a driving force in developing countries entails transforming the tourism students of today into the leaders of tomorrow by providing them with a system of values from a constructivist, competence-based perspective. The transfer of knowledge from educational settings to the tourism industry can foster innovation and enable different managerial approaches in the tertiary sector. Moreover, the impacts on third-world societies at the economic, sociocultural, and environmental levels can facilitate sustainable development. In the case of the Dominican Republic, the need to rethink the bachelor's degree in tourism has been the key to change.

INTRODUCTION

How does educational leadership impact the reality of a developing country? What is the transformational power of education in tourism-related learning environments? These issues will be dealt with in the following article, which focuses on a curriculum design project promoted by the Ministry of Higher Education, Science, and Technology of the Dominican Republic. This article is therefore concerned with educational leadership and the way Dominican university students can become the potential leaders of their local tourism industry. Under the umbrella of this country's government, in accordance with its strategic lines for tourism development, the project aims to empower future professionals by developing their competences through a new degree in tourism. The resulting curriculum is to be implemented in the forthcoming academic years, and the principles and considerations underlying it can be considered a springboard for discussion not just in the Caribbean, but also in other similar contexts.

THE ROLE OF TOURISM IN THE DOMINICAN REPUBLIC

The Dominican Republic is in a continuous process of creation and renewal. The economic development of this emerging country nowadays relies on growing tourism receipts to offset the decline in the agricultural and manufacturing industries (Padilla & McElroy, 2010). At present, tourism is regarded as the main source of income and socioeconomic interaction with other countries.

In the context of the Caribbean, after a decline in 2009, tourism arrivals were estimated to have risen 4% in 2010, with three of the major destinations recording new peaks: Jamaica (+5%), Cuba (+4%), and the Dominican Republic (+3%; United Nations World Tourism Organization [UNWTO], 2011). More specifically, in the case of the Dominican Republic, international tourism receipts in 2010 accounted for US$4,240 million (a share of 2.3% of total receipts for the Americas).

The construction of hotels on the island to host an international summit of heads of state in the mid 1950s gave birth to tourism in a country immersed in a delicate political situation, which provided further impetus for the Dominican Republic to show the world its best image. The Dominican hotel industry was gradually built up. In the 1980s, a major boom took place with the arrival of Spanish and American entrepreneurs, mainly hoteliers. The Ministry of Tourism was created and the professional international promotion of this Caribbean destination began (Miolán, 1998). The need for trained professionals was ignored until the 1980s, when the international private companies operating in this country started to train the people working in the tourism industry to meet their needs for qualified top- and middle-management positions (Olivares, Lladó, & Díaz, 1996).

In 1981, the Pontificia Universidad Catolica Madre y Maestra initiated the Hotel Administration educational program, supported first by Cornell University and later by the University of Nevada. In 1990, a bachelor's degree was created to provide the Dominican tourism industry with human resources with the knowledge, skills, and values needed to boost the economic and social development of the various regions that have based their economies on hotel, restaurant, and tourism services. Tourism studies have been offered at the Universidad Autónoma de Santo Domingo (UASD; n.d.) since 2005.

Market preferences currently focus on tourism that is compatible with the environment and the local community and culture. Meanwhile, the Dominican tourism industry seeks to enhance the pattern of sustainable development across the nation by establishing rules and regulations and strengthening social responsibility. It aims to involve the local communities in tourism activities, as well as create social and institutional capital to foster human progress.

The Dominican economy is facing great challenges, and the country requires strong environmental preservation policies. Padilla and McElroy (2010) have identified external pressures to expand development into protected, fragile coastal areas, as well as increased pressures on already weak environmental and planning governmental structures. These authors highlight the explosive growth of tourism in the South and East of the country, in contrast to a decline in the North. The result has been a subsequent rise in crime and pollution, followed by deep discounts that attract a lower class of tourists motivated by all-inclusive offers. Padilla and McElroy point out the heavy demands on infrastructure, but there is also a need for strong measures to protect minors from exploitation and sexual abuse, and for institutional consolidation. Furthermore, the decentralization of the market from tour operators, increased income per tourist and hotel room, and improved labor supply are regarded as essential.

Concerning the education of human resources and the promotion of entrepreneurship in the hospitality and tourism industry, the existing academic programs do not serve the current needs. According to the Dominican Consortium for Tourism Competitiveness, this sector demands diversified, competence-based training at all levels, as the lack of appropriate skills affects not only the basic operational staff, but also the managers (Consorcio Dominicano de Competitividad Turística, 2011). Given the increasing demand for competitiveness in the Dominican Republic, the labor market requires all levels of education and training in the areas of tourism, hospitality, and gastronomy, as well as the progressive specialization of professionals. Linking institutions of higher education with the production sector is a must so that today's students can have direct contact with the industry they will eventually be a part of tomorrow, and curriculum design procedures need to take this into account.

Tourism Studies in a Higher Education Context

It is taken for granted that universities should educate a highly skilled workforce to cater to the needs of the fast-changing tourism industry. Thus, tourism students should master different competences to be able to face a number of challenges, such as increased cultural diversity, a concern for sustainability, constant technological evolution, and supply innovation (Sheldon, Fesenmaier, & Tribe, 2011), as well as the ever-changing patterns of tourism behavior, which nowadays seem to be mainly related to experiential consumption (Morgan, Lugosi, & Ritchie, 2010).

To prevent faculties from offering their graduates ephemeral knowledge and training rather than solid, long-lasting expertise and principles, educational systems require a paradigm shift in terms of form and content of curriculum design, organization, and management (Wan & Gut, 2011). Tourism programs in higher education, in particular, ought to reconsider the current conceptualization of tourism and its implications and interrelations with the societies where it takes place. To achieve this, the present structure and foundations, as well as the way expertise is developed, must be questioned.

The concept of tourism from a scientific perspective must be incorporated into curricula, even though its precise nature is still a subject of discussion. Having analyzed its scientification process, Jafari (2001) concludes that tourism shows the features typically associated with consolidated scientific disciplines, as the study of tourism has evolved from a practical field to one present in higher education and well-founded scientific research publications. According to Jafari, its maturity as a social science implies the advance of the tourism industry thanks to applied research.

Nevertheless, the recognition of tourism as a clearly identified academic discipline in its own right at present seems to be contested by the views of those who consider that knowledge about tourism originates within and across other fields of study. In this sense, Tribe (2004) advocates for tourism "business inter-disciplinarity" parallel to and complemented by "non-business related tourism" (p. 50). Grounded on the previous work of Gibbons et al. (1994), Tribe distinguishes tourism-related knowledge from extradisciplinary knowledge. The former is produced within a specific academic discipline and can encompass both multidisciplinary and interdisciplinary traits. The latter is not usually generated at universities, but rather within the public and private sectors, for practical purposes.

In any case, tourism studies must be reappraised. Research approaches nowadays should try not to "address contemporary subjects (such as tourism) through outdated and ageing frameworks for scholarly activity and academic administration" (Coles, Hall, & Duval, 2009, p. 81). Tourism studies must be based on a set of values and principles that should characterize the undertaking of tourism-related activities. Sheldon et al. (2011) suggest that future tourism graduates ought to embody five principles: ethics, stewardship, knowledge, professionalism, and mutuality. A consistent educational approach, grounded on constructivist learning theories, should lead to the development of tourism students' competences and the fostering of lifelong learning to underpin their prospective careers.

Facilitating Knowledge From a Learner-Centered Perspective

Constructivist learning theory, represented by Dewey, Montessori, and Kolb, among others, and based on experiential learning, derives from constructivism as depicted by authors like Piaget and Vygotsky. Summing up some of the main aspects of constructivist learning and teaching according to Wilson and Cole (1991), Lebow (1993), Jonassen (1994), Ernest (1995), and Honebein (1996), learning situations, environments, skills, content, and tasks are relevant, realistic, and contextualized, and the learning process is learner-centered, so educators play the role of facilitators of knowledge.

Knowledge construction sustained on the learner's previous knowledge, beliefs, and attitudes takes place through social negotiation, collaboration, and experience. Multiple perspectives and representations of content are presented and encouraged, and knowledge complexity is reflected with an emphasis on conceptual interrelatedness and interdisciplinarity. In addition, a wide range of activities, opportunities, tools, and settings are provided to promote metacognition, reflection, and awareness, sometimes through autonomous exploration and through errors, which are regarded as part of the process.

At present, the focus on the development of the learner's competences is aimed at facilitating applicability in real-life professional environments, and preparing students for their future role in society in terms of employability and citizenship. In this sense, three outstanding projects set a valuable frame of reference: the proposal formulated in 2005 by the Commission of the European Communities on Key Competences for Lifelong Learning, Tuning Educational Structures in Europe, and Tuning Latin America.

Tuning Educational Structures in Europe started as a project in 2000. The purpose was to link the political objectives of the Bologna Process to the higher education sector (i.e., to foster citizens' mobility and employability, as well as Europe's overall development, by strengthening its cultural, social, scientific, and technological dimensions through the construction of the European Higher Education Area). In 2004, Tuning Educational Structures in Europe originated the Tuning Latin America project to identify and exchange information and to improve collaboration between Latin American universities to enhance the quality, effectiveness, and transparency of their educational systems (Beneitone et al., 2007). The main objective was to facilitate the mobility of students and professionals in Latin America and worldwide. According to Tuning Educational Structures in Europe (González & Wagenaar, 2005), "competences represent a dynamic combination of cognitive and meta-cognitive skills, knowledge and understanding, interpersonal, intellectual and practical skills, and ethical values" (p. 1). Three types of generic competences can be distinguished: instrumental, interpersonal, and systemic.

Education as a Transformational Tool for Sustainable Tourism Development

By following a constructivist, competence-based approach, tourism education can be aligned with the reality of the tourism industry so that the transfer of knowledge from educational settings can benefit not only the people who are directly involved in the sector, but also the local society by contributing to a nation's economic growth at both micro and macro levels. For many developing countries, tourism is one of the main sources of foreign income and the No. 1 export category, creating much needed employment and opportunities for infrastructure development (UNWTO, 2011). Moreover, the social and environmental impacts of ethically practiced tourism should have relevant consequences for regional and global progress.

The global forces driving tourism cannot be restrained, but tourism stakeholders have the opportunity to "fashion the future to their needs rather than simply to regard future events as beyond control" (Dwyer et al., 2008, p. 55). Educators and administrators are thus required to assume active, responsible leadership roles to enable change through the power of education and the potential of tourism both as a transformational tool and as a means to a higher end. To that effect, tourism students should be trained to eventually become responsible leaders and stewards for the hospitality- and tourism-related companies and organizations operating in their local destinations (Sheldon et al., 2011).

This transformational process is a particularly relevant issue in developing countries, because to become competitive, they require coherent policies, effective and efficient institutions, and a proactive private sector. A national tourism development strategy must address issues that affect the tourism industry and establish linkages with other sectors of the economy. Governments ought to be fully aware of the implications of different tourism developments and should encourage growth models accordingly. Comprehensive tourism development ought to imply targeted support programs, investment in infrastructure, and increased community involvement. In addition, stronger domestic markets should lead to benefits for the domestic economies, while at the same time integrating with global tourism networks (United Nations Development Program, 2011).

METHODOLOGY

Analyzing the Academic and Professional Needs of the Dominican Tourism Sector

The considerations and background mentioned in the previous section have defined the conceptual framework underlying the redesign of the university studies of tourism in the Dominican Republic. In 2011, the

Dominican Ministry of Higher Education, Science, and Technology commissioned the School of Hospitality and Tourism Management CETT-UB (Escola
Universitària d'Hoteleria i Turisme CETT-Universitat de Barcelona [EUHT
CETT-UB]) from the University of Barcelona (Spain) to carry out this project
with the aim of drawing up a formal and methodological basis for redefining
the bachelor's degree in tourism. The project was founded on the premise
that higher education in the Dominican Republic must meet the internal
needs of higher education institutions, the needs of the Dominican society,
and the requirements of both national development and international integration. In this sense, the guidelines provided by the State Secretariat for Higher
Education, Science, and Technology must be followed (Secretaría de Estado
de Educación Superior, Ciencia y Tecnología de la República Dominicana,
2008).

In terms of academic needs, the Dominican universities should address
the growing demand for technical and managerial expertise in tourism by
incorporating the multidisciplinary and interdisciplinary nature of this field
of study in the curriculum of the bachelor's degree with a constructivist,
competence-based approach. Moreover, research and postdegree studies
should be developed to advance the science of tourism.

To identify the needs of the Dominican society in relation to the tourism
industry, as well as the role of this sector in this country's development,
a series of workshops and visits were conducted. These actions were carried out at UASD, the pilot institution that will serve as a model for other
Dominican universities. The participants included a number of representatives from the Ministry of Higher Education, Science, and Technology,
the Ministry of Tourism, the Faculty of Economics and Social Sciences, the
Association of Hotels and Tourism in the Dominican Republic, and a team
of researchers from EUHT CETT-UB.

In these sessions, the current situation of the Dominican tourism sector
and the ministerial strategies were presented, as were the main goals and
trends within the private sector. In addition, an overview of the educational
system was provided, with a special focus on higher education, the structure of the management schools from the Faculty of Economics and Social
Sciences at UASD, and the curriculum for the bachelor's degree in Tourism
and Hotel Management, referred to as Plan 14 (UASD, n.d.). Such presentations were complemented by a number of practical workshops aimed at
identifying the professional profiles that tourism studies in the Dominican
Republic should target. Moreover, the syllabi of each subject included in Plan
14 were analyzed in detail. The initial needs analysis was supplemented by
visits to the regional schools where Plan 14 is offered and by interviews with
several teachers and students.

The growth potential of the Dominican tourism industry was forecast
and taken as a baseline for future educational needs, because Plan 14 was
deemed unfit and in need of urgent redesigning. Rural tourism, for example,

should be fostered by generating basic accommodation in inland areas, while the complementary offers of tourism services need strengthening in both coastal and inland areas. This will require setting up transport and logistics companies; consulting firms; institutions involved in tourism planning, development, and marketing; leisure centers; tour guide companies; travel agencies; and catering providers. Furthermore, as mentioned earlier, sustainable planning and development is a priority, and a wide range of tourism subsectors should be promoted as an alternative to the traditional sun-and-beach option, particularly those related to culture, cruises, sports, adventure activities, health, congresses and events, nightlife and entertainment, second homes, and ecotourism. Higher education programs should cater to the diversification that these new trends reflect. The specialization could be achieved by linking specific subjects to the local development of tourism in different geographic regions of the Dominican Republic.

The needs analysis also showed some education and training deficits that the new curriculum should address. The general lack of foreign language skills underscores the need to develop the communicative competence of university students of tourism in English and at least one other foreign language. Another weakness is the inadequate technical skills at a basic operational level in different areas of the hospitality industry. Moreover, there is a shortage of qualified professionals in the fields of marketing, congress and event organization, and cultural heritage management. Finally, entrepreneurs offering complementary services such as tour guides, tourist information officers, tour operators, and transport providers are scarce. All these shortcomings must be dealt with.

Curricular Foundations and Strategic Lines

The next stage of the methodological procedure consisted of another series of workshops in which further work on the foundations of the new curriculum was undertaken. A team of teachers from UASD traveled to Barcelona and took part in these sessions, along with a number of teachers from EUHT CETT-UB who teach a degree in tourism at this school. The work carried out in Spain by the National Agency for Quality Assessment and Accreditation to adapt the Spanish studies of tourism to the European Higher Education Area was taken as a foundation (Agencia Nacional de Evaluación de la Calidad y Acreditación, 2004). The target professional profiles for the Dominican Republic were subsequently categorized keeping in mind the development needs of the Dominican tourism industry.

After taking into consideration the key competences for lifelong learning and tuning competences, the transversal and specific competences associated with each professional profile were selected. More specifically, nine transversal competences were identified and are connected to the five values that should be integrated in tourism education programs as drivers for change

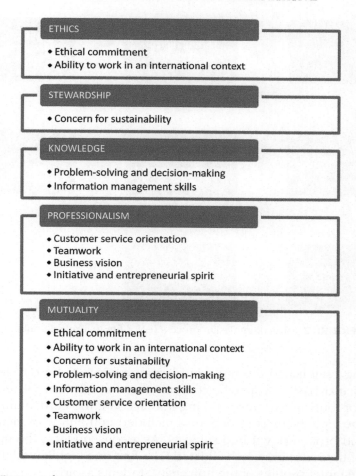

FIGURE 1 Transversal competences related to TEFI principles (color figure available online).

toward responsible leadership according to Sheldon et al. (2011). Figure 1 shows which transversal competences are related to each TEFI principle. Assuming that mutuality is the basic principle that underlies a constructivist approach and involves open-mindedness as well as empowerment, tourism students ought to develop their ability to work in a diverse, international context and to be ethically committed. They should also be able to engage actively in sustainable practices to achieve stewardship. In addition, knowledge as a principle is linked to managing information and to thinking critically in problem-solving and decision-making processes. Last but not least, professionalism is intertwined with several competences, such as proactivity, entrepreneurship, teamwork, customer service orientation, and business vision.

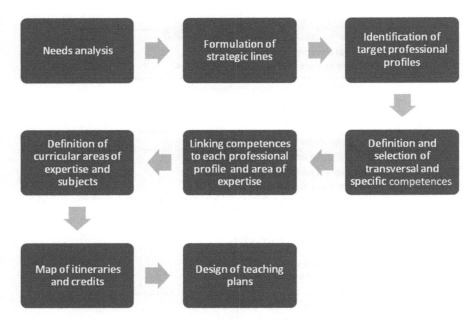

FIGURE 2 Curriculum design process (color figure available online).

Having established the transversal competences to be developed on a cross-curricular basis, 13 specific competences were in turn related to different areas of tourism expertise. Taking into account the curriculum design of Plan 14, the various areas of expertise included in the new curriculum were defined and broken down into subjects. As a consequence, the main strategic lines of the redesign were validated. The first one highlighted the need to expand the target profiles of the university students aspiring to reach middle- and top-management positions in new areas of professional development apart from the traditional hotel and catering industry-related work contexts, such as public destination planning and management, mediation, transport and logistics, tourism products and activities, and training and research. The second strategic line of the new curriculum design focused on the need for "touristification," minimizing those basic subjects that were not related to tourism, integrating tourism-oriented transversal subjects, and increasing the number of credits allocated to tourism-specific subjects. The main stages of the curriculum design process are depicted in Figure 2.

CURRICULUM DESIGN OF THE DEGREE IN TOURISM

The redesign of the university studies of tourism was ultimately undertaken by the team of researchers at EUHT CETT-UB, who endeavored to configure a curriculum that would guarantee the homogeneous planning and development of the new degree in tourism. The curriculum must be consistent with global needs and must be based on standards of quality that should be manageable and achievable in any UASD schools that offered such educational programs.

By working on the same objectives and contents and using similar, coherent methodologies and assessment procedures in the classrooms of each one of the schools, the accreditation value of the syllabi across UASD was enhanced. The new curriculum incorporated new fields of tourism-related study and restructured the credits. It also allowed for a wide range of specialization options to meet the professional needs of the students and to capitalize on the potential of each region's tourism industry. As a result of analyzing the professional profiles targeted by the new degree in tourism and their associated competences, 12 areas of study were considered essential: 9 global areas complemented by 3 specialization areas. Each 1 of the 12 areas of study encompassed different types of subjects. Figure 3 shows the curricular areas of study included in the new degree in tourism.

A specific, detailed learner-centered teaching plan for each subject was drawn up in turn and included the following sections: (1) a description of the subject (its designation, teaching period, and number of credits); (2) the competences related to it; (3) the expected learning outcomes; (4) the interconnected subjects; (5) the learning-teaching methodology; and (6) the procedures devised to assess competence development following a

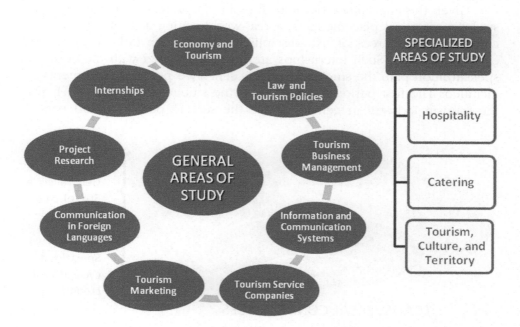

FIGURE 3 Curricular areas of study (color figure available online).

constructivist competence-based approach in accordance with the Tourism Education Futures Initiative (TEFI) principles guidelines portrayed by Sheldon et al. (2011).

The development of the learners' key competences that may not be directly linked to tourism was enabled through basic subjects. Adapting general or transversal subjects to the reality of the tourism industry made it possible to develop transversal competences. Specialized education and training referring to different subsectors (depending on each school's location and the students' preferences) were provided by means of both compulsory tourism-based subjects and optional tourism specialization subjects dealing with specific competences. Two alternative paths were offered: on the one hand, hotel and catering management, focusing on the administration of hotels, restaurants, and other tourism service providers; on the other hand, tourism management, geared toward managing tourism products and destinations. The four different types of subjects included in the curriculum of the degree in tourism are shown in Figure 4.

The new degree in tourism is meant to be a 4-year program, and the total number of credits has a balanced distribution during that period of time. The interrelations between different subjects have been clearly identified and limited to allow for interdisciplinary consistency. Even though some advanced subjects require prior knowledge acquired from other basic subjects, prerequisites have been kept to a minimum to make sure students can complete their degrees in 4 years of steady progress.

Given the importance of internships in the professional training of the students, practical placements in a real-world setting are integrated in the curriculum as sources of extradisciplinary knowledge and are given specific credit value. Such internships are to be associated with the curricular specialization path the students have chosen. Two practical placements are included: The first period should enable the students to get in touch with the tourism industry in general, while the second period should provide

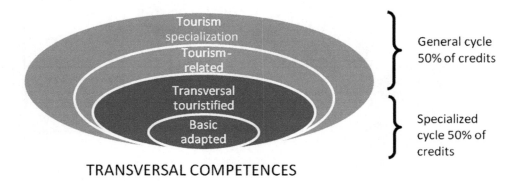

FIGURE 4 Subjects in the new degree in tourism (color figure available online).

the opportunity for them to gain experience in a specific area. A key issue involves standardization and consistent regulation of the internship periods.

The Dominican tourism industry needs professionals who can communicate in foreign languages with tourists and customers, suppliers, and other professionals, particularly those in managerial positions. Being fully proficient in Spanish as a mother tongue, in English as a lingua franca, and in a second foreign language is a must. Therefore, the international scope of the new curriculum involves using three languages with different degrees of communicative competence: Spanish at a native level, English from a false beginner level, and a second foreign language from an elementary level. The second foreign language could vary according to the geographical region where each school is located.

To improve the students' research skills, a number of credits can be fulfilled by conducting a research project, which qualifies as a subject in its own right in the new curriculum. A project tutor should ensure the appropriate quality standards regarding the format and methodological approach of this work.

Main Aspects to Be Considered in Curriculum Implementation

To optimize the new curriculum design, a number of recommendations were put forward by the team of researchers. Higher education in tourism at UASD has been provided by management schools from the Faculty of Economics and Social Sciences. The creation of schools of tourism with their own identity, under the administration of the same faculty, was highly recommended. Each school should be structured within departments based on the areas of study included in the curriculum of the new degree in tourism and should be composed of qualified, specialized teachers and coordinated by department heads. One of the school's departments ought to be devoted exclusively to handling internships. The individual responsible for that department should be in charge of orienting the students and should have a direct relationship with the Dominican tourism stakeholders.

To increase the students' professional competitiveness and employability, academic mobility must be encouraged. To support this, cooperation agreements that enable students to take part in domestic and international academic exchange programs should be considered. Moreover, policies that raise the students' awareness of responsible behavior and environmentally friendly practices in the educational context should be pursued. This line of action might have a positive impact on sustainability within the Dominican tourism industry and may contribute to the building of a more balanced society.

Finally, the design and implementation of a consistent system to monitor academic quality standards would make it possible to assess the adequacy of the degree in tourism, the fulfillment of the curricular objectives, and the effectiveness of the academic services. This, in turn, would allow for systematic review and improvement.

CONTRIBUTION OF TOURISM STUDIES TO THE DEVELOPMENT OF THE TOURISM SECTOR AND THE BROADER PROGRESS OF THE DOMINICAN REPUBLIC

This section presents some additional considerations related to tourism studies in the Dominican Republic. The new degree in tourism intends to meet the educational needs of the Dominican tourism sector at a tactical level to provide future top and middle managers with the necessary competences to succeed. However, the employees who carry out basic operational tasks in the tourism industry also require some degree of training. Such training is not to be provided in a higher education environment, but rather at an earlier stage in the educational system. Consequently, offering technical studies in tourism, which might be followed by the new degree in tourism, should be seriously considered.

Furthermore, some professionals, after having obtained a bachelor's degree in tourism, still require supplementary education and training that enable them to face high-level strategic responsibilities. This fact suggests that master's and postgraduate programs should be designed. These types of programs would facilitate the further specialization of graduates interested in pursuing careers in top management in various areas of the Dominican tourism industry. Designing a master's degree with a special focus on research might give birth to a doctorate program in tourism.

The future of the tourism sector depends heavily on initiatives derived from research projects, which therefore must be stimulated. The creation of a tourism observatory aligned with academic research should contribute to the scientification of tourism in the Dominican Republic. Resources should be devoted to research, development, and innovation in the field of tourism to enable dialogue between academia and industry, so that the research skills of tourism graduates and postgraduates and the outcomes of their work have direct applicability in the sector. This way, tourism studies could truly become a driver for socioeconomic transformation in this country.

CONCLUSION

This article has dealt with the issue of transformational leadership and its practical implications in a developing country. The scope of this curriculum proposal is limited to addressing real problems in a very specific field at an early stage of development. The outcomes of its implementation are to be evaluated in the years to come. At the same time, this project might also be particularly relevant for societies in other geographical areas that share similar characteristics. For first-world regions, it might serve as a reminder of past scenarios. Whatever its relevance, in today's era of globalization, the interrelationships between distant societies must be taken into account, and the repercussions of local policies at a macro level cannot be disregarded.

Transformation may indeed take place at various levels. In the context of the curriculum that has been presented, the transformational effects in relation to different types of leadership should be considered. Educational leadership may take several forms. In an educational institution such as the UASD, the informed decisions of the administration have top-down consequences, as the principles inherent in the curriculum are transmitted from the department heads to the teachers, who in turn transmit knowledge to the students. From a more bottom-up perspective, this proposal was grounded on TEFI values and a Competence-Based Education approach, instilled with the concept of empowerment.

The needs analysis took into consideration the views of all the stakeholders who might have a say in changing the way tourism has been developed through educational programs so far. This bottom-up process encompassed visits to schools throughout the Dominican Republic so that the voices of administration staff, teachers, and students in each regional center could be heard.

Empowerment was a key concept underlying the foundation of this proposal. The project was commissioned by the Ministry of Higher Education, Science, and Technology, with the outstanding collaboration of the Ministry of Tourism. The Minister of Education encouraged the active involvement in the curriculum design process of institutional agents representing different hierarchical layers. Fruitful teamwork resulted from the enthusiastic contributions of all the participants, based on mutuality. Participants also benefited from the exchange of cultural insights and pedagogical notions that derived from international cooperation.

One of the side effects of this project involved launching a teacher-training master's degree program for Dominican UASD teachers so that they can transfer their newly acquired knowledge to future tourism graduates effectively, both in and outside the classroom. Educational leadership would therefore be fostered at three levels: firstly, at a teacher–student level; secondly, at a teacher–teacher level, as new tourism-related pedagogical knowledge and approaches are spread among peers within school departments; and thirdly, at a professional–student level, through internships that take place in a real workplace.

This entails decentralizing the classroom as a learning context and promoting the development of key competences and values in a professional setting to provide the learners with meaningful knowledge and experiences to shape each individual's personal and professional evolution. Public and private tourism companies and organizations can thus play an active role in the process of educating future graduates.

From there, tourism graduates can take the lead as citizens behaving in accordance with their system of values when interacting with and influencing others. As professionals, the graduates' performance within the tourism industry has implications that transcend their immediate areas of influence. Educational leadership from both higher education providers and collaborating organizations can therefore have a direct effect on the reality of a developing country like the Dominican Republic. The broader economic, social, environmental, political, technological, and legal impacts could in turn affect the sustainability of the regions where tourism graduates live once they have become tourism professionals.

The transformational power of education has the ability to not only turn tourism graduates into influential industry leaders, but also to turn them into influential academicians and researchers. Educational leadership may thus revert to academia and also benefit the tourism sector, because the industry can take full advantage of applied research as a source of innovation.

REFERENCES

Agencia Nacional de Evaluación de la Calidad y Acreditación. (2004). *Libro blanco. Título de grado en turismo* [White book. Degree in tourism]. Retrieved from http://www.aneca.es/var/media/359791/libroblanco_turismo_03.pdf

Beneitone, P., Esquetini, C., González, J., Maletá, M. M., Siufi, G., & Wagenaar, R. (Eds.). (2007). *Reflexiones y perspectivas de la Educación Superior en América Latina. Informe Final Proyecto Tuning América Latina* [Final Report ALFA Tuning America Latina Project: Reflections on and outlook for Higher Education in Latin America]. Bilbao, Spain: University of Deusto, University of Groningen. Retrieved from http://www.deusto-publicaciones. es/ud/openaccess/tuning/pdfs_tuning/tuning05.pdf

Coles, T. E., Hall, C. M., & Duval, D. T. (2009). Post-disciplinary tourism. In J. Tribe (Ed.), *Philosophical issues in tourism* (pp. 80–100). Bristol, UK: Channel View.

Commission of the European Communities. (2005). *Proposal for a recommendation of the European Parliament and of the Council on Key Competences for Lifelong Learning*. Retrieved from http://ec.europa.eu/education/policies/ 2010/doc/keyrec_en.pdf

Consorcio Dominicano de Competitividad Turística. (2011). *Mesa de formación y sus aportes* [Contributions of the education commission]. Retrieved from http://www.turismocdct.org/noticias-generales/438-mesa-de-formacion-y-sus-aportes-.html

Dwyer, L., Edwards, D., Mistilis, N., Scott, N., Cooper, C., & Roman, C. (2008). *Megatrends underpinning tourism to 2020: Analysis of key drivers for change*. Gold Coast, Queensland, Australia: Cooperative Research Centre for Sustainable Tourism. Retrieved from http://www.crctourism.com.au/wms/upload/images/

disc%20of%20images%20and%20pdfs/for%20bookshop/documents/80046%20 Dwyer_TourismTrends2020%20WEB.pdf

Ernest, P. (1995). The one and the many. In L. P. Steffe & J. Gale (Eds.), *Constructivism in education* (pp. 459–486). Hillsdale, NJ: Lawrence Erlbaum.

Gibbons, M., Limoges, C., Nowotny, H., Schwartzmann, C., Scott, P., & Trow, M. (1994). *The new production of knowledge: The dynamics of science and research in contemporary society.* London, UK: Sage.

González, J., & Wagenaar, R. (Eds.). (2005). *Tuning educational structures in Europe: II. Universities' contribution to the Bologna Process.* Bilbao, Spain: University of Deusto, University of Groningen. Retrieved from http://www.unideusto. org/tuningeu/images/stories/documents/General_Brochure_final_version.pdf

Honebein, P. C. (1996). Seven goals for the design of constructivist learning environments. In B. G. Wilson (Ed.), *Constructivist learning environments: Case studies in instructional design* (pp. 11–24). Englewood Cliffs, NJ: Educational Technology Publications.

Jafari, J. (2001). The scientification of tourism. In V. L. Smith & M. Brent (Eds.), *Host and guests revisited: Tourism issues of the 21st century* (pp. 28–41). New York, NY: Cognizant Communication Corporation.

Jonassen, D. H. (1994). Thinking technology: Toward a constructivist design model. *Educational Technology, 34*(4), 34–37.

Lebow, D. (1993). Constructivist values for instructional systems design: Five principles toward a new mindset. *Educational Technology Research and Development, 41*(3), 4–16.

Miolán, A. (1998). *Datos para la historia del turismo de la República Dominicana* [Data for the history of tourism in the Dominican Republic]. Santo Domingo, Dominican Republic: Editora de Colores.

Morgan, M., Lugosi, P., & Ritchie, J. R. B. (Eds.). (2010). *The tourism and leisure experience: Consumer and managerial perspectives.* Bristol, UK: Channel View.

Olivares, M., Lladó, J., & Díaz, C. (1996). *Capacitación y entrenamiento en la microempresa dominicana* [Training in the Dominican microenterprise]. Santo Domingo, Dominican Republic: Fondo Para el Financiamiento de la Microempresa.

Padilla, A., & McElroy, J. L. (2010). The three Cs of Caribbean tourism: Contexts, characteristics, and consequences. *Ara (Caribbean) Journal of Tourism Research, 2*(2), 78–90.

Secretaría de Estado de Educación Superior, Ciencia y Tecnología de la República Dominicana. (2008). *Plan decenal de educación superior 2008-2018* [Decennial plan for higher education 2008-2018]. Retrieved from http://www.seescyt.gov. do/plandecenal/Paginas/Documentos.aspx

Sheldon, P., Fesenmaier, D., & Tribe, J. (2011). The Tourism Education Futures Initiative (TEFI): Activating change in tourism education. *Journal of Teaching in Travel & Tourism, 11,* 2–23.

Tribe, J. (2004). Knowing about tourism: Epistemological issues. In J. Phillimore & L. Goodson (Eds.), *Qualitative research in tourism: Ontologies, epistemologies and methodologies* (pp. 46–62). London, UK: Routledge.

United Nations Development Program. (2011). *Tourism and poverty reduction strategies in the integrated framework for least developed countries.*

Retrieved from http://portal.unesco.org/en/files/48503/13045122901Tourism_Poverty_Reduction_LDCs_web.pdf/Tourism_Poverty_Reduction_LDCs_web.pdf

United Nations World Tourism Organization. (2011). *Tourism highlights* (2011 ed.). Retrieved from http://mkt.unwto.org/sites/all/files/docpdf/unwtohighlights11enlr_3.pdf

Universidad Autónoma de Santo Domingo. (n.d.). *Licenciatura en Administración de Empresas Turísticas y Hoteleras. Plan de estudios 14* [Bachelor's degree in Tourism and Hotel Management. Plan 14]. Retrieved from http://uasd.edu.do/desc_carreras/?periodoV=200920&programa=P-ADMT&plan=000014&valor=R&lugar=1

Wan, G., & Gut, D. M. (2011). Introduction. In G. Wan & D. M. Gut (Eds.), *Bringing schools into the 21st century* (p. 1). London, UK: Springer.

Wilson, B., & Cole, P. (1991). A review of cognitive teaching models. *Educational Technology Research and Development, 39*(4), 47–64.

Interdisciplinarity in Higher Education Courses for Tourism: The Case of Croatia

EDNA MRNJAVAC, NADIA PAVIA and VIDOJE VUJIĆ

University of Rijeka, Opatija, Croatia

This article aims to demonstrate the similarities and differences between undergraduate tourism curricula in Europe and the Republic of Croatia from an interdisciplinary perspective. Research has revealed similarities relating to the duration, titles, and number of courses. The frequencies of occurrence of noneconomic subjects in European and Croatian courses are alike, although the scope of interdisciplinarity in European courses is much broader. The article puts together a model of an undergraduate tourism program based on interdisciplinarity and multidisciplinarity in Croatia. A scenario for developing interdisciplinarity in tourism curricula, which pursues a holistic approach and the general systems theory, is selected.

INTRODUCTION

Focused on numerous special-interest forms of tourism that are promoted on the tourism market through high-quality integrated destination products, dynamic tourism development requires highly professional and creative tourism staff in all tourism sectors and at all levels of organizational activity. In this, the education of staff in the tourism industry plays a key role, bringing tourism development into a significant positive correlation with education development (Airey, 2002).

Curriculum development depends directly upon the development of science (Tribe, 2005). Tourism's rapid development has made higher education tourism studies appealing to many. The mounting pressure of potential students on higher education institutions has been a disincentive to academic research into the tourism phenomenon, with institutions prioritizing teaching to meet the demand for education. Tourism research, however, is very important, because the curriculum should bring together new knowledge in correlation with the practical needs of actors in the educational process (enterprises, ministries of tourism and education, employment mediators, higher education institutions, employees, students; Airey & Tribe, 2005; Tribe, 2005).

Although the interdisciplinarity of tourism has been widely accepted, highly professional staff members are educated mainly at faculties of economics and schools of professional higher education (Saayman & Geldenhuys, 2002). This is a result of former tourism development based on tourism enterprises, which were dominantly focused on profit achievement (Ayikoru, Tribe, & Airey, 2009; Ladkin, 2002).

MULTIDISCIPLINARITY, INTERDISCIPLINARITY, AND SYSTEMS THEORY—APPLICATION TO TOURISM

The ongoing search for a comprehensive definition of the term "tourism" (and the term "tourist") has resulted in differences in approaches to the study of tourism—differences that have affected, in turn, the design of curricula. In the development period spanning some three decades, views can be singled out that have had a profound impact on tourism research. Even the very first definitions of the term "tourism" were an indication of the need to study this phenomenon from a variety of perspectives.

Jafari and Ritchie (1981), as cited by Echtner and Jamal (1997), point out disciplines that frequently engage in tourism research, such as economics, psychology, sociology, geography, and anthropology. Within the context of academic debate about whether tourism should be researched by a single discipline or by a field consisting of a number of disciplines, in 1981, Jafari and Ritchie, as cited by Leiper (2004), proposed a model of multidisciplinary tourism studies comprising 16 disciplines. This model sought to bring together different perspectives present in tourism research, and it had a significant impact on exploring the multidisciplinarity and interdisciplinarity of tourism.

Multidisciplinarity involves the input of a variety of disciplines but without any significant interaction or synthesis of these different perspectives (Weaver & Oppermann, 2000). The results of research by other disciplines of the same scientific problem cannot be synthesized or can be synthesized only to a very limited extent. Conclusions obtained in this way cannot be considered scientifically relevant. According to Echtner and Jamal (1997), a multidisciplinary approach involves studying a topic by including information from other disciplines but still operating within disciplinary boundaries. The extent to which information from other disciplines is present in a multidisciplinary approach depends upon the previous education of researchers and their personal scientific interests. Keeping in mind contemporary trends in science development, the likelihood of exploration being carried out within the framework of "pure" unidisciplinary research is becoming increasingly smaller. Hence, the application of multidisciplinarity to tourism research can be considered an important advancement in studying this complex phenomenon.

Interdisciplinary research involves studying a problem from the perspective of a variety of disciplines. Research is conducted by teams of researchers and headed by a team leader responsible for defining the scientific problem and the theoretical basis. Each researcher belongs to a different discipline and brings to the team the concepts, techniques, and methodologies of their own discipline. The team leader is also responsible for defining samples, locations, and criteria that will be acceptable and comprehensible to all team members. A compatible theoretical basis allows for the synthesis of research results and provides a more integrated, holistic understanding of the scientific problem (Echtner & Jamal, 1997).

An interdisciplinary approach is linked to a number of difficulties. Team members need to be knowledgeable in the other disciplines involved in the research. Przeclawski (1994) introduces the term "metalanguage," which refers to a language that team members should use to understand one another, formulate a common view, and have the same opinion regarding research results. Teamwork implies having an identical or similar philosophical view of the world and of tourism. Researchers are expected to be open to new knowledge, reasoned debate, and consensus concerning the vital elements of research.

One problem linked to the interdisciplinary approach is much greater than it may appear at first glance. It is not possible to synthesize knowledge or formulate scientific perceptions of tourism to augment the existing theoretical basis without the conscious efforts of researchers to make advancements in developing their academic potential toward interdisciplinarity. Tourism research models such as those presented in this article can never fully articulate the attitudes and actions of researchers, and herein lies the threat to their realization. It is up to each researcher and scholar to take an open approach to the world that surrounds them to search for new scientific insight and continuously push back the boundaries of their knowledge. Only in this way will they be able to better understand their colleagues and, in this spirit, increase the quantum of scientific insight into tourism.

The concepts of transdisciplinarity, extradisciplinarity, and postdisciplinarity have been introduced to additionally strengthen the advantages of a holistic approach. The term "transdisciplinarity" has mostly given way to the term "extradisciplinarity" to avoid confusion with the term "interdisciplinarity." Unlike interdisciplinarity that emerged and developed in academic circles, extradisciplinarity is linked to studying and providing solutions to concrete problems in practice. The disciplines involved in the research of a specific problem will determine the character of that problem. The quality of the proposed solution is proportional to the successful resolution of a concrete problem.

Postdisciplinarity is linked primarily to the basic factors of the postindustrial era: science and technology (Gibbons et al., 1994, as cited by Tribe, 1997). Science is becoming more and more complex and is therefore driving the rapid development of technology. Complex scientific research is become increasingly more expensive, with funders expecting a return on their investment. Hence, technological progress is determined by profitable technologies—technologies that ensure the greatest results with the least investment. This criterion has become a measure for what type of research will be conducted, and teams of researchers are created accordingly. A profitability assessment is carried out prior to research. Problems that do not promise a profit are simply not researched (for example, in the pharmaceutical industry regarding less widespread diseases).

A holistic approach to tourism studies that correlates with interdisciplinarity is closely linked to a systems approach. Studying complex phenomena by defining them as systems and then examining them using tools of the general systems theory makes it possible to define functions and purposes of phenomena—and not only their structure and external appearance, as in the case of research from the perspective of a single discipline. Because generations of scholars have been educated in the spirit of unidisciplinary research, they encounter difficulties when trying to apply a systems approach to defining and studying complex phenomena. Hence, the easiest way to study phenomena as systems is to begin by establishing the structure of the system. In this case, the system's structure is the starting point for further research.

The next issue that needs to be resolved is the selection of an optimal level of simplification that ensures the system is a credible reflection of the phenomenon under research, while making certain that the scale of its complexity is such that the price of research does not call the research into question. Another important issue that may often seem superfluous deals with establishing the system's boundaries. As a rule, researchers encounter a number of quandaries when trying to accurately establish a system's boundaries.

Complex phenomena whose nature calls for an interdisciplinary and multidisciplinary approach are a particular challenge to the application of a systems approach, as the only way they can be completely studied is by applying the methodology of the general systems theory.

Interdisciplinarity and multidisciplinarity are vital features of systematic thinking that call for teamwork in studying phenomenon using the general systems theory, while quantitative methods are especially important in studying systems, besides "traditional" scientific methods.

The general systems theory involves the following considerations:

- A system is part of a larger whole.
- Links with the environment are explored and defined.
- The function of a system within the whole is identified.
- A system's elements are investigated with regard to their interaction and with regard to how the system functions within the whole.
- A system's performance can be enhanced by linking its elements in a different way.
- A system's behavior is monitored for a longer period.

The vital elements of any system are its objective of existence, input, outputs, boundaries, environment, components, links between components, and restraints.

Tourism is highly complex and, as a system, very dynamic. Its dynamic nature is reflected in numerous processes. Interdependent elements underline the complexity of its structure. As a rule, every system is a part (subsystem) of a larger system. Tourism is an open system because of the impact that factors from the environment have on tourism and the feedback effect that tourism has on the environment. As a system, tourism belongs to the group on anthropogenic systems, which additionally augments its complexity, while the multitude of unpredictable factors places it in the group of stochastic systems that are particularly difficult to study due to their unpredictability.

THEORETICAL GUIDELINES IN DEVELOPING INTERDISCIPLINARITY IN TOURISM CURRICULA—THE BROADER CONTEXT

A sound understanding of tourism is required to identify the types of knowledge students need to acquire to improve tourism in the future. But how do we go about researching tourism, when there is such a large diversity of approaches and methodologies used? Is it even possible to establish what type of tourism knowledge is essential? Is there a methodology characteristic of researching the tourism phenomenon? These are only some of the issues researchers have been seeking to address in recent decades in an attempt to define basic guidelines to designing tourism curricula.

In the 1980s, curricula dealt with the elements of tourism from a variety of perspectives. Course titles reflected the most important development guidelines of tourism, while the global expansion of tourism initiated and fed the idea of tourismology, a scientific discipline that studies tourism (Leiper, 1981). The 1990s were marked by the realization that none of the efforts to develop a specific methodology for tourism research were successful. This became a major obstacle in establishing tourism science as a distinct discipline and impeded the development of higher education programs for tourism.

Academic research of the tourism phenomenon began to involve a holistic, as well as an interdisciplinary approach, together with a variety of methodologies taken from other scientific disciplines (Echtner & Jamal, 1997). Curricula sought to identify basic tourism knowledge, primarily referring to the tourism phenomenon and its impact on the environment. Flexible curricula were the result. Creating a distinct discipline aimed at tourism research did not seem likely to be possible.

The "wide-open doors" of interdisciplinary and multidisciplinary approaches were soon to highlight the problem of determining the extent to which the academic disciplines of economics should be present, and of determining their mutual interdependence, to act as a consistent whole of knowledge required in tourism (Tribe, 1997). New tourism knowledge gained through an interdisciplinary and multidisciplinary approach is referred to as a "cognitive bridge," a set of new understandings that expand existing tourism knowledge, on the one hand, while creating, on the other, a core upon which tourism science can develop—this being new knowledge to which other scientific disciplines cannot lay claim. Courses are very flexible and diverse, with a high degree of interdisciplinarity and multidisciplinarity.

The prevailing opinion in the first decade of the 21st century was that tourism should be viewed as both a vocation and a phenomenon and that courses should provide the required professional knowledge to ensure good employment prospects, together with a much broader liberal approach to understanding the phenomenon of tourism and planning its development. This gave rise to the concept of the "philosophical practitioner" (Tribe, 2002), which brings together vocational and liberal knowledge, reflection and action, and interdisciplinary and multidisciplinary approaches and sees tourism science as the only possible scientific framework. The objectives of courses—theories and concepts explaining tourism, understanding the intercultural dimensions of tourism, and understanding the cultural role of tourism for tourists and society (Airey, 2002)—are also the objectives of a liberal reflection of tourism through academic research.

In the previous development of courses, efforts were made, to a greater or lesser extent, to define the contents these courses should hold, and this was, in certain associations, promoted as a standard of tourism education (Peršić, 2001; Steynberg, Slabbert, & Saayman, 2002). Contrary to this, today's course development based on vocational knowledge and tourism philosophy has brought about diversity in courses with regard to their titles and has brought about elasticity with regard to the group of courses that students are free to choose. The opinion that there are no "untouchable" courses in programs (Fidgeon, 2010) bears witness to the extent of course elasticity. Interdisciplinarity and multidisciplinarity are considered special assets of tourism—attributes that ensure the well-designed development of tourism science and programs for tourism. They help to create new knowledge that is part of tourism research.

Program development, however, is still plagued with numerous dilemmas: the balance between vocational and liberal contents, the level of interdisciplinary and multidisciplinary contents, how to reconcile the requirements of various actors with stakes in program contents, etc. (Airey & Tribe, 2005).

DEFINING THE SCIENTIFIC PROBLEM AND FORMULATING A SCIENTIFIC HYPOTHESIS ON THE INTERDISCIPLINARITY OF TOURISM CURRICULA

The Croatian experience in higher education for tourism spans more than 50 years (Vujić, Galičić, & Črnjar, 2010). All tourism courses, with the exception of one, are taught at faculties of economics and business colleges. As a result, efforts in developing and designing tourism curricula have been based exclusively on, and within the framework of, economics.

Despite the fact that tourism is considered an interdisciplinary field in Croatia (Peršić, 2000), the extent of interdisciplinary and multidisciplinary approaches in designing tourism curricula in Croatia has not been researched. Contemporary trends in tourism development have given rise to new challenges in designing curricula, urging the Croatian education system to establish the extent of interdisciplinary and multidisciplinary approaches in tourism curricula. The later this happens, the greater will be the discrepancy with regard to European programs and the actual knowledge requirements of future bachelor's of science—and the harsher the consequences.

The scientific research problem is defined as follows: Although efforts have been made, for several decades around the world and in Europe and Croatia, to develop and perfect tourism curricula, tourism programs are still mostly focused on the theoretical and applicative research of the tourism phenomenon. This implies numerous adverse effects in enabling multidisciplinary competencies in creative and operational human resources in the tourism industry across all levels, from the national to the global.

The scientific research hypothesis is formulated as follows: Theoretical, applicative, disciplinary, interdisciplinary, and multidisciplinary knowledge, understanding, and skills in evaluating tourism curricula in undergraduate university studies in Europe and Croatia represent a scientific paradigm for designing a new model for teaching creative and operational staff in the modern tourism industry based on a general systems theory in combination with interdisciplinary and multidisciplinary curricula.

This article aims to highlight the similarities and differences in under-graduate tourism curricula in Europe and Croatia with regard to inter-disciplinary and multidisciplinary approaches. It seeks to demonstrate the correlation between a scientific understanding of tourism and the level of interdisciplinarity and multidisciplinarity in curricula.

The article's purpose is to define an undergraduate tourism curriculum model based on an interdisciplinary and multidisciplinary approach, while taking into consideration the European experience, Croatia's specific tourism-development resources, the existing level of interdisciplinarity in Croatia's tourism curricula, and the state of science classification in Croatia.

ANALYZING AND EVALUATING TOURISM CURRICULA IN EUROPE AND CROATIA—MATERIALS AND METHODS

The undergraduate programs of renowned European universities form the material basis of this research. An attempt was made to include as large a number as possible of European countries, as well as universities that stand out for the high quality of their programs. This approach was selected with the aim of exploring different educational concepts generated by the specific traits of university environments and to draw conclusions on the universal achievements gained, regardless of these influences. Such an analysis could help in suggesting a line of development for tourism programs in Croatia.

Considering that developments in science have a direct impact on the design of programs in Croatia, the documentation basis has included the *Regulations on Scientific and Artistic Fields and Branches, National Council for Science* (Ministry of Science, Education and Sports of Republic of Croatia, 2005, 2008, 2009) to help establish similarities and differences with other European countries and define the influence of scientific classification on the level of interdisciplinarity in curricula.

Research concerning the level of interdisciplinarity focused on a sample of some 15 renowned European institutions and some 10 higher education institutions in Croatia. Included in the study were 3-year programs at faculties and schools of professional higher education. Graduate and specialist study programs were omitted.

The teaching programs of undergraduate studies at the schools of higher education listed in Table 1 that were accessible via their Web pages were examined (Web pages listed in Appendix). Although being aware that min-imum deviations from the actual state are possible, the authors believe the data on the Web pages can be considered credible due to the reputation of the institutions. As such, these data present a solid documentation basis.

The analysis method was applied to the programs of European and Croatian higher education institutions, meaning that a detailed examination was made of all undergraduate programs related to tourism—regardless

TABLE 1 Overview of European and Croatian Higher Education Institutions' Undergraduate Study Programs

Ordinal Number	Country	Institution	Program Title
1	Italy	University of Bologna, Faculty of Economics, Rimini	– Tourism Management – Tourism Markets
2	Italy	Free University of Bozen, School of Economics and Management, Site in Brunico	– Tourism, Sport, and Event Management
3	Italy	University of Naples Federico II, Faculty of Economics	– Tourism Sciences for Managers
4	Italy	Second University of Naples, Faculty of Economics and Faculty of Arts and Philosophy	– Tourism Sciences and Cultural Heritage
5	England	University of Surrey, School of Management	– International Tourism and Hospitality Management – Tourism Management
6	England	Leeds Metropolitan University	– Many courses
7	England	Manchester Metropolitan University	– Many courses
8	England	Liverpool John Moores University, Faculty of Education, Community and Leisure	– Tourism and Leisure Management – Event Management
9	England	University of Central Lancashire	– Event Management – Hospitality Management – Sports Event Management
10	Germany	Heidelberg International Business Academy	– Tourism Management – Event Management
11	Germany	Cologne Business School	– International Tourism Management
12	Austria	Modul University Vienna	– Tourism and Hospitality Management
13	The Netherlands	Breda University of Applied Sciences	– International Leisure Management – International Tourism Management (ITM and Consultancy; IT and Travel Industry)
14	Belgium	Brussels School of Business	– Tourism and Hospitality Management
15	Slovenia	University of Primorska, Faculty of Tourism Studies	– Tourism – Management of Tourism Destinations – Mediation in Tourism – Business Systems in Tourism

(Continued)

TABLE 1 (Continued)

Ordinal Number	Country	Institution	Program Title
16	Croatia	University of Zagreb, Faculty of Economics and Business	– Tourism Operations
17	Croatia	University of Dubrovnik	– Tourism
18	Croatia	University of Split, Faculty of Economics	– Tourism
19	Croatia	University of Zadar	– Culture and Tourism
20	Croatia	Juraj Dobrila University of Pula	– Tourism
21	Croatia	University of Rijeka, Faculty of Tourism and Hospitality Management	– Business Economics in Tourism and Hospitality
22	Croatia	Polytechnic of Karlovac	– Hospitality
23	Croatia	Polytechnic of Šibenik	– Tourism Management
24	Croatia	Business School of Višnjan	– Tourism Management
25	Croatia	Business School Utilus	– Tourism and Hotel Management
26	Croatia	Zagreb School of Management	– Tourism and Hotel Management

Note. Made by the authors according to data available on the Web pages of the schools of higher education.

of the programs' design and structure—at the listed institutions. Because detailed programs were not available for all courses, and some of the programs were more detailed than others were, minor inaccuracy in making comparisons is possible. It is a fact that courses with identical titles prevail. Particularities in research results are presented separately.

Absolute comparability is also not possible because institutions design programs in accordance to the requirements of the competent state authorities who verify programs, and criteria differ from country to country. Further research in this direction could involve obtaining uniform descriptions of courses belonging to multidisciplinary and interdisciplinary areas from all institutions included in the research. This would help to increase accuracy. However, the problem of subjectivity and the levels of multidisciplinarity and interdisciplinarity discussed in detail in this article's section "Theoretical Guidelines in Developing Interdisciplinarity in Tourism Curricula—The Broader Context" would remain, calling absolute comparability into question.

The method of comparison was used to compare programs with regard to the titles, number, duration, and presence of "noneconomics" subjects. The method of synthesis was applied to derive conclusions pointing to regularities in the interdisciplinarity of tourism curricula, ultimately, to help define guidelines for designing programs in Croatia. The methods of induction and deduction were used to derive, from individual conclusions concerning individual curricula, a general conclusion on the presence of interdisciplinarity in programs and to apply this to a program development model for Croatia.

ANALYZING AND EVALUATING THE COMPATIBILITY AND COMPLEMENTARITY OF TOURISM CURRICULA IN EUROPE AND CROATIA—RESEARCH AND RESULTS

Research has demonstrated differences between European and Croatian higher education programs. Similar to Croatian programs, most European undergraduate programs last 3 years, although some last 4 years.

The titles of European curricula differ considerably. One group of institutions remains committed to business economics, with programs usually linked to tourism management and hospitality management and only occasionally with event management, leisure management, travel management, etc. Another group of institutions applies titles to programs based on tourism phenomena or seeks to imply, in the program's title, the interdisciplinarity of tourism and other scientific disciplines (tourism and foreign languages, sociology, information science, logistics, history, education, chemistry, cruising, etc.). Interestingly, some institutions (e.g., the University of Naples, Italy) seek to emphasize, in the names of their programs, the interdisciplinary approach on which they are based, resulting in programs called tourism science with a focus on management or a focus on cultural heritage.

With regard to the number of programs, most of the institutions provide two programs. Some institutions, however, provide up to a dozen programs, in particular in Great Britain (Leeds Metropolitan University and Manchester Metropolitan University). Their programs have not been included in our research, because tourism-related interdisciplinarity and a precisely determined number of disciplines can be identified from their very titles. The diverse concepts of these programs, together with their numbers, make comparison with the programs of other institutions difficult. Nevertheless, they should be emphasized as they represent possible lines of development of interdisciplinarity in tourism programs.

Differences also exist in the titles of Croatian courses. The titles of most courses emphasize business economics or management, therefore revealing the prevailing presence of economics-based subjects. Most institutions provide two programs—one for hospitality and one for tourism. An exception is the Faculty of Tourism and Hospitality Management of the University of Rijeka providing a program with five more-conventionally named modules: Tourism Management, Hotel Management, Entrepreneurship in Tourism and Hospitality, International Tourism and Hotel Management, and Event and Leisure Management. This institution offers the largest number of fields of study in Croatia. Another exception is the Department of Tourism and Communication Sciences of the University of Zadar offering a course entitled "Culture and Tourism," which is also the only course of its kind in Croatia provided by an institution not belonging to the economics group.

Table 2 illustrates the frequency of noneconomics subjects in European and Croatian programs included in the research.

TABLE 2 Frequency of Noneconomic Courses in European and Croatian Tourism Programs

Programs	High-Frequency Courses	Medium-Frequency Courses	Low-Frequency Courses
European programs	Foreign Languages Law Travel Informatics	Geography Ethics, Mathematics Art, Sociology History (of tourism), Culture Environmental Protection	Architecture Archeology Sports Air Transport (airport operations) Museology, Literature
Croatian programs	Foreign Languages (predominantly English) Law Transport Informatics Geography, Mathematics Cultural-Historical Heritage	Ethics, Sports Environmental Protection Nautical Tourism History	Sociology Culture Psychology Spatial Planning

According to the frequency of interdisciplinarity and multidisciplinarity, interdisciplinary contents fall into three groups with high, medium, and low frequency of occurrence in programs. High frequency of occurrence means the presence of a subject in 50% of programs or more; medium frequency indicates a presence in 25%t to 49.99%; and low frequency indicates a presence in 0% to 24.99%.

This distribution is accepted because of the differences that exist in the frequency of multidisciplinary subjects between European and Croatian programs. It is characteristic of Croatian programs that subjects with the highest frequency of occurrence are present in almost all programs. In European programs, subjects with the highest frequency are present in only 50% of programs. The reasons for the great similarity of interdisciplinarity in Croatian programs lies in the fact that these are programs, within a country, that emerged and developed under the influence of the same factors. Of the 11 programs examined, half are professional programs carried out in schools of higher professional education founded in the recent past. It is, therefore, understandable that they have based the design of their programs on the faculty programs of institutions with several years of experience.

Much greater differences in the interdisciplinarity of European programs result from the fact that they were developed in different countries that sought to adjust the programs to meet the specific needs of their tourism development and the specific features of their higher education systems, and in accordance with their relation toward interdisciplinarity in tourism in particular and in science in general.

Subjects such as foreign languages, law, transport, and information science have a high frequency of occurrence in European programs. In addition to these subjects, the high-frequency group in Croatian programs also includes geography, mathematics, and cultural and historical heritage.

While foreign language-learning courses are not provided in some European courses, others offer several foreign language-learning courses, including Russian and Chinese. All Croatian programs provide English language-learning courses, as well as courses like German, Italian, and French. There are plans to introduce courses of the Czech and Russian language. Transport in European programs often appears together with agencies, which is not the case in Croatia. European programs typically use the term "travel." In some European programs, air travel, land transport, and cruising are taught separately, while in Croatian programs, this is valid for nautical tourism. Cultural and historical heritage as a subject is specific to Croatian programs, as heritage constitutes the greater part of Croatia's tourism offering.

Subjects such as geography, ethics, mathematics, art, sociology, history, and culture have a medium frequency of occurrence in European programs. In Croatian programs, ethics, sports, ecology, history, and nautical tourism belong to this group. In both cases, quantitative methods are often tied to mathematics. The history of tourism is taught in place of history in European programs, which is not the case in Croatia.

Subjects such as architecture, archeology, sports, literature, and museology have a low frequency of occurrence in European programs. In Croatian programs, sociology, psychology, culture, and spatial planning belong to this group.

Croatian programs do not include subjects such as art, literature, architecture, museology, archeology, or special kinds of transport mentioned earlier. On the other hand, European programs include neither cultural and historical heritage nor nautical tourism as subjects.

It can be concluded that the greatest similarity between the undergraduate tourism study programs of European and Croatian higher education institutions can be seen in subjects with the highest frequency of occurrence, suggesting the existence of a common interdisciplinary basis. Greater differences in subjects of medium and low frequencies are the results of differences in educational systems, the needs of tourism, the understanding of multidisciplinarity and interdisciplinarity, and in staff potential.

PROPOSED MODEL OF UNDERGRADUATE PROGRAM AND ACTIVITIES WITH REGARD TO INTERDISCIPLINARITY IN CROATIA—DISCUSSION

Interdependence of Science Classification and Interdisciplinarity in Tourism Curricula in Croatia

Research has confirmed the assumption that interdisciplinary and multidisciplinary contents are present to a lesser extent in Croatian higher education programs than in European programs.

Research also shows that while the Croatian higher education system includes faculty programs and programs of schools of professional higher education, both types of programs have interdisciplinary contents. No essential difference was discerned between the programs by the frequency and scope of interdisciplinary contents, although according to their mission, schools of professional higher education should prepare professionals for immediate employment, while faculties provide courses that are a combination of academic and professional knowledge. A process of differentiation is underway, and university courses could be expected to develop the academic component to a greater degree.

Croatian laws governing higher education and scientific activities are very consistent in giving priority to disciplinary fields, while discouraging the development of interdisciplinary areas. During the past 10 years, the science classification system of Croatia has begun to recognize interdisciplinary fields, each new classification including a greater number. Despite this, scholars in these fields repeatedly come across obstacles and therefore find it necessary to explain the research they are doing.

Croatia's science classification places tourism, together with trade, in the scientific field of economics, and only in recent years has tourism been mentioned and presented as a special branch of this field. Croatian scholars in the field of tourism are discouraged from working outside the scientific field of economics, as this would prevent them from meeting conditions required for their selection to research and teaching professions and their continued work at higher education institutions. The result is a somewhat paradoxical situation: On the one hand, the interdisciplinarity of tourism is recognized, while on the other, rigid academic and educational structures make the actual application of an interdisciplinary approach impossible. Researchers often work on interdisciplinary contents in higher education programs for tourism as a supplementary job. Because of their position, they are unable to fully dedicate their time to research in this field as they derive their basic employment-related rights from their jobs at main institutions.

Despite a continuity of research and development in tourism education in Croatia, much of this research focuses on ensuring the quality of education programs and establishing the types of knowledge needed for employment in tourism (Peršić, 1997). As long as tourism education continues to exist within the field of economics, its primary goal will be educating managers. In addition to providing students with competencies that will make them employable, tourism curricula also need to ensure the development of tourism in alignment with contemporary European and world trends. Considering the current state of science and higher education in Croatia, there are two scenarios of curriculum development (see Figure 1).

There are two ways in which to increase the presence of interdisciplinarity and multidisciplinarity in courses:

• The first way is by developing science in Croatia, which is formalized every several years in the *Regulations on Scientific and Artistic Fields and*

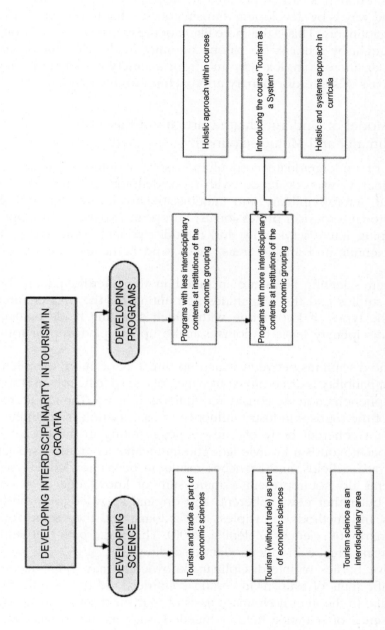

FIGURE 1 Scenarios for developing interdisciplinarity and multidisciplinarity in undergraduate tourism courses in Croatia.

Branches, National Council for Science. Although the number of interdisciplinary scientific fields is growing, this is not likely to occur in tourism, as tourism research is carried out almost exclusively by economists.

- The second way is by developing tourism courses that have a greater level of interdisciplinarity. This is the more likely of the two scenarios, as courses are also taught by scholars from noneconomics fields who study tourism in a broader, more complex way and from a variety of perspectives and who can pass this interdisciplinary approach on to their students.

Proposed Model of Undergraduate Curriculum Based on Interdisciplinarity and Multidisciplinarity

The model of undergraduate curriculum based on interdisciplinarity and multidisciplinarity was designed with consideration of the theoretical and practical, interdisciplinary and multidisciplinary knowledge and skills required in today's tourism professionals; European experience in applying and developing interdisciplinarity and multidisciplinarity; and the classification of scientific and artistic areas, fields, and branches in Croatia (see Figure 2).

All seven scientific areas are included in the interdisciplinary basis, with social studies and the humanities accounting for the greater number of fields. The types of knowledge with which scientific fields participate in the interdisciplinary basis of courses make up the platform for tourism research.

Scientific disciplines between which no direct association, complementarity, or compatibility is discernible but which play a specific role in studying the tourism phenomenon are considered multidisciplinary. The requirements and needs of the tourism industry influence the association of scientific disciplines into a coherent body of knowledge, resulting in the design of a system of specific tourism knowledge. The interactive, cognitive association of scientific areas, fields, and branches results in new knowledge systems. These systems do not represent a mere sum of knowledge of scientific disciplines, but rather new, coherent, and original knowledge at the level of concepts and methods, principles, and axioms, and they stand for the interdisciplinarity of sciences (Zelenika, 2000). This is the path that leads to making tourism science an independent discipline.

Cognitive bodies of interdisciplinary knowledge may differ according to the specific traits of tourism in certain countries, and this is reflected in their curricula. In the interdisciplinary basis of tourism curricula in Croatia, a greater presence of scientific fields is needed, such as history and art history (cultural and historical tourism), kinesiology (sports, recreation, and adventure tourism), forestry (hunting tourism), medicine (medicinal tourism), biology (various forms of ecotourism), religious sciences and theology (religious tourism), and agriculture (rural tourism).

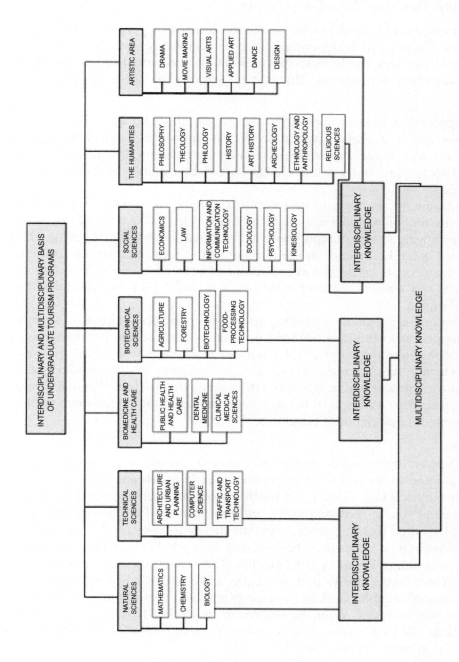

FIGURE 2 Interdisciplinary and multidisciplinary basis of undergraduate tourism courses.

Holistic and Systems Approach to Designing Undergraduate Tourism Programs Based on Interdisciplinarity

Program designing should focus heavily on a holistic approach. To prevent program designing from depending upon the knowledge and personal inclinations of teachers, the holistic approach should be formalized and made a component part of programs. This may be achieved in various ways:

- by applying a holistic approach to every course. The issue here is the consistency and actual application of this approach, particularly where teachers with longer employment records are concerned, who would first need to acquire holistic knowledge before being able to pass it on to students.
- by introducing a course in undergraduate programs in which the general systems theory would be applied to tourism and which would provide students with a more comprehensive, interdisciplinary understanding. This has not been the practice in the programs of European countries, as there was no need because the classification of sciences is less rigid than in Croatia and was not a constraining factor in developing interdisciplinarity in programs.
- by designing programs according to holistic principles. This is not likely to happen at institutions teaching economics because the previous training of teachers does not enable them to teach "noneconomics" courses. Introducing new courses would also be difficult, as this would entail employing new teachers. It is reasonable to say that such institutions would sooner employ a person from the economics field who would develop the economics component of programs.

While taking into account the definition of tourism as a system (Leiper, 1995, as cited in Weaver & Oppermann, 2000; Przeclawski, 1994) based on the five fundamental elements of tourism (tourists, tourist-generating areas, transit areas, tourist-receiving areas, and the travel and tourism industry), it should be noted that the general systems theory focuses on the function of a phenomenon. It views the phenomenon as a whole consisting of continuously interacting complex components. The whole also interacts with its environment and is always part of a larger system. Because phenomena are always highly complex and, in the case of tourism, very dynamic, constructing a model that can cover the system in its totality is difficult and often impossible. In such cases, it is necessary to resort to selecting criteria by which the system will be defined.

Leiper (2004) argues that other approaches to defining tourism as a system also exist. Students studying economics but not familiar with the general systems theory might find an approach based on the hierarchical structure of

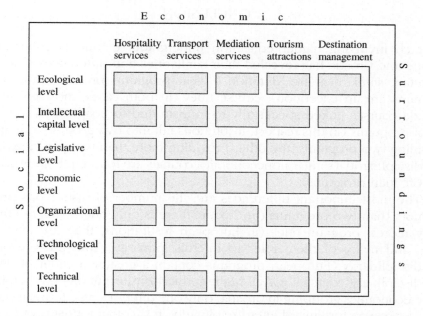

FIGURE 3 Structure of a tourism system (according to basic activities).

systems easier to understand, because it is grounded in the modern theory of organization (Perić, Radačić, & Šimulčik, 2000, pp. 9–65), which relates to the scientific area of economics. This is shown in Figure 3.

The starting point for defining and studying tourism systems should be the activities that make up the tourism and travel industry: hospitality, traffic, travel agencies and tour operators, attractions, and destination management (Mrnjavac, 2001, 2002, pp. 59–62, 2006, pp. 51–61). As a rule, because these are economic activities, they should be explored based on the elements and goals of business processes, with research including the technical, techno-logical, organizational, economic, and legal elements, human capital, and the environmental dimension.

A course on tourism as a system, designed on a systems approach to tourism based on organizational and economics principles, would enable students of economics studies to:

- rationally position the economic dimensions of tourism relative to its other dimensions;
- understand the interdisciplinarity of tourism, without underrating its economic dimension;
- experience interdisciplinarity as an advantage rather than a disadvantage;
- accept other interdisciplinary contents in courses; and
- acquire the knowledge needed for developing the concept of tourism science.

CONCLUSION

Research involving higher education undergraduate tourism programs in Europe and Croatia has revealed their similarities and differences. The most important similarities are: duration (3-year programs prevail, while 4-year programs are an exception); course titles (in both cases, most institutions provide courses linked specifically to tourism and to hospitality); the number of programs (in this respect, institutions fall into two groups—one group providing two programs, the other providing more than two programs); and interdisciplinarity (similar noneconomics courses are found in both European and Croatian programs).

The most important differences are: the number of institutions providing more than two programs (in Croatia, there is only one, while in Europe, many more); program titles (in European institutions, they are more creative, and many of them refer to interdisciplinarity); and the breadth of interdisciplinarity (European programs contain a greater number of diverse interdisciplinary courses). Of all higher education institutions not belonging to the economics grouping in Croatia, only one offers a single tourism course.

The reason for limited interdisciplinarity in Croatian tourism courses lies in Croatia's classification of scientific areas, in which tourism, together with trade, is set within the economics research area, thus discouraging scholars from working in other scientific disciplines.

A model of undergraduate tourism curriculum based on interdisciplinarity and multidisciplinarity was designed taking into consideration European experience in applying and developing interdisciplinarity and multidisciplinarity, as well as the classification of scientific and artistic areas, fields, and branches in Croatia.

Developing interdisciplinarity within curricula is proposed as a more acceptable scenario than positioning tourism outside of the economics framework in the classification of science. Introducing the general systems theory in curricula, together with a holistic approach, is also suggested. Studying tourism as a system would provide students within the economics discipline with a more comprehensive, interdisciplinary, and multidisciplinary understanding of the phenomenon of tourism.

REFERENCES

Airey, D. (2002). Growth and change in tourism education. In B. Vukonić & N. Čavlek (Eds.), *Rethinking of education and training for tourism* (pp. 13–22). Zagreb, Croatia: University of Zagreb, Graduate School of Business and Economics.

Airey, D., & Tribe, J. (2005). Issues for the future. In D. Airey & J. Tribe (Eds.), *An international handbook of tourism education* (pp. 501–506). Amsterdam, The Netherlands: Elsevier.

Ayikoru, M., Tribe, J., & Airey, D. (2009). Reading tourism education: Neoliberalism unveiled. *Annals of Tourism Research*, *36*(2), 191–221.

Echtner, M. C., & Jamal, B. T. (1997). The interdisciplinary dilemma of tourism studies. *Annals of Tourism Research*, *24*(4), 868–883.

Fidgeon, R. P. (2010). Tourism education and curriculum design: A time for consolidation and review? *Tourism Management*, *31*, 699–723.

Ladkin, A. (2002). The relationship between employment and tourism education: Issues for debate. In B. Vukonić & N. Čavlek (Eds.), *Rethinking of education and training for tourism* (pp. 45–55). Zagreb, Croatia: University of Zagreb, Graduate School of Business and Economics.

Leiper, N. (1981). Towards a cohesive curriculum in tourism: The case for a distinct discipline. *Annals of Tourism Research*, *8*, 69–84.

Leiper, N. (2004). *Tourism management* (3rd ed.). Frenchs Forest, Australia: Pearson Hospitality Press.

Ministry of Science, Education and Sports of Republic of Croatia. (2005). *Regulations on Scientific and Artistic Fields and Branches, National Council for Science*. Retrieved from http://narodne-novine.nn.hr/clanci/sluzbeni/2005_06_76_1500.html

Ministry of Science, Education and Sports of Republic of Croatia. (2008). *Regulations on Scientific and Artistic Fields and Branches, National Council for Science*. Retrieved from http://narodne-novine.nn.hr/clanci/sluzbeni/2008_07_78_2563.html

Ministry of Science, Education and Sports of Republic of Croatia. (2009). *Regulations on Scientific and Artistic Fields and Branches, National Council for Science*. Retrieved from http://narodne-novine.nn.hr/clanci/sluzbeni/2009_09_118_2929.html

Mrnjavac, E. (2001). Traffic and tourism systems in complex interdependence. In K.-H. Breitzmann (Ed.), *Economy, transport and tourism in the Baltic Sea region preparing for EU accession* (pp. 185–199). Rostock, Germany: The Baltic Sea Institute for Marketing, Transport and Tourism, University of Rostock.

Mrnjavac, E. (2002). *Traffic in Tourism*. Opatija, Croatia: University of Rijeka, Faculty of Management in Tourism and Hospitality.

Mrnjavac, E. (2006). *Traffic in Tourism* (2nd ed.). Opatija, Croatia: University of Rijeka, Faculty of Management in Tourism and Hospitality.

Perić, T., Radačić, Ž., & Šimulčik, D. (2000). *Economics of traffic system*. Zagreb, Croatia: University of Zagreb, Faculty of Traffic Sciences.

Peršić, M. (1997, September–October). Training of tourism professionals in Croatia. In W. Nahrstedt & T. P. Kombol (Eds.), *Leisure, culture and tourism in Europe* (pp. 379–394). Proceedings of the 10th ELRA Congress, Dubrovnik, Croatia.

Peršić, M. (2000). Education in Croatian tourism policy. In V. Vrtiprah (Ed.), *Tourism and Transition* (pp. 327–340). Proceedings of International Conference, Faculty of Tourism and Foreign Trade, Dubrovnik, Croatia.

Peršić, M. (2001). Quality of university's tourism education. *Tourism and Hospitality Management*, *6*(1/2), 73–84.

Przeclawski, K. (1994). Tourism as the subject of interdisciplinary research. In D. G. Pearce & R. W. Butler (Eds.), *Tourism research—Critiques and challenges* (pp. 9–19). London, UK and New York, NY: International Academy for the Study of Tourism.

Saayman, M., & Geldenhuys, S. (2002). An analysis of skills required for selected sectors of the tourism industry. In B. Vukonić & N. Čavlek (Eds.), *Rethinking of education and training for tourism* (pp. 419–430). Zagreb, Croatia: University of Zagreb, Graduate School of Business and Economics.

Srića, V. (1990). *Informatics engineering and management*. Zagreb, Croatia: Society for Development of Informatics.

Steynberg, L., Slabbert, E., & Saayman, M. (2002). Setting the stage: A global curriculum for tourism—A proposed curriculum. In B. Vukonić & N. Čavlek (Eds.), *Rethinking of education and training for tourism* (pp. 89–100). Zagreb, Croatia: University of Zagreb, Graduate School of Business and Economics.

Tribe, J. (1997). The interdiscipline of tourism. *Annals of Tourism Research*, *24*(3), 638–657.

Tribe, J. (2002). The philosophic practitioner. *Annals of Tourism Research*, *29*(2), 338–357.

Tribe, J. (2005). Tourism, knowledge, and the curriculum. In D. Airey & J. Tribe (Eds.), *An international handbook of tourism education* (pp. 47–60). Amsterdam, The Netherlands: Elsevier.

Vujić, V., Galičić, V., & Črnjar, K. (2010). Human resources development in tourism as feature of Croatian identity. In V. Vujić (Ed.), *Knowledge management and human development in tourism* (pp. 21–58). Opatija, Croatia: University of Rijeka, Faculty of Management in Tourism and Hospitality.

Weaver, D., & Oppermann, M. (2000). *Tourism management*. Brisbane, Australia: Wiley.

Zelenika, R. (2000). *Methodology and technology of scientific and professional research*. Rijeka, Croatia: University of Rijeka, Faculty of Economics.

APPENDIX

Web Pages

- Undergraduate, University of Bologna, Italy: http://corsi.unibo.it/CLET/Pagine/PianiDidattici.aspx?AnnoAccademico=2011&codCorso=0908&Orientamento=000&Indirizzo=798&Progressivo=1
- Free University of Bozen, Italy: http://www.unibz.it/en/economics/progs/bacs/majortourism/internship/Documents/Manifesto_L-18_BK_e_2011.pdf 710
- University of Naples Federico II, Italy: http://www.unina.it/studentididattica/segreteriastudenti/corsiStudio/dettagli.jsp?id=40
- Second University of Naples, Italy: http://www.study-in-italy.it/php5/scheda_corso.php?ambiente=offf&anno=2009&corso=78438
- International Hospitality and Tourism Management 2012, University of Surrey, England: http://www.surrey.ac.uk/undergraduate/courses/ihtm
- Tourism Management 2012, University of Surrey, England: http://www.surrey.ac.uk/undergraduate/courses/tourism
- Undergraduate, Leeds Metropolitan University, England: http://www.leedsmet.ac.uk/study/Undergraduate.htm720

- Undergraduate, Manchester Metropolitan University, England: http://www.mmu.ac.uk/study/undergraduate
- Undergraduate Factfile 2012 Entry: Tourism and Leisure Management BA (Hons), Liverpool John Moores University, England: http://ljmu.ac.uk/courses/undergraduate/2012/course.asp?CourseId=NN28725
- International Tourism Management, University of Central Lancashire, England: http://www.uclan.ac.uk/information/courses/ba_international_tourism_management_ft.php
- International Studies in Tourism Management, Heidelberg International Business Academy, Germany: http://www.hib-academy.com/programme/tourism-730management/tourism-management-studies.asp
- Cologne Business School, Germany: http://www.cbs-edu.de/en/study-programmes/bachelorprogramme/international-tourism-management
- Modul University Vienna, Austria: http://www.modul.ac.at/thm/bba/curriculum
- Breda University of Applied Sciences, The Netherlands: http://www.nhtv.nl/ENG/bachelors/toerisme/international-tourismmanagement/course-characteristics/course-planning.html
- Brussels School of Business, Belgium: http://www.brussels.uibs.org/study programs_undergraduate_bachelor_tourism_hospitality_management.html
- University of Primorska, Slovenia: http://www.turistica.si/downloads/BROSURAwebbb223332bb.pdf
- University of Zagreb, Croatia: http://www.efzg.unizg.hr/default.aspx?id=14000740
- University of Dubrovnik, Croatia: http://www.unidu.hr/datoteke/126izb/Izvedbeni_plan_Odjel_za_ekonomiju_i_pos.ek.-2011.-2012.-predd iplomski_studij.pdf
- University of Split, Croatia: http://www.efst.hr/content.php?k=studiji&p=115&stu=TU
- University of Zadar, Croatia: http://www.unizd.hr/LinkClick.aspx?fileticket=QDWFi883Gmk%3d&tabid=2532745
- Juraj Dobrila University of Pula, Croatia: http://www.efpu.hr/fileadmin/dokumenti/Vazni_dokumenti/StudijskiProgrami/NastavniProgram5.pdf
- University of Rijeka, Croatia: http://www.fthm.uniri.hr/index.php?option=com_content&view=article&id=97&Itemid=139
- Polytechnic of Karlovac, Croatia: http://www.vuka.hr/index.php?id=214
- Polytechnic of Šibenik, Croatia: http://vus.hr/index.php?page=fckeditorx
- Business School of Višnjan, Croatia: http://www.manero.hr/index.php/strucni-prvostupnik-menadz75
- Business School Utilus, Croatia: http://www.utilus.hr/Upisi/Program_studija.html
- Zagreb School of Management, Croatia: http://www.zsm.hr/hr/program-i-smjerovi/index.aspx

Reforming Higher Education: The Case of Jordan's Hospitality and Tourism Sector

DONALD E. HAWKINS

The George Washington University, Washington, DC, USA

JOSEPH RUDDY and AMIN ARDAH

USAID/Jordan Tourism Development, Amman, Jordan

This case cites efforts by Jordan's higher education sector to reform policies and practices related to tourism- and hospitality-specialized programs. Technical assistance was provided during the period 2009 to 2011 by the United States Agency for International Development (USAID)-funded Jordan Tourism Development Project. The methodology employed a value-chain approach. Based upon study findings, strategic initiatives, and implementation, actions were recommended to the Ministry of Higher Education and Scientific Research and the Ministry of Tourism and Antiquities in Jordan. The article concludes with future directions relevant to tourism education outlined in Jordan's National Tourism Strategy.

INTRODUCTION

Jordan received 4.6 million visitors in 2010—a 23% increase over 2009. In 2011, this growth has slowed due to volatility in the Middle East and North Africa. A major increase in construction of more than 17,000 hotel rooms,

The authors acknowledge substantial contributions made by the following colleagues from the USAID/Jordan Tourism Development Project: Ibrahim Osta, chief of party, and Dr. Suzy Bouran, value-chain survey researcher.

however, is forecast between 2011 and 2014 in Amman, Dead Sea, Petra, and particularly Aqaba, where an estimated 10,000 rooms will be added.

Faced with this escalation of hotel and tourism activity throughout Jordan, the call for action is urgent. Construction of new hotels and resorts is occurring without a comprehensive workforce development strategy and action plan. Jordan can learn from other countries that have also experienced sudden growth, particularly those in the Middle East. This tourism boom will tax the pool of qualified personnel. To meet this demand, the higher education sector needs to prepare well-educated young people to meet the urgent need. Educators and employers must work together to ensure that university programs prove relevant both for the present and future.

The USAID-funded Jordan Tourism Development Project used a value-chain approach to recommend ways in which higher education can respond to tourism industry needs. This report was approved by the Tourism Industry and Academic Steering Committee (TIASC) in collaboration with industry, community college, and university stakeholders. Higher education working with government and industry requires policies and strategic actions to supply professional talent to establish and maintain Jordan's competitive position in the global tourism marketplace.

Research was conducted to assess the current hospitality and tourism education programs and curricula for each of the 11 value-chain processes, as illustrated in Figure 1.

Questionnaires and checklists were administered to academic institution managers (deans, department heads, registrars, and placement specialists), current students, graduates, and industry human resource directors. The study included 11 universities and 9 community colleges offering hospitality and tourism programs in Jordan.

The USAID/Jordan Tourism Development Project staff organized a meeting with university deans and department heads to review the questionnaires and checklists in this study. The staff also trained a team of researchers from the education and industry sectors and deployed them to collect data at universities and community colleges in Amman, Zarqa, Kerak, Aqaba, Wadi Musa, and Irbid. Team members interviewed 11 university deans and department heads and 10 registrars, as well as 5 deans and department heads and 6 registrars at community colleges. Two hundred and seventeen university students completed questionnaires. Additional data came from 12 interviews with human resource managers from hotels and one tour operator, 173 questionnaires from students in industry internship programs, and 128 phone interviews with graduates from universities and community colleges. Researchers used the Statistical Package for the Social Sciences statistical analysis to analyze questionnaires.

Quantitative estimates for industry demand and college and university supply were based upon the Human Resources Plan for Tourism in Jordan 2009–2012, developed by the USAID/Jordan Tourism Development Project

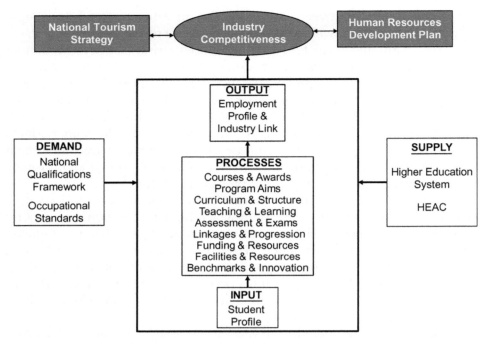

FIGURE 1 Value-chain approach for reforming Jordan's higher education in the tourism and hospitality sector (color figure available online).

in collaboration with the Ministry of Tourism and Antiquities, Ministry of Labor, and other government agencies. The data were obtained from extensive secondary literature searches and interviews held in mid-2007 with a sample of public- and private-sector institutions, hotel and tourism companies, professional bodies and trade associations, and educational institutions. Consultation workshops included government representatives, hotel and tourism employees, education and training institution delegates, and other industry stakeholders.

SUMMARY OF FINDINGS

Demand

The estimated annual demand for executives, managers, supervisors, and senior and junior team staff totals 6,355 new entrants from the labor market described in Table 1.

Universities and community colleges are major sources for meeting the demand for managers. Throughout the world, hospitality and tourism programs are popular with students, but paradoxically, the numbers of graduates that actually get jobs in the industry are disappointing. This preemployment

TABLE 1 Annual Demand by Level for the Hospitality and Tourism Sector

Sector	Annual Total Demand by Level					
	Executive	Manager	Supervisor	Senior	Junior	Total
Hotel operation departments	80	165	330	410	655	1,640
Hotel support functions	40	130	240	230	180	820
Accommodation sector total	120	295	570	640	835	2,460
Restaurant subsector	65	125	250	440	378	1,258
Fast food subsector	55	110	215	375	322	1,077
Restaurant sector total	120	235	465	815	700	2,335
Tourism amenities	5	5	10	25	45	90
Tourism services	40	40	85	255	425	845
Tourism transport	25	25	50	145	240	485
Tourism administration	5	10	15	40	70	140
Tourism sector total	75	80	160	465	780	1,560
Total Annual Demand	315	610	1,195	1,920	2,315	6,355

Source: USAID/Jordan Tourism Development Project (2009; data are from 2007).

attrition, then, must be factored into the target number of tourism graduates. Preemployment attrition can be particularly high among females due to parental influence, marriage, and cultural traditions. The estimated attrition for universities and community colleges in Jordan is estimated at 30% compared with 25% in the Middle East. The annual graduation potential, including preemployment attrition, is 420 from universities and 170 from community colleges (Table 2).

It is estimated that university graduates join the industry as management trainees and replace those internally promoted as managers or executives. Community college graduates enter as supervisor trainees and replace personnel promoted internally. These combined needs can then be compared to the adjusted output from educational institutions, resulting in a shortfall of 505 executives and managers and 1,025 supervisors (Table 3).

Because the government permits 5% of hotel staff and 35% of restaurant staff to be non-Jordanian, an allowance for international labor can be deducted thus reducing the shortfall to 360 executives and managers and 835 supervisors (Table 4).

TABLE 2 Potential Annual Supply from Education Institutions

	University	College
Graduates	600	220
Attrition	180	50
Adjusted output	420	170

Source: USAID/Jordan Tourism Development Project (2009; data are from 2007).

TABLE 3 Demand Less Adjusted Output from Higher Education

Annual Targets	Executives/Managers	Supervisors
Combined demand	925	1,195
Adjusted output	420	170
Initial shortfall	505	1,025

Source: USAID/Jordan Tourism Development Project (2009; data are from 2007).

TABLE 4 Shortfall of Higher Education Output Less International Labor Supply

Annual Targets	Executives/Managers	Supervisors
Initial shortfall	505	1,025
International labor	145	190
Adjusted shortfall	360	835

Source: USAID/Jordan Tourism Development Project (2009; data are from 2007).

Supply

Currently, 11 universities and 9 community colleges offer hospitality and tourism programs in Jordan. Four universities are public and 7 are private. Student enrollment in 2009 was 2,633 for community colleges and universities (Table 5).

During the past 5 years, higher education hospitality and tourism programs have experienced a dramatic increase in enrollment. Universities and community colleges predict that during the next 3 years, they will enjoy growth of 24% and 10%, respectively. These targets will be difficult to achieve without improvements in marketing, course delivery, and international links.

Curricula, faculty and staff development, student recruitment and placement, industry-based professional experiences, and enhancement of strategic alliances all urgently require policy reform in higher education. To systematically address this challenge, we analyzed each of the 11 value-chain elements

TABLE 5 Enrollments of University and Community College Programs 2009

Institutions	Hospitality	Tourism	Hotel & Tourism	Culinary Arts	Sustainable Tourism	Total
Universities						
Private	396	63	681			1,140
Public	279	105	0		380	764
Subtotal	675	168	681		380	1,904
Community Colleges						
Private	393	85	0	33		511
Public	116	102	0			218
Subtotal	509	187	0	33		729
Total	1,184	355	681	33	380	2,633

to determine needed reforms. A reform agenda was then formulated based upon recommendations from industry and higher education interviewees as well as internationally accepted standards and best practices.

This value-chain analysis confirmed anecdotally based criticism that many higher education hospitality and tourism programs have been unfocused and overly theoretical. Indeed, feedback from higher education and industry has revealed the following challenges:

- lack of relationships and insufficient involvement by employers in the design and implementation of curricula and practical training;
- higher education that is too theoretical with insufficient practical content;
- inadequate opportunities for supervised practical training and internships through cooperative industry and higher education collaboration;
- lack of basic knowledge, skills, and attitudes needed by college and university students to cope with workplace demands, such as languages, technical competencies, customer service, grooming, teamwork, creativity, commitment, and overall professionalism;
- unclear career paths and placement opportunities for community college and university graduates, particularly for women; and
- working conditions and salaries not competitive with other service industries, which lead to recruitment, placement, and retention problems.

To bridge these gaps, industry must invest in people. Because the new workforce needs a combination of education and experience, a partnership between educators and employers must move forward. Finally, this value-chain assessment indicates that higher education needs to conduct self-assessment of its specialized programs in hospitality, tourism, and related areas. This is particularly urgent if the system is to meet demand with locally supplied executives, managers, and supervisors and break the dependence on foreign-sourced personnel.

Findings indicate that the following strategies could address supply shortfalls of supervisors and managers:

- University consolidation: The number of 4-year degrees should be reduced or consolidated to offer only high-quality programs that result in higher rates of managerial placement. New curricular areas must be developed to meet Jordan's needs in areas like destination management and event management.
- Community college expansion: The number of students enrolled in diploma programs needs to be substantially increased to meet demand for supervisory and technically qualified graduates in the years ahead.
- Enhanced articulation: Linkages between community colleges and universities for credit transfer need to be articulated and enhanced. Opportunities

should be provided for industry employees to pass the Tawjihi require-ments (high school graduation examination) to gain entrance into higher education programs; linkages to higher education though the Vocational Training Corporation (VTC) program should also be explored.

- Graduate education: To produce instructors and highly qualified managers, the system needs master's- and doctoral-level programs, which are being planned but not yet available.
- National qualifications: Higher education curricula should prepare grad-uates to meet the proposed National Qualification Framework under consideration by the Jordanian Ministries of Labor and Higher Education.
- National accreditation: The accreditation of specialized programs by the Higher Education Accreditation Commission (HEAC) has been revised to reflect guidelines based on the higher education value chain for the hospitality and tourism sector.
- International accreditation: External international accreditation programs should supplement HEAC's quality assurance and licensing functions.
- Effective coordination: Higher education reform requires coordination of government and industry. International and national benchmarks for public- and private-sector partnerships should be followed.

NEXT STEPS

A partnership between the Ministry of Higher Education and Scientific Research and the HEAC under the leadership of the public–private TIASC was established to enhance competitiveness of Jordan's tourism industry.

This partnership recommended the following guidelines for Jordanian community college and university officials:

- Periodic performance monitoring should track student progress in pursuit of learning outcomes.
- Fifty percent of core subjects should be taught in English.
- Field-based practical training should involve a minimum of 12 credits and a formal internship of 6 credits, combined for a total of 1,200 hours of practical training.
- Curricula should teach students problem-solving skills in a tourism industry context.
- Teacher and academic counselor performance should be regularly evaluated.
- Universities and community colleges should describe their academic pro-grams on their Web sites in both Arabic and English. They should include course descriptions for each subject in the study plan.
- The program should have sufficient financial stability to enable it to achieve its educational objectives for a reasonable future period.

- Academic departments should conduct self-assessments at least every 5 years.
- Employers should codesign practical training, internships, and work-placement opportunities.
- Reforms should take into consideration best practices and benchmarks applicable to Jordan. Several examples follow:
  - Accredited Prior Learning to allow students to receive academic credit for on-the-job learning;
  - customized textbooks written to teacher specifications, which cover exactly what must be taught;
  - adopting the proposed National Qualifications Framework and incorporating occupational profile standards into program development and curriculum revisions; and
  - partnering with overseas institutions to expose faculty and students to new ideas and knowledge.

On February 28, 2011, the USAID/Jordan Tourism Development Project and the Ministry of Higher Education and the Ministry of Tourism and Antiquities convened the National Conference on Innovation and Reform of Hospitality and Tourism Education in Jordan (2011b). More than 200 representatives from industry and academics together created a road map for educational innovation to address today's challenges and meet tomorrow's needs.

This conference occurred while upheavals took place in Tunisia, Egypt, Morocco, Yemen, Libya, and, to a lesser extent, Jordan. Conferees agreed to:

- launch a strategy for reforming higher education in Jordan's hospitality and tourism sector to ensure its relevance to today's challenges and tomorrow's changes;
- create a road map that integrates innovation, reform goals, and priorities; and
- integrate the role of higher education in meeting labor force development needs in the Jordan National Tourism Strategy (NTS) for the period during 2011 to 2015.

FUTURE DIRECTIONS FOR TOURISM EDUCATION

Many regions at the forefront of tourism development (e.g., Hong Kong and Singapore) invest heavily in creating an awareness of the value of tourism as a career and encouraging young people to pursue postsecondary studies in this field. In recent years, Jordan has learned from European, American, and Asian higher education approaches and practices and then adapted them to its educational system and cultural traditions.

In terms of future challenges facing higher education in Jordan, we examined the extent to which the 11value-chain elements in our survey might relate to the core values and attributes identified as important for higher education by Sheldon, Fesenmaier, and Tribe (2009) for the Tourism Education Futures Initiative (TEFI). TEFI represents an effort by major educational institutions and leading educators throughout the world to improve the quality of the student experience by focusing on tourism education values—stewardship, knowledge, professionalism, ethics, and mutuality. For all 11 value-chain elements, significant challenges would need to be addressed for Jordan's higher education system to integrate TEFI values and attributes. These challenges are described in Table 6.

As described in the higher education value-chain map (Figure 1), human resource development involving higher education should appear in Jordan's

TABLE 6 TEFI-Related Challenges Identified in the Jordan Value-Chain Survey

TEFI Values and Attributes	TEFI-Related Challenges Identified in the Jordan Value-Chain Survey
Stewardship: critical thinking, innovation, creativity, networking	• *Student Profile*: Additional staff resources are needed to provide counseling, mentorship, and networking opportunities for an increasingly diverse student body. New modes of learning need to be introduced to encourage students to think critically and understand the social, economic, and environmental impacts of tourism—both positive and negative. • *Funding Options*: Higher education institutions need to increase their sources of income to supplement tuition revenues to upgrade staff development, scholarships, and community services.
Knowledge: critical thinking, innovation, creativity, networking	• *Program Aims and Objectives*: Collaborative curriculum development is needed to align employer needs with higher education outputs. • *Curriculum and Course Structure*: Knowledge disseminated through challenging coursework needs to be enhanced through practical training relevant to industry needs. • *Benchmarks and Innovations*: Benchmarks must provide clear indicators of progress as well as areas that need improvement.
Professionalism: leadership, practicality, services, relevance, timeliness, reflexivity, teamwork, proactivity	• *Courses and Awards:* A lack of consistent standards for specific course requirements in community college and university programs has created concerns about the practical application and relevance of educational offerings. • *Facilities and Resources*: Facility deficiencies and limited resources in some community colleges and universities give the appearance that this field is irrelevant and unprofessional, thus hampering the attraction of quality students. • *Employment Profile and Industry Links*: Clearly defined measureable goals and operational guidelines are needed for internships and practical training.
Ethics: honesty, transparency, authenticity, authentic self	• *Assessment and Exams:* The level of transparency in student selection procedures, grading policies, and internship placements needs to be increased to create a more favorable image of higher education institutions by major stakeholders (students, parents, employers, and government).

FIGURE 2 NTS pillars (2011) (color figure available online).

NTS to enhance its overall competitiveness in the global tourism marketplace. Spearheaded by the Ministry of Tourism and Antiquities, a team of more than 65 representatives of tourism investors, entrepreneurs, professionals, industry associations, and other governmental institutions developed the Jordan NTS 2011–2015 with technical assistance and funding from the USAID/Jordan Tourism Development Project. The new strategy builds on the success of its antecessor (2005–2010), which exceeded its target of JD 1.7 billion (US$2.4 billion) by JD 0.3 billion (US$0.4 billion) by 2010. The new tourism strategy seeks to more than double this figure by 2015.

The NTS assumes that quality service can only be achieved with a skilled workforce. Labor market development was designated as one of four pillars of the NTS (Figure 2). The NTS (USAID/Jordan Tourism Development Project, 2011a, p. 9) provides direction for tourism stakeholders with a "clear path forward to underpin future growth. Its development and implementation will be guided by a vision and a mission that are adapted from those within the first NTS to focus attention on the need to further develop a distinctive, unique and competitive tourism industry."

The NTS continues to depend on its four-pillar framework, which has proven successful in the past. Its range of indicators should assist the documentation of achievements to date in Jordan's tourism sector and raise overall industry competitiveness for its long-term sustainability.

According to the NTS (USAID/Jordan Tourism Development Project, 2011a), under Pillar 3—labor market development—direct employment in tourism increased by almost 85% by the end of 2010. Other important achievements under the previous NTS are as follows:

- The Jordan Applied University developed an accredited hospitality program with a public vocational high school located on its campus.
- Female participation in the workforce has grown to an estimated 10%.
- Eleven vocational training centers were upgraded to offer international standard skills training for hotel and restaurant students.
- An awareness campaign highlighting tourism benefits to the economy reached more than 2 million Jordanians.

In the labor-intensive tourism industry, professionalism of its people is essential to the unique Jordanian experience. To improve this quality, the NTS set the following targets for 2011 through 2015:

- Create 25,000 additional direct jobs.
- Increase female participation in the workforce from 10% to 15%.
- Train 5,000 students in the 11 VTC centers.
- Provide hospitality skills training to 40,000 employees.

The plan identifies the following priorities for higher education.

1. The NTS (USAID/Jordan Tourism Development Project, 2011a) urgently calls for a national entity to update the National Tourism Manpower Strategy and coordinate all labor market and human resource activities in tourism. The entity should "operate independently, with members drawn from industry, education, and government, with oversight from a board of directors. As a public–private partnership, the entity will be action-oriented and focus on delivering added value to the industry" (USAID/Jordan Tourism Development Project, 2011a, p. 64). The entity should offer a range of products and services in five dimensions:
   - tourism awareness and promotion;
   - professional and management development;
   - training in industry;
   - research and planning; and
   - human resource management.

2. The NTS emphasizes that the industry needs to be an attractive career choice for young people and adults. It must also increase the active participation of females to meet demand for workers. In Jordan, tourism competes with other industries for qualified workers. According to the NTS (USAID/Jordan Tourism Development Project, 2011a, p. 65), Jordan's "efforts are constrained by its poor image and a lack of understanding among Jordanians about the nature of jobs and careers in tourism. There is confusion about how certain cultural issues are handled in the industry, and what the expectations of employees are. Although much work has already been done in this area, these issues need to be continuously clarified to the general population, potential employees and their families. Family decision-makers need be targeted to improve the participation of youth and women. Creating greater awareness and positive attitudes will help improve the image of tourism, which will encourage Jordanians to take up jobs and careers in the sector and thus alleviate existing labor shortages."

3. The NTS (USAID/Jordan Tourism Development Project, 2011a, p. 66) advocates for the development of world-class tourism education services. Educators and employers should "work together to ensure that the programs offered by secondary schools, vocational education, colleges and universities address today's needs and prepare students to

meet the changes that will come tomorrow." Specific measures to be undertaken are:

- improve recruitment to make hotel and tourism programs more accessible, both financially and geographically;
- upgrade the national secondary school vocational stream in tourism and hospitality, known as the Fundukia Program, in the 26 secondary schools;
- reform curricula for universities and community college and introduce accreditation and internships for tourism programs;
- establish university and community college strategic alliances with industry, international institutions, and external accreditation bodies; and
- upgrade faculty, staff, training facilities, and educational centers to: (a) increase numbers and improve teaching skills of staff, (b) promote foreign-language skills among staff and students, and (c) create opportunities for teachers to gain industry experience.

4. Improve hospitality skills for tourism employees at all levels especially management, including compliance with the UN World Tourism Organization Code of Ethics.

CONCLUSION

This value-chain analysis confirmed anecdotally based criticism that many higher education hospitality and tourism programs have lacked focus and been overly theoretical. Indeed, surveys and feedback from higher education and industry have revealed substantial gaps including:

- lack of relationships and insufficient involvement by employers in the design and implementation of curricula and practical training;
- higher education that is too theoretical with insufficient practical content;
- inadequate opportunities for supervised practical training and internships through cooperative industry/higher education collaboration;
- lack of basic knowledge, skills, and attitudes needed by college and university students to cope with workplace demands—language facility, technical competencies, customer service, grooming, respect, teamwork, creativity, commitment, and overall professionalism;
- poorly prepared academic staff;
- unclear career paths and placement opportunities for graduates, particularly for women; and
- working conditions and salaries not competitive with other service industries leading to recruitment, placement, and retention problems.

Higher education providers need to better communicate their students' qualifications to potential employers. Employers and educators in partnership must first ensure the quality of higher education. Existing programs have not been entirely successful in meeting their goals. Emphasis needs to shift to innovation and reform.

In the future, Jordan needs a relevant, comprehensive higher education system integrated with industry-based professional experience that generates employees with applicable (a) technical skills, business knowledge, and service mentality; (b) communication and interpersonal skills; (c) positive attitudes; and (d) entrepreneurial spirit. These qualities will arm the workforce to face the challenges of increasing competition, sophisticated and varied consumer expectations, rapidly developing technology, and continual change.

REFERENCES

Sheldon, P. J., Fesenmaier, D. R., & Tribe, J. (2009). The Tourism Education Futures Initiative. *e-Review of Tourism Research*, 7(3), 43.

USAID/Jordan Tourism Development Project. (2009). *Human resources plan for tourism in Jordan: 2009–2012*. Amman, Jordan: Author.

USAID/Jordan Tourism Development Project. (2011a). *Jordan national tourism strategy: 2011–2015*. Amman, Jordan: Author.

USAID/Jordan Tourism Development Project. (2011b). *Reforming higher education: Jordan's hospitality and tourism sector*. Amman, Jordan: Author.

The Tourism Education Futures Initiative: The Way Forward

DIANNE DREDGE

Southern Cross University, Gold Coast, Australia

CHRISTIAN SCHOTT

Victoria University of Wellington, Wellington, New Zealand

The book's introductory chapter told the story of TEFI's evolution over the last seven years while the ensuing chapters have unpacked theoretical and conceptual issues, as well as applications and case studies of tourism education. These chapters illustrate the depth and breadth of work undertaken since TEFI's inception to build a more rigorous and well-justified platform for values-based tourism education. However in attempting to understand and appreciate these contributions, and before laying out the challenges ahead, it is also important to consider the context in which these developments have occurred.

Seven years is a long time in higher education where, across the world, reform has been deep, unrelenting and transformational (CHEPS, 2004; OECD, 2012). In many Western developed economies, higher education has been increasingly tied to economic policy where governments are implementing policies and prescriptions to increase levels of educational attainment and improve educational quality and standards in the hope of driving economic innovation and national competitiveness (Australian Government, 2009; European Science Foundation, 2007).

In developed economies, higher education has also become increasingly subject to the hegemonic forces of neoliberal economic management, which has resulted in the delivery of higher education becoming more industrialised, market-driven, client focused and globalised. In the 1990s the globalisation of higher education opened up new markets, and large numbers of students from developing economies flowed into European countries, Canada, Australia, the UK and the US (UNESCO, 2006). Higher education institutions in these countries saw opportunities to expand and diversify the programs they offered, and were often helped along by governments eager to extract foreign exchange earnings from international students. Under these conditions, higher education prospered and tourism programs grew in both the number of institutions offering programs and in student enrolments. The vast majority of these programs and their associated curricula were founded as professional programs aimed at delivering industry ready graduates who would contribute to an increasingly robust, competitive and innovative industry. More recently, tourism education has continued to mature with a strong stream of social science research influencing program design, curricula and delivery (Airey, 2008).

By 2007, when TEFI was born, concerns were already being raised about the "seismic changes" taking place in higher education (see Sheldon et al., Chapter 2), arguing that "Tourism educational programs need to fundamentally retool and redesign—not incrementally by adding new courses or simply by putting courses on-line—but by changing the nature of what is taught and how it is taught" (Sheldon et al., Chapter 2). A key theme in TEFI's evolutionary story is that its goals and aspirations quickly found wide-spread support, not only because they resonated with a large number of tourism academics, but also because of the vision, passionate commitment and tireless energy of a few early "TEFI-ites". The early "TEFI–ites" did not put the idea of radically re-examining tourism education aside as 'too hard,' but instead incubated their ideas into discussion points that could be shared, debated and critiqued by other tourism educators. The other dynamic which has seen TEFI gain momentum year on year is that TEFI is a continuously evolving collective of passionate and committed tourism educators from many different countries. Both the depth and breadth of TEFI-inspired projects have grown over the years mirroring the growth and global distribution of the TEFI community.

Tourism and Higher Education Futures

In 2013 TEFI entered a new phase with the appointment of a new leadership team to take forward and build upon the accomplishments to date. In this new phase of development we are cognizant that higher education "reform" is a continuous process and that higher education systems in most countries today look very different to the systems in place when TEFI was born. In three, five, ten or twenty years time, they will look quite different again. For instance, UNESCO (2013) estimated that there were nearly two million internationally mobile students in 2000, which grew to 4.1 million in 2010, and this number is predicted to be around seven million in 2020. Students from China, India and Korea make up the majority of foreign students abroad. Increasing wealth in Asia (particularly China), India, Brazil and Russia will drive demand for quality higher education, and, while demand for English language qualifications will remain dominant, these qualifications might be delivered in English in non-English speaking countries. Further, this internationalisation and increased mobility of students, institutions and programs will also have a significant effect on the mobility of educators, curriculum content, teaching and learning pedagogies and practices. And importantly, new technologies that facilitate learning and collaboration present an additional force, and the full impacts of these on global education have not yet been imagined.

So, after a period of rapid growth and expansion in many developed countries, public funding and investment in higher education have tightened since the mid 2000s. Rationalisation and extensive restructuring are now commonplace and private sector involvement is increasing. Unsettling forces are at play (OECD, 2009b). The growth of investment in higher education in countries such as Brazil, China, India and Russia, but also in Latin America and Asia more broadly, is reshaping student demand and mobility characteristics; and global economic conditions that affect exchange rates, levels of employment, foreign investment and so on, are also affecting student demand in ways that no country, institution or government can provide leadership or control over. These trends have resulted in the slowing of student flows from developing countries to developed countries, and, if investment in higher education in countries such as China, Singapore, Malaysia, Indonesia, India and Brazil continues to materialise, global patterns of student movement will shift dramatically (OECD, 2009b). Moreover, as the number of institutions and programs in higher education in these countries continue to expand, there will be a shortage of educators to staff these programs. So while rationalisation and restructuring are now the norm in developed countries, countries like China and India are optimistic about their expansion.

All this demonstrates that the academic workforce, students and institutions are increasingly mobile, and by corollary, the policy ideas and solutions to confront higher education challenges are also on the move. Globalisation is bringing with it a certain amount of homogeneity and policy diffusion. But there is also ambiguity: the privileged place of higher education, as an ivory tower and site of knowledge, creativity and innovation, is being both dismantled and reinforced at the same time. On one hand barriers to participation in higher education are being removed, and on the other hand the importance of a knowledge society, as a performative ideology underpinning and justifying higher education, is increasing. It seems that Bauman's liquid modernity (Bauman, 2000), where everything is on the move, and there is greater freedom of choice and opportunity, is increasingly evident in global higher education. Sohail Inayatullah sums up this transformation eloquently:

> The extent of the transformation higher learning is undergoing is yet unknown and may remain so for years to come. However, what we can be sure about is that the challenges that higher learning is facing are not going to go away. Globalisation, privatisation, virtualisation, democratisation (peer to peer learning and assessment), among other drivers, are turning business-as-usual into business-was-usual. Dramatic changes in the world economy - from the rise of East Asia and potentially India - to climate change, not to mention revolutions in genomics, nanotechnology and the brain-mind nexus, all augur for more and not less change in the future (Inayatullah in Universiti Sains Malaysia, 2007, p. xii).

What does the future look like for tourism education in this liquid, transmutable context? There are a number of reports that describe future scenarios for higher education and these provide important insights and prompts for our thinking (see Kehm, Huisman, & Stensaker, 2009; OECD, 2009a; Universiti Sains Malaysia, 2007). Three key observations resonate and help to inform how we can seek to shape tourism education. The first point is that higher education is suffering an identity crisis, and tourism as a field of transdisciplinary study is very much subject to a lack of recognition as a result. The multiple pathways to university, the different contributing disciplines, the rise in degree granting private education providers, the blurring of boundaries between vocational and professional studies within universities and the increasing social and geographical diversity of students are some of the conditions that are challenging the identity of tourism programs within the higher education environment. The opportunity and the key challenge for TEFI is to address this issue, to build an epistemic community of like-minded people that reinforces and consolidates tourism education, its contribution and purpose in world-making. To this end, TEFI's mission is *"to be the leading, forward-looking network that inspires, informs and supports tourism educators and students to passionately and courageously transform the world for the better"*.

The second point emerging from discussion about the future of higher education is that the nature and relationship between knowledge and society, and the role of higher education within this relationship, remains highly contentious. Under prevailing neo-liberal public management ideologies that dominate in most countries in the Global North and increasingly in the Global South, the role of higher education institutions is to teach and undertake research that empowers a "knowledge economy" and that contributes to economic growth and prosperity. In tourism, the alignment of "industry relevant" programs that produce graduates who are "work ready" illustrate this objective. However, competing interpretations of the role of knowledge in society highlight the danger of unthinking acceptance of this "knowledge economy" lens. Sociologists have proffered a "knowledge society" and educators have put forward a "learning society" (Välimaa and Hoffman, 2007). These two alternative framings value knowledge differently and highlight that higher education institutions have an important role in contributing to a broader conceptualisation of knowledge for the public good, one that extends beyond economic productivity to include social, environmental and political dimensions. TEFI, as a global network, seeks to acknowledge and take seriously these competing performative ideologies about the role of knowledge in society and the contribution that tourism education can play. In particular, the idea that tourism is a world-making activity, with the potential to promote tolerance, peace, intercultural understanding, alleviate poverty, address issues of equity and disempowerment has resonated strongly, not only in the preceding chapters, but also in the development of the initial TEFI values. To this end, TEFI seeks to balance the historical focus on the knowledge economy by placing a stronger emphasis on the knowledge society and the learning society as the *raison d'etre* for tourism education.

The third point arising from debates about the future of tourism higher education is related to the previous two points. The abovementioned identity crisis and the need for greater clarity around the role of tourism education and its relationship to knowledge and society highlight the importance of building a stronger, networked community of practice around such issues, and in clarifying and articulating the values that underpin tourism education applied in this context. Drawing more broadly from the scenario building exercises in higher education mentioned above, and increasing debate about the role of higher education in addressing societal issues (Nussbaum, 1997, 2010), an ethical, value-centred approach to tourism higher education has resonated as a promising sustainable solution moving forward.

In Chapter 2, Sheldon et al. identify six key challenges that are contributing to rapid and sustained change and that set the context for the future of tourism. They warn us against thinking about reproduction of past solutions and tourism models, and argue that new creative solutions must be forged to address challenges we are not yet able to fully appreciate. Under these conditions, the central task for tourism education is to equip graduates not only with skills and expertise for the workforce, but also to contribute to their moral development with respect to big questions that they will inevitably confront in their professional lives. Such questions include what kind of tourism is to be developed, how 'good' decisions can be made, what can be done to optimise the positive effects and mitigate the negative effects of tourism, and what power do they have as tourism professionals to shape the tourism world. Indeed, all the authors in the preceding chapters have started from the point that to answer these questions within the varied contexts that graduates might find themselves requires explicit and reflexive engagement with values in order to lead what Aristotle might call a virtuous life and undertake good actions in tourism (Jamal and Menzel, 2009; Tribe, 2002).

It is the development and nurturing of this debate about what constitutes good actions in tourism, and the role of tourism education within this, that provides the key focus for TEFI in the future. Such a debate will take place in diverse forums, be generated from multiple perspectives and be guided by a range of values. It is not TEFI's role to determine an overarching set of values, but rather to provide a network within which this debate can flourish. It is our intention that tourism educators, institutions, industry and other stakeholders can be inspired, supported and encouraged to engage the key social, ethical and spiritual questions confronting society and consider the role of tourism within this larger and more complex world. This positioning reinforces the original framing of TEFI as a network of educators and practitioners that seek to further global citizenship and the world-making potential of tourism (see Belhassen & Caton, 2011; Hollinshead, Ateljevic, & Ali, 2009).

TEFI Engagement and Activities

At the 2013 TEFI7 conference on the theme *Tourism Education and Global Citizenship,* both historical contributions and the future positioning of TEFI were at the forefront of discussions. During the conference, which was held in Oxford, the four priority areas formulated a year earlier at TEFI6 in Milan were refined into four succinct and easily-transmitted themes:

· Tourism teaching and learning
· Tourism education advocacy
· Tourism education scholarship
· Tourism education futures

And, a fifth theme was added:

· Tourism and social enterprise.

This additional theme emerged as a result of considerable discussion about the need for action, and a call for delegates to use their "heads, hearts and minds" and to put front and centre "action over words". Social enterprise was seen as a theme that provided opportunities for putting into action the commitments contained in teaching and learning, advocacy, scholarship and futures.

The discussion at TEFI7 also focused on dialogue about actions, with the specific intent to build action groups that bring the above five themes 'alive'. A strong drive for new initiatives developed early in the conference and culminated on the final day in the formation of five fluid action domains. The breadth and depth of these action domains far exceeded initial expectations, which is testament to the passion, skills and commitment of the tourism scholars, industry and third sector leaders that were present. The five action domains embody a strong drive to 'activate' as reflected by the headings:

Demonstrate!

This action group's vision is to "change tourism education through the creation of and connection to resources, experiences/practices that support values based learning". Numerous activities and initiatives have been proposed in pursuit of this vision. They include promoting the rationale for values-based education (Harland & Pickering, 2011) in tourism, the dissemination of a values inventory, the production of intellectually provocative and inspiring short videos, the sharing of effective teaching practices, research on teaching and learning, and discussion about innovative teaching techniques that harness the evolving opportunities of a rapidly changing world.

Consolidate!

The consolidate action group seeks to physically connect interested groups with TEFI and its mission and values by organising regional workshops in different corners of the world. These workshops are intended to not only present TEFI's mission but to also offer curriculum design workshops supported by targeted resources and experienced facilitators. Additionally, Consolidate! is envisaged to incorporate the development of stronger relationships with kindred organisations across the globe.

Disseminate!

This action group focuses on advocacy for tourism education and research, as well as sharing TEFI's work and goals with international audiences. As evidenced by the previous chapters, a diverse range of projects have been undertaken, inspired by TEFI discussions, and the development of this book exemplifies one of a range of channels we consider important to disseminate TEFI's work. The theoretical and conceptual contributions, innovative teaching applications, and case studies discussed in the previous chapters are important tools that enrich debates about tourism education, that critically assess the role and application of values, and unpack complex future challenges.

The "Disseminate" group also seeks to further expand TEFI at the international level by being more accessible to interested individuals and groups in a variety of different countries and linguistic spheres. This desire has evolved in response to strong interest in TEFI's work from the Indian subcontinent, South America and East Asia. This internationalisation agenda is complemented by advocacy initiatives which seek to promote the critical role of tourism in society (Hollinshead, 2009) and to communicate in an accessible fashion what tourism is and why the study and research of tourism are significant to society, and by implication, higher education.

Activate!

The aim of this action group is to activate and maintain effective channels to promote and communicate with a wide-ranging audience about TEFI and its activities. A particular focus is the refinement of a communication strategy that balances the needs of different audiences, with the reach of the channels and the necessity to foster dialogue and dynamic exchange. While social media has been identified as a pivotal tool in this context, due to its pervasive role in the lives of future academy and industry leaders (our students) coupled with the capacity for instant, media-enriched dialogue, the more traditional channels and media will also play a key role. This said, there is a strong drive to make 'public-ations' public again through the fostering of open-access outlets and the compilation of white papers.

Move and Shake!

The focus of this action group is the most specific of the TEFI initiatives. It explores the role of conferences and other experiential initiatives to drive change. This group is developing the concept of a "Change Conference" into an experimental event planned to take place in 2014. It is an innovative initiative to provide a forum for dialogue about tourism education and pedagogical research in a setting that aligns with the TEFI7 theme of global citizenship. Key foundations of the Change Conference concept are the importance of learning from communities and their experiences; from those that are affected and the self-empowered. As such, the concept of walking papers instead of working papers is seen as crucial to promoting dialogue and the notion that learning and knowledge exchanges are processes.

The fluid nature of the initiatives described above needs to be emphasised, as it is a natural dynamic of this action process that ideas may be revised and that new ideas will emerge and develop into innovative projects. The intention of TEFI, and the growing number of projects and activities that the TEFI community is undertaking or proposing, is not only to critically review current paradigms and practices, but also to agitate and use the power of positive disruption in mindful and innovative ways.

Conclusions

Finally, it is pertinent to consider TEFI, its organisational characteristics, roles and relationships with other stakeholders in the tourism academy. In many ways, TEFI is an organic organisation (Burns & Stalker, 1961). At present it has an informal, networked structure and relies on horizontal cooperation and task sharing as opposed to vertical hierarchical structures, routines and the rules of a "mechanistic" organisation. The TEFI network has emerged out of the drive and passion of individuals who have moved in and out of the network and the lack of a formal structure has allowed an ebb and flow of creative, constructive and passionate engagement over those issues that matter to the participants at each TEFI conference. It has also allowed the network flexibility to deal with the changing environment.

Indeed TEFI is an emergent organisation, its momentum drawn from what many see as a crisis in academia more generally (Saccarelli, 2011). No doubt, its community of scholars, industry and third sector representatives have quite varied interpretations of what a public intellectual should be (and here, inspired by Gramsci, we interpret public intellectuals in the organic sense that they exist inside and outside the academy (Hoare & Nowell Smith, 1999)), but it is fair to say that many are motivated by, and find solidarity in, the need to move outside the walls of the academy and to activate tourism change inside and outside their institutions, communities and industries. The TEFI network provides access to a community of like-minded individuals wherein our political agency to drive change in tourism education can be explored and supported. So what form will this organic organisation take in the future? There is no prescription for what makes a "good" organisation, and we are cognizant that this fluid structure is adaptive and flexible. However, in the future and as the momentum continues, we anticipate there will one day be a need to devise a more formal TEFI structure in order to support the professional development and self-actualisation of tourism world-making educators, in sharing our own and learning from others' stories of practice and, ultimately, to enhance TEFI's collective political agency. This, however, requires that we build network capacity, recognise difference and diversity of challenges across the globe, and we continue to devote our energies to making tourism the world-making force it can be.

References

Airey, D. (2008). In search of a mature subject? *Journal of Hospitality, Leisure, Sports and Tourism Education*, 7(2), 101-103.

Australian Government. (2009). Transforming Australia's Higher Education System. Canberra: Australian Government.

Bauman, Z. (2000). *Liquid Modernity*. Cambridge & Malden: Policy.

Belhassen, Y., & Caton, K. (2011). On the need for critical pedagogy in tourism education. *Tourism Management*, 32(6), 1389-1396.

Burns, T., & Stalker, G. (1961). *The Management of Innovation*. London: Tavistock.

CHEPS. (2004). The 20th Anniversary CHEPS Scenarios: European higher education and research landscape 2020. Netherlands: Center for Higher Education Policy Studies.

European Science Foundation. (2007). Higher Education Looking Forward: Relations between higher education and society: European Science Foundation.

Harland, T., & Pickering, N. (2011). *Values in Higher Education Teaching*. Abingdon: Routledge.

Hoare, Q., & Nowell Smith, G. (1999). *Selections from the Prison Notebooks of Antonio Gramsci* (Transcribed from the edition published by Lawrence & Wishart, 1971). London: ElecBook.

Hollinshead, K. (2009). The 'worldmaking' prodigy of tourism: The reach and power of tourism in the dynamics of change and transformation. *Tourism Analysis*, 14(1), 139-152.

Hollinshead, K., Ateljevic, I., & Ali, N. (2009). Worldmaking Agency - Worldmaking Authority: The Sovereign Constitutive Role of Tourism. *Tourism Geographies*, 11(4), 427-443.

Jamal, T., & Menzel, C. (2009). Good actions in tourism. In Tribe, J., *Philosophical Issues in Tourism*. (pp.227-243). Bristol: Channel View Publications.

Kehm, B., Huisman, J., & Stensaker, B. (2009). *The European Higher Education Area: Perspectives on a moving target*. Rotterdam: Sense Publishers.

Nussbaum, M. (1997). *Cultivating Humanity: A classical defense of reform in liberal education*. Cambridge: Harvard University Press.

Nussbaum, M. (2010). *Not for profit: Why democracy needs the humanities*. Woodstock: Princeton University Press.

OECD. (2009a). Four Future Scenarios for Higher Education: OECD/CERI Centre for Educational Research and Innovation, OECD Publishing. Paris.

OECD. (2009b). Higher Education to 2030. Volume 2 Globalisation. OECD/CERI Centre for Educational Research and Innovation, OECD Publishing. Paris. Retrieved 10 June 2013, from http://www.mfdps.si/Files//Knjiznica/higher%20educational%202030%20OECD.pdf

OECD. (2012). Education at a Glance 2012: OECD Indicators. Retrieved 29 May 2012, from HYPERLINK "http://dx.doi.org/10.1787/eag-2012-en" http://dx.doi.org/10.1787/eag-2012-en

Saccarelli, E. (2011). The Intellectual in Question. *Cultural Studies*, 25(6), 757-782.

UNESCO. (2006). Global Education Digest 2006: Comparing Education Statistics Across the World. Montreal: UNESCO Institute of Statistics.

Tribe, J. (2002). Education for Ethical Tourism Action, *Journal of Sustainable Tourism*, 10(4), 309-324.

Universiti Sains Malaysia. (2007). *Constructing Future Higher Education Scenarios: Insights from Universiti Sains Malaysia*. Palau Pinang: Universiti Sains Malaysia.

Välimaa, J., & Hoffman, D. (2007). Higher education and knowledge society discourse, in European Science Foundation Higher Education Looking Forward: Themes on the Changing Relationship between High Education and Society. Retrieved 29 May 2013, from http://www.esf.org/fileadmin/Public_documents/Publications/HELF.pdf

Index

Note:
Page numbers in **bold** type refer to figures
Page numbers in *italic* type refer to tables
Page numbers followed by 'n' or 'a' refer to notes
or appendices

Related titles from Routledge

Tourism Governance
Critical Perspectives on Governance and Sustainability

Edited by Bill Bramwell and Bernard Lane

This book explains and evaluates critical perspectives on the governance of tourism, examining these in the context of tourism and sustainable development. Governance processes fundamentally affect whether – and how – progress is made toward securing the economic, socio-cultural and environmental goals of sustainable development. The critical perspectives on tourism governance, examined here, challenge and re-conceptualise established ideas in tourism policy and planning, as well as engage with theoretical frameworks from other social science fields. The collection brings insights from leading researchers, and examines important new theoretical frameworks for tourism research.

Bill Bramwell is Professor of International Tourism Studies at Sheffield Hallam University, UK. He is co-founder and co-editor of the *Journal of Sustainable Tourism*.

Bernard Lane is Visiting Research Fellow at Sheffield Hallam University, UK, and co-founder and co-editor of the *Journal of Sustainable Tourism*.

December 2011: 246 x 174: 288pp
Hb: 978-0-415-58771-6
£85 / $145

Available from all good bookshops

Related titles from Routledge

Social Tourism: Perspectives and Potential
Edited by Lynn Minnaert, Robert Maitland and Graham Miller

In this volume, international specialists on social tourism present perspectives from different disciplines and geographical contexts. The book highlights the multitude of interpretations and implementations of social tourism that make the concept so multi-faceted: examples reviewed in this book include holiday vouchers in Hungary, charity initiatives in the UK, tourism schemes for senior citizens in Spain and state provision in Brazil.

Seven themed chapters and two case studies explore the potential of social tourism from a range of perspectives. Should tourism be a right that is available to all? Is social tourism indispensable in a sustainable tourism strategy? The book provides a critical reflection on these and other questions, and is therefore a key resource for social tourism researchers and practitioners.

This book was originally published as a special issue of *Current Issues in Tourism*.

November 2012: 246 x 174: 136pp
Hb: 978-0-415-52378-3
£85 / $145